D1595313

Continental Divide

Ernst Cassirer and Martin Heidegger at the Hotel Belvédère in Davos, Switzerland, Spring 1929. Photo reproduced from the Privatarchiv Dr. Henning Ritter, courtesy of the Dokumentationsbibliothek Davos.

Continental Divide

HEIDEGGER, CASSIRER, DAVOS

Peter E. Gordon

HARVARD UNIVERSITY PRESS

Cambridge, Massachusetts, and London, England · 2010

Copyright © 2010 by the President and Fellows of Harvard College
All rights reserved
Printed in the United States of America

Library of Congress Cataloging-in-Publication Data
Gordon, Peter Eli.
    Continental divide : Heidegger, Cassirer, Davos / Peter E. Gordon.
      p. cm.
    Includes bibliographical references (p.   ) and index.
    ISBN 978-0-674-04713-6 (alk. paper)
    1. Heidegger, Martin, 1889–1976.   2. Cassirer, Ernst, 1874–1945.
  3. Continental philosophy—Switzerland—Davos.   I. Title.
B3279.H49G5922   2010
193—dc22   2009050714

Anybody may take part in discussions; philosophers are those who are never involved in them. Wisdom is beyond the desire to win.

A philosopher who is not taking part in discussions is like a boxer who never goes into the ring.

—*Two remarks by Ludwig Wittgenstein*

.

Contents

Preface

This book was conceived a long time ago. Its incubation and eventual completion took many years, no doubt because in the interim my attention was drawn toward other themes and problems in the history of modern European thought. It seems relevant to note that the present study grew almost organically from my last book, in which I tried to explain the philosophical kinship between the German Jewish philosopher Franz Rosenzweig and his contemporary, Martin Heidegger.[1] The comparison between these two unlikely cousins of interwar philosophy first came to my attention thanks to a short commentary that Rosenzweig wrote at the very end of his life about the 1929 disputation between Ernst Cassirer and Martin Heidegger at Davos, Switzerland. It would of course be foolish to believe that Rosenzweig was ever much more than a minor curiosity within the larger drama of Continental philosophy. Reflecting on the book today, it seems altogether evident to me that its protagonist always stood at the periphery of the main action. A similar trick of perspective can be found in Tom Stoppard's play, *Rosenkrantz and Guildenstern Are Dead,* which brings to the foreground two of the lesser characters in Hamlet's life. The present book now closes the parentheses and returns our attention to the drama as it was played out at center stage: its major protagonists—Ernst Cassirer and Martin Heidegger—are indisputably two of the greatest philosophers of the twentieth century. In this book I have assigned myself the task of explaining to the very best of my ability just why, even today, the confrontation between them continues to loom so large in philosophical memory.

No doubt there are many ways one might answer this question. The Davos encounter has been so frequently cited and commented on by so many scholars of varying philosophical commitments that it has come to signify

almost everything and anything in the history of European ideas. There
have been, of course, a number of prior works that have grappled seriously
with the debate. Most important of all are the volume of essays in German
edited by Enno Rudolph and Dominic Kaegi, *Cassirer—Heidegger. 70 Jahre
Davoser Disputation,* and the excellent book by Michael Friedman, *A Parting of the Ways,* which devotes far deeper attention than I will here to the
role Rudolf Carnap played in the debate.[2] Generally speaking, however, the
Heidegger-Cassirer dispute has often come to serve as a philosophical allegory, a dramatization for all manner of concerns, not only philosophical but
also cultural and, perhaps most of all, political. And, because it was after all
a *confrontation,* it is frequently taken to symbolize various dualistic struggles: reason versus unreason, epistemology versus metaphysics, liberalism
versus fascism, Enlightenment versus anti-Enlightenment, and so forth. Let
me state outright that I regard such allegorical readings with deep suspicion,
for two interrelated reasons: they are typically evasive, insofar as they reduce issues of great philosophical complexity to mere slogans or simplistic
worldviews, and they are occasionally offensive, insofar as they suggest that
intellectual questions are best settled once and for all by decomposing
them into nonintellectual battles waged under this or that ideological flag. It
is indeed one of my hopes that this book may help us to better understand
just *why* the Davos disputation has been so frequently transformed into an
allegory. But this is an ancillary purpose. My chief task here is a combination of historical narrative and philosophical reconstruction: I wish to
deepen our philosophical and historical comprehension of the debate itself,
and for this reason I try, wherever necessary, to *de*-allegorize, to promote
understanding in place of polemic.

Let me note further that in the contest between Cassirer and Heidegger
I have tried to remain a more or less neutral bystander, insofar as such a
stance is possible. Although I have contributed elsewhere to ongoing discussion concerning Heidegger, I am by no means an unthinking partisan of his
philosophy. Nor do I believe my qualified sympathy for certain facets of his
work prevents me from taking a deeply sympathetic view of Cassirer's intellectual achievement. It should be admitted that, since his death a half-
century ago, Cassirer's reputation has suffered a precipitous decline, especially
in the Anglophone world. His most prominent student, Susanne Langer,
author of the popular *Philosophy in a New Key,* is rarely remembered today.

If Cassirer's legacy survives at all, it is chiefly because he was the author of several now-faded classics in the history of ideas, notably *The Philosophy of the Enlightenment* and *The Myth of the State*. Some readers may otherwise recall his name because the American philosopher Nelson Goodman invokes him as an inspiration in the book *Ways of Worldmaking* (the first chapter of which was presented at the University of Hamburg on the hundredth anniversary of Cassirer's birth). But Goodman himself seemed unable to muster full-throated enthusiasm: "Countless worlds made from nothing but symbols," he wrote, "so might a satirist summarize some major themes in the work of Ernst Cassirer."[3]

It deserves mention that in Europe, unlike North America, Cassirer has remained an important figure in philosophical discussion. In recent years he has even enjoyed a certain renaissance of interest, thanks chiefly to the efforts of John Michael Krois at the Humboldt University in Berlin, who, along with several of his colleagues and students, has worked tirelessly over many years to produce the new edition of Cassirer's collected works. Notwithstanding this renewed enthusiasm, however, the fact remains that there is something about Cassirer that seems to belong almost irretrievably to the past. Perhaps this is because his own life and intellectual commitments call to mind the larger tragedy of mid-twentieth-century Europe. And if the philosophical encounter between Cassirer and Heidegger still haunts us even today, this is in part because we associate it with the political failure of liberalism and the triumph of illiberal authoritarianism in Germany. It therefore seems worth adding that while writing this book I have come to a far greater appreciation of Cassirer's merits. Although my admiration for Heidegger has accordingly diminished, it has by no means been entirely extinguished. Overall, however, this is not a work in which I have given free reign to my own philosophical sympathies. Readers seeking a definitive verdict as to who "won" and who "lost" in this debate, inappropriate as these terms may seem, will be disappointed to learn that my purposes are largely critical and expository.

It is perhaps my luxury as an intellectual historian that I am disburdened of the requirement for a final judgment as to who was right and who was wrong. It may also be that I am by temperament disinclined to believe that philosophical arguments are ever settled once and for all. If they were, it seems to me that the history of ideas would have come to an end a long time ago. The Davos disputation endures in philosophical memory not because it offers definitive answers, but rather because the questions it raises are still felt to be compelling. My modest hope is that the reader will come away from this book with a renewed understanding of the Davos disputation and a deepened appreciation of its continued significance for the history of Continental philosophy—its past as well as its future.

Montmartre, Paris
Steingenberger Hotel Belvédère, Davos-Platz
Harvard University, Cambridge

Continental Divide

Introduction

Un jeune étudiant pouvait avoir l'impression qu'il assistait à la création et à la fin du monde.

—EMMANUEL LÉVINAS, describing the Davos encounter

Heidegger and Cassirer at Davos

In the spring of 1929, two philosophers—Martin Heidegger and Ernst Cassirer—met for a public conversation in the town of Davos, Switzerland. At the time they were arguably the most important thinkers on the European continent, and the words they exchanged were granted an epochal significance of such proportion that, even today, philosophers and historians of Continental thought have yet to take full stock of their true magnitude. It is widely understood that the Davos disputation cast in relief some of the most fundamental and divisive issues in the history of modern philosophy. In this book I offer a reconstruction of this conversation, its origins, and its aftermath.

For more than half a century the Davos disputation between Cassirer and Heidegger has remained an important touchstone in philosophical memory. It frequently plays a divisive and allegorical function in the history of Continental philosophy. Scholars from a variety of disciplines and ideological camps are tempted to regard it as a final moment of rupture—between humanism and anti-humanism, enlightenment and counter-enlightenment, or rationalism and irrationalism—as if the defining struggles of twentieth-century thought were crystallized within this single event. The accomplished Kant-scholar Michael Friedman has used it with great effect to illustrate what he has called "a parting of the ways" between analytic and Continental philosophy. The sociologist Pierre Bourdieu made it the centerpiece in his rather more dubious effort to decompose Heidegger's thought in terms of a so-called political ontology. More boldly still, the German intellectual historian Hans Blumenberg once suggested that it be read as a secular reprisal of the theological dispute between Luther and Zwingli. There is nothing prima facie wrong about such interpretations, and they are, perhaps, inevitable. Even at the time, anecdotal accounts of Heidegger's meeting with Cassirer were much-burdened with symbolism: newspaper reports and academic journals referred to the dispute in generational terms as a representative encounter between "the old and the new thinking." Heidegger's student, Otto Friedrich Bollnow, would later recall that "one had the sublime feeling, to have lived as witness to an historical moment, precisely like that of which Goethe had spoken in his 'Campagne in Frankreich': 'From here and now a new epoch of world-history begins,'—in this case, of philosophical history." And Emmanuel Lévinas, at that time living in Germany as an apprentice to Edmund Husserl, recalled in a later interview his sense that Cassirer's uninspired performance meant "the end of a particular type of humanism." A "young student," he added, "could have had the impression that he was witness to the creation and the end of the world."[1]

The debate between Heidegger and Cassirer is often remembered as a pivotal moment in the history of Continental ideas. Just why this should be the case deserves careful scrutiny. The conceptual content of the debate continues to arouse philosophical interest, and justifiably so. But it can only partly explain why the debate continues to feature so prominently as a reference point in debates over the past and future of European philosophy. A more satisfactory answer must address the way that philosophical concepts and historical significance have become almost incorrigibly intertwined.

In this study of the Davos disputation, I have therefore tried to provide two different but interlocking perspectives. First, I offer a detailed philosophical reconstruction of a pivotal debate in the history of ideas; and second, I explore the broader and more perplexing phenomenon of philosophical memory, the complicated and overdetermined process whereby philosophy comes to understand itself by telling itself stories about where it has been. What follows, then, is both a historical reconstruction *and* a philosophical analysis.

The book begins with general portraits of both Cassirer and Heidegger in the present introduction. This is followed, in Chapter 1, by a general account of philosophical trends in the 1920s and, in Chapter 2, by a detailed discussion concerning both the origins and the events of the Davos *Hochschul-kurse*. Readers impatient with this sort of narrative may wish to turn immediately to Chapter 3, where I discuss the independent lectures by Cassirer and Heidegger, and Chapter 4, where I provide a philosophical annotation to the debate itself. Chapter 5 deepens this analysis by examining the dialogue between Cassirer and Heidegger in the years leading up to their debate. Chapter 6 explores what happened in the years that followed. Finally, in Chapter 7, I consider the manifold ways the debate continues to signify in the memory of Continental philosophy. To state the matter with great brevity, the overall argument of the book is that the Davos debate illustrates the way that philosophical ideas "ramify," how they take on a variety of cultural and political meanings. I explain this phenomenon as follows.

How Concepts Ramify

It is a distinctive trait of Continental philosophy that it exhibits an acute consciousness of its own historical condition. Kant believed that his was an "age of Critique." Hegel considered his own philosophy to be nothing less than the contemporary world comprehended in thought. Nietzsche adopted a more oppositional stance, declaring his insights too advanced for his own time: when the madman in *The Gay Science* declares that "God is dead," he quickly falls into despair when he realizes his announcement is premature. This understanding of philosophy as an event whose meanings unfold in time has remained a defining characteristic of philosophy in the Continental mode. Indeed, one might even say it is *historical consciousness* above all that marks off Continental philosophy as a distinctive tradition alongside of, but separate from, "analytic" philosophy.[2] This sort of historical consciousness is a phenomenon at once less formal, but also more expansive, than "historicism" *stricto sensu*. But how does this historical awareness actually inform philosophical argumentation? How does philosophy establish its own historical meaning?

A chief task of this book is to explore what happens when philosophers begin to imagine the manifold of connections between their own arguments and the world they inhabit. There is nothing unusual about this process. It is, I would submit, a commonplace strategy of interpretation and conceptual elaboration, whereby philosophy effects its own movement from concepts to

culture so as to claim for itself a larger and seemingly more elaborate significance. To observe this strategy is to understand nothing less than the historical inscription of ideas. To understand this movement, however, is *not* to
deny the inner life of the concepts themselves or to substitute for philosophy
a reductive sociology of ideas. Rather, it is to follow philosophical concepts
themselves as their meanings branch out into the wider world to which they
already implicitly belong. It is to understand how concepts ramify. The ramification of any given concept is of course multiple and forever open to change.
The connections and associations by which philosophical arguments take on
added significance are the fruits of argument but also of imagination, and in
tracing their development one tracks not necessary entailments but strategies of interpretation by which the potentialities of a given idea are developed, transformed, and revised. Paradoxically, however, a concept begins to
ramify the instant it is conceived; there is no moment of pure thought that
does not immediately take on a further meaning. Conceptual ramification is
therefore nothing "external." It is the concept itself, conceived according to
one of its historical possibilities.

Now, in Continental philosophy during the interwar era, I would submit,
philosophers were unusually attentive to the historical inscription of their
ideas, no doubt because so many of them understood their age to be one
of historical transformation or crisis. Indeed, the intellectual situation of
interwar Germany seemed almost to *require* that philosophers take a stand
on the meaning of their ideas, that they explain the relation between their
philosophical claims and the surrounding world. In different ways, both
Heidegger and Cassirer understood themselves as philosophers whose
work emerged from and was responsive to the crisis of the modern condition. Both sought to explain this crisis, to diagnose its problems, and to
disclose prospects for a different and more salutary manner of historical being. But because they were both so conscious of their historical moment, a
proper understanding of the disagreement between them cannot remain at
the level of conceptual analysis alone. Their disagreement was irreducibly
philosophical, but it was also a disagreement concerning the very meaning
of philosophy as a human activity. Ultimately, they found themselves locked
in a deep and ongoing philosophical discussion that returned again and again
to a single question: *What is it to be a human being?*

Two Images of Humanity

To explain what I take to be the fundamental disagreement between Cassirer and Heidegger, I would like to introduce the notion of a "normative image of humanity." I shall appeal to this notion throughout the book in order to bring together various of the more local points of the dispute and to emphasize its most important and definitive tension. But first a rudimentary explanation is in order.

A normative image, as I intend it here, is an intuitive notion that provides an initial sense of orientation for philosophical argument. A relevant illustration for this idea can be found in Kant's 1785 essay, "What Does It Mean to Orient Oneself in Thinking?" in which Kant suggests that just as there is a sense of fundamental orientation that first serves to orient the individual body in space (an orientation indicated by such everyday terms as right, left, up, and down), so, too, there is a kind of mental orientation that lies at the very root of philosophical reflection. Such an orientation is a precondition for concept-formation, although it is not itself conceptual in form. Now, it was Kant's claim that this initial orientation is given by *reason*. On Kant's view it is human rationality itself that grants our thinking its original sense of direction. On my own definition, however, I shall propose the broader notion that this orientation *may* be rational but need not necessarily be so. A normative image of humanity more often takes the form of an intuition, an a priori conviction or deeply held belief. I will refer to it as an *image* largely because I wish to underscore the point that intellectuals often ground their argumentation in a basic picture, the character of which is as much aesthetic and metaphorical as it is rational.[3] In the *Philosophical Investigations,* Wittgenstein makes reference to a "picture" of the mind that can hold philosophy captive, preventing us from properly understanding the way the mind actually works. This point is both too restrictive and too ambitious, since it implies we are trapped in *false* images of ourselves, images from which we can and should escape to arrive at an unobstructed view of the way things really are. Here I would suggest instead that a normative image of humanity may just be a condition for thinking about ourselves at all. However, I should caution against a possible misunderstanding: I would not claim that such an image is *nothing but* an aesthetic device. My point is rather that the orientations that lie at the very heart of conceptual argument seem so powerful one would be hard-pressed to explain their attraction as exclusively conceptual. The images that first provide orientation *for* thinking often seem to precede thinking; they are first evident to us not through concepts but at a level we might call preconceptual, at a primitive stratum that embraces, even if it is not limited to, metaphor and affect.

A guiding premise of this book is that philosophical arguments are animated by images in this special sense. But it is not merely an image of what the world *is* like. An image plays an added and indeed crucial role insofar as it motivates and inspires us with a sense of what the world *should* be like. In this sense an image is not just descriptive but also normative. Now, I am not suggesting that we regard normativity as *nothing but* a picture we wish to see realized. My point is simply that normativity, whatever its true sources, is something that holds us in its grip thanks in part to the metaphors and examples we use when explaining its implications. But clearly this is not a matter of strict determinism. Intellectuals change their metaphors just as they change their minds, by working themselves out of one image and into another. In this process concepts prove indispensable, because they are the vehicles through which we ramify our intuitions and, sometimes (though less frequently than we might care to believe), convince ourselves to modify them entirely.

Thrownness and Spontaneity

At the core of the debate between Cassirer and Heidegger was a fundamental contest between two normative images of humanity. For Cassirer, the human being is endowed with a special capacity for spontaneous self-expression: to be human is to create in complete freedom whole worlds of meaning, and these self-created worlds become in turn the objective spheres we experience as beautiful, moral, and true. Cassirer derived this insight into our constructivist or formative capacity from Kant, whose theory of transcendental conditions served as the initial pattern and inspiration for Cassirer's philosophy of symbolic forms. The American philosopher Nelson Goodman spoke of this self-creative capacity as "worldmaking." Cassirer himself called this worldmaking capacity by its originally Kantian and more technical term, *spontaneity,* a term whose meaning for Cassirer, as for Kant, was at once epistemological *and* ethico-political.

For Heidegger, human beings are understood to be defined first and foremost by our finitude, which is to say we discover ourselves in the midst of conditions we had no share in creating and cannot hope to control. To be human in Heidegger's view is to be gifted with a special sort of *receptivity,* or openness to the world. This phenomenon of disclosedness lies at the very core of human existence, deeper than our rationality and before any and all practical action. Not infrequently, critics have noted that this image of human life has its roots in the religious experience of dependency upon God. But it is an important characteristic of Heidegger's thinking that this sense of dependency remains fundamental to human existence well after the collapse of traditional religion. Although we moderns may persist in trying somehow to ground our metaphysical principles (in reason, nature, power, and so forth), our efforts to do so are merely strategies for evading the central fact of human life, that our existence is ultimately historical and therefore *groundless.* Heidegger called this groundless condition by various names, but most typically he referred to it as *finitude* or "thrownness."

The disagreement between Cassirer and Heidegger's turns upon this fundamental distinction between spontaneity and receptivity, between the human capacity for worldmaking as against our openness to the world. Cassirer forges his philosophical system with an eye toward the unconditioned, the inexhaustible, and even the "infinite" spontaneity of human expression. Heidegger works out his own philosophical ideas from the basic premise that the human being is a creature of essential finitude, limited by time and history, which finds itself thrown into conditions it did not create. Now, there are many ways one might characterize the essential tension between these two visions of humanity. For economy's sake I will most often describe it as a contest between *thrownness* and *spontaneity.*[4]

Although the contrast between these two normative images of the human being is indeed profound, we should note that it is by no means absolute. They are interrelated most of all by virtue of a shared philosophical insight that derives ultimately from Kant and his doctrine of transcendental idealism. Briefly, this is the doctrine according to which the world is intelligible to us as human beings at all only thanks to certain conditions that we impose upon it a priori. Both Cassirer and Heidegger subscribed to some variant of this idea. Cassirer saw reality itself, in all its diverse meanings, as a symbolic creation of the human mind. The primitive human being's mythic nature, the artist's aesthetic realm, the scientist's theoretical model of the cosmos—these were all in a very deep sense *constructions,* bearing witness to the human being's distinctive capacity for world-formation. To be sure, in his *Philosophy of Symbolic Forms* Cassirer also acknowledged a place for what is sensually given. His special idea of "symbolic pregnance" was meant to explain how our experience of a meaningful reality depends on a phenomenon of meaning that lies beyond the distinction between subject and object. Cassirer's commitment to spontaneity thus does not imply a reversion to Platonism or other species of rampant idealism. But it is an insight closely bound up with the theory of transcendental conditions he derived from his neo-Kantian teachers and, *via* their instruction, from Kant himself.

Meanwhile, Heidegger saw the human being as constituted by worldliness and temporality, and he accordingly rejected as metaphysical error any doctrine that promoted a view of the human subject as a world*maker* gifted with cognitive and practical mastery over its creations. Still, his own philosophical inquiry into Being was meant to illuminate the human *understanding* of Being that first lends our world its fundamental intelligibility. Heidegger could thus describe the human being as an entity that is distinguished from all others in the world by a special capacity for "worldforming" *(Weltbildung).*[5] In *Being and Time* he went so far as to acknowledge *idealism* as the only acceptable point of departure for his philosophical commission. Ultimately, then, the account of "Being" as laid down in Heidegger's earlier work bears a close and acknowledged resemblance to the Kantian doctrine of transcendental conditions. To be sure, neither Heidegger nor Cassirer considered their own philosophical work as merely extending the principles of transcendental idealism. But they share a common point of departure in Kant's basic insight that the way the world presents itself to us depends ultimately on conditions we bring to it. The contrast between thrownness and spontaneity should accordingly be understood as working out two distinct approaches to the problem of transcendental conditions. It should not be and cannot be understood as a radical opposition.

It is also crucial to note that Cassirer and Heidegger were to a significant degree allies in the contemporary struggle to expand the scope for philosophy *beyond* what they considered the methodological constraints of both phenomenology and neo-Kantianism. Heidegger started out as an apprentice to Edmund Husserl, whose phenomenological investigations provided a model for how to practice philosophy as a rigorous science of mental intention. But Heidegger soon felt the need to break from what he saw as Husserl's idealistic commitment to studying acts of consciousness in isolation from the manifest phenomenon of being-in-the-world. Heidegger wished to broaden phenomenology so that it might be applied to the analysis of human existence itself in all its worldly forms—the moods and practical skills through which the world is first revealed, the cultural and historical understandings that first constitute our understanding of who and what we are. In his later years Heidegger turned even further against the scientific conception of philosophy; he sought instead to understand the limitations of both science and technology, and he fastened his attention on language, poetry, and art as richer modes of "world-disclosure." Cassirer, for his part, received his initial training from Hermann Cohen and the Marburg School of neo-Kantianism, and his earliest studies in epistemology and philosophy of science are a enduring testament to the Marburg legacy. But by the 1920s Cassirer felt the need to expand beyond Cohen's neo-Kantian vision of philosophy as a transcendental critique of scientific knowledge, and he turned toward far broader fields of study—anthropology, language, religion, and the arts. Later, he would draft the foundations for a new sort of philosophical method oriented toward an analysis of so-called basis-phenomena, a late turn in his method that some have likened to the phenomenological techniques of Merleau-Ponty.[6]

All too frequently, the relationship between Cassirer and Heidegger is characterized as a violent clash of antipodes or worldviews. But as the above observations have already shown, the contrast between them should not be overdrawn. In fact, we can only make sense of their disagreement if we understand how much they shared in common. First and foremost, we must take note of the fact that both Cassirer and Heidegger were part of a broader turning away from transcendental-idealist method in the decade following World War I. In their earliest training, both of them had been schooled in what one might call the "science paradigm" in philosophy. The Husserlian paradigm saw philosophy as modeled *after* science and in possession of its own equally scientific standing; the neo-Kantian paradigm saw philosophy as a transcendental groundwork *for* science. It should be noted that neither of these paradigms proposed a rigid scientism, though it was not uncommon to hear especially neo-Kantians accused of incipient positivism. Although both Cassirer and Heidegger absorbed a great deal from their teachers (Cassirer from Cohen, Heidegger from both Rickert and Husserl), in their maturity they both grew dissatisfied with the science paradigm and came to embrace a more expansive ideal of philosophy as a discipline that might cast light on the full spectrum of human experience, from language to art and from ancient religion to modern science. The consequences of this shift in philosophical method can hardly be exaggerated. Whereas the science paradigm had emphasized the singular importance of the *Naturwissenschaften* or "natural sciences," the expansive paradigm allowed for a generous understanding of the epistemic and metaphysical foundations of the so-called *Geisteswissenschaften* or "cultural sciences." Cassirer's studies of myth (which aroused Heidegger's interest) in the second volume of *The Philosophy of Symbolic Forms* and Heidegger's own analysis of mood-states such as fear and boredom in *Being and Time* were clear signs that by the mid-1920s the science paradigm was losing its sovereign status.

Finally, we should not neglect to note that, as they turned from the science paradigm, both Cassirer and Heidegger became far more intensely concerned with the problem of how philosophy is conditioned by history. The Husserlian paradigm tended to discourage this kind of historical awareness because it imagined that as a science phenomenology was disclosing ahistorical truths. In contrast, the neo-Kantian paradigm encouraged a more generous understanding for how knowledge develops over time: in his 1921 study of Einstein's relativity theory, Cassirer explained that the Kantian notion of fixed transcendental rules for scientific knowledge would have to be abandoned, because it was clear that the mathematical groundwork for science was not immune to historical transformation. But by the mid-1920s both Cassirer and Heidegger had moved toward a far richer understanding of how philosophical questions are grounded in the essential historicity of human experience. For Heidegger, philosophy aims to disclose an understanding of Being that has been forgotten or even suppressed over the span of millennia, and it is an essential lesson of his analysis that Being has a temporal-historical character. Ultimately, the human being must come to recognize that philosophizing itself is a hermeneutic event that discloses not eternal truths but rather the truths of one's own historical condition. For Cassirer, too, history came to play a crucial role in his conception of what philosophy can and should strive to be. Nearly all of his works were structured as *histories* of thought, but his was not merely an expository preference. Rather, Cassirer came to conceive of the philosophy of symbolic forms itself as a phenomenological *narrative,* which told the tale of how humanity broke from myth finally to arrive at a stage of modern and enlightened self-consciousness: the analysis of symbolism itself thereby became a *historical achievement.*

As the above observations suggest, Cassirer and Heidegger were united most of all by a deeply historical awareness that modern European philosophy was embarking on a phase of radical transformation. Thanks to this self-awareness as philosophical modernists, they looked to one another first as possible allies and later as competitors (especially when the anti-modernist strain in Heidegger's philosophical modernism became vividly apparent). In noting these broader resemblances, of course, I hardly wish to imply that these two thinkers were alike in all respects. But it is crucial that we recognize the broad commonalties between them, because it is only against this shared background of Continental philosophy that we can begin to appreciate why Cassirer and Heidegger eventually found themselves so much at loggerheads. The very intensity of their conversation, which spanned more than two decades, would not have been possible were it not for a common language.

Cassirer's Philosophy: An Excursus

Ernst Cassirer was beyond doubt one of the greatest philosophers and intellectual historians to emerge from the cultural ferment of modern Germany. Born in 1874 into a prosperous German-Jewish family, Ernst combined the temperament of a scholar with the topical promiscuity of an artist. Among his cousins were the art dealers Paul and Bruno Cassirer. Ernst himself forged an intimate association with the art historians Aby Warburg and Erwin Panofsky, and throughout the 1920s he remained an affiliate of the Warburg Library in Hamburg. To his admirers as well as his critics, Cassirer stood as the very embodiment of central European liberal culture: his many contributions to the history of science, culture, and epistemology bespoke a robust attachment to the rationalist spirit of the *Aufklärung* and the cultural legacy of German classicism. He wrote extensively, not only about Leibniz, Kant, and their significance for later developments in the philosophy of science up through the Einsteinian revolution, but he also wrote about poets and cultural critics and philosophers of culture, such as Schiller, Goethe, and Humboldt. Cassirer was first introduced as a student in Berlin to the life-philosophy of Georg Simmel, from whom he learned a capacious style of thinking that embraced all fields of cultural expression. He was more closely identified with the neo-Kantian epistemological doctrines of Hermann Cohen, with whom he later studied at the University of Marburg. Cassirer was the author of an immense variety of philosophical texts, such as the early studies of modern scientific explanation, *Substance and Function* and *Einstein's Theory of Relativity;* a synthetic history of epistemology, *The Problem of Knowledge;* a Kant-biography, *Kants Leben und Lehre;* and a new, scholarly edition of Kant's collected works. This astonishing output culminated in the 1920s with Cassirer's own, independent contribution to modern philosophy and his definitive turn from science to culture in the three-volume masterpiece, *The Philosophy of Symbolic Forms,* which was published over the span of six prolific years: the first volume, *Language,* appeared in 1923, the second, *Mythical Thought,* in 1925, and the third, *The Phenomenology of Knowledge,* in 1929, just a few months after the debate with Heidegger.

Although his Jewish origins inhibited his pace of professional advancement, by 1919 Cassirer had assumed a chair in philosophy at the newly founded University of Hamburg. When he appeared at Davos he was professionally well established, having served as a leading editor at *Kantstudien,* which was at that time one of Germany's most prominent journals for philosophy. He was widely esteemed not only in Germany but throughout Europe as a philosopher of enormous consequence. Some years later, he and his wife would be forced to emigrate, first to England (from 1933 to 1935), then to Sweden (from 1935 to 1940), and finally to the United States, where he taught at Yale (from 1941 to 1944) and then at Columbia (1944–1945), until his death in 1945.

The Spontaneity Thesis

That Cassirer was himself by no means the embodiment of neo-Kantian philosophical orthodoxy was obvious. He had long before taken the decisive step—as announced in the first volume of *The Philosophy of Symbolic Forms*—from "the critique of reason to the critique of culture." Yet despite the clear originality of his symbolic-form theory, we would be mistaken to neglect the enduring influence in Cassirer's work of certain neo-Kantian premises, which he had absorbed while studying with Cohen at Marburg.

The essential creed of the entire neo-Kantian tradition is transcendental-ism, according to which the human mind is said to be an essentially sponta-neous and creative faculty that is capable of laying down necessary and a priori conditions for its own surroundings and, therefore, of shaping the experienced world according to its own basic forms of intelligibility. Cohen anchored this moment of transcendental spontaneity in logic and he re-served its highest application for scientific explanation. Cassirer, by con-trast, is often credited with having relaxed the implicit scientism in Cohen's thinking in favor of a more generous and pluralistic theory of cultural expression. Most importantly, he introduced the phenomenon of *historical* variation, such that the Kantian a priori was no longer fixed but was un-derstood to change over time (a modification that was especially important for explaining advances beyond the strictures of Euclidean geometry).[7] But it is important to recall that even Cohen had attempted, after Kant's exam-ple, to write a purely idealist ethics as well as an idealist theory of aesthetic judgment. The core premise of transcendental creativity proved highly flex-ible in its application, and Cassirer found it possible even after his turn to culture in the 1920s to adapt it for the interpretation of nonscientific phe-nomena such as language and myth.

Cassirer's greatest contribution to the philosophy of culture, *The Philoso-phy of Symbolic Forms,* represented a bold effort to interpret all of human creativity after the transcendental model. Culture, Cassirer claimed, is an ever-expanding and pluralistic field of symbolic expression. Its apparent di-versity, however, nonetheless obeys certain formative laws, the expressive and a priori structuring principles of the human mind. Cassirer thus wished to show how an essentially Kantian theory regarding the formative powers of transcendental consciousness might guide his own inquiry into the na-ture of scientific symbolism as well as the "deeper" and historically prior modes of symbolic expression such as language and myth. The fundamen-tal premise for this project was laid out in advance in a programmatic essay from 1922, "The Concept of Symbolic Form in the Construction of the Human Sciences," which Cassirer offered as his inaugural publication for the Warburg Library (where he was to carry out research for much of the decade). The essay contains one of the earliest and most important definitions of symbolic form:

> By "symbolic form" [is meant] that energy of the spirit [*Energie des Geistes*] through which a mental meaning-content is attached to a sensual sign and inwardly dedicated to this sign. In this sense language, the mythical-religious world, and the arts each present us with a particular symbolic form. For in them all we see the mark of the basic phenomenon, that our consciousness [*Bewußtsein*] is not satisfied to receive impression [*Eindruck*] from outside, but rather that it permeates each impression with a free activity of expression [*mit einer freien Tätigkeit des Ausdrucks*]. In what we call the objective reality of things we are thus confronted with a world of self-created signs and images.[8]

Now, this theory of a self-created human symbolic order as elaborated in the three volumes of *The Philosophy of Symbolic Forms* might appear to promote a generous regard for "primitive" or even "irrational" modes of symbolism. Indeed, Cassirer's inquiry into myth and magic drew inspiration from Warburg's library, where the unusual arrangement of books on the shelves presented the visitor with a rich panoply of exotic rites and beliefs, folklore, astrology, magic, and esoteric wisdom, all of which seemed to inspire a heightened appreciation for the diversity of human culture. Yet Cassirer's attraction to cultural variety had little to do with multicultural promiscuity. The apparent pluralism of his approach was held firmly in check by a developmentalist theory that confined the diverse forms of symbolic expression to an unapologetically linear and developmentalist narrative. From myth to science, Cassirer claimed, human expressive capacities trace a single, world-historical path such that the history of symbolic expression became a quasi-Hegelian history of spiritual self-cultivation.[9] The entire theory of symbolic form thus culminated in the third and final volume with an analysis of science that Cassirer, in homage to Hegel, termed a *phenomenology* of knowledge.

Given this fundamentally developmentalist premise, Cassirer's theory of form thus cannot be credited with a nonhierarchical pluralism. Indeed, the internal logic of philosophy required that humanity awaken from mythic devotion to acknowledge its own responsibility in creating the symbolic order. Cassirer was therefore unabashedly a modernist, and self-reflexively so, insofar as his theory of symbolic development seemed to underwrite his own theoretical labor. A true "philosophy" of symbolic form demanded insight into the inner constitution of symbols and was thus only possible given the breakthrough from myth to modernity. As Cassirer claimed, philosophy "first constitutes itself by this very act of transcendence."[10]

Cassirer's robust allegiance both to Kantian transcendental premises and to the primacy of science thus remained more or less unshaken even after his turn to culture in the 1920s. Indeed, in the third volume of *The Philosophy of Symbolic Forms,* largely completed toward the end of 1927, Cassirer affirmed that science alone represented the culminating stage of human symbolic achievements. The hallmark of modern scientific thinking was that any remaining attachment to the explanation of things as "substance" had been dialectically supplanted by explanation in terms of pure "function" alone. Elaborating on ideas set forth in *Substance and Function* and applied explicitly to modern physics in his 1921 study of Einstein's relativity theory, Cassirer charted a gradual transformation in scientific explanation from the dogmatic metaphysics of "substance" to the "purely symbolic theory" of relations: whereas classical physics anchored its claims in material masses and so cleaved, if only surreptitiously, to a kind of metaphysical realism, modern science had reached a point of thoroughgoing intellectual abstraction where the coherence of purely internal relations dispensed with any and all appeals to the supposed nature of nonconceptual "reality." Thus, for example, Euclidean space is absorbed into Riemannian space (where Euclidean space is "functionalized" as space with a curvature of zero), and the rules of Euclidean geometry are absorbed into group theory (of which Euclid's rules are now merely one operational set).[11] The entire movement of science aims toward supplanting naïve realism with a kind of conceptual coherentism. As Cassirer explained, "the basic concepts of natural science no longer appear as mere copies and reproductions of immediate material data" but are now "represented as constructive projects of physical thinking." It followed that "the concept of the symbol has become a center and focus of the whole epistemology of physics."[12]

All of Cassirer's major interventions in the history of science contribute to this basic observation, summarized in a 1931 address, that in theoretical knowledge, human consciousness eventually supplants "the *concept of being*" with "the *concept of order*."[13] Scientific modernization, in sum, is a process of abstraction.[14] Incidentally, it is worth noting that this same conviction was also to guide Cassirer's 1932 work of historical synthesis, *The Philosophy of the Enlightenment,* in which Cassirer declared that mathematics remained throughout the eighteenth century, the "prototype of reason."[15] For example, in the opening chapter on Newton and his eighteenth-century natural-scientific descendants, Cassirer claimed that the "real achievement" of science lay not in its "new objective content" but rather in "the new function" which it attributed to the mind. "The knowledge of nature," he added, "does not simply lead us out into the world of objects; it serves rather as a medium in which the mind develops its own self-knowledge." Here Cassirer affirmed once again his essentially Kantian faith in the mind as a lawgiver unto nature. He also reiterated the explicitly anthropomorphic principle guiding his symbol-philosophy, according to which the entire field of human experience, from science to aesthetics, is structured a priori by the expressive spontaneity of the human mind.

Substance, Function, Form

It is no exaggeration to say that the entirety of Cassirer's philosophical labor takes as its founding premise the Kant-derived insight that all objectivity presupposes mental spontaneity, the principle according to which the world only shows itself to be an objective and ordered domain because it is shaped in advance by forms projected spontaneously by the human mind. Cassirer acknowledged various anticipations of this insight as early as the ancient Greek notion of non-Being, without which "intellectual mastery of empirical reality is not to be attained."[16] And he discerned a more modern precedent in Descartes' theory of geometry according to which spatial substance is intelligible only because it answers to the mind's own mathematical rules.[17] Yet on Cassirer's view the crucial advance was achieved only through Kant's Copernican Revolution with its insight that objectivity itself is conditional on a priori forms of sensibility and intuition. All of Cassirer's own philosophical studies, early to late, presuppose this principle of spontaneity. His principled commitment to the idea is still evident even in the third volume of *The Philosophy of Symbolic Forms,* which introduces the phrase "symbolic pregnance" to describe the saturation of perception by categorical form.[18] But the idea is already evident as early as *Substance and Function,* in which Cassirer observed that "The 'spontaneity' of thought is . . . not the opposite but the necessary correlate of 'objectivity,' which can only be reached by means of it."[19]

For Cassirer, the idea that objective reality is only intelligible as a system of conceptual rules is most apparent in the advances made by the physical sciences and mathematics, culminating in Einstein's relativity theory. With the revolutions of modern physics, the older metaphysical dogmas of invariant and ultimate substance are no longer valid: in place of things that are considered invariant or merely given, such as the sun for Copernicus or the stars for Galileo and Newton, Einstein recognized that "no sort of things are truly invariant but always only certain fundamental relations and functional dependencies retained in the symbolic language of our mathematics and physics." But this recognition did not belong to Einstein alone. The "radical resolution" of sensually given objects into conceptual functions and relations was the most advanced step forward in the modern scientific assault on all dogmas of metaphysical substance. It signaled the "logical conclusion of an intellectual tendency characteristic of all the philosophical and scientific thought of the modern age."[20]

The practical and political implications of this thesis were revealed most explicitly in Cassirer's 1916 collection, *Freedom and Form: Studies in German Intellectual History.* Most of the essays in this volume had been composed well before World War I, but Cassirer understood quite well that their focus on political and metaphysical freedom would hold a special meaning for his German contemporaries in the midst of the present conflict. The essays address key thinkers in the central European tradition—Leibniz, Kant, Goethe, Schiller, Fichte, Humboldt, and Hegel—and they are linked thematically through the correlative concepts of freedom and form, the opposition and eventual reconciliation of which furnished the ground for a distinctively German Idealist conception of political life. What permits this reconciliation is the theme of "spontaneity" *(Spontaneität),* a concept with ramified significance, at once metaphysical and practical, that Cassirer adumbrates in various ways throughout the book as Leibniz's concept of truth, Lessing's theory of genius, and Schiller's theory of freedom, all of them converging on Kant's philosophy with its "fundamental concept of autonomy" and "self-legislation of the spirit" *(Selbstgesetzlicheit des Geistes).*[21]

The chief burden of the book is to demonstrate how modern German thought shares a basic commitment to spontaneity, as theorized with unparalleled clarity in Kant's philosophy, which unites both theoretical and practical reason in a single *Grundthema* or foundational theme, "the thought of autonomy, the promotion of the self-legislation of knowledge and will." For Kant, both our theoretical knowledge of nature *and* our practical action as moral agents in the world require, for their possibility, the very same rational spontaneity. "Thought and deed," Cassirer wrote, "hang together and point back to their deepest root. The necessity of the logical, like that of the practical, are grounded in an original self-determination of reason. All formedness [*Geformtheit*]—the region in which it confronts us—has its origin in an 'act of spontaneity.'"[22] In a passage remarkable for its brevity, Cassirer seeks to explain how this spontaneity reveals itself as a mental action behind any object of human meaning: "Every contractual bindedness [*Verbundene*] must be traced back to an act of binding [*Verbindung*], all contentful structure of consciousness to the lawfulness of formation [*Gestaltung*] itself, all that is given [*Gegebene*] to the pure act [*Tun*]."[23]

Although Cassirer's concept of a pure and absolutely unconditioned mental spontaneity as the constitutive force behind all objective order is most obviously traceable to Kant, Cassirer's general argument is that the principle of spontaneity underwrites nearly all of the major intellectual contributions of modern German thought, from Luther's affirmation of individual faith to Leibniz's monadology and on to Goethe, Fichte, and Hegel. Nor was this principle limited to philosophy. In a central chapter Cassirer sought to explain how even the poetry and aesthetic theory of Friedrich Schiller drew its needed energy from Kant's principle. As Cassirer observed, Schiller had confided to his friend, the jurist and aesthetic theorist Christian Gottfried Körner, that, "regarding mortal man surely no greater word has been spoken than the Kantian, which is also the content of his entire philosophy: *Determine yourself from yourself.*"[24] In Cassirer's eyes it was Schiller perhaps most of all who demonstrated the continued appeal of the Kantian theory of freedom for German intellectuals. "Freedom," according to Schiller, was "the pure form of spirituality as such," and it reached its highest realization in the experience of beauty. The beautiful in nature and in works of art reflected the idea of self-determination, such that every beautiful object seemed to call out, "be free, as I am."[25]

In the years following 1916, Schiller would remain for Cassirer a theorist of central and even paradigmatic significance. First and foremost, Schiller served as an important model as Cassirer began to develop a theory of culture and aesthetics grounded in Kantian principles. Thanks to his poetry, Schiller also came to play a symbolic role in Cassirer's philosophy as a kind of oracle for what one might call the generalized *ethos* of German Idealism. Cassirer would on occasion quote particular passages from Schiller's poems so as to illustrate general intellectual lessons and attitudes that he warmly endorsed. During the debate at Davos and in years that followed, Cassirer would more than once invoke the poet's luminous phrases to lend metaphoric force to his own philosophical convictions and to annotate his disagreement with Heidegger. As we shall see, this is one way Cassirer tried to ramify his concepts, magnifying both their rhetorical force and their cultural-historical significance.

The Turn to Culture

Cassirer's emergent interest in a philosophy of culture during the 1920s drew intellectual nourishment and material support from Aby Warburg (1866–1929), the founder of the Warburg Institute. Warburg was an art historian and scholar of iconography who borrowed much of his earliest inspiration from Jacob Burkhardt's studies of renaissance culture. Thanks to his family's tremendous financial resources, Warburg had begun as early as the 1880s to create a vast personal collection of world artifacts, which he eventually named the Warburg Library of Cultural History and which officially opened its doors in Hamburg in 1921. Initially under the direction of Fritz Saxl (in his later years Warburg fell quite ill and for several years remained abroad, in sanatoria in Switzerland), the Warburg Library served as a massive storehouse of ethnographic knowledge, all of it organized according to its founder's idiosyncratic classificatory scheme, which moved in an ascending order through the building, from "image" (symbolism and art, first floor), "word" (language and literature, second floor), "orientation" (that is, world belief systems from magic through religion to philosophy and science, third and fourth floors), and "action" (society and politics, fourth floor). Saxl was joined at the Warburg Library by the art historian Erwin Panofsky (1892–1968) and by Ernst Cassirer, all three of whom also sustained professorial affiliations with the University of Hamburg. With the Nazi seizure of power in 1933, the Warburg

Library's holdings were transferred to London, first to a basement in Thames House and, ultimately, in 1944, to the University of London, where the Library was rechristened the Warburg Institute. Under subsequent directors such as Henri Frankfort and E. H. Gombrich, the Institute continued long after the war, operating as a major center of research and scholarly support for preeminent students in the humanistic tradition, such as Paul Oskar Kristeller, Frances Yates, and Arnaldo Momigliano.[26]

Cassirer himself became acquainted with the Warburg Library in 1920 shortly after his appointment as professor to the newly founded University of Hamburg. Fritz Saxl would later speak of Cassirer's arrival as "a day memorable in the annals of the Warburg Institute":

> He was a gracious visitor, who listened attentively as I explained to him Warburg's intentions in placing books on philosophy next to books on astrology, magic and folklore, and in linking the sections on art with those on literature, religion, and philosophy. The study of philosophy was for Warburg inseparable from that of the so-called primitive mind: neither could be isolated from the study of imagery in religion, literature, and art. These ideas had found expression in the unorthodox arrangement of the books on the shelves.[27]

The classificatory system of the Warburg Library clearly struck a chord with Cassirer's own conception of cultural history. "This library is dangerous," Saxl recalls Cassirer saying. "I shall either have to avoid it altogether or imprison myself here for years. The philosophical problems are close to my own, but the concrete historical material which Warburg has collected is overwhelming." Cassirer soon became one of the most productive and intimate members of the Warburg Library; in fact, the very first publication to be issued in its name was Cassirer's own lecture on "primitive culture." For Cassirer the association proved enormously advantageous. Not only could he discover in the collection all of the requisite materials for his new philosophy of cultural history, he could also imagine it as an architectural realization of his principles. Indeed, the entire structure of Cassirer's multivolume *Philosophy of Symbolic Forms* might well be seen as a providing a formal conceptual apparatus or transcendental groundwork to the Warburg Library's empirical collection.

The impact of Cassirer's symbolic-forms philosophy on his Warburg Library colleagues is especially evident in the case of the art historian Erwin Panofsky, whose pathbreaking essay, "Perspective as 'Symbolic Form,'" was published by the Warburg Library in 1927.[28] The essay is noteworthy not only because it represents the earliest attempt to introduce categories borrowed from Cassirer's philosophy into art history. More importantly, its brilliant though stringently teleological conception of the history of perspective—Panofsky calls it a "breakthrough to the 'modern'"—may help us to further appreciate the historical inscription of Cassirer's own philosophy into the context of Weimar modernism. For Panofsky, the rise of perspective required a "detheologized" conception of space and the installation by means of abstract thought of a notion of spatial "infinity." The result was an unprecedented elevation of art into a "science" and, more specifically, "translation of psychophysiological space into mathematical space; in other words, an objectification of the subjective."[29] Although the details of this analysis resist synopsis, Panofsky's concluding message was that perspective should be understood within the larger narrative of humanism as a triumph of consciousness over its surroundings:

> Perspective, in transforming the *ousia* (reality) into the *phainomenon* (appearance), seems to reduce the divine to a mere subject matter for human consciousness; but for that very reason, conversely, it expands human consciousness into a vessel for the divine. It is thus no accident if this perspectival view of space has already succeeded twice in the course of the evolution of art: the first time as the sign of an ending, when antique theocracy crumbled; the second time as a sign of a beginning, when modern "anthropocracy" first reared itself.[30]

Such claims closely track Cassirer's idea that human history exhibits a gradually expanding "anthropomorphism" of the world and the consequent displacement of "substance" concepts by purely "functional" concepts (as, for example, in the shift from the bounded and pragmatic space of everyday experience to the infinite and theoretical space as conceived by mathematics).

At stake more generally was a shared conviction that in the history of human expression, and even in artistic expression, the rise of conceptual abstraction marked a salutary and indeed necessary advance. Panofsky's application of Cassirer's categories in the study of art thus helps to reinforce the sense that Cassirer's philosophy was itself imprinted with an unmistakably modernist cultural-historical character. Admittedly, in marked contrast to Aby Warburg's own belief that mythological thought remains alive in modern culture, Cassirer's progressivist doctrine seemed to require that modernity be understood as both a *triumph over* and a *displacement of* myth (a theme to be explored in greater detail later). Still, Cassirer shared Warburg's celebratory appreciation for the variety of human expressive forms. Cassirer remained in this sense a philosophical as well as cultural-political moderate. Notwithstanding his teleological commitment to science as the highest stage in human consciousness, he eschewed the more reductivist trends of positivism and scientism represented by more militant philosophical contemporaries such as Rudolf Carnap (for whom cultural modernism was anchored in political socialism).[31] Rather, Cassirer remained firmly committed to the constellation of values associated with the Warburg Institute and its predominant ethos of cultural pluralism and renaissance humanism.[32] All such values also informed Cassirer's essentially progressivist and democratic political sensibility, as would become especially evident in the later 1920s when the Weimar Republic faced increasingly militant opposition on both the left and the right.

Leaving aside for a moment the venomous political beliefs that may have helped to fuel Heidegger's hostility toward the neo-Kantian movement, it would be fair to say that he was mostly correct to discern something like a loose correlation between neo-Kantianism and German liberalism. It is a fact that many of the most prominent philosophers associated with the neo-Kantian schools during the Weimar period were, in one way or another, democratic and constitutionalist in their political commitments. Hermann Cohen had been a socialist (albeit a very moderate one), and his student and colleague Paul Natorp was likewise affiliated with liberal-socialist causes, most especially the movement in *Sozialpädagogik,* or social pedagogy. From the Baden, or Southwestern School, too—despite its more conservative temperament of its core philosophers, Windelband and Rickert—there emerged a number of noteworthy advocates of Weimar democracy, including the humanist Albert Schweitzer, who had studied ancient philosophy with Windelband, and the Protestant theologian Ernst Troeltsch, Windelband's colleague at Heidelberg, who moderated his earlier conservatism after witnessing the horrors of the war. Even Max Weber, despite his grim reservations concerning the rise of noncharismatic modes of authority, gave his qualified endorsement to the fledgling Republic at the end of his life. [33]

But it is Cassirer himself who was perhaps best known, even before the encounter with Heidegger, for his statements on behalf of liberal-democratic principles in Germany. On August 11, 1928, he delivered a public address at his home institution, the University of Hamburg, celebrating the ninth anniversary of the Weimar Constitution. Cassirer was then at the height of his reputation, and his status helped to confer on the occasion a solemnity appropriate for an academic institution that owed its own founding in April 1919 to the Republic. Cassirer himself was hardly a politician. Nor was he widely recognized for any major contributions to political theory or jurisprudence (despite his study of the politics of German Idealism and classicism, *Freedom and Form*). Yet while he remained largely aloof from Weimar political debate, he nonetheless stood as a representative for the diverse collection of progressive intellectuals in the 1920s whose political and personal aspirations bound them to the new democracy and its constitution.

Cassirer delivered his address, "The Idea of a Republican Constitution," for the *Verfassungsfeier* on August 11, 1928, at a moment when the ultimate collapse of the Republic was still unforeseen. The Nazis had held their first party rally at Nuremberg in August 1927, and by the time of the Reichstag elections of May in the following year, they had won more than 2 percent of the overall national vote—their highest electoral victory thus far. At this point, they were by no means a threat to the system, but while Cassirer remained engrossed in his studies, he was not so myopic as to think that all was well in the new democracy. He was especially alert to critics on the nationalist right who condemned the Republic as fundamentally un-German, and it was a guiding theme of his address that the very idea of a republican constitution derived from principles native to German philosophy in general and German Idealism in particular (the latter in his expansive use, designating the whole span of German metaphysics and epistemology from Leibniz through Kant to Hegel). "The idea of a republican constitution," Cassirer declared, "is by no means an alien presence in the whole of German intellectual history, let alone an intruder from beyond." The ideal of a republic was therefore native-grown, nourished by Germany's "most authentic tradition of philosophical idealism."[34]

The address for the Weimar constitution is revealing perhaps most of all for the rare passion Cassirer displayed in his defense of the fledgling democracy. But evident in this speech—as in all of Cassirer's writing—was a tone of rational moderation, even in the midst of political conflict. A great many of his critics were to fault Cassirer for this moderation in which they detected yet another sign of the impotence and naïveté of the liberal tradition in Germany. However, before we can even begin to assess the political significance of Cassirer's work, we must first understand more about his interlocutor.

Heidegger's Philosophy: An Excursus

Martin Heidegger was born in 1889, the oldest child of Friedrich Heidegger and Johanna (née Kempf), in the small town of Messkirch located in the Black Forest region of Baden-Württemberg in southwestern Germany. The Heideggers were a Catholic family of modest means—Friedrich worked as a sexton for the local church—and when the young Martin excelled at Gymnasium, first in Constance and then at Freiburg, it was only natural for his parents to consider him destined for the priesthood. By 1907 he had already received his initiation into philosophy with a gift from Conrad Groeber (the future Archbishop of Freiburg, at that time head of Heidegger's boarding school in Constance) of a work by the Catholic phenomenologist Franz Brentano, *On the Manifold Meaning of Being According to Aristotle.* Although for a short while the young Heidegger trained as a novice for the Jesuits, by 1911 he had decided against a Church career and had chosen instead to study mathematics and philosophy. His early work at the University of Freiburg under the neo-Kantian Heinrich Rickert culminated in a doctorate in philosophy *summa cum laude* in 1913. The war brought only a short interruption in Heidegger's studies—he was dismissed from service due to poor health—and by 1919 he met the great phenomenologist Edmund Husserl, to whom he quickly became a cherished disciple and assistant. In the same year he also announced to a friend that he had resolved to break from the Church (a decision no doubt fortified by his marriage in 1917 to Elfride Petri, a Protestant). In the years that followed, his philosophical reputation spread at a dramatic pace: In 1923 Heidegger assumed a professorship at the University of Marburg, where his seminars probed the most intractable questions in logic, phenomenology, ontology, and hermeneutics. In 1927 he published his first (though still incomplete) and arguably his most important work of original philosophy, *Being and Time,* and the following year, on the basis of this manuscript, he was appointed professor of philosophy at Freiburg, where he remained for the rest of his career. In the spring of 1929, when he met Cassirer for the public disputation in Davos, Switzerland, Heidegger was already among the most celebrated philosophers in central Europe. He also showed a prodigious energy: in a few brisk months following the disputation, he completed the draft of his second book, *Kant and the Problem of Metaphysics,* which was published before the year's end.

But with the Nazi seizure of power in 1933, the period of relative innocence in Heidegger's life came to a close. With evident zeal he joined the party and accepted its invitation to serve the Third Reich as rector at Freiburg. During his tenure, he went so far as to debase his philosophy by drafting existential vocabulary into speeches on the new regime's behalf. He resigned the rectorship the following spring, but while many say he grew disillusioned, his political behavior over the following years was ambiguous at best. The scandal of his early support for the Nazis still arouses great controversy. For some it was a grievous mistake and an insult to the true meaning of his thought; for others it revealed internal flaws in his work and damaged his philosophical legacy beyond repair. But Heidegger himself lived on for many years and his philosophy underwent a marked transformation: already in the mid-1930s Heidegger had begun to abandon not just the technical language but also the methodology and scientific pretensions associated with Husserlian phenomenology. He turned his gaze backward to the most consequential figures in the history of philosophy (Nietzsche, Plato, Parmenides, Heraklitus), and he began to describe the history of Being as if it were a kind of destiny whose unfolding human beings could only witness but were powerless to change. Such themes were already evident as early as *An Introduction to Metaphysics* (1935), and in his Nietzsche lectures (during the later 1930s), in which he suggested that "European nihilism" arose from the will-to-power in the broadest sense. In the postwar years, while the greater share of his countrymen took satisfaction in Germany's economic gains, Heidegger warned of the perils of humanist self-assertion and coun-seled against contemporary civilization's uninhibited confidence in tech-nology. In a language that grew ever more elegiac, his attention strayed from the conventional questions of professional philosophy toward the deeper insights into the human condition now lost to the world and preserved only in poetry and the arts. In 1954 he published *Was heißt Denken?* (What Is Called Thinking?), a meditation that called for receptivity in the face of what there is. Thinking, he wrote, is an expression of gratitude: *Denken ist Danken.* In a 1966 interview for the German periodical *Der Spiegel,* he seemed to deny altogether the possibility of human control over the course of history, declaring "Only a God can save us." When he died in late May 1976, he was buried with a Catholic Mass in the Messkirch churchyard near St. Martin's, where his father had once worked as sexton.

The Idea of an Existential Analytic

Although the confrontation between Heidegger and Cassirer spanned more than two decades, the focal point of their dispute lay in the particular contrast of philosophical doctrines both men had developed during the 1920s. In fact, at the time of their 1929 meeting at Davos, both philoso-phers remained deeply engrossed in their work. Only the first two vol-umes of Cassirer's *The Philosophy of Symbolic Forms* had appeared by April 1929; the third volume would be issued later that same year. Mean-while, only two years before, Heidegger had published an incomplete por-tion of *Being and Time.* The book immediately established its author's reputation for boldness and originality of purpose, but there was no ques-tion the philosophical community had barely begun to fathom its deeper implications.

Being and Time was an almost uncategorizable book. It was ostensibly an exercise in the phenomenological method as developed by the author's men-tor Husserl: all of the inherited prejudices of the philosophical past were to be swept aside, and the fullest attention was to be brought to bear on the basic task of describing the phenomena—"the things themselves"—just as they show themselves to be within the horizon of lived experience. But nothing could prepare the reader for its unusual style—its frequent neolo-gisms and confounding abstraction—which had been crafted especially to address an unfamiliar yet somehow urgent concern: "the question of Being," or *Seinsfrage.*[35]

As early as the Greeks, Heidegger explained, philosophers had suffered a fateful misunderstanding of this question if they saw fit to recognize its significance at all. Ontic questions, or questions of fact about a given entity, were easily dispatched. But ontological questions—that is, questions as to an entity's *manner of Being*—seemed at once too obscure and too obvious. Of course, any acknowledgement of the reality or existence of an entity necessarily involved reference to that entity's Being. Typically this reference remained tacit, though on occasion it became the theme of an explicit statement, as, for example, in the existential affirmations, "This rose is red," and even, "There is a God." The problem, however, was that Being seemed to be at once the highest yet the most empty of universals. By definition it was applicable to everything, both real and imaginary. But this did not mean it remained wholly an abstraction: by virtue of the copula, the shop-worn conjugate *is,* our everyday language necessarily makes reference to Being, and we may therefore assume that some vague if barely articulate understanding of its meaning is already embedded in human understanding. Indeed, human beings may be too close to Being to properly grasp its meaning. The existence that we ourselves *are*—our temporal existence or "Dasein"—is *itself a manner of Being:* Dasein is in fact "being-in-the-world." It is indeed a distinction of Dasein that "in its very Being, that Being is an *issue* for it." And so, in virtue of the fact that we cannot exist without conferring some intelligibility on our existence, it follows that we already bear an "average" and "everyday" understanding of Being that is evident in our very own manner of existence. However, notwithstanding its familiarity, the philosophical status of Being remains enigmatic. Heidegger went so far as to suggest that because Being had been misunderstood throughout the philosophical tradition, it was therefore a crucial task for philosophy to break the spell of the past by means of so-called destruction, an aggressive and systematic rereading of the canonical texts so as to bring to light its moments of suppressed awareness. Philosophy had forgotten what humanity had always known. "The very fact that we already live in an understanding of Being and that the meaning of Being is still veiled in darkness," wrote Heidegger, "proves that it is necessary in principle to raise this question again."[36]

Philosophers misunderstood the question of Being in part because they failed to take the "average everyday" understanding of Being as their point of departure. Their usual assumption was to understand Being (or, in Greek, *ousia*) in the same fashion they understood a perceptual or mental object, as a stable phenomenon presented for experience before a human subject. But this was in fact a distorted understanding of reality. More typically, Heidegger explained, the world reveals itself for human experience within a context of concern for the accomplishment of some task. The entities that show themselves to us within such a context have as their primary manner of Being *not* the context-independence of discreet theoretical items that are merely presented to us (or *vorhanden*), their manner of Being is instead the context-*dependence* of pragmatic instruments, the significance of which arises from their being on hand (or *zuhanden*) for our daily comportment and use within a holistic environment of similar entities. The world with which Dasein is most familiar, in other words, is not the dissociated world of merely present-to-hand or occurrent things as described by science but, rather, the practical environment (or *Umwelt*) whose innermost significance cannot be understood apart from Dasein's own manner of being. The practical environment therefore has its very own spatial and temporal structure— existential space and existential time—a structure that is grounded in Dasein's own concern for its being-in-the-world and is thus more "original" than the space we measure by a standard rule and the time we count by clocks.

Heidegger claimed that from the phenomenological point of view it made little sense to distill something like an essence to human nature: "Dasein's 'essence,'" he explained, "lies in its existence." To understand Dasein's own manner of being, it was therefore necessary to examine the entire structure of human existence as nothing less than an ongoing phenomenon of environmental practice, which he called "being-in-the-world." Dasein simply *was* its being-in-the-world: its overall integrity was conditional on the care it took in its own existence and that therefore served as the ultimate purpose behind all of its action. Dasein was quite simply a *care-structure*. The analysis of this phenomenon was the "existential analytic," a title that paid homage to Kant's "transcendental analytic" while expressing Heidegger's antipathy for any metaphysical language that intimated a transcendental moment of origin behind lived experience. The existential analytic purported to show that Dasein could not be understood at all if one began with the idealist's conception of the human being as a pristine mind or will, because Dasein was typically immersed in its worldly affairs even to the point of inauthenticity: it understood its own selfhood in terms of its world. At the same time, Heidegger was inclined to agree with Kant's deeper insight that the phenomena given for human experience were only intelligible in virtue of certain structures that belonged to the human condition itself. For Kant, these were the so-called categories, mental rules whose a priori application was the ground for the world's appearance. For Heidegger, these were the "existentials," the basic modes of existence through which Dasein's understanding of Being served as the condition for the world's disclosure. This, Heidegger suggested, was the deeper truth hidden within all those modern idealist theories that vaunted the world-shaping powers of the thinking self: not the mind, but human existence itself was the site by virtue of which Being could be understood and the world thereby disclosed. Without Dasein the very *Being* of the world as such became an impossibility. Nothing itself would reign.

Heidegger's ontological inquiry thus proposed a novel answer to the old Leibnizian question, "Why is there something rather than nothing?" But Leibniz could still believe that the ultimate reasons for existence were given through God, whereas Heidegger had abandoned the traditionalist's belief in any kind of ultimate ground. Dasein was therefore an existence that lacked not only an essence but also a metaphysical support: it was a "nullity" *(Nichtigkeit)* through and through. Yet, as this anti-foundationalist statement made plain, *Being and Time* itself was in its own fashion a study in metaphysics. Barely suppressed in its argument was a constellation of themes Heidegger had carried over from his earlier work in scholastic and Protestant theology. From Augustine in particular, Heidegger had developed a sophisticated understanding of the character of human sin, and in *Being and Time* he portrayed human existence as structured in such a way as to make its fallen condition nearly inevitable. Because Dasein always understood itself in terms of its world, it could not help but "fall towards" the world. Its receptive stance toward its own existence was therefore constitutive, and even the most resolute action could not wrest oneself free of the thrownness that belonged to Dasein's very manner of being-in-the-world. On the one hand, this seemed to condemn Dasein to being something other than its authentic self: "In falling [*Verfallen*] Dasein *itself* as factical being-in-the-world, is something *from which* it has already fallen away." On the other hand, there was no Being for Dasein *apart from* its being-in-the-world: "Falling," Heidegger concluded, was "a definite existential characteristic of Dasein itself."

Here it seemed that Heidegger made use of religious experience as a clue for describing Dasein's existential structure (a strategy not unlike the "demythologization" practiced by the Protestant theologian Rudolf Bultmann, Heidegger's colleague at the University of Marburg). Just as sinfulness, for example, was a constitutive condition for *homo religiosis,* so too, "Being-in-the-world is in itself *tempting* [*versucherisch*]."[37] Heidegger insisted throughout the existential analytic that such language played the restricted role of formal indication; it designated ways of Being but remained neutral with respect to conventional problems of theology and morality. But many critics, including Cassirer, would observe that even if the *answers* Heidegger gave were not those of traditional religion, the *questions* he asked nevertheless made sense only if one granted a certain prima facie legitimacy to religious expectations and concerns. A case in point was the extensive analysis of Dasein's being-toward-death and the radical "anxiety" (*Angst*) that was said to accompany one's anticipation of the end: for awakening philosophy to the importance of anxiety, Heidegger expressly credited Augustine and Luther, and, perhaps most of all, Kierkegaard, whose writings enjoyed a new fashion in Germany in the 1920s.[38] A further example was the analysis of Dasein's fall into public understanding, which Heidegger characterized as an anonymous sphere governed by ambiguity, leveling, and "idle chatter" (*Gerede*). The suggestion that human understanding might depend on a background of shared discourse and practice was hardly controversial. But Heidegger also claimed that Dasein's fall into the social world necessarily brought a concealment of authentic selfhood, for which the sole remedy was the "call of conscience" whereby Dasein could be restored to the singular truth of its very own "potentiality-for-Being." The provenance of this claim was clearly religious: the analysis of anxiety as an instrument for separating the genuine self from the public masses drew extensively from Kierkegaard's characterization of religious consciousness, while the understanding of idle talk as a public language that leveled all distinction was informed by the Dane's indictment of "chatter" (*snak*) in *Two Ages.*[39] The specific term *authenticity,* which played so pivotal a role for Heidegger, first emerged in his 1921 seminar on Augustine's *Confessions,* in which God was understood as a voice calling the wayward soul back from "the many" to "the authentic" and "the One."[40]

But what most distinguished Heidegger's existential analytic from any of its religious antecedents was its principled denial that there could be any hope for redemption from human mortality. Dasein was for Heidegger a phenomenon marked by an incorrigible *finitude* in its very manner of being. Finitude was indeed a technical term for Heidegger. It appeared with notable frequency in his 1929 summer seminar on "The Fundamental Concepts of Metaphysics" and in his book *Kant and the Problem of Metaphysics,* published that same year. (Its proper meaning was also a major bone of contention in the debate at Davos, as will be discussed later.) Finitude is not to be confused with mortality, although Heidegger clearly understood the two concepts as mutually supportive. Finitude designates the essential *dependency* of the human being on what is disclosed within experience: the contrast between divine understanding and a human understanding is that the former is the creative source of all phenomena whereas the latter remains dependent on and responsive to the phenomena as they are given. This dependency is ultimate in the sense that there is *no metaphysical ground* or principle that we can grasp so as to assert our independence. As Heidegger would explain, even Kant was a philosopher of human finitude, insofar as the first *Critique* suggests that for beings such as ourselves, all knowledge remains bound to sensible intuitions by virtue of which *the world shows itself to us.* Heidegger went so far as to claim that the first *Critique* assigns a hidden role to *time,* thereby exposing (despite its own rationalist pretensions) the apparent sovereignty of human reason to be an illusion, a claim he would develop at great length at Davos and especially in the Kant-book. For Heidegger the problem of finitude was not merely one philosophical theme among many. It was in fact *the* problem of the history of philosophy, insofar as it was the essential if unsettling truth about existence against which philosophy had rebelled. Almost from its inception, Heidegger claimed, philosophy had committed itself to a fundamental misunderstanding of Being as a metaphysical presence or ground. Conventional philosophical wisdom characterized Being as something eternal: the ultimate foundation for reality. This misunderstanding, however, was not merely a philosophical mistake; it was an *evasion,* which served to cover up and, if possible, to forget the temporal groundlessness of our being-in-the-world. The history of philosophy was therefore nothing less than a history of the forgetting of Being, or *Seinsvergessenheit.* To retrieve what had been forgotten, Heidegger promised a "destruction" of the history of ontology: a vigorous and even violent reinterpretation of the philosophical tradition that would demonstrate, in stepwise fashion through key moments in the canon, just how humankind had fallen into error.

Thrownness, History, Fate

In his 1929 lecture "What Is Metaphysics?"—his inaugural address as professor at the University of Freiburg—Heidegger characterized the human being as a "lieutenant of the nothing [*Platzhalter des Nichts*]."[41] For his auditors at the time, the message was clear: those philosophers who celebrated the human capacity for worldmaking and cultural achievement were only helping to obscure the deeper phenomenon of human finitude—a phenomenon that could not be surmounted by an act of free will but could only be experienced as anxiety before the possibility of one's own nothingness. "We are so finite," said Heidegger, "that we cannot even bring ourselves originally before the nothing through our own decision and will. So abyssaly [*abgründig*] does the process of finitude entrench itself in Dasein that our most proper and deepest finitude refuses to yield to our freedom."[42] The nothingness at the core of human existence was something more original than the "negation" described by logic. Its exposure came only in such moments when the human being was awakened through anxiety to the recognition of its own condition as *uncanny (unheimlich),* when it could get no "hold on things" and Being as a whole seemed to recede into indifference. In these moments the human being experienced its own "transcendence," not as an elevation beyond finitude but precisely as "being held out into the nothing."[43]

Although Heidegger denied that this finitude could ever be mastered, in *Being and Time* Heidegger characterized Dasein as a being who is nevertheless burdened with responsibility or guilt for the facts that constitute its existence. Indeed, Dasein could understand itself *only* as delivered over to its facticity. To designate this condition, that is, Dasein's predicament of being "always already" caught up in some particular manner of Being, Heidegger introduced the term *thrownness* or *Geworfenheit*. "Dasein is something that has been thrown," he explained, "it has been brought into its 'there', but *not* of its own accord." He hastened to add that thrownness was *not* to be understood as some kind of misfortune that might be undone. Thrownness was rather the *constitutive* condition whereby Dasein first came upon itself as *always already delivered over to a given "basis" or state of affairs*. Even Dasein's possibilities for the future were contingent upon the facticity into which it was thrown. Dasein "projects itself upon possibilities into which it has been thrown" even while it "can *never* get that basis into its power." This *negative* condition—the *impossibility* of wholly mastering possibility—was a defining theme of human existence:

> In being a basis—that is, in existing as thrown—Dasein constantly lags behind its possibilities. It is never existent *before* its basis, but only *from* it and *as this basis*. Thus "Being-a-basis" means *never* to have power over one's ownmost being from the ground up. This *"not"* belongs to the existential meaning of "thrownness" [*Geworfenheit*].[44]

For Heidegger thrownness, or *Geworfenheit,* was a defining feature of human existence. For Cassirer, as we shall see, it was the most consequential and characteristic theme in Heidegger's entire philosophy. Whether this judgment can be sustained must await further discussion. What is certain is that thrownness expressed an insight crucial to Heidegger's broader conception of historical existence.

Heidegger had learned from his neo-Kantian mentor Heinrich Rickert to appreciate the importance of history as a special mode of human experience, the investigation of which demanded methods distinct from those of the natural sciences. As Charles Bambach has observed, neo-Kantianism's understanding of history as a realm of unique significances rather than generalizable laws left a deep imprint on Heidegger's own theory of historical being. But as Bambach shows in detail, Heidegger disagreed with neo-Kantianism's primarily epistemological conception of history as a realm of observable phenomena.[45] For Heidegger it was critical to acknowledge that history was not only a sphere of human action; history was in fact *constitutive* of the human way of being. As a being thrown into its own facticity,

Dasein was marked to its very core by an irresistible "historicity" or *Ge-schichtlichkeit*. This implied that Dasein might not be able to resist the gravitational force of thoughtless convention. The problem that consumed much of Heidegger's attention in the second major portion of *Being and Time* was to explain how it was nonetheless possible for Dasein as a historical being to understand both its past and its own self in an authentic fashion.

If the essence of Dasein was nothing other than its existence, it followed that Dasein could only derive an understanding of its being from the facticity into which it was thrown. Significantly, Heidegger never suggests that resoluteness can *overcome* one's thrownness: whatever freedom Dasein may exhibit in its resolute seizure of existential possibility, this freedom occurs "always within the limitations of its thrownness."[46] From a historical perspective, this meant that Dasein had to rely upon what was given to it as its *heritage*. Yet this did not entail an uncritical acceptance of historical convention. In fact, Heidegger insisted that to rely upon the past without authentic understanding would be to abandon oneself to what was most average and commonplace in the historically given. It was necessary instead to take over the possibilities of one's past in full awareness of their significance for Dasein's authentic being. But this required first that Dasein come to a deeper recognition of its finitude. Only then could Dasein be recalled from its dispersal in the "one." Heidegger described this recognition as a "call of conscience," but it was evident he did not think of it as a call with any determinate content. It was intelligible only as a revelation of Dasein's being from *within* the confines of Dasein's own existence. And its ultimate meaning was nothing other than the disclosure of Dasein's potentiality for being itself: the call of conscience "calls Dasein *back* to its thrownness," Heidegger wrote, "so as to understand this thrownness as the null basis which it has to take up into [its] existence."[47] With this recognition Dasein could now resolve upon its possibilities, which it understood not as mere artifacts of historical convention but rather as options for life that were genuinely its own: "The resoluteness in which Dasein comes back to itself, discloses current factical possibilities of authentic existing, and discloses them *in terms of the heritage* which that resoluteness, as thrown, *takes over*."[48]

Certain themes in these arguments concerning the historicity of human existence implied an ethic of stark confrontation. Heidegger was convinced that authentic understanding could arise *only* where Dasein was wrested from its everyday complacency to confront the fact of its own mortality. To resolve in an authentic manner upon one's heritage and to take over this heritage for the future therefore required a brutal awakening to the possibility of death:

> The more authentically Dasein resolves—and this means that in anticipating death it understands itself unambiguously in terms of its own-most distinctive possibility—the more unequivocally does it choose and find the possibility of its existence and the less does it do so by accident. Only by the anticipation of death is every accidental and "provisional" possibility driven out. Only Being-free *for* death, gives Dasein its goal outright and pushes existence into its finitude.[49]

The anticipation of death awakens human existence from its passive acceptance of what is given at random, and it serves as the occasion for Dasein to embrace its "ownmost" historical Being. Some critics believe that this train of associations, with it somewhat grandiose image of a mortally-endangered human being finding historical truth only *in extremis*—may help to explain why Heidegger was later drawn to the militancy of the Nazi program. During a discussion in Rome in 1936, Heidegger confirmed to his student Karl Löwith that "his concept of 'historicity' was the basis of his political 'engagement.'"[50] It is worth noting that this statement hardly warrants the conclusion that the whole of Heidegger's philosophy is permeated by "Nazi politics." At most it indicates what Heidegger himself believed about his political choices (and he could have been wrong); or it may indicate a largely formal justification (for instance, that authenticity only demands that one resolve upon *some* aspect of one's own historical heritage, even while it does not say *which* aspect one should prefer).[51] Some critics have tried to distill from Heidegger's early philosophy some sort of *determinate* political orientation, but any closure to their efforts seems unlikely, given that even Heidegger's most precise philosophical purposes are a matter of endless contention.

I will not pretend to be capable of resolving here the complex matter of Heidegger's political choices, let alone elucidating what might be termed his "political philosophy." But it would be naïve to insist that his conception of history lacked any and all political meaning. For my purposes it may suffice to note that for Heidegger, a truly authentic mode of historical life could only arise from the bracing experience of mortal confrontation. On his view such a confrontation, moreover, was only possible if one resisted certain kinds of enticements, such as flights into high culture or the superficies of public discourse, that were likely to induce historical and cultural complacency. This message seems evident at many points in *Being and Time,* but it is most especially evident where Heidegger brings his theory of historicity to a dramatic conclusion: "Once one has grasped the finitude of one's existence, it snatches one back from the endless multiplicity of possibilities which offer themselves as closest to one—those of comfortableness, shirking, and taking things lightly—and brings Dasein into the simplicity of its *fate.*"[52] This stated antipathy to complacency of any kind, rather than a candid affirmation of political doctrine, constitutes what we might call the existential *ethic* of Heidegger's early philosophy. The key to its message is that certain ways of living amount to an evasion of the finitude we must confront if we are to be authentic. Heidegger insists that this confrontation necessarily belongs to the *individual* because it requires a recognition of mortality—a recognition which by definition cannot be shared and is therefore in his technical jargon "non-relational." He also confirms the need to realize one's authenticity within the horizon of historical possibilities shared in common with one's "people" and one's "generation."[53]

Heidegger was often reluctant to state outright that his philosophy implied anything like an ethico-political program. Still, it seems right to say that he cleaved to a normative image of being human that afforded the highest virtue to authenticity, that is, the recognition and resolute embrace of one's own thrownness. This emphasis on an authentic confrontation with thrownness was to play a strong role in Heidegger's ultimately negative assessment of Cassirer's philosophy, which seemed to Heidegger a supreme example of cultural evasion. Surprisingly, as we will see in greater depth later, this judgment also had a personal dimension in that Heidegger seemed to believe that Cassirer himself was insufficiently confrontational (a complaint he confided to a student after the meeting at Davos). Heidegger would also claim there is a "lazy" aspect to anyone who appealed to "the works of the spirit." Throughout much of his early writing, there is no doubt an unusual emphasis on polemic.[54] But it would be wrong to draw any explicitly political conclusions from Heidegger's frequent language of confrontation.

At least at Davos, the "confrontation" between Heidegger and Cassirer remained confined to matters of philosophy alone.

A World in Common

The philosophical sketches offered above are merely provisional, but they afford us a helpful beginning to our story. Much of the drama now attached to the memory of the encounter between Cassirer and Heidegger in Davos derives from the mistaken impression that this was a unique meeting between two men of wholly dissimilar philosophical temperaments. Those tempted by vivid contrasts in cultural symbolism might stress the outward signs that separated the two men: Cassirer was an acculturated and well-to-do German Jew, while Heidegger was a lapsed Catholic of provincial and *petit-bourgeois* origin. The family name *Cassirer* itself marks a connection with merchants and cashiers; the name *Heidegger* carries a trace of woodsmen and uncultivated terrain. Observers to the Davos disputation were even struck by their contrast in personal appearance: the urbane and mild-tempered Cassirer older by fifteen years and his white hair rose vertically from his head (as one student recalled) "like an ice-cream cone."[55] Heidegger was more nimble, dark-haired, and compact. He spoke with a regional accent that marked him as an outsider to university life, a role he seemed to cultivate. On at least one occasion, he lectured before the assembly in his ski suit. Students delighted in these dissimilarities. One night they even reenacted the dispute, with "Cassirer" chattering on about "Humboldt" and "Kultur" while his rival "Heidegger" declared that "interpretation is to turn a thing upside down."

This reenactment furnishes a vivid clue as to why the Cassirer-Heidegger encounter remains susceptible to allegorization. In the many years since their meeting, unsteady progress has been made in clearing aside these caricatures to fasten our attention on the actual substance of their debate. It is therefore instructive to recall that the conversation between Cassirer and Heidegger in fact spanned many years and it was punctuated by personal meetings that passed without acrimony or incident. It is even more important to note that this was primarily a philosophical *conversation* and not a struggle between bitter adversaries. It is of course true that over time their philosophical disagreement grew ever more pronounced and it would eventually assume

an overwhelming political significance. But one can understand the true
nature of their disagreement and its ultimately political denouement only
by first recalling the philosophical world they shared. It is one of the deeper
lessons of the relationship between Heidegger and Cassirer that, just as in
geometry a bisecting line cuts across a single plane, a philosophical division
can only appear within a larger context of shared philosophical concerns.

Cassirer and Heidegger were not intimate friends but their acquaintance-
ship was far from casual. They had first met on December 17, 1923, when
Cassirer invited his younger colleague to Hamburg, where the latter addressed the local chapter of the *Kant-Gesellschaft*. Cassirer himself had been
a co-founder of the Hamburg chapter several years before, and in this period he served as its chair, facts that suggest he must have played some role
in determining who would be an appropriate choice for a scholarly presentation.[56] The actual manuscript of Heidegger's lecture, "The Tasks and Paths
of Phenomenological Research," has not survived. But we can surmise that
it most likely did not stray far from the topic of the first lecture course, "Introduction to Phenomenological Research," which Heidegger was conduct-
ing that very winter at Marburg, where, after spending years in Freiburg as
an apprentice to Husserl, he had just received an appointment as associate
professor *(Extraordinarius)*. In the Marburg course Heidegger provided an
overview of phenomenological method that began with a painstaking etymological discourse on the Greek meanings of both *phenomenon* and *logos*
and a subtle note that in Greek philosophy "there is no concept of consciousness." But in Husserlian phenomenology, Heidegger observed, consciousness
came to enjoy a "peculiar prerogative" (an emphasis especially notable in
Husserl's *Ideas*) such that phenomenology came to be defined as the "descriptive eiditic science of transcendentally pure consciousness." For Heidegger this transcendental emphasis had an obvious advantage insofar as its
"purification" allowed for an understanding of ideal meanings. But Husserl's method also suffered from a peculiar disadvantage because it neglected "the genuine object of concern: human existence."[57]

This was a harbinger of the radical innovation Heidegger would bring
to phenomenology when he transformed it into a nonidealistic method directed toward the given evidences no longer of consciousness but of *existence*.
His departure from the idealistic or "eiditic" understanding of phenomenol-

ogy sponsored by Husserl would eventually contribute to the personal and professional rift between teacher and student (which we will explore later). But this makes it all the more interesting that Heidegger apparently spoke about his *existential* modification of phenomenological method during his 1923 Hamburg lecture. One might have imagined that Cassirer would have taken particular exception to Heidegger's existential turn, given his own schooling in the transcendental-idealist doctrines of neo-Kantianism. By this point Cassirer was himself effecting a comparable departure from his neo-Kantian training to embrace the richer domain of human cultural expression. To be sure, this was not a domain of "existence" in Heidegger's sense, but the impression of a shared philosophical orientation was apparently sufficient for Cassirer to register his approval for Heidegger's proposal. Several years later Heidegger would include a brief note in *Being and Time* recalling that "In a discussion between the author and Cassirer on the occasion of a lecture before the Hamburg section of the *Kant-Gesellschaft* in December 1923 on 'Tasks and Paths of Phenomenological Research,' it was already apparent that *we agreed in demanding an existential analytic such as was sketched in that lecture.*"[58]

It is hardly surprising that Heidegger took care to record Cassirer's "agreement" concerning the need for an existential analytic, especially in light of the fact that, when *Being and Time* was published in 1927, Heidegger still looked on Cassirer as a colleague of some seniority whose approval might help to confer greater legitimacy on the younger philosopher's innovation. But even at the time the philosophical consensus between them was only partial. The full text of Heidegger's note referred to the second volume of Cassirer's *Philosophy of Symbolic Forms, Mythical Thought,* which had appeared in 1925, and there Heidegger already registered his growing concern that Cassirer's ethnographic investigations remained too strongly bound to Kantian principles: it remained an "open question," Heidegger observed, whether the doctrine of Kant's first *Critique* could furnish the instruments for "primitive" phenomena or whether "a new and more primordial approach may not here be needed."[59] This modest hint at a deeper disagreement would be made explicit when Heidegger published his first serious criticism of Cassirer's philosophical commitments in a 1928 review of *Mythical Thought.*[60] Generally speaking, we can conclude that Heidegger was quick to discern only the inadequacies in Cassirer's philosophy, which appeared in Heidegger's eyes as merely another illustration of the broader failure to arrive at a deeper and properly ontological understanding of the human being. Heidegger's own model of language as disclosure, for example, had little in common with Cassirer's own expressivist theory. In *Being and Time* Heidegger made only the briefest mention of Cassirer's theory of language (as developed in the first volume of *The Philosophy of Symbolic Forms*), and he ranked it alongside other theories, all of which have failed to work out an "adequate" understanding of the ontologico-existential structure of language as grounded in the analytic of Dasein.[61]

Meanwhile, during this same period Cassirer was also familiarizing himself with the details of Heidegger's philosophy. The third volume of *The Philosophy of Symbolic Forms,* which appeared in print in late 1929 (several months after their encounter at Davos), contains several brief notes addressing Heidegger's "existential" analyses of space and time, and they reveal Cassirer's emergent sense that Heidegger's philosophical achievement was legitimate but also gravely limited. What Heidegger described as "existence," Cassirer warned, was a wholly subjectivistic phenomenon that could not account for the human being's capacity for universal and objective knowledge. As we shall see, this would also be an important theme in the conversation at Davos.

Throughout this period and well after their meeting at Davos, personal relations between the two philosophers remained more or less cordial. Their professional careers, meanwhile, ran on a parallel course. They were two of the most admired philosophers in all of Germany, so it was only natural that they were considered for the same academic posts, but it is quite remarkable that this happened on at least *three* separate occasions. When Husserl vacated his chair at Freiburg in 1928, Cassirer was the only other candidate under serious consideration. Heidegger and Cassirer were also discussed as successors to Heinrich Rickert. And in 1930 they stood out as the only real contenders for the high honor of a philosophy chair in Berlin: Cassirer's name was put forward first, and only once it was vetoed did the faculty suggest extending an invitation to Heidegger, who, however, ultimately declined. Both philosophers were indeed widely esteemed by their colleagues throughout Germany, a fact that helps to explain why they were the two obvious choices for a public debate at the international conference in Switzerland. They were also natural candidates for the high honor of leading their own universities: Cassirer was appointed as rector at the University of Hamburg for the length of the academic year 1929–1930. Three years later, Heidegger would himself be appointed—by the Nazis—to serve as rector at the University of Freiburg. For both philosophers, these were moments of great symbolism, marking their professional achievements but also a stark divergence in political commitments.

Until the Nazi seizure of power, the two philosophers sustained a critical dialogue, though with an ever-growing awareness of the intellectual divide between them. When the substance of Heidegger's Davos lectures on Kant were published later in 1929 in the book *Kant and the Problem of Metaphysics,* Cassirer wrote a long and searingly negative review in the early spring of 1931 in the prestigious journal *Kantstudien.* Heidegger might have felt wounded by the attack. But he responded instead by inviting his colleague to Freiburg, where Cassirer delivered a lecture on Rousseau. Cassirer's own memories of the occasion suggest that he passed the time with Heidegger and other colleagues there in friendly conversation. But this was the last time the two would ever meet. In the spring of 1933, Cassirer was forced from his post and he began his final phase of life as an exile, traveling from country to country throughout Europe and ultimately arriving in the United States in 1941. Meanwhile, he continued to labor on what he hoped would be a fourth volume of *The Philosophy of Symbolic Forms.* This work remained unpublished in his lifetime, but the various notes reveal that Cassirer was still struggling to articulate his disagreement with Heidegger. By this time, however, the once-subtle disagreement over philosophical principles had erupted into something far more pronounced: during his last years as a professor at Yale, Cassirer completed a draft of what would be his final and most political work, *The Myth of the State.* In its culminating chapter Heidegger made a final appearance, as a theorist of historical fatalism whose ideas had further weakened Germany's confidence in political autonomy and encouraged its surrender to barbarism.

Although the conversation between Heidegger and Cassirer came to an end in 1945, the memory of that conversation and the interpretation of its meaning was only beginning. For generations afterward, stories of the encounter at Davos would circulate and spread, assuming an ever more elaborate significance within the larger history of modern Continental philosophy. To understand both that conversation *and* its philosophical afterlife, we can begin by recalling some of the salient features of the intellectual world they inhabited.

1

Philosophy in Crisis

Nous autres, civilisations, nous savons maintenant que nous sommes mortelles.

—PAUL VALÉRY, *La Crise de l'esprit* (1919)

The Language of Crisis

"We later civilizations . . . we too now know that we are mortal." These cheerless words serve as the opening to "The Crisis of the Mind," the 1919 essay by the Symbolist poet and conservative cultural critic Paul Valéry.[1] Much has been written about the mood of intellectual crisis that seized European culture in the years following World War I. Even in the midst of the war, the sociologist Georg Simmel warned of a "crisis of culture" that was deeper than the war itself and that no treaty could heal.[2] Crisis, it seemed, was everywhere. When the military battles concluded, the violence of the war spilled over into peacetime, bequeathing the new Republic a legacy of bitter division. Much that had once seemed enduring now lay in ruins or seemed destined to collapse. The Allied victory and German defeat spawned a variety of conservative laments for the decline of Western culture, from Oswald Spengler's monumental and neo-romantic philosophy of history, *The Decline of the West* (1918 and 1922), to Thomas Mann's self-doubting but rashly nationalistic polemic, *Confessions of an Unpolitical Man* (1918). But the chorus of fatalism was offset by more hopeful voices on both the left and the right calling for radical change. Among Rosa Luxemburg's last writings was an essay on war and socialism, *The Crisis of Social Democracy* (1919); Marxist "crisis-theory" spawned studies of the interwar inflation such as Eugene Varga's *The Crisis of the Capitalistic World-Economy* (1921);[3] analysts of international diplomacy testified to *The Crisis of Weltanschauung* (1923); and the sociologist Alfred Weber diagnosed *The Crisis of the Modern Idea of the State in Europe* (1925).[4] Soon there were crises in almost every intellectual domain, in the arts, religion, and psychology.[5] In France, too, the greatest names in aesthetic modernism—from Valéry to Proust—were invoked as symptoms for "the crisis of our literature."[6] Rudolf Pannwitz took in the entire Continent in his 1917 book *The Crisis of European Culture.*[7]

"Crisis"—the word is Greek for separation or division—was both used and abused to describe the intellectual predicament of postwar Europe.[8] Most prominent, perhaps, was the so-called crisis of historicism, first diagnosed by the historian Ernst Troeltsch in 1922.[9] As Troeltsch explained, the theory that meaning is conditional upon historical context posed a grave challenge to philosophical or religious conceptions of transcendent truth and value, as it opened up the relativistic possibility that all meaning was restricted to its time.[10] The crisis of historicism appeared to threaten not only philosophical truth but religious truth as well. Reacting against the liberal theologies of the nineteenth century, the Swiss pastor Karl Barth inaugurated "crisis theology" with his 1919 *Epistle to the Romans,* which inveighed against historicism and declared revelation an irreducible fact.[11] Mathematics, too, was seized by a so-called *Grundlagenkrise,* or "crisis of foundations," Hermann Weyl's 1921 term for the problems that now beset modern mathematical premises in light of recent developments in set theory and relativity.[12]

Philosophy, too, was seized by crisis. During the war, new voices arose to challenge the primacy of academic epistemology, quickening rumors of a "crisis in the modern theory of knowledge."[13] But the crises came in various kinds, not all of them traceable to the same philosophical origins. Perhaps the most prominent conflict turned on the question of how modern philosophers might wrest genuine problems from the heritage of German Idealism. The problem afflicted Hegelians as well as Kantians, neo-Hegelians, and neo-Kantians, but was felt most acutely perhaps in the philosophical debate over Kant's epistemology.[14] In his rectoral address, *The Present Philosophical Crisis* (1914), Karl Joël faulted the neo-Kantians for neglecting the bridge between "knowledge" and "life," while Arthur Liebert, in *The Intellectual Crisis of the Present Age* (1923), reproached philosophers who betrayed the Kantian sovereignty of philosophical reason for historicism and relativism.[15]

But the Kantian and neo-Kantian theory of knowledge was only one theme within an increasingly polarized field of debate. Most philosophers saw that the crisis had assumed global proportion and that there was little hope of returning to an earlier consensus. For Heidegger himself, the foundations-crisis that afflicted physics, mathematics, and philosophy appeared as a herald of radical innovation. "The real 'movement' of the sciences," observed Heidegger in *Being and Time,* "takes place when their basic concepts undergo a more or less radical revision." Similar crises had beset physics, biology, history, and theology, in which it was now clear that intellectual achievement could no longer be realized after the pattern of slow and steady advance. Crisis was a necessary precondition to future change. As Heidegger declared:

> The level which a science has reached is determined by how far it is *capable* of a crisis in basic concepts. In such immanent crises the very relationship between positively investigative inquiry and those things themselves that are under interrogation comes to a point where it begins to totter. Among the various disciplines everywhere today there are freshly awakened tendencies to put research on new foundations.[16]

For Cassirer, meanwhile, the crisis in philosophy was only a local symptom of the larger crisis of European civilization. His 1944 summary of his philosophy, *An Essay on Man* (published in exile in the United States), opens with an inquiry on "The Crisis of Man's Knowledge of Himself." The whole of human culture, Cassirer wrote, is conditional upon "the process of man's progressive self-liberation." Failure to recognize this unifying task had plunged philosophy into "a complete anarchy of thought" that now posed "an imminent threat to the whole extent of our ethical and cultural life."[17]

Whereas Heidegger welcomed crisis as a harbinger of radical innovation, Cassirer saw it as little more than a symptom of cultural disorientation and moral collapse. The disparity reflected not only a difference in temperament but also a difference in historical experience. With the Nazi seizure of power, what had seemed a localized struggle over technical matters in philosophy was easily construed as a battle for Europe's future, and defenders of philosophical "idealism" frequently saw themselves as defending European civilization itself. Many—though not all—of these scholars were German Jews (either by conviction or merely descent) who conceived of the German Idealist legacy as the reminder of an earlier tolerance in an increasingly intolerant society.[18] Foremost among them was Edmund Husserl, who first delivered portions of his final and incomplete work, *The Crisis of the European Sciences*, in public addresses in Prague and Vienna, though he sent portions of the manuscript to Belgrade to be published in the inaugural volume of Arthur Liebert's journal-in-exile, *Philosophia*. The Vienna lecture of 1935 opened with a dramatic declaration that there were only two solutions to "the crisis of European existence." Either it would end in Europe's downfall and its "estrangement from its own rational sense of life" or it would lead to "the rebirth of Europe from the spirit of philosophy." For Husserl philosophers had a special role to play in this crisis: it was their task to uphold the "heroism of reason" by restoring to Europe its intellectual foundations in rational-transcendental phenomenology.[19]

But the language of crisis was hardly the exclusive province of rationalists threatened by fascism. It also proved advantageous to the Right. In fact, conceiving of one's cultural-political situation as a *crisis* implied that conventional methods were no longer adequate and that the only possible salvation lay in swift and decisive action. Proponents of moderation, such as Fritz Jellinek, an Austrian Jew, continued to address "the crisis of the bourgeoisie" on the implicit though increasingly contested premise that bourgeois civilization merited defense.[20] But the general pattern was otherwise. The language of crisis ultimately worked to fortify the ideological credibility of extremists on both the left and the right who issued wholesale condemnations of bourgeois life and called for an extrasystemic solution. Thus by the early 1930s, the chief ideologue of the Nazi party, Alfred Rosenberg, was to author his own zealous inquiry into the *Crisis and Reconstruction of Europe* (1934).[21]

Although the path from lectern to political platform was hardly determined, scholarly rhetoric sometimes prepared the ground for ideological commitment. As Hans Sluga notes in his book *Heidegger's Crisis*, philosophers who saw their situation in terms of crisis proved far more vulnerable to the Platonist fantasy of a philosopher-king, and not a few felt tempted to quit the sanctuary of academic life and to assume an activist's role in the political education of the citizenry. For intellectuals such as the political theorist Carl Schmitt and the ardently pro-Nazi educational theorists Ernst Krieck and Alfred Baeumler, the perception of crisis furnished an explanatory bridge for uniting theory with practice.[22] A similar logic helped pave the way for Martin Heidegger to assume the rectorship at Freiburg, where he devised schemes to restructure the university and even nourished the hope that he might somehow "lead the Leader."[23]

The language of crisis serves as a helpful introductory framework for understanding the cultural context of interwar German philosophy. And it is especially useful for appreciating the atmosphere surrounding the Heidegger-Cassirer debate, because much of what makes their encounter so compelling in philosophical memory today is the sense of urgency that struck so many participants at the time. The *Bildungskrise,* or "crisis in education," was in fact an official theme at Davos. Joachim Ritter, a student who had attended the 1929 meeting and helped draft a transcript of the disputation, reported that at the Davos *Hochschulwochen* in 1931 the Germans were especially consumed with worry at the apparent disconnect between scholarship and "worldview": their conversation turned with great frequency to the "'crisis' of cultural formation and the "alienation of Spirit from Life."[24]

Here, then, was the great advantage of crisis-language: Weimar intellectuals who felt the absence of clear directives for how they might coordinate between ideas and substantive cultural commitments—between "theoretical knowledge" and "worldview"—could find welcome refuge in the idea of crisis. While it was unlikely to facilitate an objective report on intellectual conditions, crisis-language gave philosophers a way of lending their problems a larger and more ramified significance such that they could believe that philosophical debates were connected in some fashion to broader cultural and historical concerns. To be sure, any such interpretation would have decisive consequences for the way intellectuals understood their own ideas. And the various Weimar-era languages of crisis—in philosophy as well as natural science, in culture as well as politics—was a great liability insofar as it had the unfortunate effect of radicalizing discussion; it discouraged interlocutors from conceiving of moderate or purely ameliorative solutions to intellectual disagreement and tempted them to imagine their discussion in starkly oppositional terms. Part of our difficulty in understanding the Davos encounter, as we shall see, is that we will have to take note of how a philosophical discussion was gradually transformed into a crisis—until discussion was no longer possible.

The Problem of Generations

"It is the fate of this generation to murder its fathers," observed Fritz Heinemann in 1929. He may be partly responsible for the term *Existenzphilosophie,* which thanks to his efforts gained currency as an appellation for the
newest philosophical fashion. In his book *New Paths in Philosophy* he characterized the turn toward existence as the work of a "rising generation."[25]
But he was hardly alone. Real or imagined, the idea of generational conflict
became a common script by which German intellectuals in the interwar
years understood their own historical moment. This was indeed far more
than a shibboleth of psychoanalytic theory. Themes of generational conflict
and rebellion served as major plotlines for Walter Hasenclever's influential
expressionist play *The Son* (1914), for Kafka's short story "The Judgment"
(1917), and a great many other works of drama and literature.

Today, of course, the portrait of Weimar culture as a symbolic rupture
between fathers and sons has descended from historical insight into historical cliché.[26] But the idea of an interwar generational conflict was first born
with Weimar intellectuals themselves, many of whom believed such conflict was inevitable and even beneficial. In his 1927 essay "The Problem of
Generations," the sociologist Karl Mannheim observed that intellectual
discord between the generations was something impossible to avoid. It first
arose because, in all matters requiring interpretation, there was no such
thing as a single and eternal community of interpretation: "Cultural creation and cultural accumulation are not accomplished by the same individuals," Mannheim observed. "Our culture is developed by individuals who
come into contact anew with the accumulated heritage." Rather than la-
menting this constant overturning of past ideas, Mannheim welcomed even
*mis*understanding as a stimulus to intellectual change. "Productive misunderstanding," he observed, "is often a condition of continuing life."[27]
Even before the twentieth century, however, philosophers and theorists
gained an appreciation for the phenomenon of generational conflict. For
Wilhelm Dilthey, whose theoretical reflections on generation were published in 1924, the idea of "generation" served as a crucial explanatory tool
for writing history in the hermeneutic style. Against the scientist impulse
to divide time into objective units, a generation was supposed to be a more
promising instrument of historical description because it identified a sub-

jective feature of experience itself. As Dilthey explained, a generation was an "inner psychological unit of temporal measure." It permitted the historian to explain cultural transformations through terms available to the historical agents themselves: their consciousness of their own existence as individuals bound within what Dilthey called a "relation of contemporaneity" *(Verhält-nis der Gleichzeitigkeit).*[28]

Dilthey's theory of generational consciousness served as an important inspiration for many philosophers in the Weimar era, especially for Heidegger, who saw historical existence as a constant pattern of inheritance and creative reappropriation. "Dasein has grown up both *into* and *in* a traditional way of interpreting itself," Heidegger argued. "Its own past—and this always means the past of its 'generation' [*die seiner 'Generation'*]—is not something which *follows along after* Dasein, but something which already goes ahead of it."[29] Heidegger went on to explain that any community or people was constituted not as an aggregate of individual fates but rather as a historical totality whose inherited possibilities had to be seized upon in a moment of resolve. "Our fates," he wrote, "have already been guided in advance, in our Being with one another in the same world and in our resoluteness for definite possibilities. . . . Dasein's fateful destiny in and with its 'generation' goes to make up the full authentic historizing of Dasein."[30]

Heidegger was by philosophical conviction a holist, slow to recognize cultural fragmentation and blind to its possible advantages. The idea that history can be conceived as a succession of unified temporal blocs ignores the important truth that modern societies rarely if ever function as internally unified wholes. As Mannheim observed, "within any generation there can exist a number of differentiated, antagonistic generation-units."[31] A generation is thus rarely a neutral category of historical understanding; it conspires to obscure the true pluralism and disunity that makes cultures into the dynamic systems they are. As the Weimar-era art-historian Wilhelm Pinder observed in his volume, *The Problem of Generation in Europe's Art History* (1926), "the thinking of each epoch is polyphonous."[32]

It was nonetheless tempting for Weimar philosophers to understand complex matters of intellectual transformation in generational terms. The simplified division—between old and young, prewar and postwar, teachers and students—was no doubt appealing in part because it mirrored the factious character of politics in the Weimar Republic. Diagnosticians of the

German youth movement were quick to identify the revolutionary significance of the cultural crisis and to emphasize the special "mission of the young
generation."[33] This uneasy slippage between philosophy and politics meant
that critics not infrequently saw political meanings in the most rarefied debates. And of course sometimes they were right. By the mid-1930s the Nazis
had succeeded in politicizing nearly all of German culture. This may partly
explain why at the end of his life Edmund Husserl had come to believe that the
so-called crisis of the European sciences had its origins in "a feeling of hostility
among the younger generation."[34] But this does not mean that all generational
conflict in the Weimar period was political. And quite often the attempt to read
philosophical debates through the prism of generational conflict only conspired to obscure the seriousness of the philosophical problems themselves.

    For the Davos *Hochschulwochen,* the problem of "generations" served as
an official theme for discussion. At the 1929 meeting it was the major topic
for no less than four of the presentations, by the philosopher Karl Joël
(Basel), who claimed that centuries reveal unified but alternating styles just
as grandsons resemble not their fathers but only their grandfathers; Wilhelm Pinder (Munich), who revisited claims from his book on generational
patterns in art history concerning the theoretical significance of "contemporaneity"; the political theorist Kurt Riezler (Frankfurt), who offered a
global intellectual and generational portrait of "contemporary man"; and the
intellectual historian Eduard Wechssler (Berlin), whose lecture, "The Problem of Generations in the Human Sciences," laid down theoretical principles for conceiving historical periods according to a generational scheme.[35]
The disputation between Heidegger and Cassirer was also understood by
many as a conflict between "old and young generations." A reporter for the
Frankfurter Zeitung wrote that the dispute was "not merely an academic
struggle of the professors"; it was "a confrontation between representative
figures of the two epochs."[36] This perception soon became commonplace, as
Franz Josef Brecht observed: "For most of the participants in this year's *Davos Hochschulkurse* the public discussion between Ernst Cassirer and Martin Heidegger was the meaningful high point of the conference; for here
there stood two philosophers, as representatives not merely of two philosophical dispositions that ultimately were no longer susceptible to logical discussion, but rather, at the same time, as two philosophical generations."[37]

How can one assess the validity of such claims? Was the divide between Cassirer and Heidegger in fact a generational one? If objective years are the unit of measure, perhaps not: Cassirer was born in 1874, Heidegger in 1889, a difference of only fifteen years. According to Dilthey and Mannheim, a generational cycle required thirty years. But more important than objective criteria may be the institutional achievements that serve as markers not of chronological age but of social status and symbolic maturity. Cassirer's publishing record stretched back to the earliest years of the twentieth century, and although he suffered some delay in securing an academic post, by 1919 he had found a home as professor of philosophy at the newly established University in Hamburg. Over the next decade he grew to become an eminent figure in German scholarship as an exponent of the Kantian legacy and a historian of modern philosophy. By the time he faced off with Heidegger in Davos, he had published no fewer than eight monographs (including the monumental *Philosophy of Symbolic Forms*) and he had served as a leading editor for the German-language journals *Logos* and *Kantstudien*. Heidegger, by contrast, was still a new arrival. Although he had been teaching seminars since the start of the 1920s, when he made his appearance with Cassirer at the end of the decade, he had only just secured a permanent academic post, and, besides his 1915 habilitation, he had published just one book, *Being and Time,* which was, in fact, incomplete.

Such differences in academic achievement are notable markers of generational membership, perhaps more so than chronological age. There was also the matter of appearance, a factor mentioned with great frequency in reports of the dispute. It is of course difficult to know how seriously to take such personal factors. But it seems fair to say that generational consciousness is constituted at least in part by social recognition and subjective awareness, so it would not be entirely mistaken to see Cassirer and Heidegger as representatives for two distinctive generations. A reporter sent to Davos from the *Neue Zürcher Zeitung* even remarked that the distinction between pre- and postwar generations corresponded with the occupational rift that separated the lowly *Dozent* from the full or *Ordinarius* professor. The divide was just as much a matter of character as chronology. The postwar generation (the reporter's own) constituted "completely different stuff."[38]

The Neo-Kantian Legacy

The foregoing considerations of crisis and generation may serve as a helpful background for this chapter's discussion of the general transformation of German philosophy in the 1920s. But we must now turn from the general to the specific and from culture to philosophy. To understand the nature of the disagreement between Cassirer and Heidegger, it is especially important to know something about the status of Kant-interpretation in the early decades of the twentieth century. Intellectual interest in Kant's philosophy had gained renewed momentum in the last third of the nineteenth century, thanks chiefly to the so-called neo-Kantian movement, a diverse group that took up Otto Liebmann's call for an end to Hegelian and Schopenhauerian metaphysics—summarized in the slogan, "back to Kant"—and went on to develop important contributions to logic and the philosophy of science (e.g., Cohen, Natorp), to the philosophy of value (Windelband, Rickert), and, eventually, helped to inspire a newly rigorous method for sociology both in Germany and France (Weber, Durkheim). Of all these schools, however, "neo-Kantianism" as a term has come to be associated chiefly with the contributions of the so-called Marburg School and the work of its leading philosophers, Paul Natorp and Hermann Cohen.[39]

The special significance of Cohen's ideas for later developments in Continental thought can hardly be exaggerated. His earliest work, *Kant's Theory of Experience* (1871), established a robustly anti-metaphysical and science-oriented paradigm that would remain dominant in Kant-scholarship at least until well into the 1920s. Taking the riddle of the Kantian "thing-in-itself" as his point of departure, Cohen attempted to show that Kant's chief aim was to develop a theory of scientific discovery in which the thing-in-itself surrendered its metaphysical status to become, instead, a purely methodological idea, as the "task" *(Aufgabe),* or the as-yet-unexplained, of expanding scientific knowledge. This interpretative innovation—from metaphysics to method—became the foundation stone for Cohen's own, original contribution to philosophy, the so-called critical idealist system, which appeared from the publishing house of Bruno Cassirer (Ernst's cousin) in three successive volumes between 1902 and 1912.[40] Perhaps the most definitive innovation of Cohen's system was the argument set forth in the 1902 *Logic of Pure Knowledge* that dispensed with Kant's epistemic dualism: Kant himself had claimed that knowledge requires not only spontaneity but also receptivity—that is, it requires a union between concepts and sensible intuitions. From the very beginning, however, this dualism between concepts and intuitions had struck a great many critics as an unfortunate and perhaps indefensible compromise with empiricism, because it presupposed an unverifiably metaphysical object-independence. It was Cohen's major achievement to do away with this dogmatic reading of the thing-in-itself by suggesting that it was merely a thought-object, an object which had its origin in thought alone. Appealing to the operation in calculus whereby the infinitesimally small magnitude is generated via a mathematical operation, Cohen titled this purely idealist insight the *Ursprungsprinzip,* or principle of origins. Now, on Cohen's view, once the independent thing-in-itself had lost its metaphysical status and was transformed into a merely regulative concept of scientific discovery, there was no further need to regard sensibility as a separate faculty. The thing-in-itself was accordingly abandoned in favor of a purely conceptual coherentism that replaced the empiricist model of truth as correspondence to an independent object, with a purely intellectualistic model of truth as the systematic coherence among concepts. And it was this argument perhaps most of all that both proponents and critics saw as the defining feature of Marburg neo-Kantianism: its rejection of metaphysics.

Cohen's reputation as a philosophical radical was matched by his commanding style, in lectures as well as in politics. A vocal advocate of progressive Socialism, Cohen was also the only unbaptized Jew to hold a philosophical chair in a German university before World War I, and he was frequently drawn to the center of anti-Semitic controversies, such as the Dreyfus Affair in France, and Polish-Jewish immigration, on which he squared off against the German nationalist historian Heinrich Treitschke. Cohen's final work, the posthumously published *Religion of Reason out of the Sources of Judaism* (1919), proved an enduring though controversial inspiration for Jewish existential thinkers in the Weimar period.[41] But it is most of all the earlier and more recognizably neo-Kantian theory that has survived into the postwar world. Indeed, it would not be wrong to claim that Cohen's originally anti-metaphysical and scientific emphasis helped to set the direction and character for contemporary analytic epistemology.

For Cassirer himself, Cohen was indisputably the most consequential German philosopher of the late nineteenth and early twentieth century. In his 1912 essay, "Hermann Cohen and the Renewal of Kantian Philosophy" (which was published in *Kantstudien* on the occasion of Cohen's seventieth birthday and retirement from Marburg), Cassirer extolled his teacher as a transcendental philosopher whose major contributions built upon Kant's own theoretical insights into the intimate relation between philosophy and science. For Cohen, as for Kant, philosophy took the facts of science as its point of departure. But philosophy eschewed any and all metaphysical inquiry into the inner nature of scientific objects and instead focused its attention solely on the character of scientific judgments: "The question concerning the Being of objects remains in a transcendental sense undetermined and unsolvable," Cassirer explained, "so long as one leaves unanswered the question concerning the manner of cognition [*Erkenntnisart*] by which knowing the object secures its ground."[42] This was in Cassirer's view the fundamental innovation of transcendental philosophy, whose impact via Cohen would be felt across the rival schools, not only among neo-Kantians but also among phenomenologists, who followed Cohen's break from psychologism and naturalism to embrace what Husserl called "pure" or "transcendental" phenomenology. Perhaps the most dramatic evidence for Cohen's break from metaphysics, as Cassirer explained, was the theory of infinitesimal judgment, according to which scientific explanations involving calculus illustrated that the object of scientific knowledge was produced by thought itself, while such an object could not be understood as a sensually apprehended "existence" [*kein sinnlich fassbares "Dasein"*].[43]

This was, in Cassirer's judgment, the hallmark of transcendental philosophy as Cohen had formulated it—the "critical reduction of Being [*Sein*] to validity [*Geltung*]"—and it was this feature that most defined not only Cohen's epistemology but his ethics as well: the gesture of universalization intrinsic to the legislative form of ethical reasoning could not be derived from a merely empirical average of human behavior. Ethics had to defend itself, in Cassirer's words, "against any *anthropological* turn."[44] Here Cassirer emphasized once more the imperative to reject any and all metaphysical questions that concerned the essence or "Being" of the objects of knowledge. Philosophy would fasten its attention solely on formal and transcendental questions that concerned the validity of our own judgments about those objects. Even freedom, Cassirer observed, was to be understood in such a way that avoided any reference to a "secret ground" behind human action. Freedom retained its validity only as a conceptual *postulate*—the goal of action as posited by practical reason. The ultimate message of Cohen's critical system was that the various objects of transcendental inquiry were to be conceived each according to its specific domain: scientific knowledge required a particular transcendental grounding of its own, while ethics and aesthetics demanded their very own distinctive modes of validation. But even while the various regions of human culture could not be fused into what Cassirer called an "undifferentiated unity of validity," they nevertheless shared in common a single point of origin in the spontaneity of human *consciousness*.[45]

Well into the 1920s, and despite growing opposition, Marburg School methodology remained at the center of German philosophical discussion. Hans-Georg Gadamer recalls in *Philosophical Apprenticeships* that if a student were to announce they were "going to Marburg," this was understood to mean a commitment to the most rigorous training.[46] Although Cohen retired from his Marburg chair in 1912, the university sustained its overall reputation for philosophical excellence. But the 1920s brought to Marburg a marked shift in the winds. Heidegger assumed a post at Marburg as associate professor of philosophy in 1923, and in 1927, as part of the festivities surrounding the five-hundredth anniversary of the university's founding, he authored a brief history of the Marburg philosophical chair since the late nineteenth century. He took special note that even after both Cohen and Natorp had passed away (in 1918 and 1925, respectively), the spirit of Marburg neo-Kantianism survived thanks to the efforts of their two most prominent students, Nicolai Hartmann and Ernst Cassirer.[47]

The philosophical prestige of the neo-Kantian movement was also secured through its distinguished journal *Kantstudien*. Since its founding in 1896 by Hans Vaihinger, with an illustrious editorial board that included Wilhelm Dilthey, Kuno Fischer, Alois Riehl and Wilhelm Windelband, it had quickly grown to become one of a small handful of German academic journals whose collective verdict on new directions in German philosophy granted its authors an assumed imprimatur of academic legitimacy. Especially in the field of Kant-interpretation, its importance was widely recognized even outside of Germany. In 1898 Père Gardeil observed in the *Revue Thomiste* that "cette revue sera très utile à quiconque veut se tenir au courant du mouvement philosophique Kantien."[48] While it enjoyed a general prominence, the journal's editorial board retained a specifically neo-Kantian orientation well into the twentieth century. Beginning in 1925, its editorship passed into the hands of Paul Menzer and Arthur Liebert (the latter departing as a refugee in 1933). It is of some interest to note that a considerable number of the journal's editors were of Jewish descent, including both Liebert and Cassirer. Inevitably, there were complaints. In 1916 the established philosopher Bruno Bauch complained in a right-wing nationalist publication, *Der Panther,* that neo-Kantianism smacked of "Jewish formalism" and that because Cohen was Jewish rather than German he was unable to appreciate Kant's philosophy. The editorial board of *Kantstudien,* he despaired, was "Jew-ridden" *(verjudet).*[49] Cassirer was moved to write a rebuttal to correct Bauch's faulty conception of national identity, but once Bauch resigned from the journal's editorial board the essay went unpublished.[50] In the midst of war, nationalist passions ran high. Even the great historian of religion Ernst Troeltsch let slip the astonishing remark that under Hermann Cohen's influence, the journal had descended into "Jewish terrorism."[51] But such scandals were rare and the journal continued to enjoy an uncontested prestige well through the 1920s, even as new movements in philosophy reared their heads in rebellion against the neo-Kantian establishment.

Heidegger himself was by no means unremittingly hostile to neo-Kantianism. He had himself received serious training under the neo-Kantian Heinrich Rickert (a leading figure with Wilhelm Windelband of the so-called Southwestern neo-Kantian School). Before assuming a chair of his own at Freiburg, Heidegger worked at Marburg as an associate professor between 1923 and 1929. During this interval, his reputation as an important new voice in philosophy began to spread, and his emergence in the 1920s might well be understood as part of the wider, generational rebellion against the neo-Kantian legacy. The older ideal of philosophy as a transcendental grounding for science—an ideal best typified by the Marburg School and also by Edmund Husserl's embrace of transcendental idealism—began to yield in the face of new intellectual trends, such as life-philosophy, phenomenology, and existentialism, trends that some commentators termed the "resurrection of metaphysics."[52] It is therefore one of the small ironies in the interwar transformation of Weimar philosophy that some observed a striking intergenerational resemblance: when Nicolai Hartmann witnessed Heidegger's inaugural lecture at Marburg, he noted to the young Gadamer that "he had not seen such a powerful performance since Hermann Cohen."[53]

Southwestern and Marburg Neo-Kantianism

The powerful transformation of philosophical interests during the 1920s—from neo-idealism to existentialism—is perhaps best illustrated by attending more closely to the contemporary debate concerning the proper interpretation of Kant. The controversy was multifaceted and involved a number of schools, but at its core was the enduring rivalry between the two most celebrated institutions of neo-Kantianism at Marburg and in southwestern Germany. Whereas the Marburg School (led by Hermann Cohen until his death in 1919 and then by Natorp) saw the foremost significance in Kant's legacy as a transcendental philosophy that laid the foundations for mathematical natural science, the Southwestern, or Baden, School at Heidelberg and Freiburg (led by Wilhelm Windelband and, after his death in 1915, his former doctoral student Heinrich Rickert, along with Emil Lask) laid greatest stress on Kant's precept concerning "the primacy of practical reason" so as to ground a new philosophy of value and cultural understanding. The difference between these two orientations was indeed pronounced. As noted above, the Marburgians saw Kant primarily as a theorist of transcendental reason and they tended to regard the formal logic of scientific explanation as a methodological paradigm for any further areas of human inquiry, including ethics. The Southwestern School meanwhile drew its major inspiration from Kant's antinomy of causality and freedom, out of which it developed a crucial methodological distinction between (in Windelband's terms) the causal or "nomothetic" explanatory methods appropriate to the natural sciences, or *Naturwissenschaften,* and the individuating or "idiographic" methods appropriate to the study of uniquely meaningful events in history and the cultural sciences, or *Geisteswissenschaften.*[54]

The intensity of this rivalry notwithstanding, the schools themselves were never monolithic in doctrine. Cohen and Natorp disagreed over the place of religion in critical philosophy, while the Southwestern School, especially after Windelband's death, began to dissolve with Rickert's evolution toward a modified life-philosophy. Yet the basic contrast between the schools remained and eventually helped to reinforce the methodological split in Weimar philosophy—between transcendental rationalism and historicizing hermeneutics—which would culminate at Davos with Cassirer's attempted defense of the Marburg transcendental legacy against Heidegger's critique of its apparent scientism. This continuity was not only philosophical but a matter of educational affiliation as well. The young Heidegger had studied under Rickert at Freiburg while Cassirer apprenticed with Cohen at Marburg. The Heidegger-Cassirer dispute might therefore be seen as the final realization of the earlier, late nineteenth-century institutional and methodological rivalry between Southwestern and Marburgian neo-Kantianism.

The unusually intense nature of intellectual debate over Kant's legacy in the 1920s calls for explanation. The controversy may seem surprising, especially when one considers that neo-Kantianism first emerged as a return to "scientific" philosophy after the metaphysical indulgences of the mid-nineteenth century. As Klaus Köhnke has shown, the rise of the neo-Kantian movement was closely correlated with the rise of an academic bourgeoisie that tried to eschew ideological partisanship in favor of a strictly "professional" ethos. Notwithstanding Hermann Cohen's particular support for German Socialist principles, neo-Kantianism in general remained largely nonpolitical in character; indeed, it became the very paradigm of an ostensibly German "unpolitical" scholarship. Paradoxically, however, the neo-Kantians' dedication to intellectual practice as an end in itself and their pronounced resistance to political or "worldview" advocacy itself grew into a self-conscious and passionately defended program. By the end of World War I, it had hardened into a doctrine of political stoicism, articulated, for example, by Max Weber (an associate of the Heidelberg school) in his celebrated 1919 address, "Science as a Vocation." The Weberian distinction between fact and value, with its bitter rejection of scholarship as value promotion, was only one example of the principled hostility to "worldview" philosophy that typified the neo-Kantian movement as a whole. The earliest and most characteristic statement of this hostility was the neo-Kantian Alois Riehl's inaugural lecture, "On Scientific and Non-Scientific Philosophy," which he first delivered in 1883 upon assuming his professorship in philosophy at Freiburg, whose stringent distinction between philosophy as "science" *(Wissenschaft)* and philosophy as "worldview" *(Weltanschauung)* set the tone for the various schools of Kant-interpretation well into the twentieth century.[55]

The neo-Kantians vehemently resisted the category of "worldview" as a confusion between fact and value in part because they saw it as a threat to the status of academic philosophy as a rigorous and objective science.

Throughout the history of the neo-Kantian movement, its proponents would appeal to Riehl's statement so as to reinforce their commitment to what they called "scientific philosophy," and they were careful to explain any apparent recourse to "worldview" as incompatible with Kant's original aims. Whereas the scientific-epistemological tendency of the Marburg neo-Kantians prohibited any such justification of *"Weltanschauungsphilosophie,"* the contrasting attention to Kant's practical- (or value-) philosophy among the Southwestern neo-Kantians opened the door for a renewed discussion of its cultural significance. The task initially fell to neo-Hegelian Richard Kroner (a professor of philosophy at Kiel and author of the impressive two-volume *Von Kant bis Hegel*), who attempted to reconstruct the value commitments that had motivated Kant himself in his 1914 study, *Kants Weltanschauung.*[56] In a formula that reaffirmed the Southwestern attention to practical reason, Kroner declared that "Kant maintains the non-metaphysical but theoretical validity of mathematical science and the non-theoretical but metaphysical validity of the moral life."[57] The subordination of epistemology to ethics was necessary if ethics was to possess its own distinctive sort of "metaphysical" significance as the source of value in the world. The Kantian dualism between pure and practical reason was accordingly a prerequisite for the human experience of "meaning":

> Just as the idea of what ought to be constantly points beyond itself . . .
> so the idea of an absolute meaning also leads beyond itself. Beyond . . .
> the tension of the real and the ideal . . . all meaning seems to disappear.
> We cannot want such a meaning to exist, because it would destroy the
> meaning of our own life. Kant quotes with approval the words of the
> poet Haller: "The world with all its faults/Is better than a realm of will-
> less angels." Kant's vision of life thus demands an ethical dualism.[58]

Kroner's discussion of the Kantian "worldview" had two important consequences. The reaffirmation of Kantian dualism helped to reinforce the Southwestern neo-Kantians' separation between fact and value; indeed, it appeared to condemn the Marburg neo-Kantians for focusing exclusively on Kant's theoretical philosophy, which was bereft of "metaphysical" significance. More important, Kroner's allusion to the status of angels in Kant's ethical theory seemed to imply that the question of "worldview" or subjective meaning was only possible within the realm of finite or purely human experience (i.e., a bounded sphere in which the cleft between fact and value made "absolute meaning" an impossibility). These two conjoined themes were to reappear in the later discussion of Kant's philosophy at Davos.

To understand the deeper sources of disagreement between Heidegger and Cassirer, it is important to recognize the various ways both men struggled to define their own philosophical commitments in the twilight years of the neo-Kantian movement. Heidegger's debt to neo-Kantianism is perhaps best illustrated by considering the theory of historical interpretation developed by his earlier teacher, Heinrich Rickert (1863–1936), a prominent figure in the history of Weimar philosophy who played an especially important role in the growing rivalry between neo-Kantianism and its existential succession. Rickert first received his doctorate at Strasbourg under Windelband's direction and from there moved to Freiburg to write a habilitation with Alois Riehl. On Riehl's departure in 1896, Rickert then assumed a chair in philosophy at Freiburg, where he was an influential teacher for many of the younger students, including Heidegger. Beginning in 1911, Heidegger commenced study at Freiburg under Rickert's guidance. In 1913 he received his doctorate at Freiburg (on "The Doctrine of Judgment in Pychologism"), and two years later he completed his habilitation (on Duns Scotus's theory of categories and meaning). Alongside Windelband and Lask, Rickert was beyond doubt one of the most consequential figures in the Southwestern School of neo-Kantianism.

It is especially important to acknowledge Rickert's role in developing the Southwestern neo-Kantian doctrine of historical knowledge, as this doctrine helped to lay the foundations for Heidegger's later theory of historicized hermeneutic understanding: Rickert had laid out his most sophisticated statement of the neo-Kantian theory of history in his book *The Limits of Concept Formation in Natural Science* (1902). Building upon his teacher's famous distinction between "idiographic" and "nomothetic" modes of explanation, which Windelband had introduced at Strasbourg in his 1884 rectoral address, "History and Natural Science," Rickert further developed the idea that the so-called irrational character of historical reality might nonetheless admit of conceptual treatment.[59] In opposition to Wilhelm Dilthey (whose intuitionist tendencies Rickert faulted as a concession to antiphilosophical mysticism), Rickert insisted on a rigorous methodology specifically tailored to the noncasual and value-laden character of historical phenomena.[60]

This essentially neo-Kantian distinction between nature and culture would reappear as late as Heidegger's 1927 summer seminar, *Basic Problems of Phenomenology:*

> There are beings, however, to whose being intraworldliness belongs in a certain way. Such beings are all those we call *historical* entities— historical in the broader sense of world-historical, all those things that the human being, who is historical and exists historically in the strict and proper sense, creates, shapes, cultivates: all his culture and works. Beings of this kind *are* only or, more exactly, arise only and come into being only *as* intraworldly. Culture *is* not in the way that nature is.[61]

Yet the continuity between the neo-Kantian and Heideggerian view of historical as against natural-scientific inquiry should not be exaggerated. In Heidegger's view, the neo-Kantians seemed all too ready to grant the equality but dualistic separation between cultural and natural-scientific understanding. But Heidegger himself seemed to regard the dualism as implicitly hierarchical. In his own philosophy he argued for the primacy of historicity *(Geschichtlichkeit)* over and against the "derivative" or "deworlded" status of natural-scientific objectification, an argument that was to reemerge in his debate with Cassirer, as we shall see later on. Heidegger's celebration of the historical-cultural as against scientific understanding no doubt signaled a bold departure from his neo-Kantian predecessors. Rickert, and Windelband before him, had merely wished to demarcate the limits of natural-scientific explanatory methods, not to demote them to a lower status in the hierarchy of human understanding. Yet, although he had not meant to encourage a rejection of natural-scientific understanding, Rickert's defense of history against the natural sciences helped reinforce the divide between the Southwestern "value" philosophy and the "scientific" Marburgians and helped to pave the way for Heidegger's more radical theory of historical being.[62] This preferential analysis of historical *as against* natural-scientific understanding ironically brought Heidegger into unexpected proximity to Cassirer, who at the time was effecting his own departure from neo-Kantian orthodoxy to embrace a broader theory of cultural-historical symbolism.

Heidegger had further reasons for disputing the neo-Kantian consensus. Deeper than the aforementioned divisions between Southwestern and Marburg neo-Kantianism was their larger agreement that philosophy must take cognizance of the distinctive *regions* or diverse modes of epistemological access that partitioned human experience: the Southwestern School emphasized the distinction between the *Natur-* and *Geisteswissenschaften,* while the Marburg School emphasized the distinctive transcendental grounding for science, ethics, and aesthetics (a point Cassirer stressed in his 1912 essay summarizing Cohen's legacy). It is only against the background of this broad consensus that we can make sense of Heidegger's attempt to introduce a new line of inquiry in *Being and Time* that promised to investigate not the meaning of any particular "regional ontology" but rather "the meaning of Being in general."[63] As Heidegger explained, genuinely philosophical insight into *both* history *and* nature (an implicit nod toward neo-Kantianism's characteristic division of philosophical labor) presupposed the need for a distinctive type of ontological inquiry insofar as both required a prior working out of the *"Seinskonstitution"* of these particular regions: for history, "what is philosophically primary is neither a theory of the concept-formation of historiology nor the theory of historiological knowledge, nor yet the theory of history as the Object of historiology." Instead, "what is primary is rather the Interpretation of historical entities as regards their historicality." Similarly, for the natural sciences, Heidegger explained that, "the positive outcome of Kant's *Critique of Pure Reason* lies in what it had contributed toward the working out of what belongs to any Nature whatsoever, not in a 'theory' of knowledge. His transcendental logic is an *a priori* logic for the subject matter of that area of Being called 'Nature.'"[64] Although Heidegger was ready to grant the provisional need for this kind of regional ontology, he hastened to note that any such ontological investigation of a particular domain was insufficient if it was not grounded in a deeper and more global kind of questioning, concerning "the meaning of Being in general." This claim posed a direct challenge to *both* of the preceding neo-Kantian schools insofar as each of them appeared willing to carve up human experience into various ontological kinds: "The question of Being," Heidegger explained,

aims therefore at ascertaining the *a priori* conditions not only for the possibility of the sciences which examine entities as entities of such and such a type, and, in so doing, already operate with an understanding of Being, but also for the possibility of those ontologies themselves which are prior to the ontical sciences and which provide their foundations. *Basically, all ontology, no matter how rich and firmly compacted a system of categories it has at its disposal, remains blind and perverted from its ownmost aim, if it has not first adequately clarified the meaning of Being, and conceived this clarification as its fundamental task.*[65]

It is this theme above all—the rejection of ontological *pluralism* and the assertion of an ontological *unity* deeper than any particular object domains— that most reveals the early Heidegger's departure from the methodological consensus of neo-Kantianism. *Being and Time* thus concluded with the intriguing suggestion that notwithstanding the world's apparent fragmentation, its innermost constitution was grounded upon the single and unified phenomenon of existential temporality. This dissent from the neo-Kantians had even further and more far-reaching implications for Heidegger's conception of what it is to be a human being. Throughout *Being and Time*, Heidegger was careful to note that the temporal horizon he called "primordial temporality" should not be mistaken for a primal source of spontaneity akin to Kant's "transcendental unity of apperception." On Heidegger's view, it was the basic predicament of human existence that its thrownness meant "*never* to have power over one's ownmost Being from the ground up." This incapacity or "nullity" was indeed something like the essence of human being-in-the-world: "This '*not*,'" wrote Heidegger, "belongs to the existential meaning of 'thrownness.'" The existential temporality that served as the fundamental horizon for world-disclosure was therefore best understood not as a "ground" *(Grund)* but as an "abyss" *(Abgrund).*[66]

Cassirer, by comparison, remained essentially faithful to these two basic principles of the neo-Kantian consensus. It was indeed a guiding theme of *The Philosophy of Symbolic Forms* that there was in principle no limit whatsoever to the repertoire of human symbols. The constitutive forms of human reality exhibited a maximum of diversity; and, notwithstanding his belief that scientific symbols stood at the highest stage of abstraction, Cassirer resisted the suggestion that any one region of human experience could claim metaphysical primacy over the others. This commitment to symbolic pluralism remained a defining feature of Cassirer's philosophy from the 1920s onward. At the same time, while he insisted on symbolic pluralism, Cassirer also believed that the full range of symbolic forms all shared a common point of origin in mental spontaneity. In this respect, too, Cassirer remained faithful to what was an essential premise of the entire neo-Kantian movement: the assumption that the intelligibility of all reality as it is given in human experience depends on the spontaneous action of human consciousness.

From *Kantfeier* to *Kant-Krise*

The neo-Kantian movement remained institutionally and intellectually powerful well after World War I. But the two hundredth anniversary of Kant's birth in 1924 brought debate over Kant's philosophical and cultural legacy to a level of unusual intensity. Along with academic conferences and public speeches, the anniversary also saw the publication of Cassirer's new biography of the Königsberg philosopher, *Kants Leben und Lehre* (1918), and a new scholarly set of Kant's complete works, published under Cassirer's editorial leadership by the esteemed publishing firm Bruno Cassirer.[67] What was often known as simply the "Cassirer-edition" (though the title pages also paid homage to the late Hermann Cohen, who was supposed to have authored one of the volumes) would remain for some time the standard reference for Kant-scholarship in central Europe. Heidegger, too, owned and worked from the Cassirer edition and displayed the complete set on the shelves in his private study. Meanwhile, Cassirer's biography helped to renovate Kant's image as a thinker of immediate consequence for contemporary philosophical problems. In an admiring review, Arthur Liebert hailed Cassirer for combating the old prejudice (ratified that same year in Spengler's recently published philosophy of history, *The Decline of the West*) that "Kant's critical work was restricted to the groundlaying of natural-scientific knowledge."[68] By emphasizing the then-neglected aesthetic element in Kant's thought and recasting him as an engaging wit comparable to the French *philosophes,* the biography had in effect *modernized* Kant, presenting him in a fresh light as a broad-minded and even humanistic philosopher whose later reputation for rationalist severity was undeserved.

The 1924 bicentennial was fêted around the world, with academic festivities not only in Czechoslovakia, Denmark, England, Switzerland, and Italy, but also in more far-flung venues such as Sweden, Japan, Bucharest, Jerusalem, Sofia, and Peking. The International Congress of Philosophy in Naples devoted a special session to Kant's bicentennial with a keynote address by the esteemed neo-Kantian Arthur Liebert. The 1924 *Philosophischer Almanach* gathered a massive bibliography of all recent Kant-related scholarship. And in Königsberg itself, the philosopher's birthplace and the city where he spent all of his ironically un-cosmopolitan life, a five-day program marked the occasion with speeches on all aspects of Kant's work, including his specific historical origins in East Prussian culture and his general influence across all of modern-day philosophy. An event of such importance deserved recognition by officials of the highest order: Friedrich Ebert himself, then-president of the Weimar Republic, was listed on the program but at the last minute failed to attend and sent only a letter. In his absence there appeared two high officials: Dr. Jarres, an official in the *Deutsche Volkspartei* (DVP), at that time vice-chancellor and minister of the Interior; and Otto Braun of the Social Democratic Party (SPD), who was to serve as minister-president of Prussia during much of the Weimar era. Letters of congratulation arrived from abroad and were read during the ceremonies, from the American Philosophical Association, and from specific universities in North America, such as Northwestern and Cornell. The events marking the longevity of Kant's ideas were also the occasion for the dedication of a freshly built mausoleum, which stood beside the *Domkirche* that housed the philosopher's remains.

Apparent to all who gathered for the bicentennial was the enormity of Kant's influence on German philosophy. But conflict arose over its true meaning. In a paper addressing "Kant's legacy," Erich Adickes observed that Kant's successors had fallen into bitter factions and they had "even capitalized Kant in the interests of their own philosophic prepossessions." Some participants at the Königsberg *Kantfeier* complained in private that "the metaphysical wing" of Kant-interpreters had been given "undue prominence," a complaint that anticipated the struggle between Cassirer and Heidegger just a few years later. Cassirer himself was under the weather and barely managed to attend.[69] His colleague and coeditor at *Kantstudien,* Arthur Liebert, lectured on Kant's theory of history and read a paper on "Kant in Present-day German Philosophy" by the great Kant-scholar Hans Vaihinger (who had also taken ill), which surveyed the entire landscape of German philosophy, observing that "the spirit of Kant's philosophy . . . remains forever young" and that "today [it] manifests itself, in one way or another, in all the significant philosophical formulations and tendencies of Germany."[70]

Kant's legacy was celebrated but also fiercely disputed. As early as 1896 in the inaugural issue of *Kantstudien*, Vaihinger had observed that Kant's philosophy served as "the jousting-field for all struggles" *(Turnierplatz alle Kämpfe)* in contemporary scholarship. Even in the later 1920s, this notion remained commonplace. Citing Vaihinger's original statement from a quarter century before, Friedrich Myrho affirmed once again in the bicentennial year that his contemporaries still sought their primary orientation in Kant's philosophy: They "fought with weapons from Kant's arms-chest, or at the very least they came to understand their own meaning through opposition" to Kant's ideas. Even two centuries after his death, his philosophy remained a "jousting-field" that saw not only the occasional skirmish but also the grand battle whose victors would in the future rule vast empires spanning the philosophical globe.[71]

While the waves of scholarly canonization persisted well into the later 1920s, a rising chorus of critics complained that Kant's philosophy was no longer consonant with postwar intellectual concerns. Heinrich Rickert opened his own contribution to the bicentennial discussion, *Kant as Philosopher of Modern Culture* (1924), with a bitter acknowledgement that "Kant can in no way qualify as a philosopher of the present day." Because contemporary thinkers no longer identified with the claims of transcendental reason, they were apt to dismiss Kant as a figure of merely historical interest: "With ever increasing volume," Rickert lamented, "one hears voices announcing that Kant should finally be cast aside; that the currency of rationalistic Kantianism has lost all value and is no longer capable of speaking to our own more advanced age." The contrast with contemporary themes seemed increasingly stark: "[Kant's] most important accomplishments run in direct opposition to the extremist intuitionism and irrationalism which, as 'philosophy of life' is in our own time most admired and modern, even in the sciences."[72] But, as Rickert hastened to explain, such criticism was unfair. Contemporary disdain for Kant's philosophy was founded on the Marburgian misperception of Kant's first *Critique* as merely an epistemology. Yet epistemological and natural-scientific concerns were in fact ancillary to its core problematic: "The chief problem of this work is not a theory of the experiential sciences [*Erfahrungswissenschaften*]," Rickert explained. Instead, "it revolves upon the old but eternally recurrent problem of metaphysics." With Kant's attention to metaphysics, the foundation was laid for a "comprehensive doctrine of worldview [*Weltanschauungslehre*]," which culminated in a philosophy of religion. In Rickert's view the highest purposes of the Kantian philosophy were indeed metaphysical; its mathematical-physical theory was mere preparation.[73]

Rickert was not the only critic to oppose the Marburg interpretation of Kant's first *Critique*. By the end of the decade, such challenges were increasingly common, especially when discussion turned on the questions of theology and "worldview." Heidegger's 1929 intervention in the dispute over Kant's legacy (which is addressed in greater detail in Chapter 3) is merely the most prominent specimen of a broader philosophical trend that aimed to rescind the ban on metaphysical themes and to restore philosophy to its ostensibly higher and more relevant calling. Among the ranks of the neo-Kantian establishment this trend naturally provoked considerable unease. In his review of Cassirer's 1922 lecture for the Warburg Library, "The Concept-Form in Mythical Thought," Kurt Sternberg remarked on the "error and confusion" of controversy over the ideal of philosophy as a science. Defending the Marburg Shool against the "false" charge of one-sided scientism, Sternberg praised Cassirer as its newest representative, a philosopher whose work extended without refuting neo-Kantian doctrine by showing that even myth was grounded in a formal and conceptual structure.

Although the neo-Kantian movement persisted with some vitality well into the Weimar era, the general trend of German philosophy in the years following the 1924 centennial revealed a gradual shift away from the formalism and scientism associated especially with the classical phase of Marburg neo-Kantianism. With increasing frequency, newly emboldened critics called for the wholesale abandonment of the neo-Kantian legacy and urged philosophers to return their discipline to its theological origins. The deepening religious tenor of Weimar intellectual debate drew further strength from nineteenth-century religious writers such as Kierkegaard and Dostoyevsky, both of whom found a newly receptive audience in the 1920s. German translations of Kierkegaard's collected works, edited by Christoph Schrempf, appeared for the first time between 1909 and 1922, preparing the way for both postwar existentialism and Protestant theology.[74] In his *Psychology of*

Worldviews (1919), Karl Jaspers went so far as to name Kierkegaard the true founder of *Existenzphilosophie,* a term often applied to both Jaspers and Heidegger (despite the latter's objections).[75] Dostoyevsky, too, enjoyed a philosophical revival: Karl Löwith relates that a portrait of the Russian novelist was displayed on the wall of Heidegger's study.[76] This broadening of philosophical perspective helped to make questions of meaning and worldview once again permissible. For the partisans of theology and metaphysics, earlier efforts to prohibit the discussion of worldview as an embarrassment to scientific philosophy furnished the best evidence that the older tradition of Kant-interpretation was now bankrupt.

By the decade's end, the accomplished Jesuit philosopher Erich Przywara (himself a participant at the Davos conference) could plausibly write that a "Kant-crisis" had seized the whole of the philosophical profession.[77] In his *Kant Today* (1930), Przywara diagnosed modern philosophy as riven by a controversy that had its origins in the ancient struggle between Parmenides and Heraklitus over the capacities of the human intellect, a controversy later transformed by Aquinas, and then Kant, into an essential question: Is the mind a mere *receptivity* that remains dependent upon what is given in experience? Or, is the mind endowed with a pure *spontaneity* that shapes the objects of knowledge (even if it does not, like Kant's "intellectus archetypus," create the objects themselves)? For Przywara, the tension between these two models of cognition ran throughout Kant's philosophy, in the contrast between humanity and God, receptivity *versus* the creative mind. It was a tension no present-day philosophers had managed to resolve. Heidegger's own philosophy of existence merely performed a "destruction" of the Kantian "ideal human being," and in its stead, brought forth an equally one-sided "real human being" marked by the afflictions of care and being-toward-death.[78] For Przywara, it seemed the entire field of modern philosophy was locked in an essentially Kantian opposition between a "metaphysics of finitude" and a "metaphysics of infinity."[79]

To be sure, a great many philosophers refused to acknowledge the legitimacy of the new metaphysical fashion. As early as 1899, the aged founder of *Kantstudien,* Hans Vaihinger (1852–1933), had inveighed against any and all efforts to revive a "metaphysical" interpretation of Kant's philosophy, counsel which still seemed relevant even in the mid-1920s.[80] Philosophers faithful to the older neo-Kantian stress on methodological and epistemological argumentation concerning the validity and limits of human knowledge within specific domains, whether natural-scientific or historical, responded to the "Kant-crisis" with rueful warnings of an incipient irrationalism.

The Challenge of Philosophical Anthropology

It was a frequent complaint among philosophers in the 1920s that the earlier neo-Kantian emphasis on problems of theoretical cognition and value-objectivity had led them to neglect the key question of what it is to be a human being. In the Weimar era the question "What is Man?" assumed a newfound urgency, especially for those who identified with the emergent discipline of philosophical anthropology, which included such cultural theorists and philosophers as Georg Simmel, Helmuth Plessner, Ludwig Klages, Jacob von Uexküll, and Max Scheler. Philosophical anthropology comprised a range of doctrines and methods and remained resistant to any unifying definition.[81] Much of the empirical research associated with philosophical anthropology commenced from the evolutionist premise that the human being is a specific kind of *animal* whose capacities for rational reflection and willful action must be understood using the tools of comparative zoology. This was at any rate the starting point for von Uexküll in particular, though on the whole the philosophical anthropologists more typically moved onto a speculative terrain where biological speculations concerning humankind's natural endowment were grafted onto more metaphysical and theological claims about human existence. As Plessner explained, "When [our] ancient metaphysical and ontological guarantees are no longer regarded as beyond question, then man and humanity become a problem."[82]

For the philosophical anthropologists the threat of reductionistic disenchantment that accompanied the mechanistic and random-selection doctrines of modern evolutionary biology could only be disarmed through a newly holistic understanding of the human being. Theologico-metaphysical answers would no longer suffice. As Plessner explained,

> It is no longer a matter of questions about how God's creature could become sinful or how finite and sinful man can conceive of the infinity of God's essence, but of whether and how man, subject as he is to causal laws, asserts his freedom in the face of their determination. It is a matter

of humanity as such . . . [a matter that concerns] the question, what it means and how it is possible to be a man.[83]

Although many theorists in the 1920s claimed to represent philosophical anthropology, it was Max Scheler who played a central role as their intellectual prophet. By the end of the decade, philosophers would eulogize him for bringing to life "the first anthropology of the new epoch."[84] It was indeed chiefly through Scheler's writings that the specific doctrines of philosophical anthropology came to inform the course of Weimar thought. As we will see later, much of the disagreement between Heidegger and Cassirer turned on the question as to whose philosophy best captured the essential character of human being. Although Heidegger and Cassirer remained critical of key principles in philosophical anthropology, they nonetheless considered it a crucial factor in their own debate.

Scheler in particular stood at the crossroads of many of the various pathways of Weimar thought. Born in 1874 to a Lutheran father and an orthodox Jewish mother, as a young man he converted to Catholicism, and his works have continued to exert an especially powerful influence on Catholic phenomenology throughout the twentieth century. Edith Stein, the sainted Carmelite nun murdered in Auschwitz in 1942, was Scheler's student, and in 1954 Karol Wojtyla (the future Pope John Paul II) submitted a doctoral dissertation on Scheler's ethics. In his early years Scheler had studied philosophy and sociology with both Wilhelm Dilthey and Georg Simmel, but he later developed a close bond with phenomenology, especially the kind practiced by the Munich group that included Theodor Lipps and Moritz Geiger. He was in fact among the cofounders of the Munich-based *Jahrbuch für Philosophie und phänomenologische Forschung*, which first appeared in 1912 under Husserl's direction and served for many years as the leading journal for phenomenology throughout central Europe. Scheler was perhaps best known for his unusual attempt to supplant the formalism of Kantian ethics with a so-called material ethics of a priori feelings or values (such as sympathy, love, hate, and so forth), a theory he presented in his *Formalism in Ethics and a Non-Formal Ethics of Values,* published in two volumes in 1913 and 1916.[85] Scheler's embrace of a phenomenological method that resisted the Husserlian reduction of phenomena to consciousness thereby anticipated Heidegger's own struggle to forego the latent idealism in Husserl's various reductions and to pursue instead an existential phenomenology of the so-called natural attitude. Toward the end of his life Scheler turned with greater decisiveness to questions of philosophical anthropology and religion. Scheler's last, fragmentary work, *Man's Place in Nature*, appeared in 1928, the year he died.

In the midst of his summer 1928 lectures on "The Metaphysical Foundations of Logic," Heidegger paused to pay tribute to his departed colleague, calling Scheler "the strongest philosophical force in modern Germany, nay, in contemporary Europe and in contemporary philosophy as such."[86] The praise was no doubt sincere, as there was much in Heidegger's own manner of phenomenological description that bore the imprint of Scheler's example.[87] And, not incidentally, Heidegger also considered Scheler one of the most insightful readers of *Being and Time*.[88] Heidegger took special care to note that although Scheler "was raised a Catholic," he knew his world as "an age of collapse." From "the idea of a weak God, one who cannot be God without man," Scheler laid the groundwork for a new discipline: "Once again the question, What is man? moved to the center of his work." It was not uncommon for observers of interwar philosophy to characterize Heidegger, too, as a philosophical anthropologist after the Schelerian model.[89] However, because Heidegger aimed at an *ontology* for which any attention to the human being was merely provisional, he would insist (at Davos and on other occasions) that his own analytic of Dasein should not be mistaken for a philosophical anthropology. But he was nevertheless quick to defend Scheler's work against critics who dismissed it as a retreat into superficial humanism: "The greatness of Scheler's philosophical existence," Heidegger warned, "lay in a relentless encounter with what time only dimly lets come to us . . . an encounter with mankind that allows for no appeasement and leveling through a sterile humanism that returns to the ancients." For Heidegger it was most of all the turn against Kantian formalism and the struggle to restore the lived and worldly human being to the center of philosophy that distinguished Scheler as the most consequential thinker of his time. "There is no one among today's serious philosophers who is not essentially indebted to him."[90]

"At no time in history," observed Scheler in *Man's Place in the Cosmos,* "has the human being become so *problematic* as in our contemporary age."[91] One question had preoccupied him throughout his career: "What is the human being, and what is his place within Being? [*Was ist der Mensch, und was ist seine Stellung im Sein?*]" For Scheler, it seemed, answering this question demanded the courage to break with tradition [*Abbau der Tradition*].[92] More specifically, it required an unusual combination of biological and philosophical knowledge, much of it building upon von Uexküll's comparative investigations of human and animal perception.[93] Like von Uexküll, Scheler argued that human beings differed from animals in that animals remained locked within their *Umwelt* or sensual-instinctual environment, while human beings had a special faculty of spirit that permitted them to become *weltoffen,* or "open-to-the-world." The animal, observed Scheler, "lives ecstatically within its environment, which it in a manner of speaking carries everywhere as a structure just like a snail its house. It is incapable of making this into an object." Only the human being could be said to live within the unbounded sphere of spiritual meaning that Scheler called "world" *(Welt).*[94] With this general insight derived from theoretical biology, Scheler confirmed what was a characteristic doctrine of philosophical anthropologists, such as Ludwig Klages, who saw all human experience as riven by a near-fatal opposition between spirit *(Geist)* and life *(Leben).*[95] Yet Scheler took care to distance himself from Klages, along with the broader movement of "pan-romantic" *Lebensphilosophie* that was at that time fashionable in Germany. "It is a fundamental error," Scheler warned, to regard spirit and life as locked in primordial enmity. Although life and spirit remained essentially distinct, they were nevertheless complementary and interrelated.[96] All human achievement in fact was due to the potent combination between them: "Spirit infuses life with ideas," Scheler explained, "but only life is capable of initiating and realizing spiritual activity, from its simplest act to the achievement of a task of great spiritual content."[97]

Many of the claims set forth in *Man's Place in the Cosmos* as the special contribution of philosophical anthropology bore a striking resemblance to perspectives commonly associated with philosophers of existence such as Jaspers and Heidegger. Especially familiar was Scheler's dramatic portrayal of the human encounter with the nullity that lay at the very core of existence: Because the human being was endowed with a spiritual capacity for world-openness, he was able to turn away from the sheer matter-of-factness of his lived environment to recognize its radical contingency: "In this movement of turning around he looks, as it were, into nothingness. He discovers the possibility of an absolute nothingness, and this discovery drives him to ask: 'Why is there a world as such, and why and how do I exist?'" Jaspers had claimed an experience of a "limit situation" could burst through the psychological limitations of a given worldview, while Heidegger had claimed that authenticity emerged from the revelation of nothingness through the anticipatory condition of Being-toward-Death. Scheler now argued in similar terms that the experience of nothingness served as the source of genuine insight into the human condition: "Man discovers the peculiar accident or the contingency of the fact that there is a world rather than nothing, and that he exists instead of being nothing, at the very moment he becomes conscious of the world and himself."[98] Much like his existential contemporaries with their calls for authentic resolve, Scheler closed with the declaration that behind the palliatives of traditional religion, there lay an original experience of metaphysical insight, an experience of "self-transcendence" which demanded true courage.[99]

Given the many points of agreement between them, it was altogether natural for Heidegger to regard Scheler as an important philosophical ally. The debt to Scheler was most evident in *Being and Time,* where Heidegger introduced his basic claim that the human being should not be understood as primarily a site of mental activity or a metaphysical substance, but rather, a "unity of living-through [*Er-lebens*]" whose fundamental relation to the world was activity, not theoretical contemplation.[100] Heidegger also appealed to Scheler's example in laying down his sophisticated analysis of the existential condition of pathetic investment he called *"Befindlichkeit,"* or mood. Following Scheler's polemic against Kantian formalism, Heidegger dismissed the objectivistic stance according to which value could be understood as a secondary property superadded to a value-indifferent world. He argued instead that the world as it was disclosed for human existence was already a world of investment or care. Dasein was the sort of being that first discovered itself as caught up in a world that *mattered* in some fashion. World-disclosure itself, therefore, was said to be governed by a globalized disposition.[101] For these insights, Heidegger expressed his gratitude and enduring debt by dedicating his 1929 book, *Kant and the Problem of Metaphysics,* to Scheler's memory.[102]

Cassirer's own attitude toward philosophical anthropology was rather more conflicted.[103] He assented to Heidegger's observation that Kant's entire philosophy proposed to answer the fundamental question, "What is the human being?" But he resisted Heidegger's implication that this anthropological grounding somehow disabled the universalistic claims of theoretical and practical reason. This would later emerge as an important topic of dispute at Davos and in the following years. In 1928, Cassirer had already begun to formulate his objections to philosophical anthropology in a paper titled "On the Metaphysics of Symbolic Forms," originally intended as the concluding portion to the third volume of *The Philosophy of Symbolic Forms*. This paper deserves special notice insofar as it contains Cassirer's exposition on the meaning of philosophical anthropology according to its foremost contemporary representatives (Scheler, Klages, Simmel, and von Uexküll). Although Cassirer did not mention Heidegger by name, many of his arguments against this group bore a strong resemblance to criticism he was already developing in response to his reading of *Being and Time*. I will examine that criticism in detail in Chapter 3, but here it will suffice to discuss Cassirer's basic views on philosophical anthropology itself.

Cassirer's expository comments on philosophical anthropology stand as a typical model of what one might call his *recuperative style of interpretation*. Whereas Heidegger insisted that a true understanding involved a violent reinterpretation of a text's meaning so as to unearth its latent content, Cassirer typically drew out whatever constructive themes he could so as to ultimately confirm his own philosophical lessons. On his view one could best appreciate the true merits of philosophical anthropology by looking to its origins in Kant, for whom (at least at one phase in his development) the anthropological question stood at "the actual center" of his entire system. Even during this phase, Kant had expressed discomfort with the prevailing eighteenth-century view that a purely empirical inquiry could serve as the foundation for knowledge of human beings: as Cassirer wrote, "when Kant asked about the nature of mankind, he was thinking of something stationary, not its changing nature." Its nature was conceived "not as some mere empirical constancy, but as an ideal determination, and ideal essence." This commitment to an idealized essence of humanity had been abandoned during the long night of nineteenth-century positivism, but contemporary exponents of philosophical anthropology were now reviving Kant's question in its original form. For Scheler, as for von Uexküll, there was an essential quality to being human that gained an additional confirmation in the comparative findings of biological research. A lower animal lived forever in the confinement of its own "receptor sphere," confined to what Plessner called "the net in which it catches the world." As illustration for this confinement von Uexküll offered a whole menagerie of animal species: The *Paramaecium candatum* (a species of infusoria) "rests more peacefully in its environment than does the child in its cradle."[104]

But the human being was different. "As soon as we enter the world of specifically human consciousness and specifically human ways of fashioning the world," Cassirer observed, "the closed ring of receptivity appears to be broken."[105] This theme concerning a breakthrough from mere receptivity preoccupied Cassirer's discussion. "With this break," Cassirer observed, "mankind appears to be cast out of the paradise of organic existence so typical of the simple forms of life, which seems to surround and shelter them with loving care." On Cassirer's reading, von Uexküll's research thereby seemed to confirm Kant's original image of the human being as a creature capable of bursting the limits of its own finitude so as to attain an order of truly objective meaning. "Man comprehends a world of objects not just according to how they affect him and what they accomplish for his vital interests," Cassirer observed, "but according to what they are and mean in themselves. His 'noticing' becomes detached from dependence on his actions and sufferings; he becomes [in Kant's phrase] 'free of all interests.'"[106] Cassirer characterized this shift to a higher and more sophisticated species of experience as (in Greek terminology) a *metabasis eis allo genos*.

On this point, the contrast between Cassirer and Heidegger could hardly have been more stark. For Heidegger, philosophical anthropology furnished evidence for his own conception of the human being as governed by fundamental moods and situated within the totality of practical assignments he called the *environment,* or *Umwelt.* Cassirer, however, found validation of his own philosophic belief that the human being may begin in finitude but eventually breaks free of its limits to create a symbolic order it then understands to be *both* an objective order *and* an expression of its own spontaneous consciousness: "The turn to form," Cassirer explained, "as it is found not only in art, but in language, myth, or theoretical knowledge as well, is always a kind of returning that the subject undergoes in itself, in the totality of its sensibility to and attitudes toward life." But this self-restoration necessarily entailed the subject's further articulation and expansion beyond its finite point of origin. It followed that no philosophical definition of the human being would remain valid for all time insofar as the only essence to humanity was its unbounded capacity for new modes of symbolization. "The concept of mankind," Cassirer declared, "is defined for it not by any specific, identifiable structural features, but through the comprehensive totality of mankind's achievements."[107] The philosophical anthropologists themselves paid homage to this capacity insofar as they drew a sharp line between the closure and openness that distinguished animal from human experience: "The simplest and most pregnant definition that a philosophical oriented 'anthropology' is capable of giving for mankind would therefore perhaps be that mankind is 'capable of form.'"[108] In a striking feat of interpretation, Cassirer had managed to recuperate a species of Kantian form-giving consciousness from philosophical anthropology.

These two rival interpretations of philosophical anthropology are of crucial relevance for making sense of the encounter at Davos, where philosophical anthropology remained a pivotal theme. In fact, preceding his debate with Heidegger, Cassirer delivered a special lecture on Scheler's philosophy. As we shall see, the disagreement over philosophical anthropology as recounted above would reappear in the central questions of the dispute between Heidegger and Cassirer: Was the human being thoroughly conditioned by its worldliness and finitude? Or did the human being possess a capacity to break from the confines of its local and practical world? And if such a breakthrough were in fact possible, what was the actual relation between the everyday environment of practical concern and the nonsubjective realm of human symbolization? Was the first merely a local way station on the path to objectivity? Or was that finitude the deeper truth of human existence, and was the movement toward a higher and more theoretical sphere nothing less than an evasion of this deeper truth? Cassirer would insist on numerous occasions, both at Davos and in written criticism, that Heidegger was mistaken to consider human finitude as a permanent and incorrigible feature for his existential analytic. Cassirer did not take strong exception to Heidegger's phenomenological description of Dasein's practical environment, but, as we shall see, he insisted that this description was incomplete: Beyond the practical lay a symbolic sphere that was no longer conditioned by the finitude of everyday Dasein. Heidegger would counter this suggestion by noting that even the most sublime flights of theory retain their grounding in the practical realm of temporality and care. To imagine otherwise was to flee the constitutive conditions of the human being.

From Husserl to Heidegger

The year 1929 was not only a culmination point in the division between neo-Kantianism and phenomenology; it was also a moment of pivotal significance in the history of the phenomenological movement itself. Until that year, it might have been possible for Husserl to overlook signs that Heidegger did not intend to remain faithful to the cause of transcendental phenomenology. Throughout the young Heidegger's initial period of training at Freiburg and then, in the mid-1920s, during the early years of independent instruction at Marburg, it seemed to Husserl as if his student agreed with his own cherished philosophical ideals. As Husserl would recall in a 1931 note to Alexander Pfänder (another former pupil), Heidegger had been "constantly at my side as my close assistant. He behaved entirely as a student of my work and as a future collaborator." Moreover, toward the end of the 1920s, Husserl had fallen into a sharp depression, brought on in part by anxiety that his time was insufficient for completing the remaining tasks for phenomenological research. It is therefore understandable that Heidegger, clearly a gifted student, would have seemed in Husserl's eyes the living promise of a continued legacy.[109]

His vision clouded by such hopes, Husserl tended to ignore those others who "often enough" warned him that the existential orientation of Heidegger's work was a more or less explicit assault on transcendental phenomenology. In his letter to Pfänder, Husserl paraphrases his colleagues' warnings (not without some bitterness):

> Heidegger's phenomenology is something totally different from mine; rather than furthering the development of my scientific works, his university lectures as well as his book are, on the contrary, open or veiled attacks on my works, directed at discrediting them on the most essential points. When I used to relate such things to Heidegger in a friendly way, he would just laugh and say: Nonsense![110]

Given such admonishments, it may seem remarkable that Husserl continued to trust in Heidegger's loyalty, even after the publication of *Being and*

Time made plain the depth of the divide between them. In retrospect, Husserl ascribed this to blindness, due to his feelings of isolation, "like an appointed leader without followers."[111] At the time, however, Husserl continued to regard Heidegger's exercise in existential ontology as a faithful realization of his own phenomenological principles, and, when he taught his very last seminar at Freiburg in July 1928, he saw Heidegger as his heir apparent: "I was virtually convinced that the future of phenomenological philosophy would be entrusted to him and that he not only would become my heir but also would surpass me." No doubt the warm dedication that Heidegger wrote in ink on the frontispiece of his teacher's copy of *Being and Time*—"To Edmund Husserl, in grateful respect and friendship"—gave added reassurance of his student's fidelity. Notwithstanding the book's unusual prose style and especially the unfamiliar meaning it ascribed to that technical term *phenomenon*, Husserl suppressed whatever doubts he may have had:

> Certainly when *Being and Time* appeared in 1927, I was surprised by the newfangled language and style of thinking. Initially, I trusted his emphatic declaration: It was the continuation of my own research. . . . Faced with theories so inaccessible to my way of thinking, I did not want to admit to myself that he would surrender both the method of my phenomenological research and its scientific character.[112]

Husserl's trust in his student was so certain that he urged his colleagues to accept Heidegger as his successor for the Freiburg chair in philosophy. In his correspondence with Husserl, Pfänder confessed that he had been deeply wounded to learn that Heidegger was the preferred choice and that his own candidacy was never seriously considered. In response, Husserl tried to explain that many factors had counted against Pfänder, including age: in 1928 he was fifty-eight. Other candidates, however, were apparently considered; Nicolai Hartmann's name was at least mentioned. But of the many philosophers who might have merited the committee's attention, only two were given serious attention: Heidegger and Cassirer. "There was not much discussion among the faculty," confessed Husserl, "since from the beginning *the mood was only for Heidegger and Cassirer. Only Cassirer presented any occasion for questions . . . which I had to answer.*"[113]

All this changed in the spring of 1929. Immediately following his departure from Davos, Heidegger returned to Freiburg for the ceremonial presentation of a *Festschrift* to honor Husserl on his seventieth birthday, April 8, 1929. (Also present for the occasion were Oskar Becker, Jean Hering, Roman Ingarden, Karl Löwith, Edith Stein, Alexandre Koyré, and, also just in from Davos, Hendrik Pos.) Heidegger's speech is noteworthy both for its lavish gestures of praise and for the somewhat unsettling way it introduced themes at odds with Husserlian method: "Philosophy," Heidegger declared, "is not a doctrine, not some simplistic scheme for orienting oneself in the world, not at all an instrument or achievement of human Dasein. Rather it is *this Dasein itself* insofar as it happens, in freedom, from out of its own ground."[114] Honorable words, perhaps, but hardly in obvious accord with the philosophy they were meant to honor. By the summer of 1929, the signs pointing toward an eventual rupture were unmistakable. Heidegger had spent the intervening months completing the text of his book, *Kant and the Problem of Metaphysics,* a searching reprisal of the radically innovative interpretation of Kant's philosophy he had only just presented at Davos. On July 29, Heidegger gave his inaugural lecture at Freiburg, "What Is Metaphysics?" upon officially assuming the chair in philosophy.[115] And, shortly thereafter, he sent Husserl a copy of the Kant-book. At this time, Husserl had just returned from his lectures in Paris and had at last completed the task of guiding his final work, *Formal and Transcendental Logic,* into print. He had now decided the time was at hand "to come to a clear-headed and definitive position on Heideggerian philosophy," and he devoted two months to a scrupulous study of both *Being and Time* and the Kant-book. The scales now fell from his eyes:

> I arrived at the distressing conclusion that philosophically I have nothing to do with this Heideggerian profundity, with this brilliant unscientific genius; that Heidegger's criticism, both open and veiled, is based upon a gross misunderstanding; that he may be involved in the formation of a philosophical system of the kind which I have always considered it my life's work to make forever impossible. Everyone except me has realized this for a long time. I have not withheld my conclusion from Heidegger.[116]

We can therefore date the break in relations between Husserl and Heidegger to the summer of 1929, sometime in the four months that followed the Davos encounter, when Heidegger had gained the offer of a prestigious academic post and was riding the crest of newfound fame. Although Husserl had played an instrumental role in securing Heidegger the Freiburg chair in philosophy as his successor (apparently against others who favored Cassirer), relations between teacher and student quickly cooled by autumn: "After he took over the chair," wrote Husserl, "our exchanges lasted about two months. Then, with complete amicability, it was over."[117]

For historians of Continental philosophy, the significance of the rupture between Heidegger and Husserl remains a topic of enduring and frequently politicized debate. A great many later phenomenologists who knew both teacher and student were of the opinion that Heidegger had improved upon the Husserlian method when he broke with his teacher's more scientific and idealistic tendencies and restored phenomenology to its more worldly and embodied horizon. Yet some of the most accomplished phenomenologists (Merleau-Ponty, for example) have insisted that the ambivalence within the phenomenological school—between a transcendental as against a worldly orientation—appears already within Husserl's own doctrine.[118] Yet it would be rash to dismiss altogether the very real differences in philosophical perspective that divided the two men. Although we must forego any deeper discussion of these differences here, it was a divide much like that which typified interwar German philosophy overall, between a rationally grounded transcendentalism and an existential-anthropological hermeneutics. Husserl himself confirmed his sense of this growing fracture within the phenomenological movement, not only in his rueful remarks on Heidegger's "unscientific" thinking in the letter to Pfänder, as quoted above, but also in his marginal notations in his personal copy of *Being and Time*, where he registered his discontent with Heidegger's innovative characterization of the phenomenological method: Where Heidegger had declared phenomenology as a "way of access to . . . ontology," Husserl responded that "I would say so, too, but in an entirely different sense." And where Heidegger had written that "the ways of being and the structures of being . . . must first of all be *won* from the objects of phenomenology," Husserl penned a regretful response in the margin: "My conception [is here] given a new interpretation."[119]

Husserl's marginal notations in *Kant and the Problem of Metaphysics* are even more revealing. In them we find a teacher's frank exasperation at what he saw as his student's decision to stray from the path of a rigorously scientific phenomenology. Husserl registered explicit doubts about Heidegger's recourse throughout the book to an essentially theological contrast, between divine (creative) and human (receptive) intuition. As we will see further on, Heidegger had borrowed this contrast from Kant and his idea of an *intuitus originarus* (a creative or "infinite" intuition that brings into being its objects in the very act of intuiting them), and it had played a critical role in Heidegger's own attempt to underscore the essential finitude of human understanding. But Husserl seems to have regarded such reliance on theological categories as an illicit and foreign import: "What is infinity over against finitude?" he wrote. "Why talk at all of finitude rather than receptivity? . . . On the other hand, absolutely adequate intuition, etc. . . . is an absurdity." From Husserl's perspective, such language signaled his student's willful retreat from philosophy into the arms of crypto-theology (a charge Cassirer would echo the following year). In the Kant-book, Heidegger had tried to justify his unusual reading of Kant by appealing to the principle that "every interpretation, if it wants to wring from what the words say what they *want* to say, must use *violence*." But in response, Husserl underlined the phrase, "every interpretation must use violence," and followed this in the margin with no less than three exclamation marks and three question marks.[120] More than once Husserl expressed doubts as to the accuracy of his student's interpretation, writing his query in the margins of Heidegger's book, "Is this Kant?"

Husserl's disagreement with his student over the proper interpretation of Kant's philosophy was hardly a minor affair. Nor were the two philosophers easily reconciled. In fact, it seems fair to say that by the summer of 1929 "Husserl [had] clearly given up on seeking a reconciliation with Heidegger's general position."[121] From that point onward relations between teacher and student would only grow increasingly strained: in 1931, Husserl gave a public lecture, "Phenomenology and Anthropology," in which he accused Heidegger and others in his generation of abandoning the scientific rigor of the eiditic reduction to the purely ideational realm in favor of an anthropological study of "concrete worldly Dasein."[122] He delivered the lecture, at least three times, in different cities across Germany. That same year in a private letter, Husserl now characterized Heidegger as the sort of man who "the war and ensuing difficulties" had "driven into mysticism."[123] In Husserl's eyes, Heidegger was no longer merely a dissident; he stood together with Max Scheler as "the antipodes" to everything Husserl had struggled to achieve.[124] From a broader and historical perspective, we might accordingly understand the private rift between Husserl and Heidegger as a further manifestation of the widening divide in Weimar philosophy between those who still cleaved to the ideal of philosophy as a scientific investigation of consciousness and those who were turning instead to the new model of philosophy as an anthropological and ontological study of human being as finite being-in-the-world. At its core, this, too, was essentially a disagreement over two contrasting images of humanity as either spontaneous or thrown. It was yet another variation on the very themes that had been disputed at Davos some months before.

From Cohen to Cassirer

Just as the phenomenological movement was beginning to fracture in the mid-1920s, a comparable if less dramatic transformation also became visible within Marburg neo-Kantianism in the wake of Cohen's death in April 1918. Although *Marburg* had once served as the name for a unified philosophical doctrine, in the early 1920s internal fissures and rival factions obviated that meaning. An instructive example is the case of Paul Natorp, who received his *Habilitation* from Cohen in 1881 and remained at Marburg as Cohen's colleague until the end of the latter's life.[125] During his early years, Natorp remained an earnest expositor of Cohen's method and he devoted the greater share of his energies to working out the historical background to the transcendental theories of Marburg neo-Kantianism, especially his writings on ancient classical, chiefly Platonic, philosophy.[126]

In the 1912 *Festschrift* for Cohen's seventieth birthday published in *Kant-studien,* Natorp hastened to defend the Marburg School against the criticism by the Southwestern neo-Kantians that the Marburg emphasis on science risked naturalizing both history (Natorp) and ethics (Cohen). Natorp dismissed this criticism as a gross misreading of Marburg doctrine for which "nature" indicated not a metaphysical being *(Sein)* but merely a hypothesis. He likewise rejected the Southwestern attempt to develop a separate logic for the philosophy of culture. The methodological distinction theorized by Windelband and Rickert between the natural and the cultural sciences struck Natorp as driving an illicit metaphysical distinction where none in fact existed: "Nature as the object of philosophy," wrote Natorp, "the nature of the natural sciences, counts for us, if at all, as *an essential foundation of human culture.*" Most of all Natorp sought to defend the Marburg School against the rising chorus of fashionable critics who complained that transcendental philosophy neglected the urgent concerns of "life" itself. "Make no mistake," Natorp observed, "our age longs for nothing so much as a philosophical penetration of life." But one could best sate this thirst with transcendental philosophy itself: "We sense the pulse beat of this very life in the ostensibly marble-cold thought-constructions of the great critics of reason," he declared, "Like our antecedents, Schiller, Wilhelm von Humboldt, and all the others, for whom Kantianism was not merely a matter of the head but also of the heart and of the entirety of life, so too is it for us."[127]

Notwithstanding this muscular affirmation of Marburg principles, Natorp survived Cohen by several years only to witness firsthand the decisive shift in Weimar philosophy from neo-Kantianism to existential ontology. In 1922 he served as dissertation director for Hans-Georg Gadamer, who, having immersed himself in Heidegger's philosophy, would emerge after World War II as Europe's foremost exponent of hermeneutics.[128] In 1923, Natorp also came to Husserl's assistance to secure for Heidegger an *Extraordinarius* professorship at Marburg. In his final years, Natorp distanced himself somewhat from his earlier neo-Kantianism and solidified his role as a leading exponent in the movement known as *Sozialpädagogik.* And, in a sign of his growing disaffection with neo-Kantian doctrine, he developed themes that bore a strong resemblance to Heideggerian ontology.[129] Many critics praised Natorp for his seeming "conversion" from Marburg and they eulogized the old philosopher for his belated discovery of the fountain of youth. "It is an exquisite feature of Natorp's development," observed one writer, "that as he outgrew the narrow confines of neo-Kantianism he became ever younger, and that one hardly took him for an old man but rather for someone rejuvenated as the day that is itself reborn fresh from the night."[130]

By 1923, Cassirer, too, announced his own departure from the orthodox Marburg doctrine. In the first volume of *The Philosophy of Symbolic Forms,* he called for a shift from "the critique of reason to the critique of culture."

Drawing inspiration from the thematic inventiveness of anthropologists and art historians who gathered at the Warburg Library, Cassirer ceased defining his work primarily in relation to natural-scientific epistemology and fastened his attention instead on the endless variety of cultural and anthropological phenomena. Needless to say, this did not entail a wholesale *rejection* of neo-Kantian doctrine. It was rather an innovation and expansion of the (essentially Kantian) method of transcendental critique that looked for formal conditions behind worldly appearances. But in *The Philosophy of Symbolic Forms,* Cassirer extended this critical-transcendental method into strange and unfamiliar terrain well beyond the purview of conventional neo-Kantian philosophy, especially in the second volume, where he plunged into a wealth of rituals and myths from the world over. His interests thereby came into proximity to both philosophical anthropology and the movements collectively described at the time as *Kulturphilosophie,* or, "the philosophy of culture." It was this broadening of thematic horizons rather than any essential modification of the transcendental method that prompted his neo-Kantian colleague Kurt Sternberg to praise Cassirer's work as an inquiry into "the logic of the illogical."[131]

By the end of the 1920s it was apparent that Cassirer, too, had modified the basic character of neo-Kantianism almost to the breaking point. But his basic commitment to a transcendental mode of inquiry premised on mental spontaneity remained essentially intact, and it was this premise that aroused the greatest criticism. In 1925, Heidegger was already expressing doubt as to whether myth could be properly understood if spontaneity remained the starting point for transcendental inquiry. In 1930, Cassirer's own student Joachim Ritter (who had co-transcribed the Davos debate with Otto Bollnow) raised this concern once again in an otherwise admiring review of his teacher's just-completed three-volume masterpiece: "The transformation that the epistemological problem has experienced over the course of the last decade," Ritter observed, "reveals itself perhaps most strongly in the fact that the erstwhile meaning of the theory of knowledge and the logic of science as the fundamental discipline of philosophy overall *has now been put into question, or, at the very least has become problematic.*"[132] But even as he registered doubts concerning Cassirer's transcendental method, Ritter refused to embrace Heidegger's existential alternative. In 1933, when Cassirer surrendered his Hamburg post and Ritter ascended into an academic chair, the latter used his inaugural address to affirm the need for "rational clarity" and to issue a stern injunction against the "metaphysical turn" in recent philosophy.

It would be worthwhile comparing the specific transformation evident within the phenomenological movement with the analogous heterodoxies and heresies of the neo-Kantian movement in the decade following World War I. Against the idealistic practice that Husserl called *transcendental* phenomenology, Heidegger succeeded in asserting a legitimate place for the novel practice of *existential* phenomenology that eventually, in the eyes of many though not all disciples, surpassed the original. Cassirer, too, developed well beyond the confines of his philosophical origins, and in his first response to Heidegger at Davos, he hastened to explain that Cohen's method was valid for him only in a *functional* and not a *substantial* sense—that is, precisely as a matter of transcendental orientation but not as a "dogmatic doctrinal system." At first glance, these two patterns of philosophical transformation may seem to outwardly resemble one another, in at least two respects: First, Heidegger could not conceive of phenomenology in accordance with Husserl's ideal of a "rigorous science," whereas Cassirer, even if he did not break entirely from the natural sciences, nonetheless embraced cultural themes disharmonious with Cohen's natural-scientific emphasis. The difference, of course, is that whereas Husserl believed that philosophy could itself be a science on a par with but distinct from the natural scientific study of nonmental nature, Cohen insisted that philosophy enjoyed a specifically *meta-scientific* status by virtue of which it could serve as a critique of science. For both philosophical founders, "science" played a paradigmatic role, but they disagreed sharply regarding the means by which that paradigm was to be followed. Second, and more importantly, the modifications Heidegger introduced into phenomenology brought a change not only in *what* phenomenology could describe but also in *how* such a description could be carried out: In *Being and Time,* Heidegger made it clear that one could only practice phenomenology as a hermeneutic of factical existence, a practice that would fail entirely if one continued to believe in the transcendental ego as the constitutive principle behind all phenomena. Phenomenology, in other words, could only proceed from within Dasein's horizon as a being *thrown into the world.* The modifications Cassirer introduced into the neo-Kantian method were hardly as far-reaching in their implications. Although

he introduced novel themes borrowed (chiefly) from philosophical anthropology, Cassirer continued to cleave to the neo-Kantian notion of consciousness as *a spontaneous point of origin that both constituted and animated the
world of symbolic forms.* While Heidegger embraced thrownness, Cassirer
cleaved to spontaneity.

As this rather informal comparison suggests, the great disadvantage for
Cassirer was that his philosophy remained steeped in the language and the
values of the German Idealist tradition. But by middle of the 1920s the Idealist heritage was losing its power to inspire. Especially among students pro-
fessing an attraction to religious philosophy and radical politics, it was not
uncommon to hear the complaint that Cassirer was out of touch with present
needs.[133] He simply could not satisfy those who longed for a "philosophical
penetration of life." Even established colleagues would admit in private that
despite his tremendous erudition, Cassirer somehow failed to inspire. In a
letter to Heidegger from July 21, 1925, Jaspers ranked Cassirer as "without
question the best" alongside other candidates for a potential position. "He
admittedly bores me," Jaspers confessed, "but [he] is learned and most of all:
he has a noble manner of writing, without the hatred and secret polemics
of philosophy professors. This shows that he must also be personally quite
upstanding." It was clear Jaspers regarded Cassirer with some ambivalence:
"What I look for in philosophy I don't find in him," he wrote, "but where do
we find it?"[134] The question concerning Germany's philosophical future remained unanswered, at least for the time being.

2

Setting the Stage

This being carried upward into regions where he had never before drawn breath, and where he knew that unusual living conditions prevailed, such as could only be described as sparse or scanty—it began to work upon him, to fill him with a certain concern. Home and regular living lay not only far behind, they lay fathoms deep beneath him, and he continued to mount above them. Poised between them and the unknown, he asked himself how he was going to fare.

—THOMAS MANN, *The Magic Mountain,* chapter 1, "Arrival"

The Magic Mountain

By the time Cassirer and Heidegger arrived in 1929, Davos-Platz had already established itself as a fashionable gathering spot for travelers and artists. Set on a broad plain flanked on all sides by the Swiss Alps and the *Davosersee,* Davos belongs to Graubünden, a canton originally settled in the thirteenth century by inhabitants of the Reformed Church, and it remained a relatively placid village well into the nineteenth century. Its reputation as a *"Kurort,"* or rest spa, derives from a centuries-old folk belief that the Alpine air in the town held special curative powers.[1] Through the efforts of physicians, rest spas flourished and multiplied over the course of the later nineteenth century. As early as the 1860s, the resorts at Davos had began to attract the aristocracy and bourgeoisie from all across Europe. Robert Louis Stevenson sojourned there for his health in the early 1880s (he finished *Treasure Island* in Davos), and Sir Arthur Conan Doyle visited for a skiing holiday in 1894.

By the turn of the century, Davos was already a thriving vacation town, famous for both its skiing and its spas, where wealthy Europeans indulged themselves with rest cures and hoped for miraculous recoveries from tuberculosis and other respiratory ailments. In the 1920s, Davos had become an artists' colony and a major outpost of German Expressionism. The painter Ernst Ludwig Kirchner moved to nearby Frauenkirch in 1918, and in the following years the snow-covered mountains and steep slopes of the surrounding region would frequently reappear as favorite subjects on his canvases. The poet "Klabund" (a pseudonym for Alfred Henschke) was stricken with tuberculosis at a young age and spent much of the 1920s in Davos until his death in 1928. During this period, a little journal was born, published from 1926 onward by Jules Ferdmann in a bilingual German-French format under the title *Davoser Revue* (or, in French, *Revue de Davos*), which aimed specifically to advertise the town's latest accomplishments in painting, literature, academic scholarship, and sport. Beginning in 1928, it provided detailed reports on the daily events of the Davos *Hochschulkurse*. In the 1930s, the population of Davos would further swell with the arrival of émigrés and refugees from Nazi Germany. Long before the postwar period, when yearly meetings of the World Economic Forum prompted sociologists to theorize about "Davos culture" or "faculty club culture," Davos enjoyed a symbolic status in the European cultural imagination as a theater for events of world-historical importance.[2]

The most dramatic illustration of the town's international stature was Thomas Mann's grand novel of ideas, *The Magic Mountain,* first published in 1924. In retrospect, it may seem tempting to read the novel as an anticipation of the Cassirer-Heidegger debate: it tells the story of the young Hans Castorp, who arrives in Davos to visit his cousin, a convalescent at the International Sanatorium Berghof. But when X-ray photographs reveal a dark spot on his own lungs, Castorp opts to remain for a cure, during which time he finds himself slowly drawn into a passionate contest of ideas between two exotic personalities: the humanist Settembrini, an erudite and Pollyannaish liberal and a scholar of renaissance Italy, and his rival Naphta, a defrocked Jesuit who has transformed into a bitterly nihilistic revolutionary.

The contrast between these two characters is admittedly fantastic. Mann often freighted his novels with weighty philosophical issues, and, in this case, he might be accused of rampant symbolism: Naphta is a Jesuit but a Jew by birth (his father was a kosher slaughterer in Galicia). We also learn that since his conversion to Catholicism, he has embraced a particularly apocalyptic and severe strain of Marxism. A preacher of absolute submission, Naphta constantly fulminates against bourgeois individualism and modern rationalism. (Although Naphta seems purely imaginary, it seems Mann modeled him after the Hungarian-Jewish Marxist Georg Lukács, with Naphta's attitude toward the Church a stand-in for Lukács' troubled relationship with the Communist Party.) Settembrini is his perfect foil: blond-haired and superciliously polite, he introduces himself as a member of the "League for the Organization of Progress," which advocates the opening of universities to the common people, the abolition of war, and the "evolution of civilized humanity." He wants "to classify human suffering according to classes and categories," for "order and simplification are the first steps toward the mastery of a subject—the actual enemy is the unknown." He finds there is nothing more painful than to be prevented by our animal nature from being "of service to reason." Overall, Settembrini is the perfect bourgeois and a devoted student of the Enlightenment. As Naphta and Settembrini compete for Castorp's sympathies, their conversation lights upon a great variety of themes, constituting a kind of philosophical commentary that spans nearly the entire length of the novel. Their debate, wrote Mann, is "elegant" and perhaps "academic." But Castorp senses that his very soul is somehow at stake, "as though the matter discussed were the most burning question of the time, or of all time."[3]

Mann had in fact visited the actual town of Davos from May through June 1912.[4] That he selected it as the staging ground for his imaginary debate is hardly a surprise, as its elevated setting and dramatic peaks furnished the perfect backdrop for an inquiry into philosophical questions of pan-European significance. As in so many of Mann's novels, the stakes in this conflict are at once intellectual and mortal: Castorp's disease mirrors his own spiritual disorientation such that when, at the novel's climax, Castorp loses his way—and nearly his life—in a blizzard of snow, we are made to understand that this is a crisis not only for Castorp as an individual but for European culture as a whole. Mann thereby makes "allegorical" use of a philosophical conflict: the dispute between Naphta and Settembrini is a projection of broader, cultural problems. In this, Mann's novel was hardly alone. Notwithstanding its literary merit, *The Magic Mountain* largely reactivates (sometimes to the point of parody) themes of cultural crisis that were already commonplace by the middle of the 1920s.

The analogy to Mann's novel not lost on those attending the debate. Ludwig Englert, an attending student, described how nearly all the students who found themselves here for the *Hochschul-kursen* spent the last weeks before their departure buried in Thomas Mann's *Magic Mountain* (if they hadn't done this already) so as to be sure not to enter this mysterious atmosphere unprepared. Indeed, one must rightly say that even in the first days we were all impressed by how much the *genius loci* of Davos is captured in this novel, and we all felt ourselves drawn in by its infamous atmosphere of timelessness and eternal dialectic. For days and a great portion of the nights one saw students and professors in discussion, the high point of the daily events for us just as for Hans Castorp.... If one wished to present these discussions in a truly charming fashion, one might easily write a sort of sequel to Thomas Mann entitled "The University on the Magic Mountain."[5]

Such observations may help us to comprehend why a great many witnesses to the encounter between Heidegger and Cassirer were predisposed to see their philosophical discussion in symbolic terms. It was almost as if *The Magic Mountain* furnished a ready-made script for understanding the exchange. Nor were such comparisons always superficial. A reporter for the *Neue Zürcher Zeitung* observed that a commonplace preoccupation of contemporary philosophy—temporality—appeared as a crucial theme, both in the Heidegger-Cassirer debate and in the rambling philosophical conversations of Mann's novel.[6]

The consequences of this symbolism were ambivalent at best, for it may be the greatest failing of Mann's allegorical style that the figures in his novels often serve as representative types, with a correspondent loss of verisimilitude. Both Settembrini and Naphta are little more than ventriloquists' dolls for distinctive "worldviews" that lack intellectual precision but are therefore all the more vulnerable to Mann's withering irony. Those who appealed to Mann's novel to understand the philosophical discussion between Heidegger and Cassirer were therefore prone to a hyperinflation of cultural symbolism. Ultimately, however, the novel proved to be merely one script among many. Over the years, students and scholars would discover that there were multiple ways to read the debate and multiple ways to reimagine its meaning, though allegory would remain a serious temptation.

A Locarno of the Intellectuals

The encounter at Davos between Heidegger and Cassirer was not an isolated event. It was the centerpiece in the second annual meeting of the International Davos Conference *(Internationale Davoser Hochschulkurse),* a springtime colloquy for intellectuals from across Europe that ran once yearly and lasted a mere four years, from its inaugural session in 1928 up through its final year in 1931. For such a forum, the town of Davos was a natural choice, given its fame as a gathering point for artists and assorted literati. (Aby Warburg himself, plagued by illness throughout the 1920s, once sought treatment in Davos.) Adding to this colorful population were the ex-soldiers and students, many of them wounded in the war, who had taken up the habit of annual migrations to the sanatoria in Davos-Platz and its surrounding villages. But it is the institutional story of the *Hochschule* that really merits our attention as a small but important chapter in the larger drama of European intellectual history between the wars.

The *Hochschule* was officially founded in 1928 as a cultural bridge between the nations, especially between France and Germany. As in Mann's novel, with its long and rambling inquiries into philosophical and historical themes, the *Hochschule* was placed at a far remove from lowland affairs, the properly bucolic setting for the resolution of cultural as well as political divides. Journalists would dub it the "Locarno of the Intellectuals." Yet there was a more mundane purpose as well: A conference drawing large numbers also promised to replenish town revenues, which had been depleted due to falling tuberculosis rates across Europe. Several years before, town planners had even thought of founding an "international high-alpine University" in Davos, chiefly to convince the younger tuberculosis patients to remain for the full length of their cures. When that project proved too ambitious, a local dentist (Paul Müller) spearheaded more modest plans for a yearly academic colloquium, open to students and faculty alike, which would address topics of broadly humanistic appeal and promote interdisciplinary as well as international understanding. In preparing for the *Hochschule,* Müller was joined by several dignitaries from Davos and the Swiss government, as well as professors from Frankfurt and other leading universities in Switzerland, France, and Germany. Cassirer himself was involved in the early stages of planning.[7]

The basic format of the *Hochschule* was a simple combination of lectures and public discussion. Participants were to address the designated topic, and their lectures would culminate with a "discussion evening" in which two or three intellectuals of international stature would engage in a public dialogue. The encounter between Heidegger and Cassirer occurred in what was officially designated as a "working seminar," or *Arbeitsgemeinschaft*. The format of an *Arbeitsgemeinschaft* was relatively new. At that time, in Germany, the customary structure of an academic presentation was still almost without exception a monologue, sustained, formal, even hierarchical. A typical professor trained according to Wilhelmine custom would confront his audience from behind a podium and present his lecture as if dictating for a book. In fact, lectures were often transcribed and later published (a great number of Heidegger's lectures at Marburg and Freiburg were preserved in just this way). The traditional format had advantages as well as disadvantages: it made it possible to develop a single argument with both depth and precision and to assemble the arguments into larger systems. Yet it may also have encouraged a certain occupational tendency toward long-windedness (a feature of academic performance that has remained largely unchanged). Most of all, the conventional format put a strict limit on public criticism: the professor was supposed to hold forth; the students were expected never to interrupt, only to listen. The effect was frequently stultifying, as so many student memoirs from the period make painfully clear. A student's air of quiet respectfulness in a lecture could be offset by confessions of deep frustration in letters or among friends.

Reports and later memoirs often describe the conversation between Heidegger and Cassirer as a "disputation." But this is misleading. As William Clark explains in his study of academic charisma, the *disputatio* was a form of scholastic debate whose origins lay in the martial arts: Its complex etiquette for oral combat was expressly modeled on the rules and roles of the public joust.[8] The *Arbeitsgemeinschaft* was introduced as a way of relaxing the inhibited constraints of academic conversation. Its novelty lay in the breach of formality and the turn to a relatively unstructured and more conversational style of exchange. By today's standards, the innovation seems altogether a good thing. But the consequences depend on circumstances. A public dialogue can be a model of Socratic exchange, moving each participant to self-examination and possibly revision. But it can also descend into polarization and polemic: when confronted with objections, intellectuals often grow only more defensive and obstinate in their views. Philosophy may thrive on passionate discussion, but it can wither when intellectual exchange turns into a mere contest. Ironically, the *Hochschulkurse* had been created for the express purpose of fostering peaceful dialogue, but the dialogue between Heidegger and Cassirer seemed to illustrate not only the limits but perhaps even the risks of intimate conversation.

What distinguished the *Hochschule* from the more commonplace sort of academic conference was the pan-disciplinary prestige of the chief participants and the international composition of the guests. In the first *Hochschule* (1928), theological questions had predominated in a spirited discussion that brought together three of the most famous religious-minded philosophers of the day, Eberhard Grisebach, Paul Tillich, and Erich Przywara. Tillich was already well known as a leading Protestant theologian, while Przywara was a Jesuit philosopher who professed a strong interest in new forms of existential religion (he would return to Davos the following year). Grisebach, though now largely forgotten, was at that time considered one of the most radical and gifted of the new Protestant philosophers; his book, *Gegenwart* (published that same year) ranged broadly across religious and metaphysical themes and closed with a bold exclamation—that philosophy in its traditional, systematic form must be overturned in favor of a radically new mode of thought.[9]

In its inaugural year, the *Hochschule* attracted a large audience—more than 400 persons in all—no doubt because of the presence of Albert Einstein, who delivered a lecture on relativity. "Many a young man," Einstein observed in his prefatory remarks, "goes to this valley with his hopes fixed on the healing power of the sunny mountains and regains his bodily health." The *Hochschulkurse* would supplement this treatment with "hygiene in the sphere of the mind." "This enterprise," he added, "is admirably suited to establish relations between individuals of different nationalities, relations which help to strengthen the idea of a European community."[10] (He also played violin in a string trio: a well-known sketch by the Austrian artist Emmerich Haas depicts Einstein at Davos playing his violin.[11]) The second *Hochschule* (1929) was designed in the hopes that a public discussion between Cassirer and Heidegger would match, or even surpass, the intellectual excitement of the previous year.[12] In the subsequent two years of the

Davos conference, there is a distinct impression of lowered expectations. In the third *Hochschule* (1930), the most noteworthy participants were Werner Sombart and Alfred Weber, who engaged in a dialogue on the relationship between philosophy and the social sciences.[13] Yet notwithstanding the emphasis on worldly affairs, reporters came away from the conference remarking on the general shift in philosophical orientation. One participant recalled "how strongly these themes touched on problems in the realm of metaphysics and methodology" and that many of the participants contemplated a "return to the religious and metaphysical question of the essence and meaning of man." Even in the discipline of sociology, one sensed the spirit of "philosophical rebellion."[14] Finally, in the fourth *Hochschulkurse* of 1931, the selected theme was "culture" or "self-formation" *(Bildung)* and the relation between pedagogy and "practical man." This was the fourth consecutive year of the Davos conferences, and it was also to be the last.[15] In the 1930s appeals to international reconciliation would soon be lost in the din of conflicting national claims.

Students, Teachers, Friends

Before moving on to the actual lectures by Heidegger and Cassirer, it may be helpful to recall the witnesses to the event. But even these facts remain controversial. Some individuals are reputed to have been in the audience (and the secondary scholarship on the Davos disputation may list them as present), although records from the time suggest they were not. The discrepancy in such cases only helps to underscore the difference between history and memory: With the passage of time, the disputation has seemed only to swell in its philosophical and historical significance, and historians of philosophy have perhaps felt tempted to populate the audience with characters whose prestige makes it plausible for us to believe they were there. In some cases, individuals reputed to have seen the debate firsthand may even have misled colleagues and friends.[16]

Among the participants were some of the most celebrated scholars and authors of the day, accompanied by a vast assortment of students, friends, and reporters from newspapers across Europe. The roster (compiled by a *Hochschulkurse* official) breaks down the participants by both professional status and nationality. There were 24 regular *Dozenten;* 14 university

Dozenten; 19 academics with completed doctorates; and no fewer than 223 students (from 20 different countries). The attendees also included 952 persons from the town of Davos itself. The actual lectures were audited by more than 200 persons. Students came from all European nationalities: 117 Germans, 33 French, 27 Swiss, 12 from the Netherlands, and 34 from various other countries, including the United States, England, Greece, Italy, Yugoslavia, Austria, Palestine, Rumania, Russia, Sweden, South Africa, and Hungary. There were a total of 56 formal lectures over the three-week period.

The Grand Hotel Belvédère, the focal point for the academic events, remains even now one of the most magnificent lodgings in Davos. Perched on the hillside opposing the jagged *Jakobshorn,* since the 1920s it has been extensively remodeled and enlarged. The former lecture hall has been completely transformed: it now holds a swimming pool. But even today and despite all of the changes, the hotel seems freighted with cultural memory. It was here that all of the chief speakers of the *Hochschulkurse* stayed, including Heidegger and Cassirer (the latter with his wife Toni), along with Kurt Riezler (Frankfurt), Henri Lichtenberger (Paris), Hendrik Pos (Amsterdam), Fritz Heinemann (Frankfurt), Karl Joël (Basel), and Louis Adolphe Terracher (Dijon). Other speakers, students, and assorted guests stayed in hotels in the surrounding vicinity of Davos-Platz. Noteworthy names include the German novelist Erich Maria Remarque, the young French-Jewish philosopher Emmanuel Lévinas, Joachim Ritter (Hamburg; later an accomplished professor of philosophy), Maurice de Gandillac (Paris; later one of the most important historians of philosophy to teach at the Sorbonne, where he counted among his students both Gilles Deleuze and Jacques Derrida), Heinrich Hermann (Berlin; a professor of Protestant theology), and Ludwig Binswanger (Kreuzlingen; a student of Karl Jung and a founder of existential psychotherapy).

Some of these individuals are still remembered today, but others are mere footnotes to interwar intellectual history. One of the more fascinating was Erich Przywara (1889–1969), a Polish-born Jesuit priest and professor at Munich, whose studies in philosophy spanned the history of religion, from Augustine to Kierkegaard, plumbing the experiential depths of what he termed "Christian *Existenz.*"[17] Throughout the 1920s and well into the dark years that followed, Przywara remained active in interfaith dialogue with prominent representatives of not only German Protestant theology such as

Paul Tillich and Eberhard Grisebach but also with the foremost luminaries
of German Judaism, including Leo Baeck and Martin Buber. Although
Przywara drew inspiration from his contemporaries in phenomenology—
he was personally acquainted with both Edmund Husserl and his pupil,
Edith Stein—Przywara saw himself chiefly as Heidegger's ally in laying out
a novel philosophy of "creatureliness" that would infuse phenomenology
with theological-existential pathos.[18] Przywara's own philosophical work
made liberal use of existential terminology and frequent allusion to the
theme of intellectual crisis. Alongside Tillich and Einstein, Przywara participated in the inaugural meeting of the Davos *Hochschule* in 1928 with a
lecture on the "Crisis of the Natural Sciences." A specialist in Catholic philosophy, Przywara was also invited to engage in public debate with Tillich
and Grisebach regarding the possibility of shared theological terrain.[19]

The following year, in the *Davoser Hochschule* of 1929, Przywara was
again a participant, this time with a lecture on "The Metaphysical and Religious Problem of Existence." The lecture bespoke the new prominence of
existential themes and bore a strong resemblance to Heidegger's own philosophy. In Przywara's view, the central question of philosophy was the
question of human existence: "*was das Dasein sei.*" Philosophy in its most
traditional sense (which Przywara summarily dismissed as Platonism, scholasticism, and the pure essences or Ideas of secular modern thought) had
distanced itself from the individual existence that should have been its true
object. The danger of philosophy in the modern era was that it wished to
abstract and make rational the concrete phenomena of religion, thereby
supplanting God's living being with a mere "Idea." The new philosophy,
Przywara declared, must now abandon the methods of antique and modern
Idealism: it must no longer "forget" man in a realm of ideality but must instead move toward theology, striving to recognize man in his "creatureliness" as a being of humility and "finitude" *(Endlichkeit).*[20]

Kurt Riezler, the philosopher, political theorist, and statesman, who had
been appointed the previous year to a prestigious post as Kurator of the University of Frankfurt, was also a featured speaker at the 1929 *Hochschule.*[21]
His lecture on "The Psychological Problem of Contemporary Man" (elsewhere indicated under a variant title as "The Bondage and Freedom of Contemporary Man") spoke to the polarization of philosophical issues that culminated in that year's Heidegger-Cassirer dispute. In grandiloquent terms,

Riezler surveyed the condition of modern humanity as poised between "freedom and fatality" and between "intellect and soul." The current situation of philosophy as well as culture was characterized by a search for a new youthfulness, authenticity and immediacy at any price, as well as the search for a new "groundlaying of metaphysics." But as the quality of becoming characterizes man far more than stasis, the "fateless" cosmos would now be seen as a coming-and-going man as both creator and created *(Schöpfer und Geschöpf)*. Thus, Riezler concluded, the mutual "entwinement of fatality and freedom" belongs not only to man, but to Being itself.[22]

The political philosopher Leo Strauss (Riezler's friend and colleague) has been widely reputed to have been at Davos, but documentary evidence suggests he was not. The confusion has chiefly to do with the fact that many years later, when Strauss had emigrated to North America, he delivered a memorial address for Riezler in which he recalled his friend's impressions of the Davos disputation in seemingly eyewitness fashion.[23] The address reinforces the common impression that participants at the 1929 *Hochschule* discerned in Heidegger a representative of the ascendant philosophy: Riezler, wrote Strauss, delivered his lecture in Davos "before the same audience which immediately before had listened to a debate between Heidegger and Cassirer. Riezler took the side of Heidegger without any hesitation. There was no alternative. Mere sensitivity to greatness would have dictated Riezler's choice."[24] Strauss himself, despite his own misgivings about the ethico-political nihilism of Heidegger's position, could not deny Heidegger's clear superiority to Cassirer as a philosopher: "Cassirer represented the established academic position. He was a distinguished professor of philosophy but he was no philosopher. He was erudite but he had no passion. He was a clear writer but his clarity and placidity were not equaled by his sensitivity to the problems."[25]

Although Strauss was surely wrong in his somewhat dismissive remark that Cassirer was "no philosopher," his observations confirm the common impression of Heidegger's growing influence at the time, not only over Riezler but also over the greater portion of his contemporaries: "It would be an understatement to say that Heidegger was the greatest contemporary power which Riezler had ever encountered." (The only modern philosopher of comparable stature, Strauss suggests, was Hegel, a full century before.) "Riezler's later thought," Strauss explains, "was shaped by both the influence of Heidegger and the reaction to him. Not indeed Riezler's deepest tendency, but the way in which he expressed it or did not express it, was decisively affected by Heidegger." Heidegger's influence as Strauss describes it was nearly irresistible: "As soon as he appeared on the scene," wrote Strauss, Heidegger "stood in its center and he began to dominate it. His domination grew almost continuously in extent and in intensity. He gave adequate expression to the prevailing unrest and dissatisfaction because he had clarity and certainty, if not about the whole way, at least about the first and decisive steps."[26]

Other participants at the 1929 *Hochschulkurse* deserve brief mention. The historian of philosophy Karl Joël (Basel) presented his own philosophical-historical interpretation of the nineteenth century according to a model of generational rebellion. History, he declared, is structured as a struggle of the young against the old, and the span of a generation represents a coherent period of the Zeitgeist. The nineteenth century was a period of a "new baroque" and would be followed in the twentieth century with new philosophical reactions against both romanticism and positivism.[27] Henri Lichtenberger (Sorbonne) addressed the "psychological" aspect of cooperation and cultural difference between the French and the Germans and raised systematic doubts regarding a great number of stereotypes—artistic, philosophical, and literary—between the two nations. With specific reference to recent visits by Thomas Mann to Paris and Paul Valéry to Berlin, he expressed his hope that past divisions of culture and politics might now be bridged to mutual benefit. Ferdinand Sauerbruch (Berlin), a professor as well as physician, spoke on "the organic and mental faculties of adaptation in human beings." Léon Brunschvicg (Sorbonne) lectured on "reason and science" and "reason and religion." Armando Carlini (Pisa) delivered an erudite address on Benedetto Croce and modern Italian idealism.[28] And Hendrik Pos (1898–1955; Amsterdam), a professor of classical philology, held forth on the problem of the philosophical grounds of interpretation—a problem he raised anew in a personal intervention during the Heidegger-Cassirer debate (as will be discussed in Chapter 4).[29]

The official participants described above were joined by a great number of scholars and students from throughout Europe, who attended merely as audience members. Among them was Rudolf Carnap (1891–1970), a leading member of the Vienna School of logical positivism. The significance of

Carnap's role in the Davos disputation has been analyzed with great precision in the recent book by Michael Friedman, who remarks on the rather surprising fact that Carnap "was very impressed with Heidegger." This is remarkable given that just a few years later, in his 1932 paper, "Overcoming Metaphysics through the Logical Analysis of Language," Carnap would fix upon various phrases from Heidegger's philosophy as model pseudo-sentences. But Friedman furnishes strong evidence of Carnap's admiration, for example, in a note from March 18: "University Course. Cassirer speaks well, but somewhat pastorally. . . . Heidegger, serious and objective, as a person very attractive." In a note from March 30, Carnap wrote of taking a walk with Heidegger: "With H. walking. Discussion. His position: against idealism, especially in popular education. The new 'question of existence'. The need for a solution."[30] After the *Hochschule*, however, Carnap devoted careful attention to *Being and Time*, only to conclude that Heidegger's metaphysical ruminations "are not consistent with logic and the scientific mode of thinking."[31]

The *Hochschule* was designed in part to serve as an educational setting for the younger generation of scholars; it therefore extended financial support for both travel and lodging to students at various European universities. Yet a number of students did not receive or know they could receive such support and therefore were not able to attend. Such was the case with Heidegger's student Hans-Georg Gadamer, who (in Jean Grondin's biography) explained the reason for his absence: "No money!"[32] Yet a sizable throng of students—more than 200 in all—either managed to secure a portion of this funding or commanded private resources of their own for the journey to Switzerland. Their presence in Davos helped to transform what would have been merely another academic conference into a transgenerational event, the repercussions of which would persist through the end of the twentieth century.

Among the many talented students then enrolled at Freiburg under the direction of Heidegger and Husserl, at least three were in attendance at Davos: Eugen Fink, Otto Friedrich Bollnow, and Emmanuel Lévinas. Each of these men merits closer attention. The case of Eugen Fink (1905–1975) is especially notable because, unlike a great number of Husserl's students, he remained largely faithful to Husserl's more "classical" method of transcendental phenomenology, and he resisted the allure of Heidegger's existential innovations. Although Fink came to Freiburg in 1925 to pursue studies with Husserl and stayed to receive his promotion in 1929 under both Husserl *and* Heidegger, it is fair to say he never truly abandoned his commitment to his old master. In a well-known 1933 essay, "The Phenomenological Philosophy of Edmund Husserl and Contemporary Criticism," Fink leapt to defend his teacher against the recent neo-Kantian charge (articulated by two of Rickert's students, Rudolf Zocher and Friedrich Kreis) that phenomenology was a species of "intuitionism" that dispensed with a priori categories and lapsed into the naïve empiricism and dogmatism of the "self-given." This was an especially sharp criticism as it suggested that phenomenology, whatever its proponents claimed, had signed a fatal compact with unreason. The charge was complicated by the widespread perception that Husserl himself had incorporated neo-Kantian themes into his more intellectualist restatement of phenomenological method in the *Ideas for a Pure Phenomenology* of 1913. But Fink's extensive riposte against Husserl's neo-Kantian critics helped to clarify the true nature of the philosophical divide between the two schools: "We have not opposed [their] critique merely for the sake of polemic," Fink warned, "but rather for the sake of formulating the possibility for a true discussion between Criticism and phenomenology." Although "dialogue" was an admirable goal, Fink concluded, that, in the meanwhile, "both philosophies must be held separate."[33] That Husserl agreed with his student's defense is clear from the admiring preface he wrote to accompany the essay, in which he declared, "I am happy to be able to state that it contains no sentence which I could not completely accept as my own."[34] The peaceful and productive accord between teacher and student was to endure many years, and as Ronald Bruzina has argued, Fink should be regarded as an actual collaborator to Husserl in the latter's recasting of phenomenology during his final years (1928–1938).[35]

Fink remained faithful to Husserl's style of transcendental phenomenology and saw Heidegger's existential modification as philosophical heresy. Unfortunately, details of his experiences at Davos remain unknown. The case of Fink deserves our attention here chiefly because it may qualify the often exaggerated portrait of Heidegger at Davos as a thinker basking in the uncritical adoration of his students. Yet, as we will see in the following case, among students as well as colleagues, a general sense of admiration for Heidegger prevailed.

The Young Heideggerian

Among the many students in attendance at the 1929 Davos *Hochschule,* one deserves special mention: Emmanuel Lévinas. The case of Lévinas is instructive, not only because it provides evidence for Heidegger's tremendous popularity among his early students, but also because it offers a poignant reminder of the historical gulf that now separates that early moment of philosophical enthusiasm from our own, more chastened postwar era. Lévinas's mature reputation as an opponent of Heideggerian philosophy is well documented. But Lévinas's youthful attraction to Heidegger should not be forgotten; it tells us a great deal, both about the Davos disputation itself and also about the larger, allegorical purposes it has been made to serve.

Lévinas was born in 1906 in Kovno, Lithuania, into a family of Russian-speaking Jews. Following the Russian Revolution, in the early 1920s he journeyed to the University of Strasbourg, where he studied both sociology and philosophy. In 1928 he made his way to Freiburg, where he took up a philosophical apprenticeship in phenomenology, first seeking the direction of Edmund Husserl (who was on the verge of retirement) and then joining the growing circle surrounding Husserl's more charismatic pupil, Martin Heidegger. In a later interview, Lévinas would recall that "I went to Freiburg because of Husserl, but discovered Heidegger."[36] We may indeed credit Heidegger for initiating Lévinas into the deeper possibilities of phenomenology, as it was Heidegger who pointed the way beyond Husserl's study of intentional consciousness and toward the basic themes of "carnal" existence from which Lévinas would eventually develop his own philosophy. Lévinas's first book, *The Theory of Intuition in the Phenomenology of Husserl* (1930), served many French readers as their very first introduction to phenomenological method. It is therefore crucial to note how strongly the book already bespeaks Heidegger's impact. Lévinas noted in the introduction that in aiming to present the "simple, main inspiration" of Husserl's philosophy, "we shall not fear to take into account problems raised by other philosophers, by students of Husserl, and, in particular, by Martin Heidegger, whose influence on this book will often be felt." He further explained that "the intense philosophical life which runs through Heidegger's philosophy sometimes permits us to sharpen the outline of Husserl's philosophy by accentuating certain aporias, raising some problems, making certain view more precise, or opposing others." Lévinas saw in Heidegger not a mere disciple but rather a philosopher who had helped to clarify, even to fortify, what remained truly of value in Husserl's teaching.[37]

In 1932, Lévinas published an essay, "Martin Heidegger and Ontology," in the journal *La Revue philosophique*. The essay, a long and faithful reconstruction of Heidegger's teaching, was originally the basis for what Lévinas hoped would be an independent book. The 1932 text of the essay contains a laudatory introduction, which Lévinas himself chose to delete from the version published in his later, 1949 anthology.[38] The following passage displays the true depth of Lévinas's admiration:

> The prestige of Martin Heidegger and the influence of his thought on German philosophy marks both a new phase and one of the high points of the phenomenological movement. . . . For once, Fame has picked one who deserves it and, for that matter, one who is still living. Anyone who has studied philosophy cannot, when confronted by Heidegger's work, fail to recognize how the originality and force of his achievements, stemming from genius, are combined with an attentive, painstaking, and close working-out of the argument—with that craftsmanship of the patient artisan in which phenomenologists take such pride.[39]

The comparison between these pre-1933 lines of praise and Lévinas's occasional remarks on Heidegger written in subsequent years is indeed dramatic. Already by 1935, Lévinas confessed to feeling a need "to get out of Being by a new path." But it was really only in the postwar era that Lévinas came into his own with the bold doctrine of ethics-as-first-philosophy: in an explicit rejoinder to Heideggerian ontology, Lévinas deployed phenomenological-descriptive techniques so as to demonstrate that ethical obligation is not merely a normative value superadded a posteriori to experience but is instead a metaphysical relation. The "infinite" bond between self and other, Lévinas claimed, exceeds the self-enclosed horizon of Being and furnishes human life with an irreducibly transcendent dimension. Ethics, in Lévinas's characteristic phrase, "precedes" ontology.

The force of this argument should not be underestimated; nor should one miss the direct challenge to Heidegger. For the mature Lévinas, a critical problem in Heideggerian fundamental ontology was its neglect of intersubjective relations. Even the celebrated analysis of *das Man* (or, the "One") in *Being and Time* seemed to confirm that Heidegger saw human relations as constituted through a purely anonymous social field, a model that appeared to disallow the experience of ethical responsibility. Moreover, Lévinas claimed that this indifference to ethics on the level of theory had a political correlative in Heidegger's own life. In a 1992 interview, Lévinas observed that "the absence of care for the other in Heidegger and his personal political adventure are connected. And despite all of my admiration for the greatness of his thought, I have never been able to separate this double-aspect of his positions."[40] The remark is true; but it obscures the enthusiasm of a student who still thought only of the philosophy. It is critical to note that Lévinas only developed his criticism of Heideggerian ontology some years later, beginning with his catastrophic disillusionment when the German philosopher publicly embraced National Socialism in 1933. Before these events, however, Lévinas could still be counted among Heidegger's most admiring disciples.[41]

In March 1929, Lévinas made the journey to Davos. He did so for much the same reason as his peers, to see his teacher Heidegger engage in a public discussion with the illustrious neo-Kantian Ernst Cassirer. Lévinas was then only twenty-three years old. An old photograph from the conference shows a sober young man with black hair, in a full suit and dress shoes, supporting himself with a walking cane and flanked by his fellow students Eugen Fink and Otto Bollnow on a road in the snow some distance from the Hotel Belvédère.[42] Fink was at that time among Husserl's most intimate and faithful disciples. Lévinas himself was still virtually unknown, yet within the little universe of Freiburg phenomenology, Lévinas had already distinguished himself among his peers as a gifted exponent of Heideggerian doctrine, thanks to both his linguistic facility and his philosophical acumen. And in a European-intellectual culture still strongly divided along national lines, the linguistic skills gave Lévinas an unusual advantage. He gained an early prestige as an intermediary to French readers of the new style of existential phenomenology then emerging from Germany. The French literary critic Maurice de Gandillac, then a young *normalien,* recalls in his memoirs an initial meeting with Lévinas at Davos in 1929:

> Student at Strasbourg, Emmanuel Levinas, a young Lithuanian, my
> exact contemporary, perfectly managed the French that he had chosen

as his language. There was no better aid besides him for penetrating into the thoughts of the master, whose instruction he was then following at Marburg. How can one forget that beautiful afternoon when for some assembled Frenchmen he translated and commented upon several pages of *Sein und Zeit?* The sun was bit by bit melting away the mark of snow on the spot where Emmanuel was sitting, dressed in street clothes, healed dance-hall shoes protected in rubber galoshes. When Levinas rose, we remarked that, like the biblical Job, but without the urge to interrogate his God, he had just spoken to us of "being-there" and of "care" upon a pile of dung.[43]

De Gandillac's facts are imprecise: Lévinas was not at Marburg, but Freiburg, where Heidegger had already assumed his post. But the question remains: why does de Gandillac seem to ridicule Lévinas? Perhaps he meant to expose Heidegger's philosophical terminology as mere rubbish. But Lévinas is implicated as well, because he is the "prophet" for his teacher's existential profundities. The insult is demeaning and deserves no comment. But one should note that the insult works only because de Gandillac actually saw Lévinas as Heidegger's intermediary. In retrospect, such an impression may seem impossibly wide of the mark, but it is important to remember this moment of philosophical intimacy between teacher and student. After the war, Lévinas would come to regret his early admiration for Heidegger, to such a degree that he wished to offer Toni Cassirer a personal apology. All of this, however, will be discussed later.

Students as Scribes

The atmosphere of widespread enthusiasm for Heidegger no doubt helped to shape public and documentary memory of the debate. We therefore need to consider the two students who were entrusted with the actual task of transcribing and editing the entire exchange, Otto Friedrich Bollnow and Joachim Ritter. Bollnow (1903–1991) took up philosophy in 1925 and pursued his initial training with Georg Misch (an affiliate of the Dilthey school). But on reading *Being and Time* in 1927 (an experience he would later recall as "truly overwhelming"), Bollnow sought his teacher's blessing to transfer in mid-1928 to Marburg, where he hoped to pursue closer study with Heidegger. After one semester, he followed his new teacher to Freiburg (beginning in the winter semester of 1928–1929), where Heidegger had just assumed the chair in philosophy. In Bollnow's memory, the whole era bore a revolutionary stamp: by the 1930s and through Kierkegaard's influence, "powerful forces of existential philosophy broke forth" with the message that human life in its "essential nature and in every moment lies in crisis and can only be conceived through crisis."[44] At the center of this revolution stood Heidegger:

> I recall even now quite exactly the first hour of lectures at Marburg, which I had awaited for weeks. In his external appearance he was wholly different than I had imagined. Of the scholar he had nothing. In his compact form, in his idiosyncratic clothing of his own design, he worked an effect rather like a man from the countryside, or, to exaggerate somewhat, like a forest-worker. And so it indeed seemed to me as he began to speak . . . in these lectures one sensed a genuine, primordial philosophizing, like what I had come to know only with the classical philosophers, as an immediate and living presence.[45]

Bollnow would later describe his Freiburg period as "the happiest time of my life."[46] Too timid to enjoy much contact with Heidegger himself and lacking the nerve to penetrate Heidegger's inner circle, Bollnow remained very much an outsider. Yet even from the periphery he anticipated each of Heidegger's lectures as a promise of revelation, "like an elemental event of nature [or] a lightning storm." So one can only imagine Bollnow's enthusiasm when, toward the end of his two-semester stay at Freiburg, Heidegger extended a personal invitation for both Bollnow and Eugen Fink to accompany him to the Davos *Hochschule*. Bollnow undertook the further duty (together with Cassirer's student, Joachim Ritter) of transcribing the disputation for publication. Many years later, Bollnow could still recall how Heidegger and Cassirer seemed "the embodiment of the philosophical situation of the age." His recollection is worth quoting at length:

> With great excitement the participants waited for the . . . disputation between the two thinkers. Today, when the report which Joachim Ritter and I prepared at the time is available in print in the new edition of

Kant and the Problem of Metaphysics, I don't have to elaborate upon the substance. I can confine myself to the impression, which was truly breathtaking. For in this conversation there appeared the contrast between these two men in all its magnitude: In it one sensed the encounter between two ages: one, an inheritance that had come to its ripe unfolding, was embodied in Cassirer's imposing form, and, over and against him, the embodiment in Heidegger of a new time, breaking out with the consciousness of a radically new beginning.[47]

Bollnow's subsequent career was largely successful but not without moments of apparent compromise. He continued to teach and publish well into the 1930s and throughout the Nazi period on topics such as Dilthey's philosophy of history (1936). More important for our discussion, he published popular surveys such as *Existenzphilosophie* (1942), a book in which he sought to defend existentialism (especially Heidegger's and the now-forgotten variant developed by Hans Heyse) against the charge of "decadence" by referencing what he termed the "heroic attitude" manifest in Heidegger's notorious lecture from 1933, "The Self-Assertion of the German University." Bollnow's survey of existentialism went through several editions, and after the war, when he taught philosophy of education at the University of Tübingen, he revised it again in order to minimize the apparently favorable references to Nazism and to lay greater emphasis on the need to transcend existential despair and to embrace a new faith. He went on to suggest that *Existenzphilosophie* was tainted by its origins in the era of European crisis first diagnosed by Nietzsche, a crisis that moved many philosophers to find "joy in danger." He concluded by suggesting that for new conditions after World War II it would now be necessary to lay the foundations for an altogether new species of philosophy.[48]

Joachim Ritter (1903–1974), Bollnow's partner in transcribing the disputation, was at that time understood to be a student following in the historical-philosophical footsteps of his Hamburg mentor Cassirer. In the postwar period he would emerge as one of Germany's most accomplished historians of philosophy, best known for his 1957 book, *Hegel and the French Revolution,* and the *Historisches Wörterbuch der Philosophie,* a monument to the resurgence of German academic philosophy after the war.[49] A child of the German bourgeoisie (his father was a physician), the young Ritter was schooled in the 1920s at many of the leading universities, chiefly Hamburg, but also at Heidelberg, Marburg, and Freiburg, where he studied with Heidegger. He was only twenty-two years old in 1925 when he received his promotion with Cassirer at Hamburg with a thesis on the doctrine of ignorance in Nicolas de Cusa and then, in 1932, received his habilitation on Augustine's neo-Platonist ontology. Ritter's intimate association with Cassirer instilled an enduring preference for "critical" methods in philosophy and an aversion to the newer trends in both existentialism and philosophical anthropology.[50] He participated in the Davos *Hochschulkurse* in 1929 and once again in 1931, when he remarked on the widespread discussion concerning the so-called crisis of education and the "alienation of spirit from life."[51]

In both politics and philosophy Ritter gravitated to the left, remaining a professed Marxist at least until 1932. In her memoirs Toni Cassirer described him as "an earlier Heidegger-student" and an "erstwhile Communist" whose habilitation Ernst Cassirer defended right up until 1933 against colleagues who took a dim view of the young philosopher's communism but who soon thereafter "fell in line like a tin soldier" with the new regime.[52] However, Ritter's student Hans Jörg Sandkühler has recently shown that his teacher's political and philosophical record was thick with ambiguity. Ritter's first wife had been Jewish and a relative of the Cassirer family, a fact which in conjunction with his earlier politics branded him as unacceptable in the eyes of the Hamburg SS. The critical and anti-metaphysical character of Ritter's scholarship continued after 1933, when Cassirer was forced from his post and Ritter was simultaneously appointed professor of philosophy at the University of Hamburg. Sandkühler notes that Ritter de facto replaced Cassirer, although Ritter did not occupy Cassirer's actual chair, which was held in succession by various people, some of whom were not philosophers. During the Nazi era, the chair was transformed into a professorial post for racial science.[53]

In his philosophical orientation Ritter remained a strong critic of Heidegger's work and all it seemed to imply. In 1931 lectures he anticipated Cassirer's later critique of Heideggerian thrownness when he spoke despairingly of bourgeois philosophical-historical tendencies spawned by Dilthey that replaced deeds with mere recollection and "action with reaction, the experiencing, reflective, 'thrownness' [*Geworfenheit*]."[54] Ritter's inaugural lecture at the University of Hamburg in 1933 is noteworthy for its strenuous attack on Heidegger's thought and all forms of philosophical anthropology.[55] Speaking to the ascendancy of philosophical anthropology as manifested in its two most muscular advocates, Scheler and Heidegger, Ritter declared that anthropological investigations concerning the "essence" and "being" *(Sein)* of the human being were now "the linchpin not only of authentic philosophy, but also and more broadly, . . . the horizon of the human sciences."[56] Ritter began with Scheler's memorable statement that in the modern world the human being had become problematic because "he no longer knows, what he is; but simultaneously also *knows,* that he doesn't know."[57] Both Scheler and Heidegger wished to resolve this anthropological puzzle, but they did so in starkly dissimilar ways: Scheler, by enclosing humanity within the organic and inorganic "cosmos," and Heidegger, via the methods of fundamental ontology.[58] On Ritter's judgment, however, both paths led to the same unhappy conclusion: "to skepticism, subjectivism, and mysticism." For when philosophy turns into anthropology, he warned, it must ultimately devolve into metaphysics and surrender its bond with science. An anthropological metaphysics results in an "absolutization of one's own subjectivity" and takes on the illusory and purely subjectivistic status of a "worldview."[59] Ritter concluded:

> Metaphysics and anthropology turn . . . *against* science and against the life-meaning of scientifically secured knowledge as well. And here is the danger of the metaphysical turn, a danger which reaches beyond science itself. . . . If one wishes to determine the life-meaning of philosophy, it can only be that it secures, over and against all speculative and mystical and subjectivistic thinking, a sense of rational clarity and the broadening of our scientific experience.[60]

Ritter's inaugural address at Hamburg was a clear indictment of Heidegger's work and everything it seemed to represent. It furnishes remarkable evidence that notwithstanding the vogue for existential and anthropological philosophy in the transitional years between 1929 and 1933, dissenting voices such as his could still be heard calling for "rational clarity" and warning against the resurgence of "prophesy." In the years that followed, Ritter advanced in his career without violent reversal: he was promoted to *Ordinarius* in 1943 as a professor of philosophy at the University of Kiel, and after the war he served as professor of philosophy at Münster continuously from 1946 (except for two years in Istanbul) until his retirement in 1968.[61]

There were, of course, dozens, indeed hundreds, of participants—colleagues, students, writers, and reporters—all of whom witnessed the Davos *Hochschulkurse* in 1929 and were presumably in the room for the dramatic *Arbeitsgemeinschaft*. But Bollnow and Ritter deserve special consideration largely because they were entrusted with the joint task of transcribing the Heidegger-Cassirer debate for publication. Indeed, our best evidence regarding the debate comes from these two men, one Heidegger's student and a strong exponent of *Existenzphilosophie,* the other Cassirer's disciple and a tireless advocate for "critical philosophy." We may derive some comfort from the fact that these two, notwithstanding their apparent differences of philosophical temperament, nevertheless managed to agree on the substance of the exchange.

A final question remains: Was their transcription accurate? We can answer with a tentative affirmative because their text can be checked against the summaries published in April 1929 in the *Davoser Revue,* the local arts weekly to which both Cassirer and Heidegger entrusted the notes of their lectures. But there is also some cause for worry: In the preface to the fourth edition of *Kant and the Problem of Metaphysics,* in which the text of the *Davoser Disputation* appears as an appendix, Heidegger refers to the record prepared by Bollnow and Ritter, but he then confirms Bollnow's remark that it was "not a word-faithful protocol but a subsequent preparation based upon cooperatively written notes."[62] Still, there is a general agreement between the reports published in the *Davoser Revue* and the Bollnow-Ritter transcript. A further handwritten transcript by Heidegger's student, Helene Weiss, reconfirms almost verbatim what we find in the Bollnow-Ritter text. Other evidence may eventually come to light to challenge or at least qualify what we now know about the exchange. Naturally, not everyone left a memoir or a letter summarizing their impressions. To some of those who witnessed it, the encounter between Cassirer and Heidegger may have seemed a minor and purely academic occasion scarcely deserving mention. For many others, chiefly younger philosophers who had not yet decided on the substance of their own intellectual convictions, the *Arbeitsgemeinschaft* would be remembered as a moment of crisis, a turning point not merely in their own lives but in Continental philosophy itself.

Opening Day Ceremonies

The second annual meeting of the International Davos Conference held its opening session on a cloudless Sunday in March 1929. At this season, the sun shone strong in the lower Alps and the surrounding hills were still thickly covered with snow. Over the next three weeks, during breaks between lectures, students and professors would meet for tea in the hotel, or in the cafés in town, or they would stroll the sunlit streets to discuss the lectures of the previous day. In a letter to his wife, Heidegger confided that "Davos itself is dreadful; boundless vulgarity in the architecture, a completely random hotchpotch of guest houses & hotels."[63] Conference guests would occasionally escape from Davos-Platz to hike or to snowshoe the mountain trails. Heidegger himself found time during the conference to ski, and even invited his student Kurt Riezler to accompany him.[64] Heidegger wrote to Elfride on March 21 that he led a small band up the Parsenn mountain, climbing to 2,700 meters and skiing back into the valley. "At the beginning I was rather anxious how it would go," he confessed, "but after the first 100m. I realized that I was superior to them all, even Riezler, who has skied a lot in the Alps."[65]

The hotels in town were full to capacity, populated with a odd mixture of professors and skiing enthusiasts, reporters, and bourgeois couples on holiday.[66] The Hotel Belvédère was reserved for the professors alone, while the students sought lodging in one of the many neighboring hotels. Some found the atmosphere oppressive. Heidegger complained to Elisabeth Blochmann that "to me existence in the 'Grand Hotel' was somewhat trying. So it was pleasant when, during intervening days, I could climb up on pleasurable excursions with Riezler." Heidegger seems to have enjoyed the effect on the other guests: "In the evenings, after the whole ringing momentum of our far-ranging journey, our bodies full of sun and the freedom of the mountains, we then came, still dressed in our ski-suits, among the elegance of the evening *Toilette*."[67] Neither Cassirer nor Heidegger went to all the various presentations by the other guests. Cassirer was already ill when he arrived in Davos, and after his second talk he confined himself to his room, leaving Heidegger to wonder if the *Arbeitsgemeinschaft* would convene at all. To Elfride Heidegger wrote that "the courses themselves are fairly strenuous, but I skive off most of the things 'one' is supposed to go to. I think the non-Germans probably will be as impressed as you hope them to be."[68]

It must have been difficult to slip away. All three weeks were thick with lectures and special events, and the format remained as it had been the previous year, with the lectures scheduled Monday through Friday, both mornings and afternoons. At the center of the events was the public encounter between Heidegger and Cassirer in the *Arbeitsgemeinschaft*. In addition to broad discussion concerning the relationship between philosophy and the humanities, the main lectures were to address the central question, "What is the Human Being?" *(Was ist der Mensch?)*. Although so broad a topic would naturally speak to a variety of disciplinary interests, this question was addressed primarily to the philosophical concerns of the leading participants. For the benefit of the students, it was to be supplemented by an additional theme: "Generations." Some students remarked on the relation between these two themes: The topic of generations expressed a contemporary urgency, but so too did the question of how to relate abstract philosophizing to anthropological "reality." The basic question at Davos according to one student was quite simple: "How does philosophy stand to daily life?" In such remarks there was a hidden assumption that "abstract" thought should answer to "reality" in an unprecedented fashion.[69] And this assumption, it seems, may already have predisposed students to favor certain sorts of philosophical attitudes as against others. One reporter suggested that Heidegger satisfied the longing for a "Leader" *(Führer)* so much in evidence among the new, postwar generation.[70] Many seemed to feel that the discussions that year were marked by multiple divisions, not only the division between the prewar and postwar generations, but also that which separated *Ordinarius* professors and mere *Dozenten*.[71]

While it was rumored that Heidegger mesmerized the student auditors, Heidegger himself was dismayed by the younger generation, and he seems to have spent most of his time at Davos longing to return home. On March 23, just a few days before the final encounter with Cassirer, Heidegger wrote to Elfride:

Although there's basically nothing for me to be learnt here—I'm still very glad to join in with such things now & again—one's versatility, one's handling of people & a certain outward assurance do benefit. But

I often look forward to our house & my room. Only there can the things I have to do flourish. I also think that the young people sense that the roots of my work are to be found somewhere that today's city-dweller [*die heutige Stadtmensch*] no longer has—indeed no longer even understands. . . . It's frightful how devious, uncongenial, & lacking in security & instinct the young people are. And can no longer find their way back into the simplicity of existence. [*Und nicht mehr zurückfinden in die Einfachheit des Daseins.*][72]

It was Heidegger's familiar complaint: The deracinated urbanite was incapable of philosophy, only in the countryside was genuine reflection truly possible. Modern students had lost their way, and the world needed stern guidance. In the grip of such feelings it is hardly surprising that some witnesses would later recall Heidegger as a man stoked from within by ressentiment.[73] But immediately following the *Arbeitsgemeinschaft,* Heidegger sent another letter to Elfride, this time with restored confidence: "I've just got a two-hour public discussion with Cassirer over with," he wrote. It "went very well and—quite apart from the content—made a big impression on the students."[74] Heidegger's experiences at Davos bolstered his prestige and his personal hopes for German philosophy. Of Cassirer, by contrast, it seems fair to say this was not his best performance—he was ill throughout much of the proceedings and he was barely recovered during the *Arbeitsgemeinschaft* itself. He seems to have left Davos with an enhanced awareness of all that divided him from Heidegger, and with some determination to articulate his criticism in a more compelling fashion.

But let us return once more to the opening scene. The conference began in the Belvédère's largest hall with a ceremony of great pomp and speechifying. Every seat was taken, and a mood of expectation fell over the audience as they listened to the inaugural music, the second movement from Brahms's Piano Quintet in F minor, Opus 34. Afterward came a series of welcoming remarks by official representatives from three governments: France, Switzerland, and Germany.[75] A certain Dr. Biland strengthened the association with Mann's novel, speaking of the academic participants at Davos as "doctors of humanity."[76] The Swiss Bundesrat Motta expressed his hopes that the intellectual exchange at Davos would be carried out in a spirit of reconciliation, healing the rift between the European peoples who had been at war only a decade past.[77] Professor Sauerbruch from Germany seconded these sentiments and noted that the conference aimed expressly at educating the coming generation. Professor Terracher from France praised the town of Davos-Platz for agreeing to host so many visiting scholars and expressed his hope that the conference's unique format would provide intellectuals from all disciplines a rare occasion for a "transvaluation of values." The time spent there in abstract speculation would no doubt find concrete realization in the future world.[78] Erhard Branger, the president of the Davos *Hochschule* organizational committee, added a final word of gratitude on behalf of his colleagues and further expressed his hope that the Davos conference, enlivened by the spring sun, would do its part to strengthen the "spirit of Locarno."[79] The inaugural ceremony concluded as it had begun, with ceremonial music—the third movement from Dvořák's Piano Quintet, Opus 81. There followed the first of Cassirer's independent lectures on philosophical anthropology and Heidegger's initial lecture on Kant and metaphysics.

3

The Independent Lectures

There are ages in which the rational man and the intuitive man stand side by side, the one in fear of intuition, the other with scorn for abstraction.

—FRIEDRICH NIETZSCHE, "On Truth and Lies in a Nonmoral Sense" (1873)

Introduction

The Davos *Arbeitsgemeinschaft* between Cassirer and Heidegger was preceded with both philosophers' presentations of independent lectures. On Monday morning of the first week, Cassirer inaugurated the conference sessions with his lecture, "Foundational Problems of Philosophical Anthropology." Heidegger followed that same Monday afternoon with his lecture, "Kant's *Critique of Pure Reason* and the Task of a Groundlaying for Metaphysics." Both Cassirer and Heidegger continued their presentations on Tuesday, Cassirer being allotted two hours in the morning, Heidegger one hour in the late afternoon. On Thursday Heidegger was given an additional two-hour session to conclude his presentation. He wrote to Elfride that "my third lecture, in which I spoke for 1½ hours without a manuscript, was a great success." By this point Cassirer felt sufficiently recovered from his cold, so on Monday of the second week Cassirer concluded his own lectures in a shortened session in the late afternoon.[1] The *Arbeitsgemeinschaft* between Cassirer and Heidegger took place immediately the next morning, on Tuesday, March 26, from ten in the morning until noon. The following morning, Wednesday, Cassirer presented yet another independent lecture, "The Opposition between 'Spirit' and 'Life' in Scheler's Philosophy."[2]

The independent lectures demand careful consideration, especially as they prepared the terrain for the dispute that followed. As many commentators at the time were quick to observe, one of the most striking things about these lectures was the apparent reversal of topics: each philosopher chose to speak on an issue more customarily associated with his interlocutor. Cassirer addressed themes in philosophical anthropology, a movement more frequently named in connection with Heidegger, while the latter addressed Kant's philosophy, a topic most auditors would have expected from Cassirer. The consequence was an unexpected crossing of established boundaries, which cast in relief shared premises while heightening the likelihood of eventual disagreement. A contemporary report implies that the mutual trespass was "not accidental but was intended in the program's structure." This crossing nonetheless had the advantage of bringing the two rivals into close proximity on themes both understood, thereby "letting their relation to one another emerge with greater clarity."[3] And, of course, it also afforded both philosophers an initial chance to lay out some of the basic principles of their own work in preparation for the *Arbeitsgemeinschaft* to follow.

Cassirer's Lectures on Philosophical Anthropology

Cassirer's lectures on philosophical anthropology, as well as his specific presentation on spirit and life in Scheler's philosophy, marked out the intellectual terrain for the ensuing debate. Although Heidegger resisted the contemporary interpretation that cast him as a philosophical anthropologist, it is indeed hard to avoid the impression that Cassirer intended his remarks on philosophical anthropology as an implicit criticism of Heidegger. In any event, for the participants at Davos, the association between Heidegger and philosophical anthropology was widely understood. However imprecise it may appear in retrospect, Heidegger's contemporaries in the 1920s not infrequently characterized his existential analysis as a variant of philosophical anthropology, and they were not unaware of a certain kinship between Heidegger and life-philosophers such as Jacob von Uexküll and Ludwig Klages.

As we saw earlier, Heidegger's intimate intellectual debt to the tradition of life-philosophy, especially as developed by Wilhelm Dilthey and Max Scheler, is evident throughout *Being and Time*. One discerns it not only in the concluding discussion of Dasein's essential "historicality" (a theme modeled after Dilthey's theory of historical reason) but also in the opening methodological excursus on Dasein as a phenomenon distinct from mere "subjecthood" or "personality."[4] Here the theme of *life* (a term of art employed by both Dilthey and Scheler) plays a special role in Heidegger's analysis. Heidegger expressed particular admiration for Scheler's holistic and anti-Cartesian doctrine that a person "is never to be thought of as a Thing or a substance" but is instead "the *unity* of living-through [*Er-lebens*]." Heidegger hastened to warn his readers that philosophical anthropology remained a merely empirical answer to the question "What is Man?" and that a properly ontological "analytic of Dasein" must precede as the a priori foundation for every empirical investigation, including biology and philosophical anthropology.[5]

Despite this warning, however, it seems clear that Heidegger's own conception of Dasein as being-in-the-world bore a close resemblance to Scheler's conception of the human being as always situated in a worldly "environment" or *Umwelt,* a term originally deployed by von Uexküll, whose holistic biological theories also left a strong impression on Heidegger.[6] Heidegger's special admiration for Scheler was to endure throughout the 1920s. In the preparatory studies for *Being and Time,* Heidegger had himself employed the term *life* to indicate the holistic structure of human experience he later renamed "Dasein."[7] Especially noteworthy is Heidegger's praise for Scheler's theory concerning the unity of representation and affect (anticipating Heidegger's own conception of "mood," or *Befindlichkeit*).[8] Just after his debate with Cassirer at Davos, Heidegger dedicated his 1929 book *Kant and the Problem of Metaphysics* to the memory of Max Scheler (who had died the previous year). Although the actual resemblance may be superficial, it is important to note the widespread perception of an affinity between Heidegger and philosophical anthropologists like Scheler because this helps to explain why many participants at Davos believed that Cassirer's remarks on philosophical anthropology were also directed against Heidegger himself. The published summary in the *Davoser Revue* indicates that, notwithstanding their proposed focus, Cassirer's lectures were in fact "an engagement [*Auseinandersetzung*] with Heidegger's ontology and existential analysis."[9]

Cassirer's discourse on philosophical anthropology focused on three of its most persistent themes: space, language, and death. On Cassirer's view, philosophical anthropologists such as von Uexküll were all too strict in their theoretical insistence on the primacy of the pragmatic environment. While it was no doubt true that all experience begins with the human being's relationship to the "world of concerned action [*Welt des besorgenden*

Handelns]," or the world of "comportment with the 'ready-to-hand tool' [*des Umgehens mit "zuhandenem Zeug"*]" as encountered by "everyday Dasein [*alltäglichen Dasein*]," the philosophical anthropologists were wrong to believe that human experience remains forever bound to this pragmatic environment. In Cassirer's words, the environment of practical action served merely as a "point of departure" *(terminus a quo)* for human experience but this environment was hardly the "endpoint" *(terminus ad quem)*. Rather, humanity first achieves its "Being" and authentic purpose in what Cassirer called "the autonomous and free realm of Spirit [*Reich des Geistes*]." And such a realm was realized only insofar as the human being took a decisive step beyond the pragmatic environment, effecting a shift from a merely practical "grasp" *(Greifen)* to true "conceptualization" *(Begreifen)*.[10] This shift had a dialectical structure, in that one had first to withdraw from the sphere of action so as to then recognize the fruits of one's action in creating an objective world.

Cassirer accordingly distinguished between his own model of the human being as equipped with "symbolic, formative and spontaneous energy," and the "merely vital power [*bloß vitalen Kraft*]" as described by the philosophical anthropologists. Von Uexküll's theory of environment construed human spatial experience as merely pragmatic "life-space." But on Cassirer's view, the human understanding of space enjoyed an expressive capacity irreducible to practical action, a capacity that was already evident in the mythological image of a world populated by spirits and that was further demonstrable in both artistic and mathematical-physical conceptions of space. In the linguistic realm as well, Cassirer argued, the philosophical anthropologists were wrong to claim that the representational function of language was merely a "deficient" mode of pragmatic or "ready-to-hand" understanding, because language alone facilitates the step from the world of action to the world of pure *Gegenständlichkeit,* or "objecthood." We must acknowledge this object-world as possessing its very own "Being" *(Sein),* because it is a realm that the human being first constitutes as symbolically meaningful and thereby renders graspable in concepts.[11] So, too, Cassirer claimed, one must also grant a legitimate place for both art and science as expressive achievements within the greater "horizon of human Dasein," because both of these effect a shift from the lower sphere of action and labor to the higher realm of symbolization. In mathematical physics, moreover, the sensual realm of human intuition itself is "sublimated" into a "system of pure functions and relations."

These concepts of nonpragmatic space and language validated Cassirer's basic philosophical conviction that the human being enjoyed a "special capacity for transcendence [*eigentümliche Transzendenz*]." Philosophers who insisted on the primacy of pragmatic understanding failed to acknowledge this capacity whereby the human being, "thanks to its very own symbol-creative energies," could simultaneously "conceive itself in its world" and "conceive a world for itself."[12] This metamorphisis was a necessary feature of human self-realization: By constructing a symbolic world the human being could achieve *self*-knowledge *via* knowledge of its own activity, and it could thereby both fulfill *and* recognize it had fulfilled its very own freedom. And this endpoint of human self-realization, Cassirer concluded, was itself nothing else but "the task of philosophy."[13] Finally, the philosophical anthropologists' conception of death remained on Cassirer's view essentially at one with the "Christian-religious" image of the death-threatened individual as standing alone before his own finitude. Against this interpretation of "world-fallenness" *(Weltverfallenheit),* Cassirer insisted that although "the human being is indeed finite," the human being is nevertheless "a finite being who comprehends that finitude" *(jenes endliche Wesen, das um seine Endlichkeit weiß).* And in this comprehension (which is itself no longer finite) the human being thereby "lifts himself out and beyond this finitude."[14]

As the above reconstruction plainly shows, Cassirer's lectures were meant to foreground the broader intellectual perspective shared in common by the philosophical anthropologists and Heidegger himself. Cassirer's choice of terminology when describing the philosophical anthropologists makes this affiliation clear: "environment," "ready-to-hand," "Dasein," objectivity as a deficient mode, not to mention "fallenness" (a term that is distinct from but obviously resonant with Heidegger's existential characterization of human existence as "falling"). The surface claim in Cassirer's lectures was that the philosophical anthropologists remained caught in the merely pragmatic and environmental stratum of human understanding and failed to acknowledge the human capacity to surpass this practical stratum through expressive-symbolic "transcendence." But this claim obviously captured themes in Heidegger's philosophy as well. Following Cassirer's logic, one had to conclude that Heidegger, too, like the philosophical anthropologists from whom he tried unsuccessfully to distinguish himself, was a theorist who portrayed humanity in a condition of developmental arrest.

Spirit and Life

The implied criticism of Heidegger in Cassirer's independent lectures came to the fore in an additional presentation on "The Opposition between 'Spirit' and 'Life' in Scheler's Philosophy," which Cassirer delivered on the Wednesday morning following the disputation with Heidegger. Although this lecture transpired only *after* the debate, it nonetheless merits our attention as it elaborates on and complicates the criticism of Heidegger presented in Cassirer's prior lectures. One might even say that the Scheler lecture is the very first of several reprisals of the debate. It is crucial to note that much of this lecture repeats (in some cases nearly verbatim) the argument developed in the then-unpublished "conclusion" to *The Philosophy of Symbolic Forms*. This conclusion—titled "On the Metaphysics of Symbolic Forms"—was apparently completed in April 1928, a full year before Cassirer's Davos presentation. It consists of two chapters: the first, again titled "'Spirit' and 'Life,'" the second titled "The Problem of the Symbolic and the Fundamental Problem of Philosophical Anthropology."[15] It also bears mention that the focus of Cassirer's lecture was Scheler's philosophical essay, "Man's Place in Nature" ("Die Sonderstellung des Menschen," 1927), an essay Scheler intended to serve as the core for a longer work on philosophical anthropology that he left incomplete at the time of his death in May 1928.[16] Cassirer's lecture thus served as a kind of epitaph for the larger philosophical movement of which Scheler was perhaps the most sophisticated representative.

The lecture begins with a short excursus on the stark contrast between consciousness and nature in Heinrich von Kleist's 1810 essay "On the Marionettentheater," a contrast that prompted Cassirer to observe that "our most modern philosophical thoughts" are rooted ("consciously or unconsciously") in models first articulated in Romanticism: "Today, once again, at the centerpoint of our reflections, there stands the great antithesis between 'Nature' and 'Spirit,' the polarity of 'life' and 'knowledge.'"[17] Yet there was a crucial difference: whereas Romantics such as Schelling (in, for example, the *System of Transcendental Idealism*) still imagined an aesthetic reconciliation

between these poles, today's philosophers now saw them as implacably opposed. Ludwig Klages, for example, condemned spirit as "a power which in
its very essence is anti-divine and antagonistic to life [*widergöttliche und
lebensfeindliche*]."[18] Not surprisingly, Cassirer had very little to say in favor
of Klages, a scion of the George-Circle whose irrationalist and anti-Semitic
fulminations placed him, in Cassirer's judgment, more or less beyond the
bounds of legitimate philosophical discussion. Yet Scheler was a different
case entirely, and for Cassirer his philosophy merited sustained critical attention. Although Scheler had opposed any full reconciliation between
spirit and life, his understanding of the "original division of Being in itself"
was, Cassirer observed, "altogether different from that of traditional Western metaphysics."[19]

Opposing the merely static dualism between spirit and life, Scheler argued that human spirit only gains its reality when it asserts itself *against* the
constraints of purely organic life. Spirit was therefore primarily a principle
of *negation,* an act of "turning aside" *(Abkehr)* from the sphere of merely
vital experience and brute impulse. Animal existence (as Uexküll confirmed) remained wholly immersed in its environment. But it belonged to
the basic character of human existence that it "*has* 'world'"—Cassirer's quotation marks registered the special sense of "world" that Scheler had derived
from Husserlian phenomenology—and that it was "no longer bound to impulse or to his environing world" and was therefore "world-open" *(weltoffen).*
This freedom, on Scheler's view, was not so much a condition as an *askesis,* a
gesture of resistance or refusal. Such a resistance took many forms, among
them the capacity to represent empty space and time as merely formalistic
possibilities disconnected from actual experience. Scheler's philosophy,
concluded Cassirer, implied that the fundamental characteristic of a spiritual being was "existential disengagement" *(existentielle Entbundenheit).*[20]

Cassirer's overall complaint was that in Scheler's philosophy the actual
division between spirit and life remained dualistic notwithstanding its calls
for a dynamic relationism.[21] Scheler's distinction was therefore strongly rem-
iniscent of the older metaphysical distinctions—such as the Aristotelian,
between form and physical substance, and, more recently, between mind
and body—dualisms that made it impossible to explain their mutual traffic
or influence: "Here," Cassirer observed, there "burst[s] upon us all those questions with which the entire metaphysics and the whole psychology of the

Middle Ages, and thereafter the psychology of the Renaissance, wrestled on and on, and which even today, as the structure of Scheler's anthropology shows, seem not yet to have been definitively silenced."[22] On Cassirer's view the difficulty with any such dualism was that it remained trapped at the stage of ascetic resistance—"spirit" forever opposing "life"—such that the opposition between them eventually hardened into a metaphysical divide:

> The metaphysical concept of "Being" *(Sein)*, however, is marked by this peculiarity, that it possesses a strongly absolutist character. Within it there is basically no room for "Being" of a different stamp and different *type of meaning*. Rather we are led sooner or later to a simple "either-or"—to that "crisis" between being and non-being by which the first great thinker of Western metaphysics, Parmenides, already found himself confronted. In Scheler's philosophical anthropology, too, this fate of metaphysics is borne out anew in a rather singular and remarkable way. What Scheler gives to the Spirit he must take away from Life; what he allots the latter he must deny the former.[23]

Scheler's image of dynamic resistance therefore illustrated the larger "crisis"—a separation forbidding all reconciliation—that had afflicted ancient Greek philosophy and continued to trouble contemporary metaphysicians well into the twentieth century. Indeed, notwithstanding the strong differences between Scheler and Klages, Cassirer confirmed that the philosophical anthropologists were fundamentally alike in their drive to transform what should have been a set of *merely functional* categories for philosophical description such as "life" and "spirit" into *substantive absolutes*. Although Scheler remained in certain respects under the restraining and anti-metaphysical influence of Husserlian phenomenology, "in [Scheler] too," Cassirer declared, "the metaphysical interest in the end takes precedence over the purely phenomenological: the Spirit becomes a Being [*Sein*] *sui generis,* standing over and above the being of mere life."[24]

What this crisis-philosophy failed to explain, therefore, was how two so radically opposed metaphysical principles could ever achieve a fruitful partnership. Yet such cooperation was evident, Cassirer claimed, in all creative-expressive activity—whether mythological, linguistic, artistic, or scientific—because human expression always takes place within an "in-between" realm beyond the dualism of interior consciousness and external impulse. It was therefore wrong to characterize such expressive activity as a withdrawal from objective life into the purely subjective realm of fantasy. Symbolic expression actually created its own reality and built for itself an objective world. The products of symbolization did not "stand there like silent pictures on a blackboard; they bring themselves into being, and in their act of self-generation they afford at the same time a new intuition into 'objective' reality."[25]

According to Cassirer, the crucial philosophical instrument for understanding the simultaneously "spiritual" yet "objective" character of human expressive activity was the Kantian doctrine of productive imagination as laid out in the first *Critique*. There one found a solution to the symptomatic dualism of philosophical anthropology and a welcome means for achieving the necessary reconciliation between "spirit" and "life." According to Kant, it was the productive imagination alone that furnished the ultimate link between merely sensory perception and the categories. Only through the imagination could the categories rise beyond their merely subjective function as rules of thought to achieve genuinely objective validity. This discovery proved that knowledge itself was possible only thanks to the mediating function of form. As Cassirer observed, "the construction of the 'objective' world of experience is dependent upon the original formative powers of the spirit and upon the fundamental laws according to which they act."[26]

Anticipations of the Debate

The three general lectures and the specific Scheler-lecture afforded Cassirer an occasion not only to criticize philosophical anthropology itself but also to imply a subtle and disavowed bond between the metaphysical absolutism of philosophical anthropology and the no-less metaphysical cast to Heidegger's own work. This *sotto voce* implication was apparent throughout the lecture. Indeed, few could have missed Cassirer's intent when he complained that in philosophical anthropology the rigors of phenomenological method had been displaced by a "metaphysical interest." Even fewer could have missed his meaning when he complained of the unwarranted absolutism evident in "the metaphysical concept of Being."[27]

Yet it would be an exaggeration to read the Scheler-lectures as an un-qualified attack on Heidegger's philosophy. Despite all of Cassirer's apparent disdain for the newly emergent philosophical disquisitions on existence and ontology, much of this criticism was directed at targets other than Hei-degger himself. In fact, Cassirer's most sustained discussion of contempo-rary ontology was a 1927 review of a recent work by Nicolai Hartmann, a former student of both Cohen and Natorp from Marburg in whose "critical ontology" Cassirer detected a relapse into pre-Kantian metaphysics. There, Cassirer complained that with the first *Critique,* "the sovereignty of the old ontology and its claim to be the true, foundational science of metaphysics, was now broken: in place of the 'proud title of an ontology,' there was now supposed to step forth the more humble task of an 'analytic of pure under-standing.' Today, however, there is no lack of thinkers who, even if they be-lieve themselves to be standing on the 'critical' grounds, look upon this hu-mility in Kant as a false and disingenuous self-effacement, and once again insist on the primacy of ontology."[28] In sum, Cassirer saw Hartmann's work, and not Heidegger's, as the most important modern example of this rebirth of illicit and pre-critical ontological speculation.

Cassirer continued to believe that he and Heidegger shared much in com-mon. Behind the suggestion that Heidegger's "existential analytic" was itself a variant of philosophical anthropology lay Cassirer's own conviction that phi-losophy is and must remain anthropocentric: "As the being who alone is capable of questioning," Cassirer declared, "man is also the being who is and remains to himself thoroughly problematical, the being eternally *worthy* of questioning."[29] On this point Heidegger and Cassirer could agree: in the methodological excursus in *Being and Time* on "The Ontical Priority of the Question of Being," Heidegger, too, had argued that although one cannot mark out Dasein's "essence" *(Wesensbestimmung),* Dasein was nonetheless distinctive among all other entities in that "Being is an *issue* for it."[30] For both Cassirer and Heidegger, humanity remained "worthy of questioning" because it belonged to the essence of human being that it enjoyed a special capacity to raise the question of its own existence.

It is important to keep this common concern in mind when further exam-ining the philosophical dispute. While it would be a mistake to characterize Heidegger as a philosophical anthropologist, it is important to recognize that, much like Cassirer, the early Heidegger, too, was primarily absorbed with questions of human life. Later controversies surrounding Heidegger's departure from anthropocentric reflection (a shift already evident in the Nietzsche lectures of the later 1930s and summarized in the 1947 "Letter on 'Humanism'") have conspired to obscure this earlier and more anthropological phase in his thinking. It was nonetheless evident in 1929 that both Heidegger and Cassirer remained in a broad sense "anthropological" in their philosophical concerns, while neither could fully embrace the movement that shared this name. Indeed, the disagreement between them emerged only on the basis of this shared anthropological terrain.

Heidegger's Kant-Lectures

Heidegger's first independent lecture on Kant began on the first Monday afternoon of the Davos *Hochschulkurse* after Cassirer's first presentation on philosophical anthropology that morning. Heidegger continued the lecture on Tuesday afternoon (again after Cassirer's morning lecture), and that same Thursday he concluded with an additional two-hour presentation. The lectures provide us with crucial material for understanding the precise nature of Heidegger's disagreement with Cassirer over the proper interpretation of Kant's philosophy. Far more than their misunderstanding over the significance of philosophical anthropology, the public dispute between Heidegger and Cassirer turned upon contrasting views of Kant's critical doctrine—its original character as well as its present-day relevance. The general contents of Heidegger's lectures, like Cassirer's lectures on philosophical anthropology, are known to us thanks to a short summary-sketch of its basic claims that Heidegger may have distributed to his auditors and that he gave to the *Davoser Revue* for publication in their special *Hochschule* edition. One should also note that the lectures were not the first time Heidegger had spoken on Kant's philosophy in public. In his winter 1927–1928 seminar at Marburg he offered a "phenomenological interpretation of Kant's *Critique of Pure Reason*," followed in September 1928 with a public lecture on Kant at the Herder Institute in Riga, the contents of which seem to have closely resembled the Kant-lectures at Davos.[31] Shortly following the *Hochschule*, Heidegger would present his views in far more elaborate fashion in the book, *Kant and the Problem of Metaphysics* (1929). In his preface to the fourth edition of the Kant-book, Heidegger wrote that it was written "immediately after" the conclusion of the *Hochschulkurse*.[32]

To understand these lectures with an eye to their significance for the disputation, it is first of all important to recognize the pivotal status of Kant's philosophy in Heidegger's earlier work. This status is both historical and philosophical at once. The published sections of *Being and Time* make reference to a "Destruction of the History of Ontology," in which Heidegger proposed a critical rereading of the history of philosophy—moving in historical retrograde from Kant to Descartes to the ancient Greeks—so as to illumine the moments of ontological insight when the intimate relation between time and Being had come momentarily into view before suffering a transfiguration and renewed suppression. Heidegger's guiding aim was to work out the "temporality of Being." The challenge of this task was extraordinary, Heidegger claimed, largely because Dasein in its everyday understanding wants to evade facing up to its own thrown and temporal condition. The history of metaphysics itself was therefore a story of motivated concealment: throughout its course, the temporal character of ontology had been either concealed or simply forgotten. Consequently (as Heidegger put it in a seeming paradox), Dasein was "uprooted by tradition." This predicament required a "negative" project of "shaking off the ontological tradition."

> If the question of Being is to have its own history made transparent, then this hardened tradition must be loosened up, and the concealments which it has brought about must be dissolved. We understand this task as one in which by taking *the question of Being as our clue,* we are to *destroy* the traditional content of ancient ontology until we arrive at those primordial experiences in which we achieved our first ways of determining the nature of Being.[33]

It is well known that Heidegger never quite fulfilled this promise—the published text of *Being and Time* constitutes only the first half of the projected work. But readers customarily regard many of his early historical studies (on, for example, German Idealism—specifically, Kant, Hegel, and Schelling) as contributions to the planned-for interpretative history. This is especially true for *Kant and the Problem of Metaphysics,* which appeared in print just two years after Heidegger's *magnum opus* and seems to undertake the first step in the so-called destruction.

More importantly, however, it is indisputable that Kant, perhaps more than any other modern philosopher in the history of metaphysics, plays a decisive role in Heidegger's philosophical-historical narrative. This is because Kant's transcendental doctrine was clearly an important model for Heidegger's own existential doctrine. The Kantian view is that, if we are to arrive at secure knowledge of the world, the human mind must furnish a priori conditions for experience. The Heideggerian view is that, if we are to encounter beings, we must possess some understanding of the Being of those beings. Heidegger's major challenge to Kant was to insist that the conditions for possible experience are not mental but practical: Kant's "transcendental analytic" was replaced by an "existential analytic." While the drama of this transformation—from the rational to the existential—can hardly be denied, the underlying notion of transcendental conditions remained in crucial respects the same.[34] Perhaps the strongest proof of this resemblance is the extended discussion in *Being and Time* on the idealism-realism debate, which concludes with Heidegger's remark that because "Being can never be explained by entities but is already that which is 'transcendental' for every entity, then idealism affords the only correct possibility for a philosophical problematic." "If so," Heidegger adds, "Aristotle was no less an idealist than Kant."[35] This frankly acknowledged debt to the Kantian doctrine of transcendental conditions was no doubt one reason that, once Heidegger finished the extant portions of *Being and Time,* he turned almost immediately to a critical engagement with Kant's philosophy.

Heidegger's Quarrel with Neo-Kantianism

In *Kant and the Problem of Metaphysics* Heidegger presented his own interpretation of Kant in explicit contrast to the neo-Kantian view.[36] To understand the stakes of this contrast, we should recall our discussion from Chapter 2, in which we noted that Cohen saw transcendental idealism as essentially a "theory of knowledge" *(Erkenntnistheorie),* and more precisely, as a philosophical justification for the knowledge-claims of natural science. The linchpin to Cohen's view was the claim that if scientific knowledge is to be secure, then it must exhibit a thoroughgoing rationality that cannot in any sense depend on mere intuition but must instead find its grounding in pure a priori logic alone. Cohen accordingly rejected the Kantian separation between a receptive faculty for intuitions (sensibility) and a spontaneous faculty of concepts (understanding) and insisted instead on the autonomy of the understanding as the sole ground of knowledge. In Cohen's words, "Being" itself was "the Being of thought." As a theory of natural-scientific discovery, this meant that the thing-in-itself was to be seen, not as a meta-physical unknown or noumenon, but instead merely as a marker of the *Aufgabe*, or task, of knowledge. The ultimate consequence of this interpretation was to reframe transcendental idealism as a formalistic grounding for scientific explanation. Yet with this shift—from metaphysics to method—Kant's philosophy ironically seemed to surrender its last remaining bond to empiricism and came to resemble a species of absolute idealism. Some critics even deemed it a "panlogism."[37]

It is this distinctively Marburgian interpretation of Kant's philosophy—as an epistemological propaedeutic to natural science anchored in the thesis of mental spontaneity—that Heidegger most wished to combat. In his Kant-lectures at Davos, Heidegger indicated that his argument was meant "in opposition to the traditional interpretation of neo-Kantianism," and he insisted further that, Marburg doctrine notwithstanding, the *Critique of Pure Reason* was "no theory of mathematical, natural-scientific knowledge." Given the preeminent status of the neo-Kantian interpretation in German philosophy at the time, Heidegger's dissent from its most basic premises no doubt appeared controversial. But Heidegger clearly wished to emphasize the unprecedented character of his own argument. The traditional interpretations notwithstanding, the first *Critique* in his view was "not a theory of knowledge at all," but was instead a "groundlaying for metaphysics."[38]

The essential difference lay in the fact that the neo-Kantians saw the first *Critique* as a epistemological investigation (that is, a study of the formal conditions for empirical knowledge), whereas Heidegger now claimed the *Critique* must be understood as a preparatory investigation into the conditions for *ontological* understanding. As justification, Heidegger noted that Kant's point of departure was the set of concerns known as "traditional metaphysics," or *Metaphysica Specialis* (i.e., knowledge of the three supersensible beings: the world-totality, the immortal soul, and God). But Kant's question, "How is such knowledge possible?" depends in turn on the more foundational question as to the possibility of knowledge of beings in general. The possibility of *ontic* knowledge (knowledge of specific entities) was therefore grounded on the question of the possibility of *ontological* knowledge (knowledge of Being), or *Metaphysica Generalis.*

On Heidegger's view, such an ontological inquiry was bound from the very outset by the stricture that the investigation must concern solely *human* or *finite* reason. Human thought is in its essential character finite. "The idea of an infinite thinking," Heidegger remarked, "is an absurdity." This fundamental stricture gained further reinforcement from modern phenomenology in the theory that intentionality is not a self-enclosed structure but a relation to given or intuited phenomena. Yet even in Kant's own philosophy Heidegger could find support for the premise that "knowing is primarily intuiting."[39] Human knowledge must consist in both intuition as well as thought; indeed, intuition is primary, because for an object to be thought, it must first be given. In Kant's own system the finitude of human knowledge thus stood in fundamental contrast to an "infinite" or creative intuition *(intuitus originarus).* Such a spontaneous intuition on Kant's view would be one that spontaneously created the reality of its objects in the very act of intuiting them. For such a creative intuition no object need be "given" as knowledge would be identical with production. This contrast between a mind that produces its own objects and a mind that is dependent on objects being given proved that Kant himself saw human intuition as essentially finite.

Yet in the neo-Kantian interpretation this commitment to the finitude of human knowledge had been all but forgotten. Here it seems likely that Heidegger meant his audience to register his dissent from Cohen's theory of the "infinitesimal" (according to which, as was noted already above, the human mind itself was seen as the source the objects of scientific explanation much as in calculus an infinitesimally small magnitude is born from a mathematical operation). Yet Heidegger's more explicit complaint was that in their zealous efforts to extol the generative independence of the mind the Marburg neo-Kantians had erased from their portrait of human knowledge its most crucial feature: *receptivity.* Knowledge is always born of an orientation toward the world and a dependency upon its world by means of intuitions. A proper assessment of the first *Critique* was therefore possible only if one first acknowledged the essence of finite knowledge in general and the basic character of finitude as such. For Heidegger this meant that one must attend primarily to Kant's theory of sensibility. Against the neo-Kantian absorption of intuition into the understanding, Heidegger claimed instead that sensibility should be granted its foundational role not as a merely "sensual" or "psychological" faculty but as a truly "metaphysical" foundation for experience. It followed that the first *Critique* was an inquiry into finitude itself as the birthplace of ontology.

Kant as Metaphysician

In the Kant-lectures at Davos and again in the Kant-book, Heidegger justified his interpretation of the first *Critique* as a "groundlaying for metaphysics" by remarking upon the crucial differences between the "A" and "B" editions (first published in 1781 and 1787, respectively). On Heidegger's view, the key to understanding the relation between finitude and ontological knowledge in the *Critique* was Kant's claim that "time is the formal condition a priori of all appearance whatsoever."[40] This implied that ontological knowledge is somehow bound to temporality. This implication, Heidegger observed, found added support in Kant's claim that "transcendental imagination" must serve as the mediating faculty between the sensibility and the understanding. In securing objective validity for the categories, the transcendental imagination had to play a crucial role because it furnished the concepts of the understanding with a temporal synthesis, and thereby created "schemata," which were then applicable to pure intuition. In Kant's words, the schemata were "nothing but a priori determinations of time in accordance with rules." But even Kant seemed to admit that the precise nature of the schemata remained a mystery: "This schematism of our understanding with regard to appearances and their mere form," he wrote, "is a hidden art in the depths of the human soul, whose true operations we can divine from nature and lay unveiled before our eyes only with difficulty."[41]

Just why Kant should have admitted ignorance at so pivotal a moment in his argument has been a subject of long-standing debate. The further question was why Kant later went back to revise his classification of the transcendental imagination: In the 1781 edition he classified it as a "third" faculty, but later (in his personal copy) he renamed it a "function of the understanding." For Heidegger this revision was not merely a textual curiosity. It was integral to the broader issue of how Kant had revised the transcendental deduction itself so as to secure the sovereignty of reason. The received wisdom was that Kant had transformed his argument by replacing the "psychological" doctrine that emphasized the mediating role of the imagination in the 1781 edition with the "more logical" doctrine of the 1787 edition. But in Heidegger's view the change did not signal that Kant had actually improved upon his earlier position. Rather, it betrayed the fact that Kant had momentarily discerned the radical and potentially disruptive implications of his own argument and had moved swiftly to obscure them from view.

The more radical character of the *Critique*'s "A" edition, Heidegger explained, was twofold: First, it suggested that the transcendental imagination was independent of reason, and second, it implied that the transcendental imagination enjoyed an independent status only because it was ultimately grounded in temporality. As Heidegger noted, the "forming" *(Bilden)* action of the imagination *(Einbildung)* is in itself "relative to time." It was indeed the pure imagination that was initially responsible for the synthetic unity of intuitions. Pure imagination was therefore assigned the specified task that it must "form time." In the Kant-book Heidegger paid close attention to this idea by carefully distinguishing among the three "syntheses" necessary for knowledge (apprehension, reproduction, and recognition) in which he believed he could discern the three temporal modes ("present, having-been, and future"). And from all this, Heidegger concluded boldly that the transcendental power of imagination is "original time."[42]

On Heidegger's view, the ramifications of this conclusion were truly explosive. To identify the transcendental imagination with "original time" and to further suggest that it alone was responsible for a series of syntheses independent of reason implied that reason might not stand as the final arbiter of knowledge. But Kant (on Heidegger's interpretation) had found this implication intolerable and had hastened to redress the apparent misstep. Heidegger's conclusion was startling. Kant had revised the *Critique* so as to uphold reason's sovereign position in relation to time:

> The obscurity and "strangeness" of the transcendental power of imagination . . . and the sheer power of reason . . . were worked together so as to veil once more the line of vision into the more original essence of the . . . imagination . . . a perspective which was broken open,

so to speak, only for an instant. . . . To be sure, we should note that the ground-laying in the first edition was never "psychological" any more than the second edition was a "logical" one. On the contrary, both are transcendental . . . But in the transcendental, subjective ground-laying of the second edition, it decided in favor of the pure understanding as opposed to the pure power of the imagination in order to preserve the mastery of reason.[43]

Heidegger was clearly aware of the drama of this conclusion and he readily granted that it stood in direct conflict with Kant's stated intentions. But as Heidegger explained, it was the task of any genuine interpretation to bring out what remained "unsaid." The Kant-book intended "to make visible in this way the decisive content of [the first *Critique*] and thereby to bring out what Kant 'had wanted to say.'" Such a task was hardly straightforward: "Certainly, in order to wring from what the words say, what it is they want to say, every interpretation must necessarily use violence." But interpretative violence remained distinct from "roving arbitrariness." As with "any philosophical knowledge, what is said in uttered propositions must not be decisive." Rather, *"what must be decisive is what it sets before our eyes as still unsaid, in and through what has been said."*[44]

Heidegger's Critique of *Kulturphilosophie*

Heidegger's Kant-lectures at Davos naturally did not afford him sufficient time to present the details of his interpretation with any precision. From the published notes we can verify that the major steps of the interpretation as presented shortly thereafter in the Kant-book were already in place. (Indeed, certain passages were repeated verbatim.) Yet the spoken and public format of the Davos lecture lent the claims an additional drama. Heidegger brought the Kant-lectures to an abrupt conclusion, ending with a final riposte against both neo-Kantian rationalism and the cultural philosophy Cassirer had erected upon neo-Kantian foundations:

The point of departure in reason has thus been broken asunder.
  With that Kant himself, through his radicalism, was brought to the brink of a position from which he had to shrink back.

It implies: destruction of the former foundation of Western meta-physics (spirit, logos, reason).

It demands a radical, renewed unveiling of the grounds for the pos-sibility of metaphysics as [a] natural disposition of human beings; i.e., a metaphysics of Dasein directed at the possibility of metaphysics as such, which must pose the question concerning the essence of human beings in such a way which is *prior* to all philosophical anthropology and cul-tural philosophy.[45]

Heidegger's challenge was clear: Whereas Cassirer had claimed that the metaphysical strain in philosophical anthropology had led its proponents into error, Heidegger now claimed instead that by *denying* the metaphysical strain in Kant's philosophy, the neo-Kantians had utterly failed to grasp the deeper significance of the first *Critique*. Notwithstanding their apparent difference in subject matter, the two philosophers were in direct conflict on the question of whether metaphysical inquiry *as such* was to be considered legitimate philosophical terrain. The implicit lesson in Cassirer's lectures was that modern philosophy was *right* to dispense with metaphysical ques-tions and should instead endorse an essentially neo-Kantian model of phi-losophy as a transcendental study of spontaneous (i.e., free and rational) creativity. Conversely, the explicit claim in Heidegger's lectures was that, precisely *because* modern philosophy in general and neo-Kantianism in particular *neglected* the true character of metaphysics as a "natural disposi-tion of human beings," they remained trapped within the self-deceptive tradition of metaphysical rationalism. What they extolled as mental sponta-neity was little more than an illusion. Accordingly, a suspicious and neces-sarily "violent" reinterpretation of Kant's philosophical legacy was crucial, although it was to be only one step in what Heidegger promised would be a wholesale "destruction" of the "former foundation of Western metaphys-ics," that is, the philosophical tradition that sought its grounding in "spirit, logos, reason." In place of this tradition, Heidegger upheld "metaphysics as such," the task of which would be to pursue "the question concerning the essence of human beings" in a fashion necessarily "*prior* to all philosophical anthropology and cultural philosophy."[46]

It is now worth pausing to consider Heidegger's closing words, which articulate what was arguably the focal point in Heidegger's quarrel with

Cassirer: the claim that "fundamental ontology" takes precedence before all other philosophical concerns. This is so because, on Heidegger's view, any philosophy, no matter its domain, must begin with an understanding of the Being *(Seinsverständnis)* of the entities within that domain. A philosophy of factual achievements (including Cassirer's study of the achievements of "form") therefore of necessity presupposed a philosophy of the Being of those achievements. And because any such *Seinsverständnis* presupposed an earlier inquiry into the ontological constitution of Dasein as the specific being for whom Being itself is "at issue," it followed that all topical philosophy must be preceded by something like an existential analytic or "metaphysics of Dasein." For Heidegger, this metaphysical inquiry therefore enjoyed indubitable priority over *all* other philosophies—and, explicitly so—over *both* philosophical anthropology *and* cultural philosophy.

Here it is important to note that the claim that fundamental ontology must come *before* other philosophical pursuits need not necessarily have committed Heidegger to the further claim that fundamental ontology must be accorded greater *value*. The priority claim simply tells us where philosophy must begin; it does *not* say this beginning is of higher importance or that a cultural philosophy—simply because it is dependent—is therefore superficial or deceptive. But it is characteristic of Heidegger's understanding of fundamental ontology as a precondition to further inquiry that such evaluative conclusions appeared to follow the priority claim almost as a matter of course: if Cassirer's philosophy did not study what was foundational, this implied not only its superficiality but its complicity in perpetuating the largest errors of the rationalist-metaphysical tradition.

At Davos, Heidegger refrained from announcing these further implications. The following winter (1929–1930), in his Freiburg seminar on "The Fundamental Concepts of Metaphysics," he stated the matter without inhibition:

It is a widespread opinion today that both culture and man in culture can only be properly comprehended through the idea of expression or symbol. *We have today a philosophy of culture concerned with expression, with symbol, with symbolic forms.* Man as soul and spirit, coming to expression in forms that bear an intrinsic meaning and which, on the basis of this meaning, give a sense to existence as it expresses

itself: this, roughly speaking, is the scheme of contemporary philosophy of culture. Here too almost everything is correct, right down to the
essential. Yet we must ask anew: Is this view of man an essential one?[47]

The answer was already implicit in the rhetorical question. Cassirer's philosophy of symbolic forms neglected what was most essential in humanity,
and it was therefore complicit with the broader culture's evasion of deeper
and more "metaphysical" insight. The philosophy of symbols, explained Heidegger, "not only factically misses the essence of man, but *must* necessarily
miss it." The problem was not merely that the philosophy of form remained
dependent on an earlier ontology or was itself incapable of plumbing the
deepest levels of human Dasein. The problem was that Cassirer's philosophy
actually conspired to *obstruct* this deeper purpose: *"in itself it blocks the
path to doing so."*[48] Heidegger now saw the philosophy of culture as a mere
symptom for an affliction pervading the entire atmosphere of modern culture itself, an affliction he labeled "profound boredom."

> This philosophy of culture at most sets out what is contemporary about
> our situation, but does not take hold of *us*. What is more, not only does
> it not succeed in grasping us, but it unties us from ourselves in impart-
> ing us a role in world history. It unties us from ourselves, and yet does
> so precisely as anthropology. *Our flight and disorientation, the illusion
> and lostness become more acute.*[49]

This was indeed a stinging and far more direct rebuke than what Heidegger
offered at Davos (as we shall see momentarily). Yet as we now turn to the
disputation itself, we should keep this argument in mind, especially because
it seems probable Heidegger was already committed to its more basic claims.
It therefore furnished a kind of subtext to his conversation with Cassirer.
Moreover, it is a perfect illustration of what I want to call the cultural inscription of philosophy. The effect in any such inscription is to show how
philosophy ramifies, how it is the carrier, perhaps even despite itself, of some
broader cultural or historical significance. Heidegger ultimately responded
to Cassirer's philosophy by inscribing it into a larger and more ramified
cultural-metaphysical narrative, characterizing it as merely another way

station on the flight from ontological knowledge. At Davos such cultural inscriptions remained largely implicit, but their allegorical lessons, both philosophical and political, grew increasingly evident in the years that followed. Before we can truly appreciate these larger meanings, we must turn to the debate itself.

4

The Davos Encounter

I'll fight not with thee.

—*Macbeth*, Act 5, Scene 8

Introduction

In Chapters 1 and 2, I tried to reconstruct the philosophical and institutional context for the years leading up to the Davos debate, and in Chapter 3, I discussed the independent lectures by both Cassirer and Heidegger. In this chapter, I turn to the debate itself, offering an English-language translation of the entire *Arbeitsgemeinschaft* interlaced with my own philosophical and historical commentary.[1] To clarify the complexities of the debate, I have divided the chapter into ten thematic sections. The purpose of these sections is merely heuristic. Between the annotation, the full transcript of the debate is reproduced here as it was originally transcribed.

Cohen's Legacy

Cassirer's opening remarks in the *Arbeitsgemeinschaft* responded directly to Heidegger's three lectures on Kant. Cassirer began by raising doubt as to whether Heidegger had correctly grasped the significance of the neo-Kantian legacy and whether his noticeably vigorous rejection of this entire interpretative tradition was in fact warranted. In Cassirer's eyes Heidegger's essential *mis*understanding of neo-Kantianism on the most central issues appeared so pronounced that it suggested an almost willful distortion (hence the unusual comment that neo-Kantianism served as "the scapegoat of the newer philosophy"). The marked antagonism between phenomenology and neo-Kantianism was an illusion, Cassirer claimed, not least because he could no longer identify any "existing" neo-Kantians *sensu stricto*. In any case he was eager to rectify Heidegger's historical and philosophical misrepresentations:

Cassirer: What does Heidegger understand by neo-Kantianism?
          Who is the opponent to whom Heidegger has addressed
          himself? I believe that there is hardly a single concept that
          has been paraphrased with so little clarity as that of
          neo-Kantianism. What does Heidegger have in mind
          when he employs the phenomenological critique in place
          of the neo-Kantian one? Neo-Kantianism is the scapegoat
          of the newer philosophy [*Der Neukantianismus ist der
          Sündenbock der neueren Philosophie*]. To me, there is an
          absence of existing neo-Kantians. I would be thankful for
          some clarification as to where it is here that the difference
          properly lies. I believe that absolutely no essential differ-
          ence arises. The term *neo-Kantianism* must be determined
          functionally rather than substantially. It is not a matter of
          the kind of philosophy as dogmatic doctrinal system;
          rather, it is a matter of a direction taken in question
          posing. Though I had not expected to find it in him, I
          must confess that I have found a neo-Kantian here in
          Heidegger.

From Cassirer's perspective, the true significance of the neo-Kantian movement lay in neither a dogma nor a *substantive doctrine* but rather in a basic
orientation, a *function* and manner of posing questions. By making this distinction Cassirer made oblique reference to his own 1910 work on the development of mathematics, *Substance and Function*. What he had in mind was
the special kind of philosophical creativity that characterized the neo-
Kantian movement as a whole and the uninhibited radicalism with which it
attempted both to reactivate the original insights of Kant's philosophy and
also to apply them to new scientific problems and new domains of cultural
and historical knowledge. This definition surely describes Cassirer's own
earliest studies of modern mathematics and Einsteinian physics as well as
his later philosophy of symbolic forms.

But such a definition may also be applied in certain respects to Heidegger's
philosophy as well, a fact that may explain Cassirer's rather surprising suggestion that Heidegger, too, shows signs of neo-Kantian influence. The suggestion becomes more intelligible if one bears in mind that, between 1911
and 1916, Heidegger had trained at Freiburg under Heinrich Rickert, at that

time the leading representative of the Southwestern neo-Kantians. But education is only the beginning of the story. The deeper insight behind Cassirer's remark is that Heidegger's own investigation into the *Sinn des Seins* (the "sense of Being" that serves as the fundamental condition for the possibility of human experience) was itself to be understood as a species of transcendental inquiry and therefore belongs to the broadly Kantian tradition of transcendental philosophy. As I noted in the Introduction to this book, this transcendental motif is granted prominent space in the opening methodological portions of *Being and Time,* where Heidegger cites the medieval definition of Being as the *transcendens.* It is further evident in the later, approving remarks on idealism, where Heidegger even allowed that Being is "in the consciousness" and that "Being can never be explained by entities but is already that which is 'transcendental' for every entity."[2] More striking still are those passages in Heidegger's lectures that deploy idealist phrases congruent with Cassirer's humanistic forms-philosophy, such as the dictum from the winter semester lectures on "The Fundamental Concepts of Metaphysics" (1929–1930) that because the *concept* of the world unfolds from the *human understanding* of the world, it follows that "*Man is world-forming* [*weltbildend*]."[3] Later in the debate Cassirer would elaborate further on this affinity with an acknowledgment that Heidegger was right to indicate the crucial role played by the productive imagination within Kant's broader theory of experience. It is largely thanks to the prominence of this transcendental motif in both Heidegger's own philosophy and his interpretation of Kant's first *Critique* that Cassirer insisted on Heidegger's own philosophical kinship with neo-Kantianism.

But this was a suggestion Heidegger could hardly welcome, especially because, in his Kant-lectures of the preceding week, he had insisted on the (ostensibly) fatal errors of neo-Kantian doctrine. This may explain why in his initial reply to Cassirer one may detect a note of irritation:

> *Heidegger:* If I should first of all name names, then I say: Cohen,
>   Windelband, Rickert, Erdmann, Riehl. We can only
>   understand what is common to neo-Kantianism on the
>   basis of its origin. Its genesis lies in the predicament of
>   philosophy concerning the question of what properly
>   remains of it in the whole of knowledge. Since about 1850

it has been the case that both the human and the natural sciences have taken possession of the totality of what is knowable, so that the question arises: what still remains of philosophy if the totality of beings has been divided up under the sciences? It remains just knowledge of science, not of beings. And it is from this perspective that the return to Kant is then determined. Consequently, Kant was seen as a theoretician of the mathematico-physical theory of knowledge. Theory of knowledge [*Erkenntnis-theorie*] is the aspect according to which Kant came to be seen. In a certain sense, Husserl himself fell into the clutches of neo-Kantianism between 1900 and 1910.

The response was remarkable on several counts. Heidegger began with a short (and incomplete) list of philosophers associated with the neo-Kantian movement—Hermann Cohen, Wilhelm Windelband, Heinrich Rickert, Benno Erdmann, and Alois Riehl. In Heidegger's view, these philosophers were united in the conviction that, given the apparent supremacy of the natural sciences, the sole task left to philosophy was to furnish a theoretical groundwork for natural-scientific knowledge. Hence, in Heidegger's judgment neo-Kantianism was in the beginning and remained throughout its course a mere *Erkenntnistheorie,* an epistemology or theory of knowledge. Its tendency overall was to regard the methodology of the sciences, specifically, the mathematical-physical sciences, as the privileged and even the unique paradigm for all human understanding as such. It therefore limited itself to providing a transcendental theory of scientific explanation and, Heidegger concluded, it failed to offer any deeper ontological insight into the basic character of scientific entities in themselves.

Clearly this account of the neo-Kantian movement involves a fair measure of simplification. The general image of neo-Kantianism as inhibited by a rigid scientism (i.e., the view that all problems of philosophical significance can be adequately explained by science) does not capture the true diversity of the movement. Heidegger makes no mention of the fact that most neo-Kantians expanded their concerns well beyond a transcendental justification for natural scientific methodology and, after Kant's example, devoted serious attention to various issues in ethics, aesthetics, and history. As was explained in Chapter 1, even Hermann Cohen (whose name appears first in Heidegger's list) followed his pathbreaking work on Kant's transcendental philosophy of natural science (*Kant's Theory of Experience*, 1871) with commentaries on the central themes of both Kant's second and third *Critiques* (*Kant's Grounding of Ethics* and *Kant's Grounding of Aesthetics*) and then produced an original system covering all three domains (*The Logic of Pure Knowledge, The Ethics of Pure Will*, and *The Aesthetics of Pure Feeling*). Most surprising of all, Heidegger also characterized the Southwestern neo-Kantians Windelband and Rickert as bound by a narrowly scientist conception of philosophical inquiry. As Heidegger knew very well, both Windelband and Rickert were especially concerned with the status of value-concepts peculiar to the *human and historical sciences* rather than the natural-scientific sciences. It is thus plainly mistaken to accuse them of scientism or any more general kind of bias in favor of the "mathematico-physical" sciences.

This accusation, moreover, came as a personal affront to Heinrich Rickert in particular. Shortly after the Davos disputation, Rickert sent a strongly worded letter to his former student expressing his dismay to have read (in the typewritten Bollnow-Ritter transcript) that Heidegger had listed Rickert himself alongside others in the neo-Kantian movement, all of whom were ostensibly guilty of confining transcendental idealism to a theory of science rather than a theory of beings. In his response Heidegger explained that the transcript was reproduced arbitrarily, without giving him time to proof it for possible distortions. He further noted that he had never used the phrase "*the* Neo-Kantianism" and that he had expressly indicated in the disputation that he was only trying to explain how neo-Kantians in general interpreted the opening segment of the first *Critique,* specifically, the transcendental aesthetic and the analytic, which they saw as laying down a "theory of knowledge." This, Heidegger wrote, "nobody would dispute."[4]

This may seem like a poor defense. But to appreciate the true force of Heidegger's comments, we must understand that he meant the term *neo-Kantian* only in a very loose manner, as describing a general tendency common to many late-nineteenth and early twentieth-century central-European philosophers who laid cardinal emphasis on formalistic questions of epistemology and method. We must also take note of Heidegger's historical narrative, informed by the theme of philosophical "crisis," according to which the ascendancy of the natural sciences in the latter half of the nineteenth century

cast in doubt the very purposes of philosophy as a discipline. Bereft of any discrete objects of its own, it turned its attention toward transcendental questions of method applicable to all objects irrespective of their disciplinary domain. This characterization indeed captures a prevailing attitude even among
the Southwestern neo-Kantians, because (notwithstanding their scrupulous
attempts to distinguish between the methods of the human and the natural
sciences) they remained largely preoccupied by formal transcendental questions concerning both the limits and the validity of concept-formation.

It is only in this admittedly broad sense that we can also appreciate Heidegger's further claim, that during roughly the first decade of the twentieth
century, Husserl, too, strayed toward a kind of "neo-Kantianism." For this
was the period Husserl wrote his most idealist-epistemological works: the
Logical Investigations (1900–1901), the programmatic essay "Philosophy as a
Rigorous Science" (1911), and the *Ideas Pertaining to a Pure Phenomenology
and to a Phenomenological Philosophy* (1913). Common to all these texts was
the message that phenomenology could succeed only if it laid down an ap-
propriately formal method by which to suspend all of the psychological,
historical, and empirical commitments that encumber the so-called natural
attitude, so as to then study the absolutely pure phenomena as they present
themselves within the bounds of purely transcendental consciousness. This
formalistic emphasis on the methods appropriate to a rigorous science of
phenomena does indeed represent something of an idealist phase in the history of Husserlian phenomenology. But to describe it as verging on "neo-
Kantianism" seems an obvious exaggeration. Notwithstanding their historical variations, the actual disagreements between Husserlian phenomenology
and neo-Kantianism remained intense. As noted in Chapter 2, Eugen Fink
(Husserl's student and a witness to the Davos disputation) was so provoked
by the neo-Kantian critique (by two of Rickert's students) of phenomenology as "naïve intuitionism" that in 1933 he authored a long essay defending
Husserlian phenomenology and reconfirming the disagreement between
the two movements. We are forced to conclude that "neo-Kantianism" in
Heidegger's more relaxed sense of the term served chiefly as a pejorative. It
captured only the most vague set of family resemblances (idealism, methodological formalism, the priority of epistemological concerns, the distinction
between fact and value, and so forth) while it ignored very real variations in
philosophical substance.

In his following comments, however, Heidegger offered a more limited account of neo-Kantianism, which served to introduce his own, quite different reading of Kant's philosophy:

> *Heidegger:* I understand by neo-Kantianism that conception of the *Critique of Pure Reason* that explains the part of pure reason that leads up to the Transcendental Dialectic as a theory of knowledge with reference to natural science. For me, what matters is to show that what came to be extracted here as a theory of science was nonessential for Kant. Kant did not want to give any sort of theory of natural science [*Naturwissenschaft*], but rather wanted to point out the problematic of metaphysics, which is to say, the problematic of ontology. For what matters to me is to work this core content of the positive element of the *Critique of Pure Reason* into ontology in a positive way. On the grounds of my interpretation of the Dialectic as ontology, I believe I can show that the problem of appearance [*das Problem des Scheins*] in the Transcendental Logic, which for Kant is only negative in the form in which it first appears there, is [actually] a positive problem, and that the following is in question: is appearance just a matter of fact that we state, or must the entire problem of reason be apprehended in such a way that we grasp from the beginning how appearance necessarily belongs to the nature of human beings?

For Heidegger the defining and indeed fatal error of the neo-Kantian interpretation was that it understood Kant's first *Critique* chiefly as an epistemological inquiry into the formal-methodological foundations of the natural sciences. Here it seems evident that Heidegger had in mind Cohen's interpretation in particular, because it was the latter's study, *Kant's Theory of Experience,* that was most responsible for validating the view that "experience" in Kant's theoretical philosophy should be taken to mean "natural-scientific experience." Heidegger argued that this interpretation was mistaken insofar as the epistemology of the natural sciences was for Kant himself merely a peripheral issue. His true aim was to develop an ontology, that is, an interpretation of the Being of whatsoever makes its appearance within the bounds of human experience.

It is interesting to note that in these remarks Heidegger placed special stress on Kant's intentions in the "Transcendental Dialectic" (the latter section of the *Critique of Pure Reason* that addresses the limits of metaphysical and theological knowledge and lays down principles for the regulative use of the ideas). Many readers today will customarily read the first *Critique* only for the epistemological lessons as they are developed in the earlier portions of the book (in the "Transcendental Aesthetic," "Logic," and "Analytic"). By contrast, a distinguishing feature of Heidegger's interpretation is that he refuses to see the "Dialectic" as containing merely a *negative* theory concerning the transcendental illusions that are born if we erroneously take the ideas of reason to be fully realizable within the bounds of human experience. Heidegger claims instead that the account of metaphysical knowledge in the "Dialectic" tells us something very important about the positive doctrine animating the entirety of the first *Critique*. Even Kant's earlier introductory remarks to the "Transcendental Logic" on what he called the "logic of illusion" *(Logik des Scheins)* demonstrate that he was trying to work out, albeit in negative form, an understanding of how "appearance" *(Schein)* belongs to the "nature of human being."[5] It is this deeper view—of an underlying unity between human being and what appears—that Heidegger considered the more positive and genuinely "ontological" doctrine animating the first *Critique*.

A potential problem for Heidegger's reading is that Kant was keen to uphold an important distinction between "appearance" *(Erscheinung)* and mere "illusion" *(Schein)*. By ignoring this distinction Heidegger seems to infer that all appearances must share the same inner bond with human understanding, whereas Kant's own view was that illusions arise precisely when merely logical concepts are *mistakenly* given the status of appearances.[6] But this problem may stem from little more than a terminological confusion. Heidegger's larger claim—that the first *Critique* contains a general ontology relating all appearances to human understanding rather than a specifically epistemological groundwork for natural science—remains open for consideration. Cassirer replied to Heidegger's response with a brief comment in defense of Cohen's epistemological and natural-scientific interpretation:

> *Cassirer:* One only understands Cohen correctly if one understands
> him historically, not merely as an epistemologist. I do not
> conceive of my own development as a defection from
> Cohen. Naturally, in the course of my work much else has
> emerged, and, indeed, above all I recognized the position of
> mathematical natural science, though this can only serve as
> a paradigm and not as the whole of the problem. And the
> same goes for Natorp.

According to Cassirer, Cohen's interpretation had a far greater significance
in the history of philosophy than Heidegger seemed prepared to admit. To
appreciate the true importance of the Marburg School, one must look beyond its own epistemological doctrines to judge it from a wider historical
perspective. It is in this light that Cassirer stood ready to affirm his own
philosophical debt to Marburg, *not* because he would have accepted the
view of the natural sciences as the *sole and sufficient* sphere of legitimate
knowledge but rather because he was willing to see in the natural sciences a
necessary *paradigm* for all further inquiries into the dynamics of human
understanding. I should note that this distinction was crucial to Cassirer,
not least because it protected him as a philosopher of science from any
accusations of vulgar scientism. Just as importantly, it afforded him the
opportunity to distance himself from certain tendencies in the neo-Kantian
theory of knowledge even while he affirmed his continued debt, both philosophical and personal, to Cohen himself. It is evident from his final reply to
Heidegger's criticism of Cohen that Cassirer understood his *own* philosophy
to be an implicit target. Cassirer clearly considered much of this criticism
unfair, and his "scapegoat" remark seems to suggest that he believed the
motives for such criticism were not entirely philosophical (I shall have more
to say on this point in Chapter 6). Yet he was nonetheless eager to explain
how his own philosophy of symbolic forms transcended the narrow bounds,
real or perceived, of neo-Kantian epistemology.

Transcendental Imagination

Notwithstanding the fundamental disagreement between Cassirer and
Heidegger concerning both the philosophical and the cultural-historical

significance of Kant's philosophy, there were several points on which they seemed to agree and that marked their common identity as philosophers who had moved together beyond the constraints of neo-Kantian orthodoxy. It was characteristic of Cassirer's scholarly temperament that he began by emphasizing these points of consensus. Perhaps most significant was their shared conviction that the key to Kant's theoretical philosophy overall lay in the specifically formative role it assigned to the faculty of the productive power of imagination, or *produktive Einbildungskraft*:

> *Cassirer:* Now to Heidegger's basic systematic problem. On one point we agree, in that for me as well the productive power of imagination appears in fact to have central meaning for Kant. From there I was led through my work on the symbolic. One cannot resolve this [the symbolic] without referring it back to the faculty of the productive power of imagination. The power of imagination is the connection of all thought to intuition. Kant calls the power of imagination *Synthesis Speciosa*. Synthesis is the basic power [*Grundkraft*] of pure thinking. For Kant, however, it [pure thinking] does not depend simply on synthesis, but depends instead primarily upon the synthesis that serves the species. But this problem of the species leads into the core of the concept of image, the concept of symbol.

Kant's account of transcendental imagination played a pivotal role in Heidegger's Kant-lectures at Davos. As discussed in Chapter 3, Heidegger understood the first *Critique* as an implicitly ontological inquiry, that is, as a "groundlaying for metaphysics," and he understood the schematism chapter in particular as the true core of Kant's ontological argument. In his Davos lectures and in the Kant-book, Heidegger placed great stress on Kant's claims in the schematism chapter that the production of a schematism is "a hidden art in the depths of the human soul" and that the pure imagination that is responsible for this production lies beneath intuition and understanding as their "common root."[7] Kant had originally put forth these claims in order to explain how two essentially heterogeneous species of representation, the pure intuitions of space and time (which belong to sensibility) and the pure concepts of the understanding (which are purely discursive), could come into an essential harmony so as to furnish a transcendental grounding for human knowledge. From these claims Heidegger now inferred that the true grounds of ontology in Kant's system could *not* be credited to human reason itself (although Kant wished to make it seem so and in the second edition "shrank back" from his more radical discovery in order to "preserve the mastery of reason").[8]

Heidegger explained that ontology was born instead from the pure imagination as an original *unity* of intuition and understanding. And this led to the paradoxical consequence that the pure imagination exhibits both spontaneity *and* receptivity at once. It was (in Heidegger's phrase) a "spontaneous receptivity," a seemingly paradoxical notion to which Cassier would later raise vigorous objections.[9] Heidegger further argued that it is instead the transcendental power of imagination *itself* that lies at the very roots of ontological knowledge, insofar as it is the imagination in its nonempirical capacity that first brings temporal unity *(synthesis)* to experience. And in this sense the transcendental power of imagination could rightly be understood as "original time."[10] By Kant's own explanations, Heidegger claimed, we are brought to the quite unexpected conclusion that ontological understanding is ultimately grounded in temporality alone: time itself is now revealed as the horizon of Being. And because this temporality lies deeper than logic, deeper, even, than any pure or unconditioned mental spontaneity, the presumptive sovereignty of human reason is accordingly "broken asunder."[11]

Cassirer was perhaps right to say that he agreed with Heidegger concerning the pivotal role of the productive imagination in Kant's theoretical philosophy. But Cassirer's own interpretation as to what this role actually entailed could hardly have been more dissimilar. To see this, one need only consult the remarks on the imagination that Cassier included in *The Phenomenology of Knowledge* (the third volume of his *Philosophy of Symbolic Forms*), which he had completed near the end of 1927, though its publication was delayed until the summer of 1929. The timing of its appearance may be significant insofar as several of the footnotes make explicit reference to Heidegger's *Being and Time* (also published in 1927), and it seems somewhat unlikely that Cassirer developed these insights within the space of a few months. About those particular references more will be said in the chapters to follow. Here it is only relevant to note that Cassirer, in starkest contrast to Heidegger, interpreted Kant's theory of the productive imagination as decisive evidence for what he called the "creative action of the human spirit." While Heidegger described the pure a priori imagination as a "spontaneous receptivity," Cassirer described it as a "pure spontaneity."[12]

The terminological difference underscores a crucial disagreement in philosophical perspective: for Heidegger, the faculty of productive imagination served as the inescapably temporal horizon for all human knowledge. But precisely because time is a *horizon,* it must be considered only as a *condition* for all mental activity even though it is not itself a *source* or *achievement* of mental action. For Cassirer, however, the faculty of *productive* imagination was distinguished from merely *reproductive* imagination precisely because it effects the synthesis of experience *without prior conditioning.* It is therefore spontaneous and *not* receptive, and it is a key sign for what Cassirer called the "basic productive function of the spirit." But perhaps the most striking contrast appears in the remarks on the intuition of time, where Cassirer observed that because the possibility of our experience of an objective temporal order is dependent on the schematism as a product of pure imagination, we are therefore justified in regarding time as *"created by thought itself a priori."*[13] Temporality on Cassirer's reading therefore cannot be a mere horizon or receptive field anterior to all mental action; it is instead, as Cohen taught, a spontaneity and therefore itself a product of mental action.

As Cassirer explained in his above reply to Heidegger, the doctrine in the first *Critique* concerning the pure and unconditioned spontaneity of the imagination served as an inspiration and founding premise to the philosophy of symbolic forms. According to Kant, if we are justified in claiming to possess pure a priori knowledge, then the discrete intuitions given in sense experience must exhibit not merely an "association" but rather a true "affinity," a thoroughgoing and necessary synthesis of the manifold of intuitions. It is the imagination that is responsible for producing this synthesis (hence Kant's term for the imagination, *Synthesis Speciosa*). But in the crucial argumentative section of the first *Critique* on the "schematism of the pure concepts of the understanding," Kant had explained that any such synthesis cannot be merely empirical because the certitude of pure a priori knowledge requires that the objective validity of the categories be ascertained for any possible spatiotemporal intuition.[14] It is for this reason that the synthesis must be valid not just for specific intuitions (in which case the imagination would produce merely an image) but must instead serve as a rule for the production of images such that it is therefore valid for all possible intuitions. Any such synthesis cannot yield an image as such but must instead produce a truly transcendental *schema* or, in Kant's phrase, a *monogram of pure a priori imagination*.[15] It seems Cassirer had in mind this distinction—between empirical and transcendental synthesis—when he replied to Heidegger that pure thinking "does not depend on synthesis *as such*" but depends instead on "the synthesis which serves the *species*."[16]

The larger point for Cassirer was that Heidegger was mistaken to infer that, because the imagination serves an essential *role* in human knowledge, all knowledge is essentially dependent on imagination alone. The inference was mistaken because, as Kant had explained, "nothing can be given to the imagination other than what is conjoined through the understanding." There is, in other words, a formal and rule-like character to the activity of pure a priori imagination such that its synthesis applies not to particular intuitions but instead to the entire species, or conceptual-universal *classes* of intuition. Cassirer explained that in working out his own theory of symbolic forms he drew inspiration from this particular idea, because it helped him to distinguish between a mere image, which merely reproduces what is immediately given in intuition, and an actual symbol, which exhibits "pregnance" insofar as it fuses into a "single perceptive phenomenon" both intuition *and* form.[17] On Cassirer's Kant-interpretation, the formative spontaneity of the mind therefore retained its primacy.

Ethics and Objectivity

Until this point in their conversation, Cassirer and Heidegger had confined themselves to chiefly technical and interpretative issues in Kant's theoretical philosophy. Cassirer now broadened the discussion to address themes in Kant's practical philosophy as well. It is perhaps worth noting that it was Cassirer alone who seems to have been responsible for this shift in focus. Heidegger, in his preceding Kant-lectures, made no mention whatsoever of practical reason, though (perhaps in response to Cassirer's challenges) he would do so immediately after the debate, first in the Kant-book, and then at far greater length in his summer 1930 lecture course, *On the Essence of*

Human Freedom (see Chapter 5). With the introduction of ethical questions, one may also detect a shift in tone: Cassirer now abandoned his more conciliatory efforts to identify points of commonality, and he began instead to address the deeper and more dramatic issues about which the two philosophers would ultimately disagree:

> *Cassirer:* If we keep the whole of Kant's work in view, severe problems surface. One of these is the problem of freedom. This was for me always Kant's truly highest problem. How is freedom possible? Kant says that this question does not allow being conceived in this way. We conceive only of the inconceivability of freedom. In opposition to this, then, I might now set Kantian ethics: the Categorical Imperative must be constituted in such a fashion that the law set up is not valid by chance just for human beings, but for all rational entities [*Vewrnunftwesen*] in general.

To appreciate the force of Cassirer's remarks, one should recall several points that followed from Kant's distinction between the *theoretical* and *practical* uses of pure reason. According to Kant, any knowledge to which we lay claim in virtue of theoretical reason will necessarily be constrained by the cognitive conditions under which we experience the world. And these conditions place necessary and inviolable limits on what we can know: Insofar as we are finite beings, and therefore dependent for our experience on what is given to us through intuition, we are constrained to knowledge of only the sensible and spatiotemporal realm. But reason in its practical use is bound by no such conditions. In the *Critique of Practical Reason* we are told that what is known in virtue of practical reason has as its ground nothing else besides "the form of a pure will" itself. "It thereby happens," Kant observes, "that the practical concepts a priori in relation to the supreme principle of freedom immediately become cognitions, not needing to wait upon intuitions in order to acquire a meaning." The concepts of pure practical reason, in other words, are concepts that the pure will gives to itself *without recourse to experience*. Such concepts are known wholly independent of the cognitive conditions that necessarily obtain for pure reason in its theoretical use. But they nonetheless count as real objects of pure practical reason. Kant thus declared that the moral concepts *"themselves produce the reality of that to which they refer."*[18] He further argued that the principle of morality, precisely by virtue of its universal and formal character, can function as the law and determining ground of the will *"for all rational beings insofar as they have a will."* They obtain, in other words, for all beings that have "the ability to determine their actions . . . in accordance with a priori practical principles." The principle of morality is thus *"not limited to human beings only but applies to all finite beings that have reason and will and even includes the infinite being as the supreme intelligence."*[19] Finally, the enlarged scope of validity for moral concepts suggests that it is only by virtue of such concepts that the human being can learn "to tear himself away from all sensual attachments" and, while never denying his bonds to worldly experience, can also come to recognize what Kant calls "the independence of his rational nature."[20]

These cardinal precepts of Kantian ethical theory clearly furnished an inspiration for Cassirer's comment above, that through pure practical reason we have knowledge of moral concepts whose validity is not limited only to human beings but rather extends to "all rational entities." Behind this remark lay the deeper lesson that, notwithstanding his constant allusions to the limits of human knowledge in the *theoretical* sphere, Kant also saw that in the *practical* sphere we employ our reason unconstrained by such limits and we are thereby granted legitimate access to a higher, albeit purely "intelligible," reality. For Cassirer this distinction was of crucial importance. It meant that there was a notable and even *fundamental* aspect to Kant's philosophy (hence the much-vaunted "primacy" of practical reason) that Heidegger could not explain, although it was precisely this ethical perspective that enjoyed the *functional* status of metaphysical knowledge insofar as it lay beyond the finitude of worldly existence. As Cassirer explained:

> Cassirer: Here suddenly is this remarkable transition. The restrictedness to a determinate sphere suddenly falls away. The ethical as such leads beyond the world of appearances. This is indeed the decisively metaphysical, insofar as there now follows a breakthrough [*Durchbruch*]. It is a matter of the transition to the *mundus intelligibilis*. That holds for the ethical, and in the ethical a point is reached that is no longer

> relative to the finitude of the knowing creature, rather an
> Absolute is now erected there. This cannot be illuminated
> historically. A step, one can say, that Kant should not have
> brought to completion. But we cannot deny the fact that the
> problem of freedom has been posed in this way, [and] that it
> breaks through the original sphere [*die ursprüngliche Sphäre
> durchbricht*].

Here Cassirer introduced the image of "breakthrough" so as to illustrate his claim that the concepts of pure practical reason possessed an objective validity that extended beyond the bounds of sensible experience and that was therefore no longer relative to human finitude. On Cassirer's view, Heidegger's interpretation of Kant was inadequate insofar as it failed to acknowledge this basic fact concerning the intelligible and objective status of moral principles.

This criticism was revealing on at least two counts: First, it suggested (though only indirectly) that Heidegger had turned Kant's broader philosophy into a species of relativistic and subjective idealism. Because the Kantian-transcendental conditions (space, time, and the categories) that obtain across all possible experience stood revealed in Heidegger's interpretation as ontological conditions belonging to a specifically *human* finitude, we no longer had any assurance that such experience puts us in touch with an objectively valid world. It is worth noting that Cassirer's initial version of this complaint was that Heidegger had missed the objective validity of *moral* concepts only. Later in the debate, as we shall see, Cassirer would accuse Heidegger of missing the nonrelative character of theoretical concepts as well. Second, Cassirer's criticism also suggested that Heidegger's very definition of "metaphysics" was fundamentally mistaken: if it is only by means of our unconditioned concepts of morality that we arrive at a perspective we can describe as "the decisively metaphysical," then on Cassirer's interpretation metaphysics must be understood as a breakthrough *from and beyond* finitude. This interpretation stands in sharpest contrast to Heidegger's understanding of metaphysics as an ontology grounded precisely *in and on* the finitude of Dasein. The two definitions of the metaphysical are not merely dissimilar; they are virtual inversions of each other. Later in the disputation, the philosophers would be asked to comment further on such basic contrasts of philosophical terminology. But at this preliminary stage, Cassirer kept his attention firmly fixed on Heidegger's Kant-interpretation.[21]

Next, while acknowledging the pivotal importance of the schematism for theoretical reason (and thereby implicitly crediting Heidegger's interpretation), Cassirer once again emphasized the critical distinction in Kant's philosophy between theoretical and practical reason, that is, between the use of reason for worldly spatiotemporal knowledge and the use of reason for ethical deliberation. Although knowledge of the spatiotemporal world necessarily relies on the schematism (and hence brings into play the mysterious activities of the imagination), our concepts of freedom require no such spatiotemporal application. We think them apart from the schematism and by means of the understanding alone. In the *Critique of Practical Reason,* however, Kant suggests that practical reason appeals to something that *resembles* a schemata because practical reason must conceive of the *application* of its purely intelligible concepts to the sensible world. It conceives of this application through a test as to whether the maxim underlying one's action would still be possible if it were made into the "form of a law of nature in general." But Kant hastens to note that such a test serves only as "the *type* of a law of freedom." The test itself is purely *formal* and although it conceives of one's actions under the laws of nature, it derives nothing whatsoever from empirical nature itself. Thus Kant upholds the distinction between a true schematism (which is a necessary condition for sensible experience) and a "typic of pure practical judgment" (which has merely an intelligible status).[22] Cassirer explained this as follows:

> *Cassirer:* And this ties in with Heidegger's arguments. The extraordinary significance of the Schematism cannot be overestimated. The greatest misunderstandings in the interpretation of Kant creep in at this point. In the ethical, however, he forbids the Schematism. There he says: our concepts of freedom, and so on, are insights (not as bits of knowledge) that no longer permit schematizing. There is a Schematism of theoretical knowledge but not of practical reason. There is in any event something else, namely, what Kant calls the Typic of Practical Reason. And he makes a distinction between Schematism and Typic. It is necessary

to understand that one cannot penetrate this [realm of practical reason] if one does not give up the Schematism here. For Kant, the Schematism is also the *terminus a quo,* but not the *terminus ad quem.* New problems arise in the *Critique of Practical Reason,* and Kant indeed always adheres to this point of departure in the Schematism, but it is also expanded on. Kant started out from Heidegger's problem, but he expanded from this sphere.

Until this point in the discussion, it may have seemed as if Cassirer's primary complaint was that Heidegger had failed to acknowledge the special status of ethical concepts in Kant's philosophy. We shall see momentarily that this was merely one element within a much larger and more ramified disagreement. I will pause here to note the considerable force behind even this initial complaint.

On textual grounds alone Cassirer's argument seems nearly irrefutable. The nonrelative and purely intelligible status of moral principles is indeed one of the key messages reiterated in many ways throughout both the *Groundwork to the Metaphysics of Morals* and the *Critique of Practical Reason.* The essential dualism between theoretical and practical reason—between "the starry heavens above me" and "the moral law within me"—can be understood to mean that although Kant's system has its *terminus a quo* (point of departure) in a theory of human limitation, it reaches its *terminus ad quem* (point of arrival) in a theory of infinite human worth. Hence the ringing conclusion to the second *Critique,* in which Kant observes that although the human being must recognize its finitude as a member of "the external world of sense," it is also given to comprehend its legitimate membership as a moral being in "a world which has true infinity." And while the former perspective reduces the human being to a "mere speck" in the causal nexus and thereby "annihilates . . . my importance as an animal creature," the latter perspective "infinitely raises my worth" and "reveals a life independent of all animality and even of the whole world of sense."[23] Cassirer's complaint— that Heidegger neglects a key theme in Kant's philosophy insofar as he gives no room to the "infinite" worth of the human being as a moral agent— seems undeniably correct. But of course the disputation was not merely about how to read Kant. As I have noted already, it is crucial that we see how the discussion about how best to interpret Kant's philosophy served as an occasion for an original confrontation—a fact which would grow increasingly evident as the debate unfolded.

Terminus a quo, Terminus ad quem

In the following remarks, Cassirer first paused to summarize his criticism so far and then posed a direct challenge to his interlocutor: keeping in mind that Heidegger had emphasized the radical finitude of human understanding, could Heidegger nonetheless explain how it is that human beings come to possess nonrelative truth and objective knowledge? It is worth noting that this challenge was no longer limited to ethics alone: Cassirer had shifted from the particular problems of practical reason to the more global problems of "reason" and "knowledge" as such. His question was especially urgent insofar as Heidegger had correctly identified human finitude as the "starting point" (or *terminus a quo*) of Kantian philosophy: The essential pathos of human reason, as Kant explains in the first *Critique,* is that it is burdened with questions that, due to its own constitutive limits, it can never answer to its complete satisfaction, yet which, due to that very same constitution, it can also never renounce.[24] In this sense Heidegger was right to discover in Kant's philosophy a theory of human finitude. But the well-known Kantian theory concerning the limits of human reason hardly prevented Kant from developing a robust theory allowing for objectively valid knowledge; instead, the key lesson of transcendental idealism was that *it is precisely in virtue of its own constitution* that human reason is indeed *justified* in its claims to objective knowledge. Thus on Cassirer's view Heidegger was perhaps right to identify finitude as the starting point of Kantian philosophy, but he was mistaken when he insisted that Kant's "groundlaying for metaphysics" never moves beyond its point of departure, for transcendental idealism reached its true culmination and its so-called point of arrival *(terminus ad quem)* with a theory that was supposed to justify the human claim to objective truth and experience:

> *Cassirer:* Summary: This expansion was therefore necessary because there is a problem at its core: Heidegger has emphasized that our power of knowledge is finite. It is relative and it is fixed.

> But then the question arises: how does such a finite creature
> as such come to have knowledge, to have reason, to have
> truth? And now to the pertinent questions. At one point
> Heidegger poses the problem of truth and says: there can be
> no truths in themselves, nor can there be any eternal truths
> at all. Rather, insofar as they occur in general, truths are
> relative to Dasein. And now it follows: A finite creature
> cannot in general possess eternal truths. [*Ein endliches
> Wesen kann überhaupt ewige Wahrheiten nicht besitzen.*]
> For human beings there are no eternal and necessary truths,
> and here the whole problem again erupts: For Kant, the
> problem was precisely: Without prejudice to the finitude
> that Kant himself exhibited, how can there nonetheless be
> necessary and universal truths [*notwendige und allgemeine
> Wahrheiten*]?

To understand Cassirer's remarks, we should recall that a central task of the
first *Critique* was to explain how judgments about the empirical world could
be valid across all possible empirical experience such that they could be said
to exhibit both universality and necessity. Hence Kant's guiding question:
"How are synthetic, a priori judgments possible?" The question was especially urgent because Kant believed that a special class of mathematical
judgments served as the requisite conceptual instruments for natural scientific explanation.[25] Judgments of this kind were said to be nonanalytic (that
is, the predicate was not simply contained in the subject), yet also enjoyed
the status of knowledge a priori (that is, their truth was ascertained independent of empirical experience). The difficulty confronting this task was
that no such judgments could possibly be justified by appealing to what is
merely given through the senses. It thus seemed that the entire foundation
of the modern sciences stood vulnerable to skepticism. The special, a priori
yet synthetic status of mathematical knowledge thus served as a crucial
premise for Kant's theoretical philosophy. Yet the solution Kant proffered
would demand a thoroughgoing revolution in the very meaning of objectivity. Thus in his *Prolegomena to Any Future Metaphysics* Kant warned readers
from rashly assuming that a mathematical judgment could be a mere "fig-
ment of our poetic fantasy," that is, a product of unrestrained imagination.[26]

He affirmed instead that mathematical propositions do indeed possess "objective reality" in the special sense that they are necessarily valid for *all possible experience.* He also warned that such propositions were valid *only* for all possible experience. For human beings, this meant that their validity was confined solely to the conditions under which our experience is possible, namely, within the bounds of time and space as pure forms of intuition. It is this conclusion that motivated Kant's more global doctrine of transcendental idealism, according to which objectivity for human knowledge can only mean the objectivity of knowledge within the bounds of possible experience.[27] In his response to Heidegger, Cassirer offered a very brief summary of this philosophical background before once again pressing his interlocutor to respond to the essential concern:

> *Cassirer:* How are synthetic, a priori judgments possible—judgments
> that are not simply finite in their content, but that are
> necessarily universal? It is therefore because of this problem
> that Kant exemplifies mathematics: Finite knowledge places
> itself in a relationship to truth that does not develop anew
> an "only." Heidegger said that Kant gave no proof for the
> possibility of mathematics. I believe that the question was
> well posed in the *Prolegomena,* but it is not and it cannot be
> the only question. But this pure theoretical question must
> first be clarified: How does this finite creature come to a
> determination of objects that as such are not bound to
> finitude? Now my question is the following: Does Heidegger
> want to renounce this entire objectivity, this form of
> absoluteness that Kant advocated in the ethical and the
> theoretical, as well as in the *Critique of Judgment?* Does he
> want to withdraw completely to the finite creature [*Will er
> sich ganz zurückziehen auf das endliche Wesen*] or, if not,
> where for him is the breakthrough [*Durchbruch*] to this
> sphere? I ask this question because I really do not yet know.
> The fixing of the point of transit, then, lies first with
> Heidegger. I believe, however, that Heidegger cannot be
> capable of abiding by it, nor can he want to. He must first

pose these questions to himself, and then, I believe, whole
new problems emerge.

For Cassirer, it was evident that, just as Kant had preserved the objectivity
of moral concepts, so, too, his transcendental argument for the a priori synthetic status of mathematical knowledge preserved its objective character.
Both ethical *and* theoretical reason thereby achieved a "breakthrough" to the
objective sphere of universal and necessary knowledge. Heidegger, however,
permitted no such breakthrough to objectivity; his philosophy remained incorrigibly bound to the sphere of the human being as a "finite creature."

For Cassirer it was clear that Heidegger's failure to embrace an objective
realm beyond human finitude signaled a violent deviation from the actual
precepts of Kantian philosophy. But whether this verdict was altogether justified remains uncertain. After all, it is a cardinal rule of Kant's theoretical
philosophy that human knowledge cannot trespass the bounds of possible
experience. One might therefore argue that according to Kant's own principles, what goes by the name of *objective* knowledge must itself retain an
ineliminable bond to those conditions of sensible intuition by which beings
of finite cognitive capability are permitted to know the world at all. If such
an inference is correct, then it seems at least prima facie plausible for Heidegger to have claimed that Kant himself never sought anything like a genuine "breakthrough" to a realm of objectivity unconditioned by human finitude. Cassirer's question—"Does Heidegger want to renounce this entire
objectivity?"—might therefore seem like an attempt to drive a wedge between a putatively Kantian objectivism and a Heideggerian subjectivism
when in fact no such divide could be found.

Cassirer himself would of course have disputed any such inference as
wildly off the mark. During the Davos encounter, he offered little explanation as to why he believed Heidegger's existential revision of Kantian principles failed to achieve the proper sort of objectivity. The precise arguments
for this charge would only take shape in the following months when Cassirer put the final touches on the third volume of *The Philosophy of Symbolic
Forms, The Phenomenology of Knowledge,* completed in July 1929.[28] Though
these arguments will be discussed in detail in Chapter 5, here one should
note that Cassirer would come to regard the Heideggerian existentials of

space and time as valid but merely provisional: what Heidegger described as the local or subjective-pragmatic ("ready-to-hand") modes of spatiotemporal understanding were acceptable, but *only* if they were seen as merely the starting point, or *terminus a quo,* for human knowledge. Cassirer's own inquiry took the existential modes of space-time as given and took up an analysis of the pure *forms* of space-time, the proper domain of which was the higher sphere of objectivity, the *terminus ad quem* that lay, in Cassirer's words, *"beyond the existentiality of 'being-there.'"*[29]

During the actual *Arbeitsgemeinschaft,* however, Cassirer failed to elaborate on his charge that Heidegger had surrendered the objectivism Kant wished to secure. Heidegger continued to insist that the compulsion to establish a species of "objective knowledge" (modeled on mathematical natural science) was little more than neo-Kantian dogma and had nothing to do with Kant's genuine aims. How one resolves this perplexity depends entirely, of course, on whether one regards Heidegger's Kant-interpretation as a faithful exposition or as a willful imposition of exotic claims. But reaching a settlement on this issue was by no means a simple matter of textual evidence. In fact, for those at Davos who had listened closely to Heidegger's exposition on the first *Critique* as a "groundlaying for metaphysics," it was by now obvious that he considered the very ideal of a faithful exposition as deeply naïve. After all, an effort at brute reconstruction would miss the fact that Kant himself was at war with his own intentions and that he had been led "to the brink of a position from which he had to shrink back." To remain at the level of mere reconstruction was thus to assure that the deeper historical significance of Kant's philosophy remained hidden. What was required was not a mere *reconstruction* but a genuine *destruction,* because ostensibly only the latter could reveal the true significance of Kant's philosophy within the larger history of Western metaphysics. It thus seems fair to say that the ultimate effect of Cassirer's challenge was to insist on the sharp distinction between reconstructive and destructive modes of interpretation. At stake in this distinction, Cassirer believed, was Kant's own investment in the objective status of mathematical and ethical knowledge, an objectivity Heidegger seemed ready to abandon so as to overcome reason's historical-metaphysical supremacy.

More broadly, we may conclude that with Cassirer's challenge the disputation had now entered a new phase: the participants would no longer focus their attention primarily on the question of how best to interpret Kant's philosophy. The question that consumed them from this point forward was the question that had consumed them all along, even if it remained unstated until now: Of what significance were Kantian themes for today? Which interpretative legacy possessed the greater authority within the terrain of contemporary European thought? Whose interpretation of the Kantian inheritance grasped with greater power and conviction the most vital insights of the philosophical past, insights that would also prove viable for philosophy's future?

Ontology and Angels

In his initial response to Cassirer's challenge, Heidegger said very little about his own philosophical commitments and instead cleaved to the interpretive question as to whether the neo-Kantians properly understood Kant's problematic. On the neo-Kantian view, Kant was aiming at a theory of "nature" understood as the realm available to mathematical-scientific inquiry. Heidegger now objected to this cherished piece of neo-Kantian doctrine on the grounds that Kant actually meant to lay down a prior and more global theory of Being, in which nature was understood as merely one region of entities, the field of the merely occurrent or "present-at-hand" (Vorhanden). Kant's larger purpose was therefore to develop nothing less than a "general metaphysics," or *Metaphysica Generalis:*

> *Heidegger:* First of all, to the question of the mathematical natural sciences. One can say that Nature, as a region of beings, was for Kant not just any such region. For Kant, Nature never signifies: the object of mathematical-natural science. Rather, the being of Nature is a being in the sense of what is at hand [*das Seiende im Sinne des Vorhandenen*]. In the Doctrine of Principles, what Kant really wanted to give is not a categorical, structural doctrine of the object of mathematical-natural science. What he wanted was a theory of beings in general. (Heidegger supports this [transciption remark].) Kant sought a theory of Being in general, without assuming objects that were given, without assuming a determinate region of beings (either

psychic or physical). He sought a general ontology that
exists prior to an ontology of nature as the object of
natural science and prior to an ontology of nature as the
object of psychology. What I want to point out is that the
Analytic is not just an ontology of nature as the object of
natural science, but is rather a general ontology, a critical,
well-established *Metaphysica Generalis.* Kant himself says:
the problematic of the *Prolegomena,* where he consequently illustrates how natural science is possible, and so
on, is not the central motive. Rather, the central motive is
the question concerning the possibility of *Metaphysica
Generalis,* or rather the carrying out of the same.

In this passage Heidegger was apparently paraphrasing Kant's remarks from
the third chapter of the first *Critique,* the "Doctrine of Method on the Architectonic of Pure Reason," which contains a systematic map of the various
tasks and domains of philosophical inquiry: Metaphysics in general, Kant
observes, is the study of a priori cognition. The "narrower" species of metaphysics, the metaphysics of nature, "considers everything insofar as it is (not
that which ought to be) on the basis of a priori concepts."[30] And this species
of metaphysics is in turn divided into transcendental philosophy and the
physiology of pure reason. Kant goes on to explain that transcendental philosophy "considers only the understanding and reason itself in a system of
all concepts and principles that are related to objects in general, without assuming objects that would be given *(Ontologia).*" The physiology of reason,
by contrast, "considers nature, i.e., the sum total of given objects (whether
they are given by the senses, or, if one will, by another kind of intuition)."
But the rational study of nature is further subdivided into "immanent" and
"transcendent" modes of study, the former applying only to objects of experience, the latter to objects that surpass all experience, whether "inner"
(concerning the cosmos) or "outer" (concerning God). With these distinctions in place, Kant would eventually suggest that the entire discipline of
metaphysics breaks down into no fewer than four subfields of inquiry:
ontology, rational physiology, rational cosmology, and rational theology.
While the details of this complex taxonomy need not concern us here, we
must take note of the most crucial implication: what goes by the name of

"nature" is *only one subdomain* within the general discipline of metaphysics. Heidegger's point was that the neo-Kantian emphasis on the "given" objects of mathematical-scientific nature remained far too narrow and did an injustice to Kant's broader metaphysical purposes.

Against Heidegger, however, one might note that in the first *Critique* Kant states plainly and with some frequency that he is *not* interested in the larger project of metaphysics that might concern purely speculative or ontological claims about beings irrespective of whether or how those beings are given. In the Transcendental Analytic, for example, Kant notes that the principles of the understanding "can never overstep the limits of sensibility, within which alone objects are given to us." Kant thus *denies* a legitimate place in his book to a purely generic *ontology* (in Latin, *Ontologia*). The principles of the understanding "are merely principles of the exposition of appearances, and the proud name of an ontology, which presumes to offer synthetic a priori cognitions of things in general in a systematic doctrine (e.g., the doctrine of causality), must give way to the modest one of a mere analytic of the understanding."[31] Thus while it is true that Kant acknowledges a general discipline of ontology, his epistemological restriction that the *Critique* can address appearances only would seem to contradict Heidegger's proposal that Kant meant to offer a broader ontology, a theory of Being as such. On this point at least, the textual evidence seems clearly to support Cassirer's neo-Kantian interpretation.

It is here that one could begin to discern the deeper truth, as Heidegger himself would later acknowledge, that the Kant-interpretation Heidegger presented at Davos served as merely a pretext for expounding his own philosophy. In the fourth edition of *Kant and the Problem of Metaphysics* (1973), Heidegger would candidly call his book an "overinterpretation" *(Überdeutung),* and he would admit that Kant's critical question was "foreign" to the question of Being. This estrangement—the actual divide between Kant and Heidegger—was readily apparent at Davos once Heidegger turned away from the epistemological discussion and began to expound on themes more closely associated with his own existential ontology. For suddenly we are in the company of angels:

Heidegger: But now to the other problem, that of the power of
imagination. Cassirer wants to show that finitude becomes

transcendent in the ethical writings.—In the Categorical
Imperative we have something that goes beyond the finite
creature. But precisely the concept of the Imperative as
such shows the inner reference to a finite creature. Also,
this going-beyond to something higher is always just a
going-beyond to the finite creature, to one which is created
(angel). This transcendence too still remains within
creatureliness [*Geschopflichkeit*] and finitude. This inner
relation, which lies within the Imperative itself, and the
finitude of ethics, emerges from a passage in which Kant
speaks of human reason as self-supporting, that is, of a
reason that stands purely on its own and that cannot
escape into something eternal or absolute, but that also
cannot escape into the world of things. This being-there-
between [*Dieses Dazwischen*] is the essence of Practical
Reason.

Cassirer had claimed that the ethical "leads beyond" the world of appearances and achieves a genuine "breakthrough" to a *mundus intelligibilus,* a
purely intellectual reality that is "no longer relative to the finitude of the
knowing creature." To this Heidegger now objected that even in practical
reason there remains an ineliminable bond to human finitude. Indeed, the
categorical imperative retains its validity *only for a finite creature:*

Heidegger: I believe that we proceed mistakenly in the interpretation
of Kantian ethics if we first orient ourselves to that to
which ethical action conforms and if we see too little of
the inner function of the law itself for Dasein. We cannot
discuss the problem of the finitude of the ethical creature
if we do not pose the question: what does law mean here,
and how is the lawfulness itself constitutive for Dasein
and for the personality? It is not to be denied that something that goes beyond sensibility lies before the law. But
the question is: How is the inner structure of Dasein itself,
is it finite or infinite [*Wie ist die innere Struktur des
Daseins selbst, ist sie endlich, oder unendlich*]?

In developing these claims Heidegger seemed to have in mind the famous passage from the *Critique of Practical Reason* in which Kant draws attention to the human being's feeling of "respect for the moral law."[32] This feeling provides the human being with a *subjective interest* or *incentive* for obedience to the moral law (the categorical imperative that one act only such that the maxim of one's will could hold as a universal law). But such notions—incentive, interest, and maxim—retain their meaning *only* on the condition that there remains a distinction between the subjective will and the objective law of practical reason. They therefore necessarily cannot apply to a "divine will" but "only to finite beings."[33] This was apparently the proof-text for Heidegger's suggestion that the very concept of an imperative referred exclusively to a finite creature. On Heidegger's view, Cassirer was therefore wrong to claim that in practical reason humanity finds a means of transcending its own constitutive limits.

The parenthetical reference to an angel is ambiguous. We cannot know from the transcript whether it was meant to reinforce Heidegger's claim that the categorical imperative applies *only* to a finite and created being (because the angel, too, might qualify as created), or whether it was meant instead as a counterexample concerning the sort of divine being who might be exempted from the categorical imperative (because an angel might qualify as divine). Elsewhere in the second *Critique* Kant suggests that the moral law must hold for "all finite beings that have reason and will" (and it holds even for "the Infinite Being," though in this case the moral does not take the form of an imperative).[34] The suggestion provoked Schopenhauer's well-known quip that "Kant here gave a thought to the dear little angels," an unwarranted appeal, in Schopenhauer's view, to a wholly imaginary class of nonhuman rational beings the purpose of which was simply to buttress Kant's dogmatic faith in reason as the indestructible essence of the human being.[35] We may assume both Heidegger and Cassirer were familiar with Schopenhauer's remark, but this hardly explains what Heidegger intended with his rather oblique reference. The ambiguity may be partly resolved if we recall the remarks on angels from the *Anthropology from a Pragmatic Point of View*, where Kant notes that the human imagination lacks sufficient creative power to represent nonhuman but rational agents: when a painter or sculptor tries to portray a higher rational being (such as an angel or a god), he or she will typically endow that being with a human form, a strategy Kant ascribes to a weakness of the imagination.[36] And in *Religion within the Limits of Reason Alone,* Kant cites Haller's poetic dictum that "The world with all its faults/Is better than a realm of will-less angels."[37] Whatever Heidegger's meaning, we should note that the very concept of an angel seems especially ambiguous because it is at once created *and* divine; it thereby provides a perfect illustration for what Heidegger called the "being-there-between" of all created life. In other words, *even if* angels are by their own nature exempt from this intermediary status, we *still* cannot conceive of them without binding them to the constraints of embodiment and finitude that are distinctively our lot as human beings.

Heidegger would again invoke the angel as a symbol of incorrigible "betweenness" in his lecture "What Are Poets For?" given in 1946 on the twentieth anniversary of the poet's death. There Heidegger described the angel from Rilke's *Duino Elegies* as an exemplary being who represents for humanity an alternative to its frenetic attempts at self-assertion and financial gain. The angel instead achieves a rare and exceptional "balance" within the "worldly whole of the Open." Humanity, too, can turn "unshieldedness" into "the Open" and so discover its own balance within "the world's inner space."[38] The crucial theme here would seem to be that *angel* is a name for the holistic understanding of the Being of beings, and it might therefore serve as a paradigm for human beings to follow as they attempt to dwell more authentically in the "between" space of worldly existence. This theme (notwithstanding its poetic opacity) seems continuous with Heidegger's earlier comments at Davos regarding the shared moral experience that unites the human being and the angel. Whatever the ambiguities of this symbolism, it seems clear that Heidegger wished to say that for humanity our finitude stands as an impassable horizon, even and perhaps especially when we conceive of moral codes that appear to transcend our existence.

God, Finitude, Truth

As the debate unfolded, Heidegger grew ever more insistent that, throughout Kant's philosophy, a certain unbreachable finitude governs its conception of the human being. Given this interpretation, it is neither surprising nor insignificant that Heidegger appealed to religious illustrations, such as the angel, to confirm his thesis. His scholastic education and his early work in the phenomenology of religion as applied to both Augustinian and Pauline texts had left him with an acute sensitivity for the theological heritage of modern philosophical categories. Indeed, in a 1921 letter to his student Karl Löwith, Heidegger went so far as to describe himself as a "Christian Theo-*logian*."[39] It is, of course, generally acknowledged that by the late 1920s, his doctrinal commitment to Christianity had relaxed considerably, but he nonetheless retained a pronounced interest in themes of an originally theological provenance. As late as 1953, he could still make reference to the "piety" of thinking.[40] The religious dimension of Heidegger's work was in any case self-evident to those who offered commentaries on the Davos disputation.[41] For those present at Davos, this impression was perhaps heightened thanks to the Jesuit Erich Przywara, whose lectures deployed Heideggerian existential methods for expressly religious ends. Nor was Cassirer unaware of his interlocutor's continued bond with religion. As noted in Chapter 3, Cassirer's lectures on Max Scheler's Catholic phenomenology were widely seen as an implicit critique of Heidegger. And in the years following the exchange at Davos, Cassirer would claim that Heidegger's philosophy carried a species of mythic-religious fatalism (a charge I will examine in further detail in Chapter 6).

Especially in the middle phase of the discussion, Heidegger made use of theological language to illustrate his claims. At first it may have seemed Heidegger used these illustrations only to bring out a logical contrast: the very idea of human finitude presupposes an idea of infinity. Thus in *Kant and the Problem of Metaphysics* Heidegger called attention to the difference between "divine knowing" and human knowledge through sensible intuition: Divine knowing is an intuition that "first creates the intuitable being." But such an intuition seizes on Being as a whole without the mediation of concepts. "Thinking as such," Heidegger concluded, "is thus already the mark of finitude." The contrast was sharp: finite knowledge is "delivered over to the being which already is" whereas infinite knowledge actually *creates* rather than merely *conforms to* that which it knows. The conformity of finite knowledge is "an intuition that takes things in stride" [*hinnehmende Anschauung*] and as such it exhibits a "dependency on" [*Angewiesenheit auf*] a worldliness it has not created.[42] At Davos, Heidegger articulated these claims with liberal use of Kantian teminology:

Heidegger: In this question of the going-beyond of finitude, there lies
a quite central problem. I have said it is a particular
question to ask about the possibility of finitude as such.
For one can argue simply in a formal fashion: As soon as
I make assertions about the finite and as soon as I want to
determine the finite as finite [*als Endliches*], I must already
have an idea of infinitude [*Unendlichkeit*]. For the moment
this does not say much. And yet it suffices to say that here
before us there lies a central problem. From the fact that
now this character of infinitude comes to light precisely in
what we have emphasized as the constitutive feature of
finitude [*als das Konstitutivum der Endlichkeit*], I want to
make it clear that I would say: Kant describes the power of
imagination of the Schematism as *exhibitio originaria*.
But this originality is an *exhibitio,* an *exhibitio* of the
presentation of the free self-giving in which there lies a
dependency upon a taking-in-stride [*eine Angewiesenheit
auf ein Hinnehmen*]. So in a certain sense this originality
is indeed there as creative faculty. As a finite creature, the
human being has a certain infinitude in the ontological.
But the human being is never infinite and absolute in the
creating of the being itself; rather, it is infinite in the sense
of the understanding of Being.

Above, Heidegger once again referred to the *Anthropology,* where Kant de-
fines the imagination as "a faculty of intuition without the presence of an
object." The imagination can be either *productive* or *reproductive:* that is, it
can be either a faculty for the production of the object that precedes any
actual experience, which Kant calls "the original presentation of the object" (in Latin, *exhibitio originaria*), or it can be a faculty for "the derivative
presentation of the object," which is to say it "brings back to the mind an
empirical intuition that it had previously" *(exhibitio derivativa).*[43] Now, Kant
claims that pure intuitions of space and time require the *productive* imagination, whereas all empirical intuitions require only the *reproductive* imagination. But Heidegger insisted that *although* the pure intuitions are original,
they *nonetheless* involve the "presentation" of an intuition to the mind.

And in this sense they require a certain dependency upon what is given, or, in other words, a "taking-in-stride" of the intuition as it is received. With this observation Heidegger meant to emphasize once again the *constitutive finitude of the human being.*[44] The human being cannot *create* what there is but instead remains *dependent* on that which is given for any and all understanding.[45] Even if it is true that the understanding of Being involves a certain creativity (because the pure forms of space and time are born from the mind itself), this seeming "infinitude" is valid *only* within our experience of what is given. This is our distinction as human beings, and it indicates the radical division between ourselves and God. Heidegger continued thus:

> *Heidegger:* But provided, as Kant says, that the ontological understanding of Being is only possible within the inner experience of beings, this infinitude of the ontological is bound essentially to ontic experience so that we must say the reverse: this infinitude that breaks out in the power of imagination is precisely the strongest argument for finitude. For ontology is an index of finitude. God does not have it. And the fact that the human being has the *exhibitio* is the strongest argument for its finitude, for ontology requires only a finite creature.

An infinite being such as God would have no need for an understanding of Being, Heidegger claimed, because God would understand the whole of what there is in a single act of unmediated and unbounded intuition. The understanding of Being—ontology—was therefore a distinctively human endowment.

This argument recalled the famous introductory statements from *Being and Time* that an "*understanding of Being is itself a definite characteristic of Dasein's Being*" and that Dasein is indeed "ontically distinguished by the fact that, in its very Being, that Being is an *issue* for it."[46] But why did Heidegger speak of God at all? At this point one might ask whether the notion of a divine understanding was truly necessary to Heidegger's argument or whether it instead served merely as a counterexample to human finitude. The question is not easily resolved, but it is at least illuminating that Heidegger introduced his theological example only to illustrate what human beings are *not*. The constant attention to human finitude carries the pathos it does in part because it stands in starkest contrast to a different, religiously derived vision of the cosmos in which humanity might at least hope for the metaphysical security of divinely given grace. It should be obvious, in other words, that Heidegger's vision of human finitude does not logically *require* God's reality. It requires only the notional *contrast* to an alternate way of being so as to deepen our understanding of the kinds of beings we are. Heidegger would make precisely this point in his private notes responding to criticism of the Kant-book by Cassirer and Odebrecht (see "Heidegger's Response" in Chapter 6).

Heidegger's further comments veered sharply from theology to the problem of truth. Cassirer had suggested that Heidegger had abandoned the possibility of eternal and necessary truths and that truth thereby lost its nonrelative character and became merely "relative to Dasein." To this Heidegger offered a long and complex response:

> *Heidegger:* Then Cassirer's counterquestion with reference to the concept of truth is elevated in importance. For Kant, ontological knowledge is what is universally necessary, what all factical experiences anticipate, and in connection with this I might point out that in other passages Kant says that what makes experience possible, the inner possibility of ontological knowledge, is accidental.—Truth itself is unified with the structure of transcendence on the most intimate level in order for Dasein to be a being open to others and to itself. We are a being that holds itself in the unconcealedness of beings. [*Wir sind ein Seiendes, das sich in der Unverborgenheit von Seiendem hält.*] To hold oneself in this way in the openness of beings is what I describe as Being-in-truth [*In-der-Wahrheit-sein*], and I go further and say: On the grounds of the finitude of the being-in-truth of human beings, there exists at the same time a being-in-untruth [*In-der-Unwahrheit-sein*]. Un-truth belongs to the innermost core of the structure of Dasein. And I believe here to have found for the first time

the root upon which Kant's metaphysical "illusion"
["*Schein*"] is metaphysically grounded.

This answer referred back to Heidegger's effort in *Being and Time* to revise the traditional concept of truth as correspondence with a more "primordial" account of truth as unhiddenness.[47] As Heidegger explained, truth is conventionally defined as an *adequatio intellectus et rei*: a correspondence between a thought and the thing to which it refers. But any such correspondence presupposes that the phenomenon must show itself as being in some way or another. This showing of the phenomenon is the "being-uncoveredness," or *Entdeckt-sein,* of the entity in question. In Aristotelian language, it is the *Aletheia,* the unveiling of the entity's way of being. Thus on Heidegger's view this uncoveredness or unhiddenness *(Unverborgenheit)* deserves the title of primordial truth because a prior uncoveredness of the phenomenon is a necessary *precondition* for truth as correspondence.[48] It is the distinction of Dasein as the being whose very transcendence (or ontological understanding) permits the world to show itself that Dasein finds itself open to the unconcealedness of beings. Because "Dasein *is* its disclosedness," it follows that "*Dasein is 'in the truth.'*"[49] Yet Heidegger also believes that human existence is marked by a nearly irresistible drive to lose oneself in public interpretations that do violence to the truth of phenomena. This tendency, which Heidegger called *Verfallen,* or *falling,* is said to distort and disguise that which has been disclosed. It follows that Dasein exists simultaneously "in truth" and "in 'untruth.'"[50] Almost as an afterthought, Heidegger added that this notion of untruth might also cast a better light on the Kantian notion of metaphysical illusion, the so-called *dialectic* whereby one falsely ascribes objective spatiotemporal reality to concepts that transcend any possible experience. The apparent similarity is that in both cases—dialectic and falling—human comprehension was said to suffer the peculiar fate that it exhibits an almost inevitable propensity for metaphysical error: it attributes to phenomena a spurious objectivity when in fact what is disclosed for human understanding is conditional upon the finitude of our own capacities.

Heidegger now explained that, because human existence is the condition for the disclosure of phenomena, it follows that truth is relative to and dependent on the human being: There could be no truth without Dasein's disclosure of truth. This does not mean there could be no "transsubjective" truths, that is, truths that hold their validity across all human beings. But it is important to acknowledge that, because Dasein's own being-in-truth is also the disclosure of its world, human existence is itself implicated in and could be transformed by the event of disclosure:

> *Heidegger:* Now to Cassirer's question concerning universally valid eternal truths. If I say: truth is relative to Dasein, this is no ontic assertion of the sort in which I say: the true is always only what the individual human being thinks. Rather, this statement is a metaphysical one: in general, truth can only be as truth, and as truth it only has a sense in general if Dasein exists. If Dasein does not exist, there is no truth, and then there is nothing at all. But with the existence of something like Dasein, truth first comes in Dasein itself. Now, however, is the question: How does it stand with the validity of the eternality of truth? With respect to the problem of validity, this question always orients us toward the previously expressed statement, and from there, we find values or the like. I believe that the problem must be unraveled in another way. Truth is relative to Dasein. That is not to say that there would be no possibility for everyone to make the entity manifest as it is. But I would say that this transsubjectivity of truth, this breaking out of the truth concerning the individual itself as being-in-truth, already means to be at the mercy of the entity itself, to be displaced into the possibility to form itself [*es selbst zu gestalten*].

It is evident that such claims could no longer be understood primarily in reference to Kant. Heidegger now in fact explained his own philosophical views on truth, Dasein, and temporality: Dasein, he explained, is the condition for primordial truth as disclosure. It followed that truth in this sense is *relative to Dasein*. But Dasein's "inner transcendence" (i.e., Dasein's understanding of the Being of entities) is only possible within the temporal horizon that belongs to Dasein's very essence as being-in-the-world. Now, if a nonrelative truth is supposed to be *that which just is the case* notwithstanding changes in local experience, it becomes clear that even what counts as "eternal truth" must show up within Dasein's temporal horizon as a certain "permanence" (in the Greek, ἀεί or "forever"). Even in the case of an apparently eternal truth, therefore, Dasein's temporality is not and cannot be dispensed with:

> *Heidegger:* What is redeemable here as objective knowledge has, according to the respective, factical, individual existence, a truth-content, which, as content, says something about the being. The peculiar validity of which he spoke is poorly interpreted if we say: In contrast to the flow of experience there is a permanence, the eternal, the sense, and concept. I pose the counterquestion: What, then, does the eternal actually mean here? From where, then, do we know of this eternity? Is this eternity not just permanence in the sense of the ἀεί [Gr., "forever"] of time? Is this eternality not just that which is possible on the grounds of an inner transcendence of time itself? My whole interpretation of temporality has the metaphysical intention of asking: Are all these headings from transcendental metaphysics, namely a priori, ἀεί ὄν, οὐσία [Gr., being that always is] accidental, or from where do they come? If they speak of the eternal, how are they to be understood? They are only to be understood and are only possible owing to the fact that an inner transcendence lies within the essence of time; that time is not just what makes transcendence possible, but that time itself has in itself a horizonal character; that in future, recollected behavior I always have at the same time a horizon with respect to the present, futurity, and pastness in general; that a transcendental, ontological determination of time is found here, within which something like the permanence of the substance is constituted for the first time.—My whole interpretation of temporality is to be understood from this point of view.

Heidegger's argument here was directed squarely against Cassirer's previous statement that through reason, human beings are capable of grasping certain truths that stand above and beyond our finite-temporal horizon. Heidegger wished to claim instead that the very notion of a permanent truth, along with its metaphysical correlative of permanent substance, is only conceivable *within* our temporal horizon. Indeed, ontological understanding *as such,* that is, *any disclosure of oneself and one's world,* is founded upon the temporality that belongs to the human being as the very essence of its being-in-the-world. And these, Heidegger noted, are precisely the claims developed at great length in *Being and Time.* The perception of his work as merely another variant of philosophical anthropology (as Cassirer had implied in his lectures) was therefore mistaken:

> *Heidegger:* And in order to emphasize this inner structure of tempo-
> rality and in order to show that time is not just a setting in
> which experiences play themselves out to make manifest
> this innermost character of temporality in Dasein itself,
> the effort made in my book is required. Every page in this
> book was written solely with a view to the fact that since
> antiquity the problem of Being was interpreted on the
> basis of time in a wholly comprehensible sense and that
> time was always assigned to the subject. With a view to the
> connection of this question to time, with a view to the
> question concerning Being in general, it is first a matter of
> bringing out the temporality of Dasein, not in the sense
> that is now worked out with any theory, but rather in the
> sense that, in a wholly determined problematic, the
> question concerning human Dasein will be posed.—This
> whole problematic in *Being and Time,* which treats Dasein
> in man, is no philosophical anthropology. For that it is
> much too narrow, much too preliminary.

For Heidegger the suggestion that his labors to date were little more than an elaboration of themes deriving from philosophical anthropology was not just mistaken, it also grievously diminished the philosophical significance of his work. As we have seen in the preceding chapters, Heidegger acknowledged the recently deceased Max Scheler as an important source of inspiration, and shortly after returning from Davos he dedicated *Kant and the Problem of Metaphysics* to Scheler's memory. But the claims set forth in Heidegger's own philosophy were by no means limited to anthropological speculations on the meaning of human life, problems of human culture, history, and the like. It was therefore a matter of some urgency for Heidegger to specify that although existential ontology offered deep insights into various problems of human experience, its aims were in fact directed primarily toward what Heidegger called the "Dasein in man." The phrase is noteworthy because it implies a distinction between *ontic* considerations regarding the human being as an entity and *ontological* considerations regarding the human *manner of being* the entity which it is. The former could be a legitimate subject for philosophical anthropology; the latter required tools and methods uniquely its own. In *Being and Time* Heidegger had insisted upon this distinction and thus concluded that anthropology along with psychology and biology all failed to give an "ontologically adequate" response to the question concerning the "*kind of Being* which belongs to those entities which we ourselves are."[51] It is nevertheless hard to overlook the fact that as the debate proceeded, both Heidegger and Cassirer grew increasingly bold in speaking to the broader anthropological and cultural ramifications of their disagreement. Their concepts ramified, and as they did, so too the arguments transfigured, perhaps notwithstanding the philosophers' own intentions, into opposed and possibly irreconcilable "worldviews," as we shall see below.

Anxiety, Culture, Freedom

As an overture to these broader themes, Heidegger began with the suggestion that the temporal character of the *Seinsverständnis,* or understanding of Being, might cast light on our "comportment toward entities," that is, the specific manner by which human beings relate to the objects around them. And this, in turn, might eventually help us toward understanding the "historical occurrence in the world history of the human being." But all of this required a preparatory analysis of the temporality of human being itself, for which a key theme would be the anticipatory phenomenon of "being-toward-death."

As Heidegger had explained already in *Being and Time,* a rigorous analysis of Dasein's temporality begins from the fact that human beings cannot make sense of a given comportment without some sense of what that activity is meant to achieve. This means that a comportment necessarily has an *anticipatory* structure: it can only be the comportment it is if it makes reference to the future. In Heidegger's terminology, this means that Dasein is always "ahead-of-itself." Now, if one wants to inquire about the being of Dasein *as such* we find that this question can only be answered with reference to the *entirety* of Dasein's existence, that is, Dasein's "being-a-whole." One's own death is a future possibility of complete individuation that every person must experience only for him- or herself. But because it puts an end to the Dasein that is in each case "mine," death itself cannot be an object of phenomenological reflection. The possibility for understanding oneself as a whole can therefore emerge only from the *anticipation* of death, the future-directed or *"not-yet"* structure Heidegger called *Being-toward-death.* Heidegger therefore insisted that his phenomenological treatment of death and anxiety should not be mistaken for morbid fascination, nor for an anthropological commentary on the centrality of death for human experience. Rather, the anticipatory anxiety of Being-toward-death lights up the temporal primacy of the *future* within Dasein's ontological structure:

Heidegger: I believe that there is a problem here of a kind that
hitherto has not been brought up as such, a problem that
has been determined by means of the question: If the
possibility of the understanding of Being, along with
the possibility of the transcendence of the human being,
the possibility of the formative comportment toward
entities and of the historical occurrence in the world
history of the human being itself is supposed to be
possible, and if this possibility has been grounded in an
understanding of Being, and if this ontological understanding has been oriented in some sense with respect to
time, then the task is this: to bring out the temporality of
Dasein with reference to the possibility of the understanding of Being. And it is with respect to this that all problems are oriented. The analysis of death has the function,

from one perspective, of bringing out the radical futurity
of Dasein but not of producing an altogether final and
metaphysical thesis concerning the essence of death.

All of these claims were already laid out with some precision in *Being and Time*. However, shortly *after* the Davos disputation, in his inaugural lecture at Freiburg, "What Is Metaphysics?" (composed in 1928, but presented publicly on July 24, 1929), Heidegger would add an additional explanation concerning the importance of anxiety for ontological inquiry.[52] Heidegger argued that when one is seized by anxiety one discovers that "beings as a whole slip away," for anxiety is not fear for one thing or another but a general apprehension in the face of existence as a whole. Anxiety brings forth the possibility of losing one's grip on all that there is, and it therefore "makes manifest the Nothing." In the *Arbeitsgemeinschaft* Heidegger explained this as follows:

> *Heidegger:* The analysis of anxiety does not have as its sole function
> the making-visible of a central phenomenon in man, but
> instead has the function of preparing for the question: on
> the grounds of which metaphysical sense of Dasein itself is
> it possible that the human being in general can have been
> placed before something like the Nothing? In answer to
> this question, the analysis of anxiety was provided so that
> the possibility of something like the Nothing is thought
> of only as an idea that has also been grounded in this
> determination of the disposition of anxiety [*Befindlichkeit der Angst*]. It is only possible for me to understand Being if
> I understand the Nothing or anxiety.

It bears repeating that in 1929 these arguments were still new. In *Being and Time* Heidegger claimed that it belongs to the essence of Dasein as a thrown projection that it is finite and it must accordingly choose *not* to realize certain possibilities. This exigency of negation is said to reveal the "nothingness" or nullity at the core of Dasein's being. And it is to this very nullity or "null ground" *(nichtiger Grund)* that one's conscience will call attention, demanding that it be gathered up into a truthful understanding of one's own existence. But nowhere in *Being and Time* does Heidegger suggest straightforwardly that the Nothing [*das Nichts*] is crucial to, and even a correlative for, the understanding of Being. This claim was first developed in systematic fashion in the Freiburg inaugural lecture. But three months earlier it was announced at Davos as if for the first time:

> *Heidegger:* Being is incomprehensible if the Nothing is incomprehensible. [*Sein ist unverständlich, wenn das Nichts unverständlich ist.*] And only in the unity of the understanding of Being and Nothing does the question of the origin [*Ursprung*] spring up [*springt . . . auf*] from the why. Why can man ask about the why, and why must he ask? These central problems of Being, the Nothing, and the why are the most elementary and the most concrete of problems. They are those to which the whole analytic of Dasein has been oriented. And I believe that from this initial grasping we have already seen that the whole supposition under which the critique of *Being and Time* stands, the proper kernel of intent, has not been encountered.

The two years between *Being and Time* and the Davos disputation thus seem to have brought a subtle shift in argument: in 1927, Heidegger saw "nothingness" as Dasein's own way of being, another name for human finitude or its lack of metaphysical ground. In 1929, he now claimed that "the Nothing" was a metaphysical condition that might be *revealed to Dasein.* Thus, by the time he presented "What Is Metaphysics?" Heidegger could argue that, when seized with anxiety, Dasein is actually "held out into the nothing," an insight that was then supposed to help answer the question, "Why are there beings at all, and not rather Nothing?" The difference is that the former awards primary attention to *human existence* whereas the latter places greater emphasis on the *question of Being* itself. The change therefore suggests that the so-called turning—Heidegger's shift of emphasis from the analytic of Dasein to nonanthropocentric ontology—may have had its beginnings already in 1929.

We are now better prepared to explain why it is that at Davos Heidegger wished to minimize the significance of anxiety for "the phenomenon of man." When faced with Cassirer's criticism of philosophical anthropology, Heidegger took pains to distance himself from *any* interpretation of his work that left it vulnerable to an anthropological reading. But what worked as a defense could also serve as polemic. By minimizing his connection to philosophical anthropology, Heidegger could amplify his own criticism of the anthropological premises animating Cassirer's philosophy of culture:

> *Heidegger:* On the other hand, I can very well concede that if, in some measure, we take this analytic of Dasein in *Being and Time* as at core an investigation of the human being, and we then pose the question of how, on the grounds of this understanding of man, the understanding of a formation of culture and a cultural sphere is to be possible, then, if we pose this question in this way, it is an absolute impossibility to say something about what is under consideration here. All these questions are inadequate with respect to my central problem.

Heidegger's conclusion was that any attempt to construe his philosophy along the lines of a philosophical anthropology was bound to fail. The analysis of existence as developed in *Being and Time* was precisely *not* intended as an "investigation of the human being." Rather, the aim was to *commence* the project of ontological inquiry by asking in a provisional fashion about that being that *already lives in an understanding of Being.*[53] And this provisional inquiry was intended *only* as a preparation for raising the question of Being as such. But this meant that his philosophical task was primarily *ontological* and it was *not* primarily concerned with "an investigation of the human being." From Heidegger's perspective, then, the anthropocentric purposes of Cassirer's philosophy (as aiming toward the formation of a "cultural sphere") seemed of little relevance. For if one's attention remained fixed solely on human cultural achievements. the general questions of ontology would likely remain neglected and perhaps forgotten.

Heidegger's dismissive remarks concerning the supposed inadequacy of Cassirer's cultural philosophy nevertheless raised the question as to whether Heidegger himself acknowledged a role for philosophy in the formation and preservation of cultural values. From this arose the much-discussed problem concerning the relationship between philosophy and worldview *(Weltan-schauung)*. In his famous 1911 essay, "Philosophy as a Rigorous Science," Edmund Husserl had argued—against then-prevalent historicist philoso-phers of hermeneutic understanding such as Wilhelm Dilthey—that world-views could have no legitimate place in philosophy: Dilthey saw human meaning as conditioned by its historical context, and it was a basic principle of his work that actions or thoughts of human beings in the past require a sympathetic "re-experiencing" *(nacherleben)* of the world as those agents would have experienced it themselves. A central motivation in Dilthey's so-called critique of historical reason was to preserve the originally Kantian distinction between the spheres of natural causality and meaningful human action. From Husserl's perspective, however, this method had the ironic consequence of dissolving the transcendental status of truth claims, best exemplified in logic and mathematics, into a plurality of historically and psychologically relativistic contexts. Husserl's conclusion was that any phi-losophy that wished to claim the title of a science must consider its claims as possessing an essentially ahistorical validity and must sunder any and all relation to a historically conditioned worldview.

For Heidegger, however, the relation between philosophy and worldview was far more problematic. Already in his 1919 review of Karl Jaspers's *Psy-chology of Worldviews,* Heidegger had expressed serious reservations re-garding Jaspers's attempt to develop a comprehensive typology of the vari-ous worldviews that condition psychic life. Jaspers had presented worldviews as "cages" *(Gehäuse)* that served individuals as defensive objectifications against the challenges confronting their existence. Only a so-called limit-situation *(Grenzsituation)* such as anxiety or guilt could break through such an objectified worldview to offer the individual a vision of unconstrained possibility.[54] Heidegger criticized Jaspers for attempting to describe world-views by means of the false objectivism of the positive sciences: insofar as humans *themselves* are historical beings (a claim for which Heidegger appealed to Count Yorck von Wartenburg's dictum, "We *are* history"), the phenomenon of human life could only be studied in a historical fashion and not in an "aesthetic" or contemplative-scientific manner.[55] In his 1925 Kas-sel lectures on Dilthey, Heidegger argued even more strenuously that "the struggle for an historical worldview" could not be left to historical study but required a genuinely philosophical confrontation with Dasein's sense of itself as a historical being.[56]

But even as Heidegger distanced himself from Husserl's radical anti-historicism and embraced historicity as a constitutive element of human existence, he nonetheless echoed his teacher's concern that philosophy and historical worldviews must remain distinct. In his 1927 summer semester lectures at Marburg, Heidegger granted that a worldview "springs in each case from a factical Dasein" because a historically determined worldview belongs to the very character of the human being *qua* historical existence. Yet he hastened to add that "the formation of a worldview cannot be the task of philosophy."[57] On the one hand, Heidegger saw historicity and historical worldview as existential foundations for factical life, and he therefore rejected Husserl's attempt to practice phenomenology as a transcendental inquiry dissociated from our all-too-human conditions of historical existence.[58] On the other hand, Heidegger shared with Husserl the strong conviction that phenomenology could only fulfill its own intrinsic ideals if it eschewed any role in the practical construction of historical values, a point he would restate even more sharply in his summer 1928 Marburg course on "The Metaphysical Foundations of Logic." There, Heidegger explained that "we do not philosophize in order to become philosophers, no more than to fashion for ourselves and others a salutary worldview that could be procured like a coat and hat. The goal of philosophy is not a system of interesting information, nor a sentimental edification for faltering souls."[59]

In his response to Cassirer at Davos, Heidegger revisited both of these claims. He embraced historical worldviews as the ground of philosophy while he denied to philosophy any active share in worldview construction. Yet he granted that a genuinely philosophical recognition of Dasein's capacity for transcendence could open the path toward a deeper and more radical relation between Dasein and its world:

> *Heidegger:* At the same time, I pose a further methodological
> question: How, then, must such a metaphysics of Dasein,
> which has the ground for its determination in the problem
> of winning the foundation for the problem of the
> possibility of metaphysics, be put forth? Is a determinate

worldview not taken as a basis for it? I would misunderstand myself if I said that I gave philosophy free of points of view. And here a problem is expressed: that of the relationship between philosophy and worldview. Philosophy does not have the task of giving worldview, although, again, worldview is the presupposition of philosophizing. And the worldview that the philosophy gives is not a direct one in the sense of a doctrine or in the sense of an influencing. Rather, the worldview that the philosopher gives rests in the fact that in the philosophizing, it succeeds in making the transcendence of Dasein itself radical, that is, it succeeds in making the inner possibility of this finite creature comport itself with respect to beings as a whole.

With this conclusion Heidegger was ready to announce that philosophy can indeed play a transformative role in human life: Philosophy is not a merely academic affair or a mode of learned discourse. It is instead an activity—"philosophizing" versus "philosophy"—that arises from the metaphysical essence of the human being. As Heidegger had explained in the 1928 lectures on logic, "philosophy remains latent in every human existence."[60] Its pursuit therefore has the potential to awaken us to a deepened appreciation of what it is to be human. But we cannot discover this essence as an object available to theoretical apprehension. Nor should we try to develop a "practical recipe for life" and derive a worldview from a given philosopher's comments on ethics.[61] Cassirer was therefore wrong to concern himself with articulating a specific conception of freedom: if philosophy was a transformative event, this was not because it works up ethical concepts but only because it works toward the "setting-free of the Dasein in man." Heidegger's implication was that philosophizing as the disclosure of Dasein's capacity for transcendence had to be considered a prerequisite to any other philosophical questions. Cassirer's "cultural philosophy" could proceed *only* if the fundamental questions of ontology were already secured:

> *Heidegger:* To turn it another way: Cassirer says: We do not grasp freedom, but only the ungraspability of freedom.

> Freedom does not allow itself to be grasped. The question: How is freedom possible? is absurd. From this, however, it does not follow that to a certain extent here a problem of the irrational remains. Rather, because freedom is not an object of theoretical apprehending but is instead an object of philosophizing, this can mean nothing other than the fact that freedom only is and can only be in the setting-free [*Befreiung*]. The sole, adequate relation to freedom in man is the self-freeing of freedom in man. In order to get into this dimension of philosophizing, which is not a matter for a learned discussion but is rather a matter about which the individual philosopher knows nothing, and which is a task to which the philosopher has submitted himself—this setting-free of the Dasein in man must be the sole and central [thing] that philosophy as philosophizing can perform. And in this sense, I would believe that for Cassirer there is a wholly other *terminus ad quem* in the sense of a cultural philosophy. Further, I believe that for Cassirer this question of cultural philosophy first receives its metaphysical function in the happening of the history of humankind, if it is not to remain and to be a mere presentation of the various regions. Rather, at the same time within its inner dynamic, it is so deeply rooted that it becomes visible, expressly and a priori, not afterward, in the metaphysics of Dasein itself as a fundamental happening [*als Grundgeschehen*].

Although Heidegger did not state the conclusion outright, the thrust of his remarks was unmistakable: The "metaphysics of Dasein" was to serve as the necessary ground and precondition for all other modes of philosophical questioning. It followed that any pursuit of what Heidegger termed "cultural philosophy" was bound to be fruitless unless it conceded to ontology a higher and a priori status. We may call this the "argument for priority." As we shall see in Chapter 5, it was to be a central feature of the disagreement between Heidegger and Cassirer that both philosophers would try to claim this priority for themselves.

Finitude and Infinity

Meanwhile, Heidegger concluded his round of remarks with three questions for Cassirer, as follows:

> *Heidegger:* 1. What path does man have to infinitude? And what is
> the manner in which man can participate in infinity?
> 2. Is infinitude to be attained as a privative determination
> of finitude, or is infinitude a region in its own right?
> 3. To what extent does philosophy have as its task to be
> allowed to become free from anxiety? Or does it not have
> as its task to surrender man, even radically, to anxiety?

Cassirer responded to each of these in turn. To the first, he appealed immediately to the principles developed in *The Philosophy of Symbolic Forms:* against Heidegger's repeated claim that all human thought and action is marked irrevocably by finitude, Cassirer insisted that human beings could achieve a kind of "immanent infinitude" thanks to their capacity for symbolization. Form first emerges from out of the finite conditions of human experience, but it then assumes an objectivity and independence in relation to those very conditions. The movement from finitude to infinity can be described as a *metabasis eis allo genos,* a transition to an entirely different plane. But it would be wrong to regard this realm of forms as a truly *metaphysical* dimension existing beyond and separate from finite human experience. It is rather a purely human creation and accordingly "immanent." Cassirer's full response was as follows:

> *Cassirer:* To the first: in no way other than through the medium of
> form. This is the function of form, that while man changes
> the form of his Dasein, that is, while he now must transpose everything in him that is lived experience into some
> objective shape in which he is objectified in such a way, to
> be sure, that he does not thereby become radically free
> from the finitude of the point of departure (for this is still
> connected to his particular finitude). Rather, while it
> arises from finitude, it leads finitude out into something

new. And that is immanent infinitude. Man cannot make
the leap from his own proper finitude into a realistic
infinitude. He can and must have, however, the *metabasis*
that leads him from the immediacy of his existence into
the region of pure form. And he possesses his infinity
solely in this form. "From out of the chalice of this
spiritual realm; infinity flows to him." [*"Aus dem Kelche
dieses Geisterreiches strömt ihm die Unendlichkeit."*] The
spiritual realm is not a metaphysical spiritual realm; the
true spiritual realm is just the spiritual world created
from himself. That he could create it is the seal of his
infinitude [*das Siegel seiner Unendlichkeit*].

To illustrate the idea of immanent infinity, Cassirer quotes (with a small
modification) the well-known concluding lines to Friedrich Schiller's poem,
"To Friendship": "Friendless was the great Master of the World, / He felt a lack,
hence souls were made, / The blessed mirrors of his blessedness!— / Yet in his
loftiest works he found no equal, / And from the chalice of this realm of spirits
/ Flows forth to him—Infinity."[62] The last two lines of the poem hold a special
significance for the history of German Idealism as they appear as the concluding lines to Hegel's *Phenomenology of Spirit*. For Hegel, they served to illustrate the fulfillment of the dialectical narrative: Spirit's self-externalization
and return. For Cassirer, however, they provide an apt illustration for the
claim that the human being itself wields a formative spiritual energy, such
that it can populate its world with symbolic forms that assume an independent and objective existence while they also testify to their author's creativity.

The difference is instructive: Hegel preserved the poem's quasi-
metaphysical status and uses it to describe the theogonic self-alienation and
reconciliation of the World-Spirit. Cassirer borrows the image of divine
self-creation but uses it to illustrate a purely immanent phenomenon of humanist self-expression. Perhaps most provocative of all was that Cassirer's
use of the poem ran directly counter to Heidegger's conception of the relation between the human and the divine. As we saw above, Heidegger on
several occasions invoked the notion of an infinite and divine comprehension, but he used it only as a counterexample to underscore the radical *difference* between the infinite and creative capacity of the divine mind (*intuitus*

originarus) and the merely finite or receptive capacity of the human being *(intuitus derivatus)*. Cassirer, too, invoked the notion of divinity, but he did so *not* to emphasize a contrast but rather to insist on a *continuity*. In other words, he recalled the creative powers of the divine mind but then reclaimed precisely those capacities for the human being. It is revealing that Cassirer made no mention whatsoever of Schiller's originally theological language: The "blessedness" of the "Master of the World" plays no role in Cassirer's illustration above. And the final phrase, "flows forth to him," appears as if its intended referent were not a divine creator but an exclusively human one.

This secular application of a religious image suggests that Cassirer believed the human being might itself enjoy a potentially limitless creativity. Thus, in response to Heidegger's second question, Cassirer affirmed that there was indeed a certain kind of "infinity" that the human being could claim as its own legitimate possession. This infinity was not to be misconstrued as merely a logical privation, that is, as an absence of limits (as the German term *Unendlichkeit* might suggest). Rather, it was best conceived as a fullness or plenitude that resulted from the expansion of human symbolic energies into every possible sphere of activity. To illustrate this idea, Cassirer quoted Goethe's well-known aphorism, *"Willst du ins Unendliche schreiten, geh nur im Endlichen nach allen Seiten!"*[63]

> *Cassirer:* As to the second. It is not just a private determination but is
>   instead its own sphere, although it is not one obtained in a
>   purely negative way in addition to the finite. In infinity, it is
>   not just an opposition to the finitude that is constituted but
>   rather, in a certain sense, it is the totality, the fulfillment of
>   finitude itself [*die Erfüllung der Endlichkeit selbst*]. But this
>   fulfillment of finitude exactly constitutes infinity. Goethe:
>   "If into the infinite you wish to stride, / Explore the finite
>   from every side." As finitude is fulfilled, that is, as it goes in
>   all directions, it steps out into infinity. This is the opposite
>   of privation, it is the perfect filling out of finitude itself
>   [*vollkommene Ausfüllung der Endlichkeit selbst*].

It is worth noting that Cassirer had already articulated this idea two years earlier in his historical study, *The Individual and the Cosmos in Renaissance*

Philosophy (1927). Celebrating Giordano Bruno's new conception of reality, Cassirer had explained that for Bruno, "man finds his true Ego by drawing the infinite universe into himself, and conversely, by extending himself into it." It follows that the infinity of the cosmos does not leave the soul with a feeling of its own limitation or inadequacy but is instead a source of fullness and self-elevation: "The Ego can face the infinite cosmos inasmuch as it finds within itself the principles by which it *knows* that the cosmos is infinite."[64] Several years later in *An Essay on Man* (1944), Cassirer would revisit these themes in language that recalled his above remarks at Davos: in ancient Greek thought infinity was a negative concept and it represented a boundless expanse that was limitless and therefore "without form." But because human reason can only understand what has form, it followed that this infinity was unintelligible. Plato typified the classical perspective with his conclusion that finitude and infinity were fundamentally opposed and mutually exclusive principles. But with the Renaissance, infinity no longer meant a mere negation or limitation. Rather, it meant the "inexhaustible abundance of reality and the unrestricted power of the human intellect." Bruno thus saw in Copernican science a "decisive step towards man's self-liberation. Man no longer lives in the world as a prisoner enclosed within the narrow walls of a finite physical universe. He can traverse the air and break through all the imaginary boundaries of the celestial spheres which have been erected by a false metaphysics and cosmology." In Bruno's philosophy Cassirer saw a dramatic breakthrough to a new conception of human dignity: "The human intellect becomes aware of its own infinity through measuring its powers by the infinite universe." Thus, although the human being cannot leave behind the conditions by which it knows the cosmos, it can nevertheless "break through" its finitude insofar as it discerns in the cosmos a reflection of its own limitless capacity for knowledge.[65]

At Davos Cassirer seemed to appeal (if only implicitly) to this Renaissance idea, although the more obvious touchstone for his remarks was the Kantian conception of the human being as simultaneously finite and infinite: As Kant explains in the famous concluding lines to the *Critique of Practical Reason*, the human being is simultaneously a citizen of two worlds, the "external world of sense" and that of the "invisible self." In fidelity to Kant, Cassirer cleaved to both of these characterizations. He accepted the critical doctrine concerning the finitude of human experience, but he also believed that the human being is gifted with an infinite dignity as a practical agent. What was most striking about Cassirer's appeal to this idea, however, was that he did not follow Kant in confining its significance to ethical reason alone. Instead he borrowed the image of infinite dignity and applied it to his conception of the human being as a creature who generates its own symbolic reality. Thus, for Cassirer, the human being was understood as a *spontaneous and creative agency* whose own activity as *animal symbolicum* cleared its path to an "immanent infinity."

From this, Cassirer moved on to address Heidegger's third and final question: "To what extent does philosophy have as its task to be allowed to become free from anxiety? Or does it not have as its task to surrender man, even radically, to anxiety?" The status of this question was unusual—Cassirer called it "radical"—and his response seemed to betray discomfort at the fact that he was supposed to provide "a kind of confession." His first answer verged on tautology: philosophy must let the human being become just as free as the human being is able. Behind this claim is a strong reluctance to use the term *freedom* in a way that would grant it any kind of robustly metaphysical status: for Cassirer, as for Kant, freedom is not a theoretical object but a postulate of practical reason, and it is therefore discovered in and through the "path of progressive freeing." In reference to Heidegger's previous comment (above) that because freedom is "not an objective of theoretical apprehending," it is knowable only in the event of "setting-free [*Befreiung*]," Cassirer concluded that Heidegger should agree with him that freedom is conceivable only as an *infinite process*.

But Cassirer naturally understood that the Heideggerian conception of becoming free ramifies differently. For Cassirer it had to imply an emancipation of the human being from "anxiety as mere disposition," terms that refer to Heidegger's own philosophy: In *Being and Time,* "disposition" (or *Befindlichkeit*) is the manner of being that typically reveals itself in everyday moods, and anxiety (or *Angst*) is the radical disposition that lights up for Dasein the entire care structure of its being-in-the-world and thereby makes possible its authentic recognition of its own finitude. To be exposed to anxiety therefore offers a kind of emancipation, because it is only in the anxious anticipation of being-toward-death that one can take on board the finitude at the core of one's existence and resolve authentically to be who one truly is. But Heidegger suggested that Dasein usually exists in such as a way as to evade this recognition: it flees from anxiety and prefers instead to live in the conformist untruth of average everydayness. Dasein's typical mode of being is therefore one of "comfortableness, shirking, and taking things lightly."[66] Now it is obvious that Cassirer could not agree with this description of human possibilities; for Cassirer, there was no deeper truth about the human condition that is to be discovered through anxiety, and so he could not assent to the Heideggerian principle that anxiety has a crucial role to play in our emancipation from inauthenticity. Cassirer instead believed that whatever else freedom might entail, it surely must involve a liberation *from* anxiety. As illustration Cassirer quoted a well-known line from Friedrich Schiller:

> *Cassirer:* As to the third. That is quite a radical question, to which one can answer only with a kind of confession. Philosophy had to allow to become sufficiently free, to the extent that man can become free. While it does that, I believe, it frees man—to be sure in a certain radical sense—from anxiety as mere disposition [*in gewissem Sinne radikal von der Angst als bloßer Befindlichkeit*]. I believe, even according to Heidegger's explanations earlier today, that freedom can be properly found only along the path of progressive freeing [*nur auf dem Wege der fortschreitenden Befreiung*], which indeed is also an infinite process for him. I believe that he can agree with this interpretation. Granted, I see that the most difficult problem is found here. I would like the sense, the goal, in the fact the freeing, to be taken in the sense: "Cast off from yourself the anxiety of earthly things! [*Werft die Angst des Irdischen von euch!*]" That is the position of idealism to which I have always confessed.

The quotation that concludes this response comes from the third stanza of Schiller's poem, "Das Ideal und das Leben" ("Ideal and Life").[67] Given its history, we should not be surprised that Cassirer considered it a suitable illustration for his philosophy. When Schiller first composed the poem in 1795, he gave it the title, "The Empire of Shadows," later changed to "The Empire of Forms." It was apparently among the poet's own favorites, and it served as a frequent point of reference for the neo-Kantian movement throughout the later nineteenth century. Kuno Fischer, in his short work *Schiller als Philosoph* (1859), describes it as the most significant example of Schiller's "poetic philosophy." F. A. Lange, Hermann Cohen's Marburg predecessor, saw it as "the most difficult of all Schiller's poems and the greatest illustration of his "poetry of ideas." And Karl Vorländer, an ally of Cohen and Natorp later famous for his 1924 biography on Kant, praised it in 1894 as "the most philosophical" of all Schiller's philosophical poetry, those "ripest blossoms of Schiller's genius" that embodied "in sublime language . . . the highest philosophical ideas as had not been achieved since Plato's day."[68] For Cassirer, too, the poem served as an apt illustration of his own philosophical principles. The broadly Kantian distinction between freedom and necessity reappeared in the poetic contrast between the ideal kingdom of "divine form" and the cramped, time-bound sphere of "dull life." In his response to Heidegger, Cassirer could therefore conclude that it was the task of philosophy to aid us in casting aside our fears as beings of temporal finitude so that we may create for ourselves an ideal world of form.

On this issue the divide between the two philosophers is indeed dramatic, for it is a cardinal principle of Heidegger's philosophy that the human being cannot extricate itself from its temporal condition as thrown *(geworfen)* into the world. Dasein's freedom is conditioned by thrownness in such a way that authentic Being-a-self cannot mean a release from this thrownness but instead means *a deepened understanding and acceptance of the thrown being one is.* And because anxiety is crucial to this understanding, there is nothing to be gained in the attempt to flee anxiety for an ostensibly ideal world. For Heidegger such an effort could be understood only as evasion.[69] Cassirer reversed these claims: Although a modicum of anxiety is no doubt common to the human condition, this anxiety can and should be "thrown off" for the sake of a freedom that transcends our earthly life: *"Werft die Angst . . . von euch"* (throw off your anxiety). Although we may at times feel ourselves as "thrown" or abandoned to temporality, this is hardly a condition we must embrace as if it were the very essence of our being. The difference could hardly be more profound: What in Heidegger's philosophy appears as an existential *condition* (thrownness as a mark of finitude) reveals itself in Cassirer's philosophy as an *action* (to throw off illustrating our emancipatory capacity as *agents*). The difference between these principles—thrownness and spontaneity—now stands revealed as the key to the entire debate.

Given the magnitude of this divide, a host of questions immediately arose: What *kind* of division was this? Was it merely a disagreement or was it perhaps an incommensurability? Was there in fact a common language in which the two philosophers could carry on their discussion? Did there remain a possibility for translation between their respective philosophies? Or was the very ideal of a common language little more than a dream?

Translation, Aporia, Difference

At this point, the Dutch linguist Hendrik J. Pos intervened with the following observation:

> *Pos:* Philological remark: Both men speak a completely different language. For us, it is a matter of extracting something common from these two languages. An attempt at translation was already made by Cassirer in his "Space for Action" ["*Aktionsraum*"]. We must hear the acknowledgment of this translation from Heidegger. The translational possibility extends up to the point at which something emerges that does not allow translation. Those are the terms that demarcate what is characteristic of one of a group of languages. In both of these languages, I have attempted to gather several of these terms that I doubt would allow for translation into the other language. I nominate Heidegger's expressions: Dasein, Being, the ontic. On the other hand, I nominate Cassirer's expressions: the functional in spirit and the transformation of primordial space into another one. Should it be found that there is no translation for these terms from both sides, then these would be the terms with which to differentiate the spirit of Cassirer's philosophy from Heidegger's.

In this remark one could detect a growing awareness that the two philosophers were perhaps separated by more than intellectual disagreement: each of them spoke a unique language with terminology so distinct as to defy the possibility of mutual translation. In his postwar recollections Pos varies this claim: "The two standpoints could be mutually clarified," he writes, "but they could not be brought any closer together."[70] Clearly, all of Pos's sympathies,

intellectual and political, lay with Cassirer (a fact that would become altogether obvious from Pos's postwar sketch of the disputation, as will be discussed later). This fact must be borne in mind because Pos may have been
inclined to exaggerate the division. It is nonetheless remarkable that a member of the Davos audience would resort to the analogy of translation between different languages.

A complicating factor is that Pos alluded to a comment from Cassirer's
independent lectures, where Cassirer made reference to an *"Aktionsraum."*
It is not hard to guess at his meaning, because his earlier discussion of
philosophical anthropology focused on the question of human versus animal spheres of action. Moreover, in the third volume of Cassirer's *Philosophy of Symbolic Forms,* one finds several footnotes to Heidegger's philosophy, the longest of which tries to reconcile the Heideggerian category
of existential space with Cassirer's own theory of scientific-mathematical
space. Briefly, Cassirer accepts that Heidegger is correct in his analysis of the
"primary experience of space" as the spatiality of what is "at-hand" *(zuhanden)* in the "comings and goings of everyday life." But Cassirer goes on
to claim that this primary everyday spatiality of action is insufficient and
that, "without challenging Heidegger's position," his own analysis will pass
"beyond it" to the nonsubjective space as pure symbolic form.[71] The details
of Cassirer's corrective will be discussed in Chapter 5. Here it suffices to
note that Pos saw this as Cassirer's attempt at "translation." What Pos failed
to mention is that this translation was also an implicit criticism, because it
judged existential space to be a merely provisional and subjective stage that
must be surpassed if one hoped to arrive at the higher station of scientific
objectivity.

Whether Cassirer's comment on Heideggerian space came across to the
Davos assembly as critical or generous is impossible to glean from the transcript itself. Pos himself obviously saw it as a magnanimous gesture that
Heidegger would be honor-bound to reciprocate. But Pos also voiced skepticism as to whether a thorough and mutual comprehension was even possible given the striking divergence of philosophical vocabulary: certain terms
could altogether defy translation. In Heidegger's language, such terms included *Dasein, Being, the ontic;* in Cassirer's language, they were the *functional in spirit, the transformation of primordial space,* and so forth. Such

terms did not signal merely a difference in philosophical doctrine; they betrayed a more profound and perhaps irreconcilable division of philosophical
"spirit." Heidegger, seizing an opportunity to sharpen the philosophical
contrast, responded to Pos's suggestion at great length:

> *Heidegger:* In the first lecture, Cassirer used the expressions *termi-
> nus a quo* and *terminus ad quem.* One could say that for
> Cassirer the *terminus ad quem* is the whole of a philoso-
> phy of culture in the sense of an elucidation of the
> wholeness of the forms of the shaping consciousness. For
> Cassirer, the *terminus a quo* is utterly problematical. My
> position is the reverse: The *terminus a quo* is my central
> problematic, the one I develop. The question is: Is the
> *terminus ad quem* as clear for me? For me, this occurs
> not in the whole of a Philosophy of Culture, but rather in
> the question: τί τὸ ὄν [Greek in original]; or rather:
> what in general is called Being? For me, it was from
> this question that the problematic of a metaphysics of
> Dasein arose in order to derive a ground for the basic
> problem of metaphysics. Or, in order to come once more
> to the core of the interpretation of Kant: My intention
> was not to bring up something new in contrast to an
> epistemological interpretation and to bring honor to the
> power of imagination. Rather, it should be clear that the
> inner problematic of the *Critique of Pure Reason,* that is,
> the question concerning the possibility of ontology, is
> pushed back toward a radical destruction of the concept
> in a traditional sense that was Kant's point of departure.
> In the attempted groundlaying for metaphysics, Kant is
> thereby compelled to make the proper foundation
> [*Grund*] into an abyss [*Abgrund*]. When Kant says: the
> three fundamental questions are led back to the fourth:
> What is Man? then the question in its character as
> question has become questionable. I attempted to show
> that it is not at all self-evident to start from a concept of

> *logos,* but instead that the question of the possibility of
> metaphysics demands a metaphysics of Dasein itself as
> possibility of the fundament of a question of metaphys-
> ics. In this way, the question of what man is must be
> answered not so much in the sense of an anthropological
> system, but rather it must first be properly clarified with
> regard to the perspective from within which it wants to
> be posed.

Heidegger's initial response simply reiterated some of the central themes
already presented in his Davos Kant-lectures and later in *Kant and the
Problem of Metaphysics:* Heidegger was most concerned, he explained, with
the fundamental question of philosophy, its *terminus a quo,* or point of
departure. This is the *Seinsfrage,* the Question of Being, the original question of philosophy as developed by the ancient Greeks. Heidegger's interpretation of Kant was developed with an eye toward this neglected metaphysical question. In the first *Critique,* Kant writes that all of the interests
of reason could be summarized by three questions: "1. What can I know?
2. What should I do? 3. What may I hope?"[72] But in the introduction to his
lectures on *Logic,* Kant suggests that all three can be related to a fourth and
final question: "What is man?"[73] This naturally raised the suspicion that
the fundamental questions of metaphysics might all find their common
point of origin in philosophical anthropology. But the thrust of Heidegger's
explanation in the Kant-book would be that nothing like a philosophical
anthropology could *ever* be adequate to the question of Being.[74] For philosophical anthropology had a predetermined response concerning the essence of the human being, whereas what was actually needed was a prior
inquiry into the human *manner of being* itself. It followed that, in Heidegger's judgment, Cassirer's appeals to "Spirit" and related themes such as
the philosophy of culture and the forms of creative consciousness were not
only irrelevant but were in fact without metaphysical foundation, for the
highest concerns of philosophy must be derived *from* and remain grounded
in their point of departure. Concerning this rule of metaphysical foundations, Cassirer appeared indifferent. The studiously non-metaphysical language of symbolic forms had no name for what existential ontology calls
Dasein:

Heidegger: And here I come back to the concepts *terminus a quo* and *terminus ad quem.* Is this just a heuristic questioning, or does it lie in the essence of philosophy itself that it has a *terminus a quo* that must be made into a problem and that it has a *terminus ad quem* that correlates to the *terminus a quo?* This problematic does not yet appear to me to have been coined clearly in Cassirer's philosophy up to now. Cassirer's point is to emphasize the various forms of the shaping in order, with a view to these shapings, subsequently to point out a certain dimension of the shaping powers themselves. Now, one could say: this dimension, then, is fundamentally the same as that which I call Dasein. But that would be erroneous.

What Heidegger considered the stark disanalogy between creative consciousness and Dasein becomes most evident in the case of freedom: For Cassirer, freedom is the capacity for "forming images of consciousness." Freedom, in this sense, is a mental spontaneity that first reveals itself in creative acts of symbolization. For Heidegger, freedom is the "becoming free for the finitude of Dasein." Here, freedom is not mental spontaneity but instead a coming-into-recognition of one's own incorrigible finitude. In Heidegger's words, it is "to come into the thrownness of Dasein."

Here was a vivid disagreement. On Heidegger's view, the specific conception of freedom animating the philosophy of symbolic forms necessarily committed Cassirer to a metaphysical notion of the human being as an "indifferent ground" that must preexist its own temporal entanglements. But for Heidegger Dasein could only be conceived as an "authentic basic occurrence." Dasein was the "existing of man," and its essence could be grasped only as a temporal event:

Heidegger: The difference is clearest in the concept of Freedom. I spoke of a freeing in the sense that the freeing of the inner transcendence of Dasein is the fundamental character of philosophizing itself. In so doing, the authentic sense of this freeing is not to be found in becoming free to a certain extent for the forming images of consciousness

and for the realm of form, rather, it is to be found in
becoming free for the finitude of Dasein [*der eigentliche
Sinn dieser Befreiung nicht darin liegt, frei zu werden
gewissermaßen für die gestaltenden Bilder des Bewußtseins
und für das Reich der* Form, *sondern frei zu werden für die
Endlichkeit des Daseins*]. Just to come into the thrownness
of Dasein [*hineinzukommen in die Geworfenheit des
Daseins*] is to come into the conflict that lies within the
essence of freedom. I did not give freedom to myself,
although it is through Being-free that I can first be I myself.
But now, not I myself in the sense of an indifferent ground
for explanation, but rather: Dasein is the authentic basic
occurrence [*das eigentliche Grundgeschehen*] in which the
existing of man [*das Existieren des Menschen*], and with it
every problematic of existence itself, becomes essential.

With this explanation Heidegger was ready to concede that Pos was correct
in surmising how meaningful translation between certain key terms might
prove impossible: Dasein does not equal consciousness. Heidegger accordingly rejected Schiller's poetic image of spirit as unshackled from body and
earth: the human being is not an a priori consciousness that can simply con-
template its worldly entanglements from a vantage external to own existence. Rather, the human being as Dasein finds itself always already thrown
and its condition might even be characterized as bondage *(Gebundenheit)* in
the midst of worldly entities. This is the condition of Dasein's everydayness
and the phenomenon of *fleeing-toward-worldly-entities* that Heidegger calls
"inauthenticity."[75] Dasein most typically remains in the mode of inauthen-
tic being, whereas even its authentic recognition via anxiety of its "ownmost" possibility is a rare and privileged disclosure that is itself *conditional
upon* Dasein's inauthenticity. Heidegger described this recognition as an
entry "into the thrownness of Dasein." But Cassirer's philosophy, he observed, allowed for no such recognition. Indeed, the very notion of *Dasein
itself* was foreign to Cassirer's entire manner of thinking:

Heidegger: Based on this, I believe we can answer the question by
           Pos concerning translation. I believe that what I describe

by Dasein does not allow translation into a concept of
Cassirer's. Should one say consciousness, that is precisely
what I rejected. What I call Dasein is essentially
codetermined—not just through what we describe as
spirit, and not just through what we call living. Rather,
it depends on the original unity and the immanent
structure of the relatedness of a human being, which to
a certain extent has been fettered in a body and which,
in the fetteredness in the body, stands in a particular
condition of being bound up with beings [*Gebundenheit
mit dem Seienden*]. In the midst of this it finds itself [*sich
befindet*], not in the sense of a spirit that gazes down
upon it, but rather in the sense that Dasein, thrown into
the midst of beings [*inmitten des Seienden geworfen*],
carries out as free an incursion into entities, an incursion
that is always historical and, in the ultimate sense,
contingent. [It is] so contingent that the highest form of
the existence of Dasein is only allowed to lead back to the
very few and rare glimpses of Dasein's duration between
living and death, [and so contingent] that man exists
only in very few glimpses of the pinnacle of his own
possibility, but otherwise moves in the midst of his
beings.

Heidegger went on to explain that his own philosophical interest was
directed toward clarifying the manner of Being *(Seinsart)* that underwrites
ontic knowledge for any given region of entities. Ontological understanding
of this kind was determined by a prior analysis of the existential-ontological
understanding that belonged to human beings simply in virtue of their
being-in-the-world. Thus to determine the manner of being of entities
within any domain required a "metaphysics of Dasein." This was no less the
case for the entities Cassirer had named "symbolic forms," the ontological
status of which required prior clarification. But this task was to avoid taking
on board without careful scrutiny any of the inherited conceptions of how
human knowledge was partitioned. Cassirer's quasi-scholastic differentiation of knowledge into various regions (myth, language, art, science, and so

forth) was a mere convention and a symptom that the genuine concerns of
philosophical inquiry had been forgotten:

> *Heidegger:* The question concerning the manner of Being that lies
> within the philosophy of symbolic form, the central
> question concerning the inner constitution of Being, is
> what the metaphysics of Dasein determines—and it does
> not determine it with an aim toward a pregiven systematic
> of cultural domains and philosophical disciplines. In the
> entirety of my philosophical efforts, I have left the tradi-
> tional shape and division of the philosophical disciplines
> wholly undecided, because I believe that such an orienta-
> tion is the greatest misfortune, in the sense that we no
> longer come back to the inner problematic of philosophy.
> Neither Plato nor Aristotle could have known of such a
> partitioning of philosophy. A division of this sort was the
> concern of the schools, that is, of a philosophy for which
> the inner problematic of its questioning was lost; and it
> requires exertion to break through these disciplines.
> Moreover, that is why if we pass through the disciplines of
> aesthetics, and so forth, we again return to the specific
> metaphysical manner of Being of the region concerned.
> Art is not merely a form of self-formative consciousness
> [*eine Form des sich gestaltenden Bewußtseins*]; rather, art
> itself has a metaphysical sense within the fundamental
> occurrence of Dasein itself [*innerhalb des Grundgeschehens
> des Daseins selbst*].

It would be hard to miss in the above remarks Heidegger's withering criticism of Cassirer's philosophical method. For it is a founding premise of the
philosophy of symbolic forms that, although the various spheres of human
formative expression (language, myth, art, and science, to name only the
most fundamental) share a common origin in the spontaneity of consciousness, they nonetheless develop this basic capacity in different ways and toward sharply distinctive ends. Cassirer acknowledged continuity across the
expressive domains but also wished to preserve the manifold differences

among them. The concern for differentiation is evident in the very structure of *The Philosophy of Symbolic Forms,* which proceeds in stepwise and progressive fashion through an analysis of the various domains of human symbolization, from myth to science. The methodological introduction in the first volume addressed precisely this concern: The philosophical critique of knowledge, wrote Cassirer, must ask whether "the intellectual symbols by means of which the specialized disciplines reflect on and describe reality exist merely side by side or whether they are not diverse manifestations of the same basic human function." If the latter premise were ultimately confirmed, the aim would then be to "formulate the universal conditions of this function and define the principle underlying it." Cassirer hastened to add that this unifying function would *not* have the character of a "dogmatic metaphysics, which seeks absolute unity in a substance to which all the particulars of existence are reducible." The task of philosophical critique would be to seek after "a rule that governs the concrete diversity of the functions of cognition." Cassirer's chief task was to identify unity in diversity, the "original, formative power" evident across several distinct fields of expression. Yet he was also careful to say that "None of these forms can be simply reduced to, or derived from, the others; each of them designates a particular intellectual approach [*eine bestimmte geistige Auffassungsweise*], in which and through which it constitutes its own aspect of 'reality' [*eine eigene Seite des "Wirklichen"*]."[76]

This concern for diversity-in-unity remained a constant leitmotif for the philosophy of symbolic forms from beginning to end. In his 1944 *An Essay on Man,* Cassirer would insist upon a sharp distinction between science and art, domains that differed in both the objects they describe and the aims they are supposed to achieve: whereas science subordinates manifold impressions to general principles and thereby commits an "abbreviation of reality," art strives toward a "revelation of [the] inexhaustibility of the aspects of things" and thereby commits a "concretion of reality."[77] It is crucial to note, however, that Cassirer consistently rejected any dogmatic conclusions concerning the character of reality itself: He emphasized the variety of symbolic forms and symbolic domains, but he denied that the diversity in *regions of objectification* might be traced back to an underlying diversity in *metaphysical objects.* But Heidegger's criticism, as quoted above, seems to impute to Cassirer just this inference: in Heidegger's view Cassirer had illicitly borrowed from the scholastics more than just "a pregiven systematic of cultural domains and philosophical disciplines." He had also inherited far deeper prejudices concerning the metaphysical character of the objects that populate each domain. Heidegger did not hesitate to call this the "greatest misfortune," because it perpetuated habits of analysis for which the genuine problems of philosophy had ostensibly been lost.

At first glance, Heidegger's criticism may seem unfair given Cassirer's express confession of metaphysical agnosticism. But from another perspective the criticism is quite revealing insofar as it casts light on a basic anthropological assumption of Cassirer's entire philosophy, that is, that all domains of symbolic reality are derived from what is an essentially human power. What authorizes this inference is Cassirer's apparently innocent methodological decision to organize the analysis of symbolic forms according to more-or-less conventional distinctions of knowledge-domains. But this decision carries with it the assumption that these domains ultimately express *human ways of knowing* and must therefore find their common origin in a single anthropological capacity, which Heidegger identified as "self-forming consciousness." Heidegger objected to this inference on the grounds that it appealed illicitly to an anthropological metaphysics, and he argued instead that the various domains of knowledge find their origin in "the fundamental occurrence of Dasein itself." Heidegger developed this objection at greater length in the following comment:

> *Heidegger:* I have intentionally singled out these differences. The task at hand is not well served if we aim toward leveling. Rather, because the problem gains in clarity only through the sharpness of exposition, I would like once again to orient our whole discussion under the sign of Kant's *Critique of Pure Reason* and once again to fasten upon the question, what the human being is [*was der Mensch sei*], as our central question. At the same time, however, [I would like to fasten upon it] as the question we pose not in some isolated ethical sense, but instead in such a fashion that both positions become clear on the basis of this problematic, so that the question of man is only essential for the philosophers in such a way that the philosopher disregards

himself completely, so that the question not be posed in
an anthropocentric fashion [*anthropozentrisch*]. On the
contrary, it must be shown that: because man is the
creature who is transcendent, that is, the creature who is
open to beings in totality and to himself, that through this
eccentric character [*exzentrischen Charakter*] man at the
same time also stands within the totality of entities in
general—and that only in this way can the question and
the idea of a philosophical anthropology have meaning.

The proposal that one might simply translate between philosophical vocabu-
laries rests upon what Heidegger saw as the naïve assumption that there are
no genuine aporias of philosophical doctrine. He thus felt compelled to announce his opposition to any such leveling of philosophical differences. Taking his cue once again from the specified theme of the disputation—the
Kantian question, "What is the human being?"—, Heidegger suggested that
this question might help to bring into sharper relief the areas of real disagreement between Cassirer and himself. Heidegger insisted that the problem should not be taken in an "isolated ethical sense" and that the philosopher must "disregard himself completely" so as to avoid an anthropocentric
bias. If there was to be any significance at all in philosophical anthropology,
it would be found only if one took as the starting point for philosophy the
essential fact of Dasein's transcendence, which is to say the ontico-ontological
priority of Dasein as *the being for whom entities are disclosed*.[78]

But no anthropological inquiry of an empirical nature could possibly do
justice to this fact. At stake was nothing less than the task of philosophy
qua philosophy: it is the essential truth of the human condition as revealed
in the anxious anticipation of being-toward-death that it has no essence
other than the nullity or *un-ground (Abgrund)* of its existence as thrown
being-in-the-world. The highest task of philosophy is to bring the human
being out from the inauthenticity of quotidian existence into a genuine
understanding of its own condition. To deny this understanding is to remain "lazy," that is, to "flee" the truth and to prefer instead the "comfortableness" of "shirking" and "taking things lightly."[79] And an idealist anthropology that celebrates the creativity of human spirit can offer a merely
superficial satisfaction:

Heidegger: The question concerning the essence of human beings is
not to be understood in the sense that we study human
beings empirically as given objects, nor is it to be understood in such a way that I project an anthropology of man.
Rather, the question concerning the essence of human
beings only makes sense and is only justifiable insofar as
it derives its motivation from philosophy's central problematic itself, which leads man back beyond himself and
into the totality of beings in order to make manifest to
him there, with all his freedom, the nothingness of his
Dasein. This nothingness is not the occasion for pessi-
mism and melancholy; it is rather the occasion for
understanding that authentic activity takes place only
where there is opposition and that philosophy has the task,
out from the lazy outlook of a man who uses merely the
works of the spirit, of, so to speak, throwing man back
into the hardness of his fate [*und daß die Philosophie die
Aufgabe hat, aus dem faulen Aspekt eines Menschen, der
bloß die Werke des Geistes benutzt, gewissermaßen den
Menschen zurückzuwerfen in die Härte seines Schicksals*].

In the entirety of the debate between Heidegger and Cassirer, the above lines
are unique in their vehemence. For it is evident that Heidegger had moved
well beyond an exposition of Kantian doctrine and even beyond the exposition of his own philosophical commitments. He was now stating what philosophy *as such* aims to accomplish and what role it should play in the
broader context of human history and life: Negatively, Heidegger warned
that philosophy should *not* tempt the human being with ennobling dis-
courses on spiritual achievement. Positively, Heidegger declared that philosophy should return the human being from its obeisance before the idols
of humanism to a genuine recognition of its own nothingness as being-
in-the-world. The contrast between these two conceptions of philosophy is
indeed pronounced and the conflict between them seemingly inevitable:
on one side, we find "the works of spirit," on the other, "the hardness of fate."
The conflict is due to Heidegger's broader, historico-philosophical conviction that the history of ontology is an escalating tragedy of motivated error,

in the special sense that metaphysical notions such as *ratio*, spirit, consciousness, and *Geist* do not proffer merely a false understanding of our existence and our place in the world, they actually conspire, by delivering us over to the palliative belief in metaphysical foundations, to *obscure* the truth of our condition. It was therefore Heidegger's view that the humanistic philosopher who invokes "the works of the spirit," is more than just mistaken. Such a philosopher is nothing less than an emissary for metaphysical error in the pan-historical drama of *Seinsvergessenheit*.

It is hard to suppress the further thought that Heidegger's description of "the man who uses merely the works of the spirit" was meant as a reference to Cassirer. If so, the reference was at least mildly insulting: the implication would have been that Cassirer *himself* was a paradigm of the humanist philosopher whose cherished ideals were symptoms of metaphysical evasion and ontological forgetting. However, there is no direct evidence to support such an interpretation (least of all evidence from the transcript itself, the language of which is at best ambiguous). But the inference does not appear altogether unwarranted given Heidegger's global criticism of Cassirer's anthropocentric and humanist tendencies. A further detail, that this unnamed man-who-uses-mere-spirit is said to possess "a lazy outlook," seems only to enhance the insult. But here we must be extremely cautious in drawing any strong conclusions. In all likelihood Heidegger was referring to the various remarks on "lazy reason" *(ignava ratio)* in the first *Critique* where Kant warns his readers against transforming regulative principles, which play a necessary and legitimate role insofar as they orient reason in its investigation of nature (such as the idea of a divine author or the highest being), into constitutive principles, which reason mistakenly grants an objective reality. To commit this error, Kant explains, is to "take refuge in a mere idea, which is very comforting to reason [*um in einer bloßen Idea, die der Vernunft sehr bequem ist, zu ruhen*]."[80] The comparison has at least a prima facie plausibility, insofar as Heidegger, like Kant, meant to criticize the erroneous but characteristically human attempt to invest metaphysical principles with an unwarranted value, thereby transgressing the worldly constraints that define us as human. That Kant refers to *theological* ideas only strengthens the analogy, because Heidegger tended to consider God (in the conventional sense) as yet another metaphysical idol alongside reason, will, *Geist*, and so forth. Still, one can rightly conclude that from Heidegger's perspective

Cassirer's philosophy of symbolic forms was indeed guilty of "laziness" insofar as it typified humanity's metaphysical attempt to seek refuge and comfort in its own intellectual creations. The very same verdict would be restated a year later in the lecture course in the winter semester of 1929–1930, "The Fundamental Concepts of Metaphysics," when Heidegger would warn his auditors that the "philosophy of culture . . . does not take hold of *us*" and more drastically that it "unties us from ourselves in imparting us a role in world history. It unties us from ourselves, and yet does so precisely as anthropology." Cultural philosophy was not a solution to the present crisis but only served to intensify "our flight and disorientation." The attempt to secure though culture a redemption from the "profound boredom" of the contemporary world must end in failure because "convoluted idle talk about culture" was in the end little more than a strategy by which we "flee from ourselves."[81] The judgment was not only against Cassirer but against all modes of cultural philosophy. For it was an essential lesson of Heidegger's philosophy that such attempts only served to distract humanity from its actual historical condition.[82]

The Final Exchange

In response to claims that had been voiced so forcefully against the very essence of his own philosophy, Cassirer now found himself in a difficult position. With characteristic equanimity he began by emphasizing his basic agreement with Heidegger: to Heidegger's claim that they should avoid any "leveling" of the differences between them, Cassirer responded (perhaps humorously, perhaps failing to recognize the irony) that he agreed with Heidegger that leveling would be unwise. But he also cautioned that philosophical understanding requires, at the very least, a recognition of what the opponent's standpoint might entail. If instead one persisted in asserting a radical division of philosophical perspective, one would ultimately be forced to abandon the very ideal of philosophical insight. But to insist upon disagreement *without* imagining a higher plane of reconciliation would be to condemn oneself to a fruitless relativism of empirical individuals, as expressed in Fichte's dictum, "What sort of philosophy one chooses depends, . . . on what sort of man one is."[83] This species of relativism must somehow be combated, Cassirer warns, because it would bring philosophy itself to an end:

> *Cassirer:* I, too, am opposed to leveling. What we both want to, and must, strive for, and also what we can achieve, is that anyone, for all that he remains with his own standpoint, would see not only himself but the other as well. That this must be possible appears to me to lie in the idea of philosophical knowledge in general, in an idea that Heidegger too will appreciate. I do not want to make the attempt to break Heidegger from his position, to force him into another direction of seeing. Instead, I want only to make his position understandable to me. I believe that where the disagreement lies has already become clearer. It is not fruitful, however, to highlight this disagreement again and again. We maintain a position where little is to be accomplished through arguments that are merely logical. Nobody can be compelled to take up this position, and no such purely logical compulsion can force someone to begin with the position that appears to me to be the essential one. For here we would be condemned to a relativity. "What one chooses for a philosophy depends upon what sort of human being one is." But we must not persevere in this relativity, which would stand the empirical man at the center [of the analysis].

What is perhaps most noteworthy in these remarks is Cassirer's poignant desire to establish a common language even in the face of mounting disagreement. As he appealed to mutual understanding, Cassirer also developed a forceful rejoinder to his opponent: Heidegger's criticism of the anthropocentric premise behind the philosophy of symbolic forms prompted Cassirer to respond that Heidegger himself cannot coherently insist upon the sheer fact of philosophical disagreement, because grounding one's philosophy in difference is itself a concession to anthropocentrism, that is, the subjectivistic differentiation of doctrines is grounded in nothing more than the empirical differentiation of philosophers as individual persons, a subjectivism Heidegger disavowed. Against Heidegger, Cassirer insisted that if the anthropocentrism of different subjectivities is to be surpassed, there must indeed be something like a common and objective world. This unity across difference is established through the "primordial phenomenon of language" because, although each individual "speaks his own language," a collective of individuals can reach mutual understanding only through a common linguistic *medium*. As Cassirer put it, "there is something like *the* language." This claim is anticipated in the first volume of *The Philosophy of Symbolic Forms,* where Cassirer already claimed that "while languages differ in their 'perspectives of the world' [*Standpunkt der Weltansicht*], *there is a perspective of language itself* [*es gibt . . . eine Weltansicht der Sprache selbst*]."[84] When confronted with Heidegger's animadversions against the ideal of mutual translation, Cassirer responded that a common medium must serve as the logical precondition for all communication, without which even the acknowledgment of difference would be impossible:

> *Cassirer:* And what Heidegger finally said was very important. His
>   position, too, cannot be anthropocentric, and if it does not
>   want to be such, then I ask where the common core of our
>   disagreement lies. That it cannot be in the empirical is clear.
>   We must search again for the common center, precisely in
>   the disagreement. And I say, we do not need to search. For
>   we have this center and, what is more, this is so because
>   there is a common, objective human world in which the
>   differences between individuals have in no way now been
>   cancelled [*aufgehoben*], but with the stipulation that here the
>   bridge from individual to individual has now been estab-
>   lished. This occurs repeatedly for me in the primordial
>   phenomenon of language. Each of us speaks his own
>   language, and it is unthinkable that the language of one of
>   us is carried over into the language of the other. And yet,
>   we understand ourselves through the medium of language.
>   Hence, there is something like *the* language. And hence
>   there is something like a unity over and beyond the infinity
>   of the variety of ways of speaking [*Und so etwas wie eine
>   Einheit über der Unendlichkeit der verschiedenen
>   Sprechweisen*].

Cassirer had now returned after several detours to what on his view was the pivotal question of the debate: even granting Heidegger's analysis of situated existence, Cassirer insisted there must nonetheless be some path to objectivity. The possibility of intersubjective communication and even the intelligibility of one's own subjective experience already presuppose some common ground. The objective-*qua*-intersubjective validity of knowledge is therefore a postulate embedded in the very medium of communication. In the first volume of the *Philosophy of Symbolic Forms*, Cassirer had already observed that all symbolic systems such as language "lay claim to objective value. They reach beyond the mere phenomena of the individual consciousness, claiming to confront them with something that is universally valid." This appeal to transsubjective validity furnished added proof that such form-systems are born from "a pure activity of spirit [*eine reine Aktivität des Geistes*]."[85] The medium of mutual understanding is itself the co-creation of individual subjectivities whose communication first establishes the bonds between them. But the network they create brings into being a higher domain that itself functions as a nonsubjective and universally valid reality:

> *Cassirer:* Therein lies what is for me the decisive point. And it is for that reason that I start from the objectivity of the symbolic form, because here the inconceivable has been done. Language is the clearest example. We assert here that we tread on a common ground. We assert this first of all as a postulate [*als Postulat*]. And in spite of all deceptions, in this demand we will not be mistaken. This is what I would like to call the world of the objective spirit [*die Welt des objektiven Geistes*]. From Dasein is spun the thread that, through the medium of such an objective spirit, again ties us together with another Dasein. And I believe that there is no other way from Dasein to Dasein than through this world of forms. There is this factum. Should this not be so, then I would not know how there could be something like a self-understanding. Knowing, too, is just a basic instance of this assertion: that an objective statement can be formulated about a matter and that it has the character of necessity that no longer refers back to the subjectivity of the individual.

Cassirer agreed with Heidegger that the fundamental question of metaphysics is the question of Being. But he resisted Heidegger's implication that this question was only to be understood through recollection of its ancient Greek origins. As Cassirer explained, the very meaning of Being underwent a profound transformation with the modernist recasting of metaphysics in Kant's "Copernican Revolution," the basic lesson of which is that the human being does not confront the objects of the world as their passive recipient but rather spontaneously determines the world in its order and its form. But it follows that the human being has an active role in the creation of objectivity itself. Cassirer had already drawn this conclusion as early as 1910 in *Substance and Function,* in which he argued that for science an object is said to possess reality if and only if it has a functional place within the conceptual system constituting the scientific world. This basic conclusion remained unchanged even after Cassirer shifted from the critique of science to the critique of culture, and his prior focus on scientific symbolism gave way to his pluralistic theory of symbolic forms. In the introduction to the first volume of *The Philosophy of Symbolic Forms,* Cassirer had observed that in science and in language, myth, art, and religion, the world of the 'real' is constructed [*die Welt des 'Wirklichen' . . . aufbaut*]."[86] In his rejoinder to Heidegger at Davos, Cassirer proposes a *modernist ontology of construction,* according to which reality is itself a symbolic construct but for that very reason also counts as objective. The question of Being as Heidegger conceived it must accordingly be revised; it must now be understood in a radically new sense as the question of the constitution of Being of objectivity:

> *Cassirer:* Heidegger rightly said that the basic question of his
> metaphysics is the same one that Plato and Aristotle defined:
> what is the being [*Was ist das Seiende*]? And he further said
> that Kant had again referred to this basic question of all
> metaphysics. This I concede without further ado. But here an
> essential difference appears to me to exist, namely, with
> respect to what Kant called the Copernican Turn. Indeed, it
> seems to me that the question of Being [*die Seinsfrage*] has in
> no way been done away with by this turn. That would be a
> completely false interpretation. But as a result of this turn,
> the question of Being now comes to have an extremely

complicated form, as it had had in antiquity. Where does the turn occur? "Previously it was accepted that knowledge must conform to the object.... But for once, we now attempt the reverse question. How would it be if it were not our knowledge that must conform to the object, but if instead it were the object that must conform to knowledge?" That means that this question regarding the determinacy of the object is preceded by a question concerning the constitution of the Being of objectivity in general [*Seinskonstitution einer Gegenständlichkeit überhaupt*]. And what is applicable to this objectivity in general now must also apply to every object within this structure of Being [*Seinsstruktur*].

Cassirer saw his own philosophy as directly in line with the modernist transformation of ontology stemming from Kant's Copernican Revolution. Whereas Being as understood by the ancient metaphysicians was a substance or *hypokeimenon* (i.e., the unformed foundation), Being as understood by Kant and post-Kantian metaphysics has merely a *functional* meaning, in that what counts as objectively real can only be determined with reference to the system of symbolic forms within which a given entity plays its role. To be sure, Cassirer has expanded significantly upon Kant's original problematic: Whereas Kant had acknowledged only a "single structure of Being," Cassirer recognized "completely varied structures of Being." He had thereby pluralized Kant's constructivist ontology but also emancipated it from its erstwhile scientific constraints:

> *Cassirer:* What is new in this [Copernican] turn, it seems to me, lies in the fact that now there is no longer one single such structure of Being, but that instead we have completely varied structures of Being [*ganz verschiedene Seinsstrukturen*]. Every new structure of Being has its new a priori presuppositions. Kant shows that he was bound to the conditions for the possibility of experience. Kant shows how every kind of new form now also refers to a new world of the objective, how the aesthetic object is not bound to the empirical object, how it has its own a priori categories, how

art also builds up a world, but also how these laws are
different from the laws of the physical. For this reason, a
completely new multiplicity enters into the problem of the
object in general. And for this reason, the new Kantian
metaphysics come into being precisely from out of ancient,
dogmatic metaphysics. Being in ancient metaphysics was
substance, what forms a ground [*das eine Zugrundelieg-
ende*]. Being in the new metaphysics is, in my language, no
longer the Being of a substance, but rather the Being that
starts from a variety of functional determinations and
meanings [*nicht mehr das Sein einer Substanz, sondern das
Sein, das von einer Mannigfaltigkeit von funktionellen
Bestimmungen und Bedeutungen ausgeht*]. And the essential
point that distinguishes my position from Heidegger's
appears to me to lie here.

It should be noted that in his contrast between ancient and Kantian versions
of Being, Cassirer was no longer speaking to the "question of Being" as Heidegger understood it. Heidegger's own inquiry into the problem of ontology
was directed toward *neither* the ancient conception of Being as substantial
ground *nor* the Kantian conception of Being as mental form; it was instead
aimed toward the sense of Being *(Seinssinn)* that inhered in the actual comportment of Dasein as an embodied and thrown entity whose own manner
of being was that of being-in-the-world. This difference was indeed profound. There was certainly no obvious commensurability that would have
permitted Cassirer to align Heidegger with either of the two historical
definitions as he had sketched them. Heidegger in fact believed that *both*
of these historical definitions betrayed a "forgetting of Being" insofar as
they conceived it according to the metaphysical model of an atemporal
presence.

It was indeed a measure of their real divergence that Cassirer seemed unable to describe the basic problem in terms Heidegger could recognize. But
this was not due to a simple failure of comprehension: Cassirer elsewhere
showed that he found little difficulty understanding Heidegger's claims. It is
simply that the disagreement was so elementary that at a certain point Cassirer could only return to a discussion of the problem as he understood it

himself, even if the unfortunate consequence was that his historical remarks seemed to speak *about* his interlocutor rather than *to* him. One might conclude that *both* Cassirer *and* Heidegger committed the very same breach of philosophical dialogue, insofar as each of them wished to dispose of the opponent's doctrine not through the force of the better argument but rather by means of a historical redescription: Heidegger wrote Cassirer's philosophy into the history of *Seinsvergessenheit*. But Cassirer responded in kind, suggesting that Heidegger's philosophy subscribed to a defunct metaphysics of substance. The result is what one might call a stalemate of mutual historicization: both philosophers seemed to believe they occupied a position of superior historical knowledge from which they could characterize the errors of their opponent. Neither had in fact shown that the opponent's philosophy was wrong on argumentative grounds alone. Their separation was complete.

Cassirer now offered a final remark on the matter of Cohen's legacy: what remained legitimate in Cohen's neo-Kantian doctrine was the basic method of transcendental inquiry, according to which one begins with a fact and then asks after the conditions for the possibility of this fact. In Cassirer's opinion, however, Cohen had failed to appreciate the greater promise of Kantian philosophy, because he understood the transcendental method too narrowly and held that it applied only to mathematical natural science. Cassirer now suggested that what was truly promising in Kantian doctrine was the insight that there might be *multiple* spheres for transcendental inquiry and that each of them (language, art, and so forth) could be shown to possess its own set of a priori forms. Cassirer conceded that perhaps not all philosophical questions could be resolved within the Kantian framework. He closed with the bold suggestion that the transcendental method should at least be taken as a general point of departure for current questions in philosophy, including the questions of concern to Heidegger:

> *Cassirer:* I stand by the Kantian manner of posing the question of the transcendental, as Cohen always formulated it. He saw it as essential to the transcendental method that this method begins with a fact; except that for him this general definition—begin with a fact in order to ask about the possibility of this fact—was further narrowed down, in that he constantly construed mathematical natural science as the

[only] genuine problematic [*das eigentlich Fragwürddige*]. With Kant there is no such constraint. Now, I ask about the possibility of the fact of language. How does it come about, how is it thinkable, that we are able to come to an understanding from Dasein to Dasein in this medium? How is it possible that now and in general we can see a work of art as an objective determination, as an Objective being [*als objektiv Seiendes*], as this meaningful whole [*als dieses Sinnvolle in seiner Ganzheit*]? This question must be settled. Perhaps not all of the questions of philosophy are to be settled from this one. Perhaps there are vast areas that are not approachable from here. But it is necessary that we pose this question in the first instance [*zunächst einmal*]. And I believe that once this question is posed, one's way is then open to the question posed by Heidegger.

It is noteworthy that Cassirer felt compelled to return in his final remarks to the issue of Cohen's legacy, because one might have thought that by 1929 the passions for debating Marburg neo-Kantianism were wholly spent. That he ended with this issue was perhaps a sign that in a climate of waning enthusiasm for neo-Kantianism, Cassirer felt it imperative to emphasize the real distance he had traveled from Marburg even as he continued to profess fidelity to its foremost sage.[87] But this issue was largely academic. More significant was Cassirer's claim that the transcendental method must serve as *the general point of departure for all philosophical problems,* even the problems for which ultimately it can provide no solution. This was a statement of unusual strength and immodesty, though it was neither more nor less defensible than Heidegger's own frequently repeated claim that the question of Being was *the preeminent question of philosophy* and that it was to take precedence over the questions of all the positive sciences.[88]

To be sure, there was a close resemblance between these two claims: Both assert the priority of a distinctive philosophical question as the necessary precondition for all other questions of philosophy. Moreover, each of them asserts that this one question must be posed *first* if the interlocutor's question is to be properly understood. The result looks very much like a game of philosophical one-upmanship. But there are internal-philosophical reasons as to why their claims appear so markedly alike: the resemblance is due chiefly to a strong parallelism between transcendental and ontological questions. Heidegger himself suggests in *Being and Time* that the doctrine of transcendental logic laid down in Kant's *Critique of Pure Reason* has an *ontological meaning* insofar as it aims to disclose the Being of nature.[89] And in both the Davos Kant-lectures and the Kant-book Heidegger suggested that the transcendental inquiry of the first *Critique* goes well beyond the concerns of natural science and is in fact an inquiry into the human capacity for ontological knowledge. The parallelism is actually quite close: The structure of a transcendental argument in Kant's sense is that one begins with knowledge as it is given and then one asks what must be true of human understanding such that this knowledge is possible. The project of existential ontology as Heidegger conceived it can therefore be said to have a transcendental structure insofar as it begins from ontological knowledge as it is given in average everydayness and it then asks after the conditions of Dasein as the being for whom the question of Being is possible. Cassirer recognized this parallelism, and it is surely on these grounds that in his opening remarks he had suggested that Heidegger, too, was a neo-Kantian.

This resemblance is something Heidegger could neither accept nor wholly disown. His own lectures on Kant's first *Critique* had the effect of bringing out the strong affinity between transcendental and existential philosophy insofar as his chief aim was to characterize the *Critique* as a groundlaying for metaphysics (i.e., Dasein's ontological knowledge). But in Heidegger's view there remained a decisive difference: the Kantian question of the transcendental (especially as understood by the neo-Kantians and by Cassirer) is directed toward mental spontaneity as the ultimate wellspring of a priori form; whereas the transcendental question as Heidegger conceived it was directed toward human finitude or thrownness as an existential-temporal horizon *prior to* mental spontaneity. Heidegger therefore could not accept Cassirer's verdict that the Kantian-Copernican Revolution renders invalid any retrieval of the ontological question in its original Greek sense. Furthermore, although Cassirer was correct to observe that Being is disclosed in manifold ways, this did not foreclose the possibility of seeking a higher unity in an overall sense of Being *(Sinn von Sein überhaupt)*. But it was crucial for Heidegger that we should not misunderstand this unity as a "creative human achievement." As

he explained, it is the essence of philosophy that even its highest aspirations
remain forever bound to the finitude of the human being:

> *Heidegger:* Cassirer's last question in Kant's confrontation with the
> ancients gives me another opportunity to characterize the
> total work. I say that Plato's question must be retrieved.
> This cannot mean that we retreat to the Greeks' answer. It
> turns out that Being itself has been dispersed in a
> multiplicity and that a central problem exists therein,
> namely, to attain the foundation in order to understand
> the inner multiplicity of the ways of Being from the idea of
> Being [*die innere Mannigfaltigkeit der Seinsweisen aus der
> Idee von Sein zu verstehen*]. For my part, I am anxious to
> establish this sense of Being in general [*Sinn von Sein
> überhaupt*] as central. Accordingly, the only concern of
> my investigations is aimed toward attaining the horizon
> for the question concerning Being, its structure and
> multiplicity. Mere mediation [*bloße Vermitteln*] will never
> amount to anything productive. It is the essence of
> philosophy as a finite concern of human beings that it has
> been confined within the finitude of human beings as
> something that is not a creative human achievement [*Es ist
> das Wesen der Philosophie als einer endlichen Angelegen-
> heit des Menschen, daß sie in die Endlichkeit des Menschen
> beschränkt ist, wie keine schöpferische Leistung des
> Menschen*]. Because philosophy opens out onto the totality
> and what is highest in man, finitude must appear in
> philosophy in a completely radical way.

With this restatement of philosophical principles, Heidegger was now ready
to impart a final summation to the assembled guests. He admonished them
to take care they did not misunderstand the debate as a mere conflict of personalities: "Do not occupy yourselves with Cassirer and Heidegger," he
warned. At issue were not problems of standpoint or empirical perspective
but rather the concerns that belonged ultimately to the "central question of
metaphysics." Notwithstanding the many differences between the two phi-

losophers, they shared a devotion to this central problem, and anyone who understood their confrontation as a mere clash of rival perspectives would have failed to grasp this problem. Of course, this confrontation was merely one small chapter in the history of philosophy. But the history of philosophy itself was not simply a plurality of possible perspectives. Here, too, one had to free oneself from the sheer plurality of different standpoints so as to grasp the "unity of the problematic." Only then could one recognize that genuine philosophy demands the *differentiation* of positions:

> *Heidegger:* What it comes down to is that you take one thing with you from our confrontation [*Auseinandersetzung*]: do not orient yourselves to the variety of positions of philosophizing human beings, and do not occupy yourselves with Cassirer and Heidegger. Rather, the point is that you have come far enough to have felt that we are on the way toward once again applying ourselves in earnest to the central question of metaphysics. And on top of that, I would like to point out to you that, what you have seen here in the smallest measure is the difference between philosophizing human beings in the unity of the problematic, that this on a large scale expresses something completely different, and that it is precisely this self-liberation from the difference of positions and standpoints that is essential for a confrontation with the history of philosophy, that it is the first step in the history of philosophy to free oneself from the difference of positions and standpoints, so as to see how it is precisely the differentiation of standpoints that is the very root of philosophical endeavor [*wie gerade die Unterscheidung der Standpunkte die Wurzel der philosophischen Arbeit ist*].

As the above remarks suggest, Heidegger was clearly aware of the epochal or historical character of the confrontation. In fact he seemed strongly concerned lest the audience recall the debate in future years as nothing but a clash of personalities or worldviews. Heidegger's concern was perhaps justified. Indeed, even during the debate critics were keen to reimagine its significance in historical-philosophical terms that transfigured the two participants as titans in a grand allegory far suprassing Mann's novel. Only a month after the debate, a reporter for the *Frankfurter Zeitung* would write that the disputation "was felt to be not merely an academic quarrel between professors but rather a confrontation of representatives between two epochs."[90]

Many interpretations of the debate have fastened upon its historical symbolism, and as we have seen, both Cassirer and Heidegger themselves helped to encourage the notion that their philosophies were inscribed into history. This is somewhat ironic, given how very much they both tried to resist any kind of historical reduction. Cassirer claimed that in philosophical discourse it is possible to achieve a plateau of understanding that is no longer relative to the empirical individual or the historical epoch of which that individual is a part. Similarly, Heidegger claimed that it is a desideratum of philosophical insight that one must effect some measure of self-emancipation from mere standpoint or worldview.

Yet it is a striking feature of their discussion that both Cassirer and Heidegger themselves *already* understood their philosophies as inscribed into history: Cassirer saw the philosophy of symbolic forms as a development of cultural and intellectual modernism and he aligned its celebration of human creativity, or spontaneity, with philosophical trends born from the Enlightenment. Heidegger saw his philosophy as an event of disclosure by which to restore human being to a deepened recognition of its thrownness in historical time. Over the course of their conversation, both philosophers made use of these rival inscriptions so as to gain a certain argumentative advantage: Cassirer cast Heidegger's philosophy as a regression to the ancient metaphysics of substance, while Heidegger implicated Cassirer's philosophy in the narrative of modern *Seinsvergessenheit*. This, one might say, was the final consequence of their encounter: what began as a philosophical disagreement acquired an allegorical significance, reinforcing the divide between them until, eventually, in the years that followed, it ramified into a historical-political crisis.

5

Before Davos: Myth, Science, Modernity

Metaphysics is the science that aspires to dispense with symbols.

—HENRI BERGSON, *Introduction à la métaphysique*, 1903

Introduction

This chapter marks an interruption. Thus far we have been trying to make sense of the Davos encounter as an event unfolding in time. We have learned who was there and what was said, and to do so we remained more or less faithful to the chronological structure of a conventional narrative. But philosophical controversy does not unfold in linear fashion: its rhythms do not follow the steady pulse beats of calendrical time. If we are to understand the Davos disputation as a *philosophical* event, we must accordingly break from history and pause to consider some of the deeper and conceptual issues that were at stake. This chapter provides a deeper look at the conversation between Cassirer and Heidegger in the years preceding the Davos disputation. Chapter 6 then turns to the period of intensified philosophical and political disagreement in the years that immediately followed it.

It may be surprising to learn how much Heidegger and Cassirer already knew of one another's work before arriving in Davos. As early as 1923, Cassirer was acquainted with Heidegger, both personally and professionally, having first met him at a local meeting of the *Kant-Gesellschaft* in Hamburg, where they had exchanged views on the significance of myth as an object of philosophical inquiry: in *Being and Time,* Heidegger explicitly recalled this meeting and he praised the second volume of Cassirer's *Philosophy of Symbolic Forms,* which had "made the Dasein of myth a theme for philosophical interpretation." And in 1928 Heidegger amplified his thoughts on the second volume in a published review. Meanwhile, Cassirer was learning more about Heidegger's work as well. The third volume of his monumental study, *The Philosophy of Symbolic Forms,* was first published in 1929 as *The Phenomenology of Knowledge,* bringing to conclusion Cassirer's expansive and multivolume investigation of human symbolic activity in all spheres of expression. It should be noted that the term *phenomenology* was meant strictly in the Hegelian sense and made scant mention of the contemporary movement promoted by Husserl and his increasingly famous disciples. In fact, any explicit discussion of rival methods in interwar European philosophy was kept to a minimum. The entire text was largely complete by 1927, and although Cassirer had originally planned to add a final critical chapter on more recent philosophies, his experience over the next two years convinced him that an adequate assessment of the newest schools required nothing less than a fourth, additional work. Clues to his debate with Heidegger appear intermittently as random footnotes and asides that seem to have been slipped into the third volume after the body of the text was complete but just before publication in the closing months of 1929.[1] These scattered comments, though modest in size, provide crucial evidence for examining Cassirer's *Auseinandersetzung* with Heidegger's philosophy.

Taken together, all of the various acknowledgements and critical reviews that passed between Cassirer and Heidegger during the period from 1923 to 1929 furnish an indispensable framework for understanding the true philosophical stakes of the dispute at Davos. What emerges from these earlier exchanges is the impression that Cassirer and Heidegger were already divided by profound differences of philosophical doctrine and method, differences that made the prospects for future reconciliation highly improbable.

Cassirer, Phenomenology, Science

To understand Cassirer's emergent critique of Heidegger before Davos, we must recall some of the larger themes in the third volume of Cassirer's masterpiece. More generally, it provides a so-called phenomenology of scientific knowledge as the culminating stage in the philosophy of symbolic forms. Specifically, Cassirer singled out the concepts of space and time as the most vivid illustrations of this transhistorical process. And, as we shall see, his early disagreement with Heidegger first emerged out of a profound difference in their respective theories concerning the status of space and time.

Since the seventeenth century, Cassirer explained, physical explanation has moved increasingly toward the view that space and time are not substances or metaphysically real containers but merely concepts of relation, a development originating already in Descartes' mathematization of space, boldly advanced by Leibniz in his polemics against the Newtonians, and brought to completion by the development of group theory and non-Euclidean space in the nineteenth century and, most recently, in relativity and quantum theory. Cassirer's theory of scientific development therefore presupposes the gradual de-ontologization of the space-time field and its replacement by a symbolized, purely conceptual theory of relations.[2]

Alongside strictly scientific models of space and time, however, Cassirer also devoted considerable attention to the nature of space-time forms in other regions of human symbolization, most notably in aesthetics and "primitive," or mythic, thought: Whereas scientific thinking gradually breaks free from substantive conception of space and time, a predominant characteristic especially of mythological thinking is that it cannot achieve any comparable degree of abstraction, because the spatiotemporal horizon remains infused with practical and emotional significance. And it is here that Cassirer's disagreement with Heidegger first comes into view: Cassirer's commitment to philosophical modernism requires that philosophy *itself* recapitulate the process of abstraction and functionalization evident in scientific explanation. Just as science must dispense with "ontological" claims about the ultimate nature of reality, so, too, philosophy itself first arises only where it has performed a decisive break from myth. Thus while generously acknowledging the importance of Heidegger's "ontological" analysis of the spatiotemporal environment in *Being and Time,* Cassirer suggested that a properly philosophical understanding of the world cannot rest content with this stratum but must press "beyond" the existential horizon toward a purely functionalist universe of symbolization. To explain this disagreement, however, we must first recall some of the essential features of Heidegger's philosophy.

Heidegger's Existential Phenomenology

It bears repeating that Heidegger's entire project in *Being and Time* was meant merely as a means of laying the groundwork for the ultimate inquiry, the so-called *Seinsfrage,* or question of Being. Heidegger believed this question had laid dormant and half-forgotten throughout much of modernity. In *Being and Time* there was little of the eschatological yet paradoxically anti-modernist attempt to receive a "message" sent by Being; this was a theme that would only emerge in the mid-1930s. Heidegger's early philosophy still remained in certain respects bound by the more scientific ambitions of Husserl's phenomenological method for intentional analysis, a method that Heidegger adapted for purposes his teacher could hardly have foreseen. Yet the relation is clear: the "sense of Being," or the *Sinn des Seins,* is the basic understanding by which the object of intention is said to be at all.[3]

Heidegger's question of Being was first and foremost an inquiry into the "sense" of Being that precedes and underwrites the intentional horizon. Like Husserl, Heidegger believed the constitutive features of this horizon might be described without recourse to the possibly prejudicial concepts and methods of the philosophical tradition. Indeed, a marked indifference, or even antipathy, toward past philosophies is something that Heidegger's early work inherited directly from Husserl, and it remains characteristic of this tradition that it aims to recover through description alone what experience is like, eschewing the frequent references to the canon that is otherwise characteristic of Continental thought. Phenomenological description, in other words, is supposed to begin with an analysis of phenomena just as they are presented to intentional consciousness. The difference, however, is that Husserl developed a method of phenomenological bracketing, or *epoché,* so as to isolate the purely transcendental features of intentionality. Through this reduction, philosophy shifted its vision from the natural to the phenomenological attitude: all features of the empirical self and all existential commitments to the everyday world were to be put temporarily out of play, if only in order to better explore the essential features of intentional consciousness. Heidegger, however, followed a rather different path by developing a phenomenology of the natural attitude itself. He wished to explore intentionality—the route of intention opening upon the world—insofar as this is manifest in the "everydayness" of human existence. Against the quasi-Cartesian project of Husserl's "transcendental" analysis, an investigation, in other words, of the a priori structures of transcendental consciousness, Heidegger termed his own project an "existential analytic."[4]

The guiding assumption of this interpretation is that Dasein "is" only in-sofar as it is "ontological." Human life, that is, carries along with it as a mat-ter of existential necessity a rudimentary understanding of what it means to be. It is this, Dasein's ontological understanding, that Heidegger contrived to examine in the existential analytic by breaking it down into each one of its elements. Of course, these elements constitute a hermeneutic unity, so the breakdown is merely a conceptual artifice, a problem Heidegger tried to ex-cuse by noting that his terms served only as "formal indications" for dimen-sions of the holistic structure. These various indications included the social quality of "being-with," the linguistic structure of "understanding-being" and "being-in" as such, and the so-called worldhood of the world.[5]

Worldhood and Involvement

The analysis of worldhood as laid down in the third chapter of *Being and Time* introduces the distinctively "existential" thematics of space and time that would especially arouse Cassirer's interest. Heidegger began by warding off a possible misunderstanding, saying that the "world" to be analyzed is that of objective "nature" enjoying ontological independence from Dasein. The world here should not be construed as what-is-*not*-Dasein, because the aim is precisely to examine that "worldhood" that is a constitutive part of Dasein's own intentional structure. Thus "worldhood" (*Weltlichkeit*) is itself, in Heidegger's terminology, an "existentiale," or existential category analo-gous at least in this respect to Kantian categories, because they are a priori constitutive conditions for possible experience, although they are not mental conditions for possible *representation* as in Kant's theory.[6] Heidegger did not wish to prejudice his analysis in favor of cognitivism or representationalism. But he believed this prejudice to be so deeply engrained in the way we habitu-ally relate to the world that it passes already for the commonsense metaphys-ics of everyday life. It would accordingly be unwise to begin by describing the "entities" (*Seiendes*) within-the-world, because any such description would necessarily presuppose the existential horizon we need to examine. We al-ways risk falling back without notice upon a particular ontological inter-pretation of these entities as "things," as objective and extended substances (*res extensa*) that are somehow "out there" and "beyond" the subjective mind (*res cogitans*) that wishes to know them. This is an interpretation, Heidegger claimed, that we have inherited from the metaphysical tradition, chiefly from Descartes. Heidegger took great pains to fend off this view, as he believed it misses the ontological character of "worldhood" that informs Dasein's own self-understanding as a being whose manner of being is being-in-the-world.

Heidegger's own analysis took as its point of departure that sense of Being that suffuses the human being's understanding of its worldly situation. The world that is closest to Dasein, Heidegger explained, is not the world of scientific explanation but instead the *Umwelt,* or "environment."[7] While cautioning the reader that the prefix *Um,* or "aroundness" should not be construed in a literally *spatial* sense, Heidegger nonetheless devoted much effort later in the chapter to distinguishing between the spatiality most customarily associated with the Cartesian, physical-scientific understanding of the world as nature and his own understanding of the world as environment. The analysis of "environmentality" begins, however, not with environmental spatiality but with our practical relation *to* that environment, which Heidegger calls our involvement or "dealings" *(Umgang).*[8] As Heidegger explained, "the kind of dealing which is closest to us is . . . not a bare perceptual cognition, but rather that kind of concern which manipulates things and puts them to use; and this has its own kind of 'knowledge.'" The basic and pre-philosophical interpretation of environmental entities therefore construes them not as "things" but rather as things-in-use, as "equipment" *(Zeug)* or, in Greek, *pragmata.* Heidegger's basic thought was that the human relation to worldly things is primarily a relation of practice and concern: we understand things not as objects of theoretical analysis, but rather only as they first appear within the context of practice, that is, in and through the context of our involvement with them. To reinforce this idea, Heidegger introduced his famous distinction between the ready-to-hand *(zuhanden)* status of things as understood in an equipmental fashion versus the present-at-hand *(vorhanden)* manner of being of entities as they are disclosed for perceptual cognition. The ready-to-hand is our "everyday" and pre-philosophical understanding, and Heidegger claimed that it is the "primordial" way things appear to us, while the present-at-hand is a consequence of theoretical dissociation from that more basic relation.

A noteworthy feature of this argument—and it is a theme Cassirer found exceptionally troublesome—is its holistic premise: Given the pragmatic relationship to the world as described above, Heidegger suggested that objects are interpreted in advance according to a teleological network, where each facet of the environment enjoys its most basic significance only because it is assigned a purpose. An environmental object is therefore a "something 'in-order-to'" *(etwas um-zu),* and this significance immediately implies its purposive interconnection with the other objects of the world. Indeed, Heidegger noted that this interconnection belongs to the very essence of equipmental things, because each thing is assigned its place only in reference to something else. Consequently, there is no such thing as "an equipment," and discrete objects are understood in advance according to a referential totality of assignments. The totality thereby assumes a transcendental status in that the whole is a condition for the possibility of understanding any one of its parts. Or, put differently, the world is encountered as always already a "totality of equipment." The environment, then, is a holistic structure of concern, in which objects are *always* practically understood in a collective fashion, before the explicit knowledge of any discrete item we may pick out for inspection. To underscore this point, Heidegger coined an additional term of art that captures the mode of understanding that accompanies our environmental relation: As against theoretical "vision," or *Sicht,* we understand in a mode of circumspection, or *Umsicht.* Accordingly, we should not think of "dealings" as explicit "tasks" that we understand theoretically in advance and then go on to complete in practice. As Heidegger explained, most of our dealings "have already dispersed themselves into manifold ways of concern." A future-oriented intention is built in to human understanding, and this implies that our practical relation to things is best understood not as an instrumentalist one that aims to fulfill some specified goal but instead as a kind of implicit investment in how things turn out and how our world as a whole will unfold.[9]

Existential Spatiality and Functional Space

Heidegger further claimed that Dasein's own sense of spatial relatedness in-the-world—"existential spatiality"—is itself conditional upon Dasein's equipmental context. Existential spatiality, or *"Räumlichkeit,"* is therefore fundamentally unlike the Cartesian notion of extension or a Newtonian idea of space as a container. The latter makes sense only in reference to present-at-hand objects. They do not apply to a being whose primary relation to the

world is one of involvement.[10] In fact, Heidegger took care to note that while
we may think of the equipmental context in a formal way as a "relational"
structure (i.e., a whole where each element gains its significance in "relation"
to the other parts), this formal definition should not be ontologized as if it
were the explicit principle actually responsible for binding together the structure: The "things" embedded in an equipmental context *resist any sort of
mathematical functionalization.*[11] In other words, contextual significance is
not the fruit of some mental effort that first brings together previously independent entities, nor are the objects of significance "merely something
thought, first posited in an 'act of thinking.'" But this means that equipmental
involvement is, in Heidegger's view, the prior condition for all functional talk
of "relation." The neo-Kantian view, Heidegger concluded, must be mistaken,
because it claimed that in mathematical-scientific explanation, substance is
wholly displaced by function. Cassirer, though not cited by name, was the
obvious target of this criticism, which Heidegger summarized in *Being and
Time* as follows:

> This "system of Relations," [is] something constitutive for worldhood
> [and] . . . worldhood . . . provides the basis upon which such entities can
> be discovered as they are "substantially" "in themselves." And only if
> entities within-the-world can be encountered at all [i.e., within equip-
> mental contexts], is it possible, in the field of such entities, to make ac-
> cessible what is just present-at-hand and no more. By reason of their
> Being-present-at-hand-and-no-more, these latter entities can [only then]
> have their "properties" defined mathematically in "functional concepts."
> Ontologically, such concepts are possible only in relation to entities
> whose Being has the character of pure substantiality. *Functional con-
> cepts are never possible except as formalized substantial concepts.*[12]

Heidegger's point is that selecting discrete "concepts" of things and relating
them to one another for theoretical explanation is only possible once things
have first been conceived as "present-at-hand," that is, as "substances" in
Cartesian space. But this conception is at odds with the spatiality by which
Dasein first understands its being-in-the-world. Relation, therefore, is not
logically prior to substance but simply its conceptual precipitate. Indeed, relation is only possible once one has effected a "break" from the equipmental

context that constitutes the true ground of human understanding. It follows, however, that we must develop a notion of existential spatiality from this sort of involvement, and we must take care to distinguish between Dasein's spatiality and the "Cartesian" space of present-at-hand things.

The spatiality of Dasein, then, is in Heidegger's view the sense of orientation that emerges out of the equipmental totality of Dasein's world. The ready-to-hand has its own spatiality insofar as equipment requires placement within the totality of assignments. This sort of placement implies an understanding of something ready-to-hand as being "close" *(in der Nähe),* but it is not closeness in the sense of measurable distance. It is more a matter of an item's "belonging-somewhere" *(Hingehörigkeit)* within the context of involvement itself. And this sense of proper fit is what first lends the context its specific orientation: everything within the context is therefore assigned a certain position, a "yonder" or "there" *("'Dort' und 'Da'"),* such that the entire context shows up for us as a spatial "region" *(Gegend).* Unlike the three-dimensional, coordinate system of Cartesian space, which possesses neither left nor right, neither up nor down, the spatiality of Dasein's involvement first lends our experience a definite orientation.[13]

The spatiality attending the equipmental context of the ready-to-hand is thus irreducible to Cartesian space. The strength of the contrast is most noticeable when one reflects on the fact that Cartesian space always places things at a measurable distance, whereas Dasein's spatiality determines distance in terms of its own context of significance. It thus picks out items of the world in such a way as to annul in advance the distance of whatsoever falls within its horizon. This is true already, Heidegger suggests, insofar as bodily orientation and directionality attends our involvement in the world. Stated more broadly, our sense of what is near is a function of significance rather than measure. The soles of one's feet, for example, tend as a rule to vanish into the inconspicuousness of the ready-to-hand, although the person encountered while walking is brought to the fore, even while she may remain at a great measurable distance. (Here Heidegger added an intriguing aside: "modern" communications equipment, such as the radio or the telephone, have the peculiar feature of conquering all remoteness, while their present-at-hand being may tend to withdraw from the horizon of involvement. We should recall that this was published in 1927, when the novelty of such devices seemed to merit philosophical comment.) To clarify this peculiar feature of Dasein's existential constitution, Heidegger introduced the term *"Entfernung,"* indicating the "undoing-the-far" that accompanies our orientation within the equipmental context.[14] It is important to note that this is not the result of an interpretative action, as if things laying at some measurable distance were brought close as a result of subjective imposition. As Heidegger explained, "de-severance" is an *existential,* and this means that Dasein's world is first *constituted* with this existential-spatial structure: *"In Dasein,"* he concluded, *"there lies an essential tendency towards closeness."*[15]

Science and Epistemic Nostalgia

As we shall see momentarily, it is this characterization of existential space as an intimate or even closed horizon that brought the underlying differences between Cassirer and Heidegger into stark relief. It was indeed characteristic of Heidegger's overall manner of thinking to posit a strong distinction between hermeneutic and natural-scientific understanding. And the analysis of space was no exception: whereas Cartesian space was that of measurable distance, existential spatiality was a horizon that "brings close." And whereas Cartesian space was a world of pure dimensionality that nonetheless lacked any determinate sense of orientation, existential spatiality "with regard to right and left" is itself based on the *"a priori* of Being-in-the-world," and yet "lacks the pure multiplicity of the three dimensions." Moreover, existential spatiality was the *precondition* for our understanding of Cartesian space, because the former was an existential condition for understanding at all. It followed that whatever formalized structures of measurement we might create in our attempt to better negotiate our surroundings, such structures were themselves merely a way of "thematizing" the spatiality of Dasein's everyday environment. There was accordingly no such thing as a "breakthrough" from existential spatiality to space:

> As Being-in-the-world, Dasein maintains itself essentially in de-severing. This de-severance—the farness of the ready-to-hand from Dasein itself—is something that Dasein can *never cross over.* Of course the remoteness of something ready-to-hand from Dasein can show up as a distance from it, . . . [and] Dasein can subsequently traverse the

"between" of this distance, but only in such a way that the distance itself becomes one which has been de-severed. So little has Dasein crossed over its de-severance that it has rather taken it along with it and keeps doing so constantly; for *Dasein is essentially de-severance.*[16]

Heidegger of course did not deny the possibility that one could *develop* a purely mental representation of formalized, Cartesian space. But he resisted the conclusion that this representation could put one in touch with something more "real" or "objective" than Dasein's spatial world. While he did not develop the point at length, the following passage clearly accords with Heidegger's more general view that existential contexts are constitutively *prior* to the conceptual schemes of science:

Space . . . can be studied purely by looking at it, if one gives up what was formerly the only possibility of access to it—circumspective calculation. When space is "intuited formally," the pure possibilities of spatial relations are discovered. Here one may go through a series of stages in laying bare pure homogenous space, passing from the pure morphology of spatial shapes to *analysis situs* and finally to the purely metrical science of space.[17]

Here Heidegger introduced a troublesome theme—the order of priority between existential conditions and scientific concepts—to which he failed to provide adequate resolution and which became a focal point for Cassirer's criticism. It remained unclear just what it could mean to "give up" an existential condition in one's passage toward abstract, scientific concepts. An existential condition by definition was constitutive and could not be abandoned. Indeed, as Heidegger himself had earlier noted, it simply wasn't possible to somehow "cross over" the interpretative horizon by which Dasein brings close the equipment of its world. "In our present study," Heidegger demurred, "we shall not consider how all these are connected." The order of connection was ostensibly a "series of stages," a term seemingly indicating a process of advance. But if this remark appeared momentarily to assign scientific conceptualization a status of greater sophistication in human understanding, the suggestion was just as quickly withdrawn in language that suggested not progress but loss:

When space is discovered non-circumspectively by just looking at it, the environmental regions *get neutralized to pure dimensions.* Places—and indeed the whole circumspectively oriented totality of places belonging to equipment ready-to-hand—*get reduced to* a multiplicity of positions for random Things. The spatiality of what is ready-to-hand within-the-world *loses its involvement-character,* and so does the ready-to-hand. The world *loses its specific aroundness;* the environment becomes the world of Nature. The "world," as a totality of equipment ready-to-hand, becomes spatialized to a context of extended Things which are *just present-at-hand and no more.* The homogenous space of Nature shows itself only when the entities we encounter are discovered in such a way that it has the character of a specifically *Unworlding* [*Entweltlichung*] of the worldliness of the ready-to-hand.[18]

Despite its seeming obscurity, the importance of this passage should not be underestimated and it will prove vital for our understanding of Cassirer's criticism. One of the core issues in Heidegger's fundamental ontology was whether the hermeneutic conditions he described were analogous to Kantian conditions, insofar as one might distinguish between the world "in itself" and the hermeneutic world as it is shaped by human understanding. If this distinction were tenable, Heidegger left himself open to the charge that hermeneutic conditions were merely "subjective" because, however deep their structuring effect, one could nonetheless appeal, if only counterfactually, to a realm of things present-at-hand and seemingly independent of Dasein's world.

The danger of this subjectivist reading, however, was considerable, because it conflicted with the fundamental premises of Heidegger's metaphysical anti-naturalism. According to Heidegger, philosophy since Plato has remained captive to a metaphysics of "presence," that is, the notion that the "Being" by virtue of which "there is" intelligible reality can only be understood as occupying some kind of metaphysical precinct beyond that reality, because only then could it serve as its self-sufficient ground. This notion of Being, however, takes its cue from the idea that time is a series of "nows," such that Being itself would naturally appear as an eternal present. It is this conception that then seems to warrant the rationalists' view that one can grasp Being itself in a complete and perfected thought. Moreover, it is a notion that tends to imagine a sharp break between the knower and the known: by disengaging from the world, this view suggests, one can ostensibly achieve a position of complete neutrality and therefore articulate what Bernard Williams, in reference to Descartes, once called "the absolute conception of reality."[19] The guiding insight of Heidegger's philosophy, however, is that this metaphysics of presence is an error, which must be vigorously combated on behalf of the "post-metaphysical" insight that Being is itself grounded in time. It follows, however, that philosophers may never again stake claims to an unmoved and metaphysical reality such as "God," "Reason," or "Nature." Heidegger sought to render such claims impermissible by recasting the inquiry into Being on anti-metaphysical (or, apparently, nonrealist) grounds.

Modern natural science thus confronted Heidegger with a serious challenge. For if science could claim to know what is "real," then the existential categories could not rise above the status of merely subjective conditions for everyday experience, and the global pretensions of Heidegger's philosophy to escape subjectivism were at best confused. Yet it is important to realize that Heidegger himself was uncertain as to how best to cope with this difficulty, as his remarks on the "neutralization" of hermeneutic horizons show: once the structures of involvement are consigned to the status of human-dependent "interpretation," the way was open for science to declare as its own domain the world as it is disclosed *without* interpretation, and so to proclaim that only through scientific "objectivity" can one gain access to what is metaphysically real. Kant himself, of course, had inoculated his own doctrine against this subjectivist reading, with the assertion that not only is transcendental idealism compatible with empirical realism, it in fact underwrites whatever passes for "reality." Scientific objectivity was, for Kant, correlative with the structures of understanding. On this point, Cassirer followed Kant, as we shall see momentarily. For Heidegger, however, this solution was not available. By insisting that *scientific* reality was itself disclosed to Dasein *as* the present-at-hand, Heidegger's transcendental-existential conditions, unlike Kant's conditions, risked taking on the appearance of being both *contingent* and *subjective*. By Heidegger's own logic, it seemed possible to break free of interpretation, to neutralize one's own existential horizon so as to encounter the scientist's field of merely "given" reality. But then, Heidegger's protests notwithstanding, his metaphysical

anti-naturalism—the doctrine that the *world as such* just *is* Dasein's interpretative world—seemed to posit a pre-critical distinction between interpretation and natural reality.

Heidegger's dilemma was poorly disguised in his recourse—most evident
in the passage quoted immediately above—to what one might call epistemic
nostalgia: The interpretative conditions of Dasein's involvement could be
"lost," "neutralized," or, less dramatically, "reduced," a process captured in
the global term *unworlding*, or *Entweltlichung* (sometimes translated as
"world-alienation"), which seemed both a condensation and intensification
of the process of rationalization Max Weber had termed *"die Entzauberung
der Welt,"* the disenchantment of the world. If unworlding were truly a kind
of loss, then it seemed Heidegger might have still plausibly insisted that the
human world of involvement is "fundamental," and the scientific world of
the present-at-hand merely "derivative." But this now seemed merely a poetic
or quasi-moralistic judgment rather than an ontological doctrine. In fact,
casting the shift from involvement to scientific objectivity in the mournful
language of disenchantment did nothing to ward off a subjectivist and
metaphysical-naturalist interpretation of Heidegger's philosophy. It implied
only that subjective involvement was preferable to the cold, but metaphysically unimpeachable encounter with the real.

But if these were indeed the implications of Heidegger's interpretation,
it now amounted to little more than a normative protest against the rise of
science and the consequent corrosion of human meaning, very much like
the protest Max Weber had ridiculed in his famous 1919 address, *Science as
a Vocation:*

> Who—aside from certain big children who are indeed found in the
> natural sciences—still believes that the findings of astronomy, biology,
> physics, or chemistry could teach us anything about the *meaning* of the
> world? . . . If [the] natural sciences lead to anything . . . , they are apt to
> make the belief that there is such a thing as the "meaning" of the uni-
> verse die out at its very roots.[20]

It was surely not Heidegger's aim to indulge in regressive fantasy about the
rich meaning now lost to the world. But the suggestion that spatial "nature"
lay both "beyond" Dasein's spatiality yet was still somehow accessible (given

a so-called loss of involvement), threatened to transform existential ontology into a doctrine that was, on the one hand, idealist and subjectivist (regarding the existential space-time which constitutes Dasein's world) and, on the other hand, metaphysically realist (regarding the realm of objective entities known through the scientific practice of "deworlding" the existential world). This potentially fatal moment in Heidegger's early thought had as its Achilles' heel an uncertain and potentially self-contradictory theory concerning the status of scientific concepts, specifically, space and time: The pragmatic structure of involvement informed a "spatiality" that, although not equivalent to space, was supposedly deeper than space and even its precondition. But this squared poorly with the idea that one could rupture the spatiality of involvement to theorize the present-at-hand field of mathematizable "Nature." The nostalgic characterization of this breakthrough as a loss of meaning did little to alleviate the possible conflict in Heidegger's metaphysical commitments.

Original Temporality and Worldly Time

Heidegger's discussion of time was more sweeping, yet just as conflicted. Whereas spatiality was merely a feature of existential involvement, Heidegger argued that temporality was its necessary precondition and an insuperable horizon of worldhood without exception. It is not surprising, then, that the argument about time would weld together all of the various argumentative layers of *Being and Time*. To be sure, the first half of the book, titled "Preparatory Fundamental Analysis of Dasein," is, in Robert Dostal's phrase, largely "static," because it lacks any rich account of Dasein's temporality.[21] The second half of the book, "Dasein and Temporality," much like Kant's schematism of the categories, explains how the static structure of "existentials" (language, social being, disposition, and so forth) actually show up in Dasein's always-temporal world. But this distinction is too stark because, as Heidegger readily admitted, his phenomenology exhibits a hermeneutic circularity such that any understanding of Dasein must rely on the structures it examines. It follows that even the "static" analysis must be inevitably temporal. Involvement itself presupposes a teleological structure of intentionality, an "in-order-to" that characterizes our practical investment in how things unfold, from past assignments to future goals. We cannot be in

the world without "care," that is, without finding our being "at issue," because this is just what it means to find our being through involvement.
Because care has a temporal orientation, it follows that this very temporality
is the ground for all care as such, and, associatively, for involvement and
spatiality as well: from this insight, Heidegger developed what was perhaps
his most far-reaching insight, that the entire "care-structure" of Dasein's
being-in-the-world is unified by a so-called original temporality *(ursprüngliche Zeitlichkeit).*[22]

Yet the entire edifice of *Being and Time* stood under a question mark. The
book began with a promissory note, the suggestion that time—Dasein's own
"original" temporality—would serve as the "transcendental horizon for the
question of Being."[23] During the exposition, Heidegger had shown how Dasein's way of understanding itself and its world is always "ecstatic," in that it
discloses the world in terms of a "temporalizing" structure uniting the three
so-called ecstases of past, present, and future. The premise of this exposition
was that original temporality is the deepest condition for Dasein's being-in-
the-world at all. On this point Heidegger repeated a view hailing from
Augustine, who considered time "an extension of the mind itself." Kant had
similarly claimed that time could not be ascribed metaphysical reality but
was instead the "pure form of inner intuition" and therefore a condition for
all appearance.[24] And Husserl, as early as his 1905 lectures, *The Phenomenology of Internal Time-Consciousness* (which were published, under Heidegger's auspices, in 1928), had identified the structures of retension (past)
and "protension" (future) that would inspire Heidegger's own theory of
original temporality. Later, in *Ideas* I, Husserl argued that "phenomenological time" is "the unitary form of all lived experience," but itself belongs
to the structure of the "egological" horizon. The time usually considered
"out there" and independent of one's own experience—Husserl called it "objective," or "cosmic" time—was itself founded on "inner" or phenomenological time, which "belongs essentially to experience as such . . . and derived from these the modally determined now, before and after, simultaneity,
succession, and so forth—[and] is not to be measured by any state of the sun,
by any clock, by any physical means, and generally cannot be measured at
all."[25] Taking his cue from Husserl, Heidegger likewise insisted that the
"worldly" time of clocks and measurable duration was derivative: It was

founded on the more "original time"—which Husserl called the "absolute stream"—of Dasein's own existential structure.

As is well known, however, Heidegger's effort at confronting the "question of Being" did not move beyond the analysis of *Dasein's* own way of being. The book concluded without conclusion by asserting that "an original mode of the temporalizing of ecstatic temporality itself *must* render possible the ecstatical projection of Being itself."[26] Just what this meant remained indeterminate: Because the *Seinsfrage* was itself a question that only Dasein could pose, it seemed trivial to repeat the claim that the "projection of Being" was possible only on the basis of human (temporal) understanding. The closing remarks seemed to imply something more, as if from the structure of human understanding, one might conclude something about "Being" as a ground separable from its preparatory horizons. The suggestion betrayed a scent of metaphysical realism, the full commitment to which Heidegger resisted only by casting the closing lines of the book in the open-ended form of three progressively sharpened questions: "How is this mode of the temporalizing of temporality to be interpreted? Is there a way which leads from primordial *time* to the sense of *Being*? Does *time* reveal itself as the horizon of *Being*?"[27]

As in his discussion of space, in which he seemed ready to admit an independent, nonexistential space, Heidegger now verged on a metaphysically realist doctrine about "Being" as *itself* constituted in "Time," where the latter appeared independent of Dasein. But this doctrine seemed compatible with the scientific-realist view of space-time as non-human-dependent continuum. To avoid this realist view, however, Heidegger slipped occasionally toward the opposite extreme of transcendental-subjectivism, where "time" meant merely *Dasein's own* temporalizing while time in this existential sense played no role whatsoever in the constitution of nature-in-itself. Two years before *Being and Time*, in the 1925 lectures titled "History of the Concept of Time," Heidegger had noted that "nature" is "encountered 'in' the time which we ourselves are." But he gave this claim a realist turn with the further suggestion that "they [the movements of nature] are as such *completely time-free*."[28] The doctrine of time was therefore at least as equivocal as the doctrine of space, because to posit a "time-free" nature meant to contrast, once again, the existential structures of Dasein's understanding, both spatial and temporal, with a metaphysically "real" object of science beyond those structures. As if to validate this possibility, Heidegger noted in the 1927 lectures titled *Basic Problems of Phenomenology* that "Nature can also be when no Dasein exists."[29]

Here, Heidegger's analysis betrayed a striking ambiguity that would become the focal point for Cassirer's criticism. The essential problem was that Heidegger seemed unable to resolve his views concerning space and time on the question of metaphysical anti-realism. On the one hand, he clearly saw existential space and time as constitutive of the world and therefore non-subjective. On the other hand, by positing a "time-free" nature independent of Dasein, he implied they were both subjective and contingent. This was perhaps merely one illustration of Heidegger's greater inability throughout his early work to theorize the relation between Dasein and Being without falling into idealism or subjectivism. The dilemma was most conspicuous in his scattered remarks on science, because it was science most of all, perhaps, that appeared, in *Being and Time,* to enjoy a monopoly on the realm of pure present-at-hand entities, that is, entities as considered apart from Dasein's existential-constitutive horizon.[30]

In his discussion of "truth," for example, Heidegger struggled to develop a distinction between the "original truth" relative to Dasein's disclosure of the world and the traditional concept of truth as correspondence, which he claimed was dependent upon original truth.[31] Here, too, Heidegger wanted to insist that even scientific truth as such is relative to Dasein:

> *"There is" truth only in so far as Dasein* is *and so long as Dasein* is. Entities are uncovered only *when* Dasein *is; and only so long as Dasein* is Newton's laws [for example] . . . are true only so long as Dasein *is.* Before there was any Dasein, there was no truth; nor will there be any after Dasein is no more. . . . Before Newton's laws were discovered, they were not "true"; it does not follow [however] that they were false, or even that they would become false. To say that before Newton his laws were neither true nor false, cannot signify that before him there were no such entities as have been uncovered and pointed out by those laws. Through Newton the laws became truth; and with them, entities became accessible in themselves to Dasein. Once entities have been uncovered, they show themselves precisely as entities which beforehand already were.[32]

This was perhaps one of the more perplexing passages in all of Heidegger's 1927 masterwork, because it seemed to give with one hand what it took back with the other: it suggested that the very Being of scientific objects was contingent on Dasein's existential horizon, while also implying that the objects thus disclosed were "already" there prior to that disclosure. Again Heidegger confronted the anti-realist implications of his method. But when confronted with a paradigmatic example from the history of science, he seemed to draw back from these very implications, by granting that present-at-hand scientific entities were not in fact contingent on Dasein at all, because they preexisted their own disclosure.

It is perhaps unsurprising if the history of scientific discovery, and, more specifically, the status of scientific claims about spatiotemporal nature, confronted Heidegger with the most obdurate challenge to his anti-realism. As examples drawn from the past, scientific truths are discovered by human beings at a distinct moment in time, and they seem thereby implicated, at least potentially, in the temporality and historicity of human understanding itself. But as truths about *nature,* their realist status seems potentially nonrelative to the context of their discovery. Not only did Heidegger fail to adequately distinguish the context of discovery from the context of justification, and, from truth status as such, but he also seemed to collapse the two into a historicist ontology with his claim that Dasein's disclosure is "prior" to scientific truth. Some of the difficulties of combining historicist ontology with a modified scientific realism would be addressed later, with perhaps greater success, by such theorists as Kuhn, Feyerabend, and Hacking. However, in *Being and Time* they remained unresolved. Heidegger himself soon abandoned the basic premise of existential ontology—that Dasein is the privileged horizon from which to first pose the question of Being. After the so-called turning, Heidegger opted instead for a "history of Being" *(Seinsgeschichte)* that was seemingly free of the transcendentalist premises of his early philosophy. A nonsubjectivist, but radically historicist, theory of Being now took over the disclosive function earlier reserved for human understanding. Whether this newly historicist ontology truly resolved the problematic relationship between scientific explanation and metaphysical realism remains an open question. In his earlier work, however, Heidegger left his argument vulnerable to the charge that existential space and time were nothing more than temporary and merely pragmatic schemata for subjective experience. This would be the opening for Cassirer's criticism.

Cassirer on Mythic Space-Time

Cassirer laid out his own analysis of mythic space-time in the second volume of *The Philosophy of Symbolic Forms,* titled *Das Mythische Denken,* or *Mythical Thought,* first published in 1925. It bears repeating that Cassirer believed the symbolic systems of language and myth are analogous to scientific symbolization in that they were also built on transcendental-formative foundations: The mythic-linguistic universe is an early manifestation of the universally human capacity for "form," that is, for constructing the representational field of intelligible experience in accordance with fundamental principles originating in mental spontaneity. It followed, however, that myth cannot be dismissed as sheer falsehood, because it lay the very foundations for science, although science itself had to pass in dialectical fashion *beyond* myth and, eventually, dispense with its substantial understanding of experience so as to realize a purely functional system of symbolization. Cassirer nevertheless insisted that myth already furnishes a vivid illustration of the Kantian principle that the world of experience owes its primal order to the projective-transcendental rules of the human mind.

For mythical thinking, Cassirer observed, there is a spatial-physical "correspondence" between the world and man, an "original kinship" that especially structures the mythic symbolization of space. *"The mere possibility of coordinating certain spatial totalities part for part suffices to make them coalesce,"* he wrote. "By virtue of this peculiar principle *mythical thinking seems to negate and suspend spatial distance."* Consequently, "the *distant merges with what is close at hand."* Moreover, Cassirer claimed that even in scientific reasoning this principle remains at work: "So deeply rooted is this trait that with all its progress, pure knowledge, the 'exact' view of space, has never fully overcome it."[33] But myth is unlike science in that "there are no purely geometrical ... no purely ideal ... distinctions," and "all thought and all sensory intuition and perception rest on an original foundation of feeling [*ruht auf einem ursprünglichen Gefühlsgrund*]." The consequence of this essentially affective foundation is that no matter how subtle and articulated it becomes, mythical space as a whole remains "embedded, or one might say immersed in this feeling." The very sense of spatial *orientation* that inheres in mythical thought was itself grounded in this "original foundation." Indeed,

> the zones and directions [*Orte und Richtungen*] in space stand out from one another because a different accent of meaning is connected with them, and they are mythically evaluated in different and opposite senses. . . . The characteristic mythical accent of the sacred and the profane is distributed in different ways among the separate directions and regions [*Richtungen und Gegenden*].[34]

The basic logic of myth, then, is such that it spontaneously transposes all significance into spatial order. "Wherever mythical thinking and mythical feeling endows a content with a particular value, wherever they distinguish it from others and lend it a special significance, this qualitative distinction tends to be represented in the image of spatial separation."[35] At its core, this process of transposition commits mythical thinking to a notion of reality that is fundamentally holistic. Each "region" and "part" owes its orientation, its basic directionality, to a relation by which it is bound to the totality. Unlike the "functional" space of pure mathematics, then, "the space of myth [is] *structural*." Consequently, no region of space could appear to the mythical mind except on its "original ground of feeling" and what Cassirer called its "negation" of distance. "Regardless of how far we divide," Cassirer concluded, "we find in each part the form, the structure, of the whole [*die Struktur des Ganzen*]."[36]

The case was similar with mythic temporality. As Cassirer explained, the temporal world of myth presupposed an understanding of sacred unity derived from the past: "The true character of mythical being is first revealed when it appears as the being of origins [*Sein des Ursprungs*]."[37] "By being thrust back into temporal distance," Cassirer continued, "by being situated in the depths of the past, a particular content is not only established as sacred, as mythically and religiously significant, but also justified as such." At the basis of mythic temporality, therefore, was a sense of temporal "origin," which then sanctified all of human intersubjective relations: "Specifically human existence—usages, customs, social norms, and ties—are thus hallowed by being derived from institutions prevailing in the primordial mythical past...this mythical 'primordial time' [*diese mythische "Urzeit"*]."[38] But given this holistic structure premised on "origin," mythic temporality is incapable of performing any decisive break in the temporal order.

Here Cassirer anticipated Heidegger's own account of the differences between existential and scientific space-time: "Myth knows nothing of that kind of objectivity which is expressed in the mathematical-physical concept or of Newton's absolute time which 'flows in and for itself, without regard to any outward object.'" Unlike the modern time of separable instants, myth construes the temporal flow without differentiation. It knows "historical time" little better than it did "mathematical-physical time" and instead construes the world of experience such that discrete instances are dissolved into pure identity:

> The stages of time—past, present, future—do not remain distinct; over and over again the mythical consciousness succumbs to the tendency and temptation to level the differences and ultimately transform them into pure identity.... The magical "now" is by no means a *mere* now, a simple, differentiated present, but is, to quote Leibniz, "chargé du passé et gros de l'avenir"—laden with the past and pregnant with the future.[39]

Mythic temporality, Cassirer concluded, is therefore relational rather than punctual. And just as mythic spatiality brings close and gives experience its primary orientation in reality, so, too, mythic time unifies temporal instants and grounds them in the sacred past. Overall, the structure of mythic space-time was thoroughly holistic; it could not distinguish pure moments or points in the spatiotemporal field apart from its own affective and normative criteria.

Cassirer had already developed these claims by 1925. However, it would be difficult to overlook the resemblance between the ostensibly "primitive" understanding of space-time as analyzed by Cassirer and the supposedly "existential" account of Dasein's spatiotemporal structures as presented by Heidegger two years later in *Being and Time*. Both mythic and existential spatiality exhibit the phenomenological effect Heidegger termed *Entfernung*, a "bringing-close" from the background of a referential context whatsoever it finds significant. Both were said to grant experience its holistic unity, thanks to which there first emerges the basic sense of orientations or "directions" *(Richtungen)*—such as "left" and "right," or "here" and "there"—as well as that indispensable sense that one could differentiate the totality of experience into "regions" *(Gegenden)*. More than any resemblance of terminology, the comparison shows us how deeply Cassirer and Heidegger were divided even at the innermost premises of their thinking. From Heidegger's perspective, mythic space-time could serve as an appropriate illustration for the pragmatic space-time that belonged to Dasein's everyday comportment. For Cassirer, meanwhile, the Heideggerian analytic of space-time looked almost as if it were a retreat into a primitive and quasi-mythic mode of understanding.

The Debate on Myth

Cassirer's earliest reflections on Heidegger's philosophy in the third volume of *The Philosophy of Symbolic Forms* directly address its ambiguous theoretical positioning between scientific realism and hermeneutic anti-realism. But these reflections only make sense against the background of Cassirer's own attempts to theorize the status of space-time symbolization in both mythical thinking and science. The similarities between their two theories were considerable. Like Heidegger, Cassirer believed that human symbolic capacities are "transcendental" in the Kantian sense: the world of experienced reality, whether mythical or scientific, is correlative to the form-giving, constitutive structures of human understanding. Moreover, like Heidegger, Cassirer was ready to grant the imagination an important if not preeminent status in the generation of these formal structures. Departing from his neo-Kantian predecessors, Cassirer wished to expand the critique of reason into a critique of culture, but this required some theory that might account for the nonrational, but nonetheless formal-symbolic, quality of nontheoretical representation—mythic, linguistic, aesthetic, and so forth.

The considerable proximity between Cassirer and Heidegger was first apparent in their common interest in the analysis of myth: Cassirer discerned in myth an early manifestation of human symbolizing capacities, and Heidegger, a simplified model of human existential structure. Heidegger's interest in myth and so-called primitive consciousness arose directly from his methodological focus on "everydayness." In *Being and Time,* in the final section of the expository chapter announcing "the task of a preparatory

analysis of Dasein," Heidegger warned readers not to mistake the philosophical attention to everydayness for a sophisticated rejection of modernity: *"Everydayness does not coincide with primitiveness,"* he explained, and
must thus be considered a constant modality of Dasein's being, "even when
that Dasein is active in a highly developed and differentiated culture." Heidegger was strongly opposed to any nostalgic efforts to locate the more
"genuine" aspects of human life in what was merely "some primitive stage of
Dasein with which we can become acquainted empirically through the medium of anthropology." By "everydayness," he wished only to draw philosophical attention to the fact that human interpretative activities are lived
for the most part in an absorbed and nontheoretical concern. Everydayness
was therefore a modality of *all* human understanding, and among other
things this implied that *primitive Dasein* exhibits everydayness no less and
no more than does any sort of "developed" culture. More importantly, Heidegger was wary of anthropological studies that tended in his view to rely
on a naïvely empiricist technique for gathering information about native
systems of meaning. "Ethnology itself," he warned, "already presupposes as
its clue an inadequate analytic of Dasein."[40]

Despite such warnings, however, Heidegger's existential analysis of myth
closely resembled the "functionalism" traceable to Bronoslaw Malinowski,
who saw in myth a universal human purpose: to render livable that sense of
"overwhelming foreboding, behind which, even for the native, there lurks the
idea of an inevitable and ruthless fatality."[41] What Malinowski called the
"pragmatic character of primitive belief" and the "backbone" of community
Heidegger now identified as the "background" to the lived-pragmatic world.[42]
Yet, like Malinowski, Heidegger saw that a certain methodological advantage
might be derived in fixing one's attention on the "life of primitive peoples,"
because

> "primitive phenomena" are often less concealed and less complicated
> by extensive self-interpretation on the part of the Dasein in question.
> Primitive Dasein often speaks to us more directly in terms of a primor-
> dial absorption in "phenomena." . . . A way of conceiving things which
> seems, perhaps, rather clumsy and crude from our standpoint [there-
> fore], can be positively helpful in bringing out the ontological struc-
> tures of phenomena in a genuine way.[43]

Thus, although Heidegger saw all of human culture as the ongoing work of self-interpretation, he noted that there might be an added benefit in attending more specifically to primitive cultures, where the basic outlines of "everydayness" remained most vivid (a claim, incidentally, that bore a strong resemblance to the arguments put forth by Émile Durkheim more than a decade before in *The Elementary Forms of Religious Life*).[44] As evidence of how philosophers might learn through the study of primitive culture, Heidegger in *Being and Time* specifically credited the second volume of Cassirer's *Philosophy of Symbolic Forms*, the volume on myth, which contained (in his words) "clues of far-reaching importance." But already he registered doubts concerning Cassirer's transcendental presuppositions: "It remains an open question," he warned, "whether the foundations of this Interpretation are sufficiently transparent—whether . . . the architectonics and . . . systematic content of Kant's *Critique of Pure Reason* can provide a possible design for such a task, or whether a new and more primordial approach may not here be needed."[45]

Although Heidegger did not spell out just what he found unsatisfactory, the drift of his remarks was clear: Cassirer's study of myth presupposed a Kantian model of subjectivity and it therefore regarded myth through the distorting lens of a spontaneous and transcendental consciousness. However, if mythological study were to have any bearing on the philosophical analysis of everydayness, it had to be anchored in a quite different model of the human being. Heidegger's focus on the practical and situated quality of "everyday" meaning offered a superior model of human being precisely because it avoided any and all reference to a spontaneous "consciousness" prior to its interpretative action. But then, a "new" and "more primordial" method was needed. For such a task, Heidegger suggested, only phenomenology would prove adequate. To strengthen his case, Heidegger noted that in the second volume to *The Philosophy of Symbolic Forms,* Cassirer had himself conceded the usefulness of a phenomenological approach. Moreover, Heidegger noted that, in his 1923 conversation with Cassirer in Hamburg, "we had agreed in demanding an existential analytic."[46]

Heidegger's doubts regarding the validity of transcendental subjectivity as applied to myth were made most explicit in 1928 when he published a lengthy critical review of Cassirer's *Philosophy of Symbolic Forms,* volume 2: *Mythical Thought.* The review was respectful, but its criticism went to the very heart of their disagreement.[47] "The neo-Kantian orientation to the problem of consciousness," wrote Heidegger, "is so disadvantageous, that it . . . hinders a firm footing in the center of the problem." The difficulty was that Cassirer had already assumed the "ontological constitution" of the subject *before* his investigation, while what was required was "a radical ontology of Dasein in the light of the problem of Being in general." Cassirer's own treatment of mana revealed this problem. Mana was the originally Polynesian notion of a supernatural force thought to be present in natural objects or persons. Cassirer discussed it at length as evidence of how human beings impregnate their own surroundings with sacred meaning. But for Heidegger the phenomenon of mana only seemed to highlight the fact that Cassirer's premise was mistaken: mythic human existence does not conceive of its meaning-systems as mere "representations" that are simply "present" *(vorhanden)* to a consciousness. Indeed, Mana showed that, for "mythic Dasein," the meaningfulness of the world simply *cannot* be understood as born from the sovereign capacities of an expressive subject:

> Which is the mode of being of mythic "life" which enables the mana-representation to function as the guiding . . . understanding of Being? The possible answer to this question of course presupposes a previous working out of the basic ontological constitution of Dasein. If this basic constitution is to be found in "care," . . . then it becomes clear that mythic Dasein is primarily determined by "thrownness" [*Geworfenheit*].[48]

For Heidegger, mana seemed to indicate precisely a mode of meaning not subject to human control. It was presumptuous, then, for Cassirer to describe mana from the point of view of a specifically "modern" and enlightened consciousness, as if it were obvious that mythic thinking expressed the disengagement and "presence" characteristic of a Kantian subject. "In 'thrownness,'" Heidegger concluded, "mythic Dasein, in its manner of being-in-the-world, is delivered up to the world in such a way that it is *overwhelmed by that to which it is delivered up.*"[49]

For Heidegger, then, the analysis of mythic meaning would only succeed if it presupposed as its methodological point of departure a human being characterized by "thrownness" and not "spontaneity." This implied, first and foremost, that one should not presume a subject that was split off on the ontological level from the objects it represented. The sense of being "overwhelmed" by representations was not, as Cassirer supposed, merely an *illusion* inflicted on primitive consciousness because it still lacked rational insight into its own powers of creation. It was instead an experience of all human existence in its "everyday" mode. Cassirer had assumed as "a basic rule which governs all development," that "spirit achieves true and complete inwardness only in expressing itself." But even this model of expression pointed *away* from the Kantian model of subjectivity as *sovereign* and toward a model of subjecthood as *dependent*. To emphasize this point, Heidegger posed a purely rhetorical question: "*What is the ontological constitution of human Dasein which accounts for the fact that it, as it were, comes to its proper self only by way of a detour through the world?*"[50]

Implicit in this question was Heidegger's essential objection to the neo-Kantian foundations animating all of Cassirer's work: Cassirer conceived of the human being as achieving its highest reality only by means of a self-expressive and self-objectifying process that expanded in all directions. But even if this were the case, Heidegger could not see why this self-alienation into the world permitted Cassirer to retain the dogma of consciousness as an absolute spontaneity preexisting its worldly manifestation: by what right could Cassirer insist upon the priority and unconditioned freedom of this human essence, especially if its was known to itself *via* its symbolic achievements? Cassirer's neo-Kantian premises blocked him from appreciating the ontological structure of myth as a *form of life*:

> The orientation of the neo-Kantian problem of consciousness is so inconducive, that it prevents us from gaining a proper foothold in the central problem. Instead of placing the interpretation of mythic Dasein in a central characteristic of the ontological constitution [*Seinsverfassung*] of this being, Cassirer begins with an analysis of the mythic consciousness of objects [*Gegenstandsbewußtseins*], its form of thought and intuition. To be sure, Cassirer clearly sees that [such form] must be traced back to the mythic "Life-form" [*Lebensform*] as the "spiritual sub-stratum" [*geistige Urschicht*]. . . . Nevertheless, the *expess* and *systematic* clarification of the origin of the thought- and intuition- form in the "life-form" [*Lebensform*] is not carried through.[51]

The drift of these remarks was unmistakable. If the human being only came to self-recognition and self-realization through the worldly "detour" of symbolization, then Cassirer had no warrant for insisting upon the priority of transcendental consciousness; the human being's disclosure in-the-world, a disclosure without foundation, was all that remained. This was a critical premise in *Being and Time*: "*The 'essence' of Dasein lies in its existence.*"[52] The idea of a human essence had *no other ground* besides its being-in-the-world.

This was a disagreement that allowed for little compromise. Nevertheless, Cassirer and Heidegger's common interest in myth sprang from a shared conviction that philosophers could not confine themselves merely to theoretical-scientific phenomena but must develop more capacious techniques so as to better appreciate the universal structure underlying the entirety of lived, human reality. This common point of departure had at its core a shared recognition of the faculty Kant had called the "productive imagination." In the conversation at Davos, Cassirer placed great emphasis on the fact that "one cannot unravel [the symbolic] without referring it to the faculty of the productive power of imagination," which Kant had called "*synthesis speciosa.*" Such a synthesis relied on the imagination in part because the mind must retain past representations and bind concepts together through time. Synthesis, Cassirer concluded, was "the basic power of pure thinking." At Davos, Heidegger had first presented his own analysis of productive imagination in Kant's system, suggesting that it revealed a fundamentally nonrational and temporal "mystery" at the heart of human existential capacities, a claim he would elaborate in *Kant and the Problem of Metaphysics*.

Despite this common point of departure, however, the rift between Cassirer and Heidegger was already apparent in their analysis of myth and its methodological premises. While applauding him for recognizing the singular importance of the imagination, Cassirer nonetheless criticized Heidegger for having reduced *all* human-transcendental capacities to this single function. This reduction carried a pronounced risk that all claims to objectivity would collapse: Objectivity in the Kantian system is guaranteed only in so far as there are pure and universal conceptual rules that govern intuition. But in his presentation at Davos, Heidegger implied that this seemingly conceptual structure was itself rooted in the imagination, and, more deeply still, in Dasein's "original temporality." In Cassirer's eyes, Heidegger had therefore substituted, in place of Kant's dualism of understanding and sensibility, what seemed to be an all-encompassing and nonrational "monism of the imagination."[53] Heidegger aimed *not* at expanding the philosophical inquiry concerning transcendental structures into a generalized critique of culture (Cassirer's "logic of the illogical") but rather at locating temporal and precognitive structures of existence *beneath* the mind's ostensibly stable forms (to disclose, as it were, the "illogic of the logical"). Despite their common interest in the basic structural features of human life—formal-symbolic or existential—the implied moment of irrationalism in Heidegger's Kant-interpretation therefore marked a decisive line of fracture between the two philosophers that would only deepen in the years after Davos.

Myth, Crisis, Science

There remained an even more profound difference between Cassirer's phenomenon of mythic thinking and the Heideggerian model of existential structure. As noted above, Heidegger cast his portrait of existential involvement as a somehow "deeper" mode of understanding, against which the scientific-conceptual mode must appear as derivative, as "loss," or, at the very least, as "reduction." This quasi-normative language of impoverishment helps to explain what I described above as Heidegger's "epistemic nostalgia," that is, the normative mood that seems to make the distinction between hermeneutic understanding and objectivist science (an otherwise neutral distinction, taken philosophically) into a quasi-historical distinction between earlier (hermeneutic) and later (scientific) modes of knowing, and, ultimately, into a narrative of epistemic disenchantment.

As shown above, similar themes of sacredness and holistic depth also pervaded Cassirer's portrait of mythical thinking, except that, for Cassirer, the sacred quality was merely definitional: it accompanied that earlier stage of thought that was explicitly classified as mythic and therefore analyzed as such. Unlike Heidegger, Cassirer described the hermeneutic condition as sacred only because that is the actual disposition of mythic thought itself, and it is restricted to *only that stage* of human symbolization. The argumentative and historical bridge connecting the second and third volumes of

The Philosophy of Symbolic Forms—that is, the movement from myth to science—therefore exhibits nothing of the nostalgia for hermeneutic conditions that accompanies Heidegger's analysis. On the contrary, as Cassirer announced at the beginning of volume 3, *"the concept of philosophy attains its full power and purity only where the world view expressed in linguistic and mythical concepts is abandoned, where it is in principle overcome."*[54] It is impossible to remain at the level of mythical thinking and develop a philosophy of myth, because it is only by means of a "crisis"—a breakthrough from myth to modernity—that philosophical reflection as well as science can first arrive on the scene:

> To achieve its own maturity, philosophy must above all come to grips with the linguistic and mythical worlds and place itself in dialectic opposition to them. . . . And natural science arrives at the mastery of its specific task in very much the same way as pure philosophy. In order to find itself it, too, must first effect the great intellectual differentiation, the *krisis,* separating it from myth and language. This act of separation marks philosophy's hour of birth, and also the starting point of empirical research and the mathematical determination of nature.[55]

As this passage makes plain, Cassirer sometimes saw the origin of science and philosophy as radical crisis. Elsewhere, however, he took pains to identify moments of "dialectical" preparation.[56] While mythical thought imbues representation with substantial versus merely conceptual efficacy, within myth itself, Cassirer claimed, one could nonetheless discern a "gradual process" by which substance and concept were separated, and "it is this separation that constitutes the beginning of the specifically religious consciousness." Religion therefore appears within the landscape of mythological thinking but gradually turns against it: "Religion takes the decisive step that is essentially alien to myth: in its use of sensuous images and signs it recognizes them as such—a means of expression which, though they reveal a determinate meaning, must necessarily remain inadequate to it."[57] The prototype for this dialectical reversal, he claimed, is the prophetic assault on idolatry, which opens a chasm previously unknown to the unreflective and "naïve" world of mythic belief. At its greatest heights the religious struggle against idolatry orients the mind in a fashion transcending representation entirely, toward an ethical "Idea of the good," which is, in Plato's memorable phrase, "beyond being [*jenseits des Seins*]."[58]

Already in his 1925 analysis of myth in *The Philosophy of Symbolic Forms,* Cassirer introduced the argument he would later direct against Heidegger at Davos, that, in the realm of ethics, which is originally born from the monotheistic idealization of the divine, the human understanding breaks through to a higher realm of the good that is "beyond being." Cassirer would later incorporate this celebratory account of monotheism's assault on myth into his political assessment of Nazism, whose anti-Semitism he would characterize as myth's vengeance against those who had first brought anti-mythic religion into the world (a theme I will revisit in Chapter 6). A similar idea was to be developed in greater depth by Emmanuel Lévinas, who theorized an ethics of "infinity" breaking free from the apparent "paganism" of Heidegger's *Seinsfrage*.[59] It is crucial to note, however, that this specifically *ethical* response to the mythical-symbolic world, and by association, to Heidegger, was by no means Cassirer's major concern. His claims against Heidegger's philosophy first emerged, not from the precincts of practical reason, but rather from the purely theoretical concerns of scientific explanation.

Space, Time, and the Politics of Reduction

The disagreement over space and time had deep roots in Cassirer's earliest work. Indeed, his philosophical interest in the epistemic status of modern-scientific concepts of space and time was evident as early as 1910 in *Substance and Function,* in which he celebrated Leibniz's philosophy for effecting a decisive advance toward conceptual "construction," the prerequisite for scientific explanation. Significantly, here, *explanation* meant precisely *reduction:*

> The evolution of modern mathematics has approached the ideal, which Leibniz established ... with growing consciousness and success. Within pure geometry, this is shown ... in the development of the general concept of space. The *reduction* of metrical relations to projective realizes the thought of Leibniz that, before space is defined as a *quantum,* it must be grasped in its original qualitative peculiarity

as an "order of co-existence" *(ordre des coexistences possibles)*. The chain of harmonic constructions, by which the points of projective space are generated, provides the structure of this order, which owes its value and intelligibility to the fact that it is not sensuously presented but is *constructed by thought through a succession of relational structures.*[60]

Leibniz was of course not the only philosopher to have contributed to this development. Descartes' investigations in analytical geometry, for example, helped to inaugurate the view that space is a function of mathematical representation, although his own metaphysics of "extension"—as Cassirer argued in his 1923 study, *The Problem of Knowledge*—construed spatial extension as a primary characteristic of material substance and therefore "some sort of absolute thing." Leibniz, however, went beyond this "metaphysical hypostatizing," with its mistaken "assumption that space is real," and instead insisted on its ideal character. This "ideality" of space, Cassirer hastened to note, "should in no way cast doubt on the objectivity of space and turn it into a 'mere idea' in the subjective, psychological sense, but rather define this objectivity in its proper and only justifiable meaning, thus establishing the inevitable validity of geometrical truths."[61]

The ideality of space was especially important to Cassirer in his early evaluation of Einstein's general theory of relativity. Ontology was to be replaced by function and metaphysics by mathematized explanation. Space thereby shed its last remaining metaphysical resemblance to a substantive entity or container. As Cassirer explained in *Einstein's Theory of Relativity:*

> Each answer [that] physics imparts concerning the character and peculiar nature of its fundamental concepts, assumes inevitably for epistemology the form of a question. When, for example, Einstein gives as the essential result of his theory that by it "the last remainder of physical objectivity" is taken from space and time, this answer of the physicist contains for the epistemologist the precise formulation of his real problem. What are we to understand by the physical objectivity, which is here denied to the concepts of space and time?[62]

In answer to his own question, Cassirer later observed that

> *We are no longer concerned with what space "is"* and whether any defi-
> nite character, whether Euclidean, Lobaschefskian or Riemannian, is to
> be ascribed to it, *but rather what use is to be made of the different systems
> of geometrical presuppositions in the interpretation of the phenomena of
> nature and their dependences according to law.*[63]

There remained, however, a crucial divide between the idealist concept of
space (which was a mental construct) and the "experience" of spatial orientation: "The space of our sense perception," Cassirer explained in *Substance and
Function*, "is not identical with the space of our geometry," but is instead "distinguished from it in the decisive constitutive properties." He continued:

> For sensuous apprehension, every difference of place is necessarily con-
> nected with an opposition in the content of sensation. "Above" and
> "below," "right" and "left" are ... not equivalent directions, ... but ...
> remain qualitatively distinct and irreducible ... In geometrical space
> [however], these oppositions are cancelled. For the element as such pos-
> sesses no specific content, but all its meaning comes from the relative
> position it occupies in the total system ... [and] further moments of
> geometrical space, such as its continuity and infinity, rest upon a simi-
> lar foundation; they are in no way given in spatial sensations, but rest
> upon ideal completions.[64]

Whereas the spatiality of everyday experience is relational, though nonetheless dependent on the "qualitative" significance of practical orientation, scientific concepts are "relational" and ideal.[65]

As Cassirer was quick to acknowledge, the historical journey of "reduction" and conceptual abstraction, leading from the scientific revolution
until the present day, was arduous and frequently contested. In *Einstein's
Theory of Relativity* he even granted that, from the popular perspective, the
"radical resolution of 'things' into mere relations" was seen as "suspicious
and alienating" because objectivity appeared to require a straightforwardly
substantialistic "thing-concept."[66] In *The Problem of Knowledge,* he further

observed that "it was feared that the first ground of 'truth' would be lost." Kant himself had warned in the first *Critique* that (in Cassirer's paraphrase), "philosophy would [now] have to *renounce the proud name of an ontology* that [had] presumed to furnish in a systematized doctrine synthetic a priori judgments on all existence," and that this goal must henceforth yield to the more "modest" goal of "a simple analysis of pure understanding." But the post-Kantian systems had brushed this warning aside: "They started from ontology and metaphysics, and every critique of knowledge that came within their purview was instinctively transformed into an ontological inquiry," a confusion, Cassirer added, that especially afflicted the problem of space.[67] Written in 1923, this complaint already signaled the divergence of philosophical perspective between Cassirer and Heidegger that over the next few years would grow only more pronounced.

Cassirer's Early Critique of *Being and Time*

By 1927, Cassirer had nearly brought to completion the third volume of his tripartite study, *The Philosophy of Symbolic Forms,* the arguments of which left little doubt that he placed scientific concept-formation at the highest stage of human symbolization. As we have seen, despite his generous attention to various symbolic spheres—not only of myth, but also of language, art, history, and so forth—he sustained an unshaken faith in the cultural and philosophical authority of science, which he believed must furnish experience with its "inevitable validity" and theoretical-objective form. Cassirer was no doubt a pluralist regarding cultural meaning, and it would therefore be wrong to characterize his admiration for science as an unreflective scientism. Yet *The Philosophy of Symbolic Forms* was nonetheless a teleological system: It presented a robustly modernist vision of philosophy as a "phenomenology" of the scientific spirit. It remained unclear just how this vision was compatible with the altogether different phenomenology of human existential structure as elaborated in Heidegger's just-published *Being and Time.* Before the publication of the third volume of *The Philosophy of Symbolic Forms,* Cassirer struggled for the first time to come to terms with Heidegger's arguments and to express his tentative admiration for Heidegger's philosophy without conceding the essential premises of his own position.

As noted above, the differences were considerable. Heidegger saw the hermeneutic structure of human understanding as constitutive rather than evolving toward scientific abstraction. He admitted "historicity" as an existential condition, but while the thrown-structure itself was historical, its composition was not: A phenomenology of that structure therefore revealed the permanent "existentials" of human life, including the existential of "historicity" itself. Accordingly, while Cassirer saw scientific "reduction" as the highest station of symbolization, Heidegger could only regard the movement—from the hermeneutic field of existential involvement to the scientific ideal of present-at-hand "objectivity"—as a reduction in significance. And, whereas Cassirer saw reduction as synonymous with cultural achievement and epistemic gain, Heidegger saw it as evidence of existential impoverishment, as what he termed an "unworlding" of the world. Given the pronounced contrast between them, one might suppose Cassirer's most likely response would have been simply to dismiss Heidegger's contribution as negligible or as merely a lapse into the pre-critical "ontology" that Kant had ostensibly destroyed. With characteristic equanimity, however, Cassirer tried to lay down an interpretation of Heidegger's work that did not conflict in any obvious fashion with the premises of his own philosophy.

In a protracted footnote adjoined to the discussion of scientific space, Cassirer wrote that Heidegger's *Being and Time* had given an incisive analysis for the "primary experience of space" (*das primäre Erlebnis des Räumlichen*), which meant "purely 'pragmatic' space." According to Heidegger, Cassirer explained:

> any characterization of what is primarily at hand, of what is present as a 'thing,' comes up against the factor of spatiality. The place and the place-manifold may not be interpreted as the where of any random presence of things. The place is the determinate "there" and "here" where a thing belongs. . . . This regional orientation of the place-manifold of things at-hand [*zuhanden*] makes up the aroundness, the around-us, of what is in our closest environment. Never is a three-dimensional manifold of possible positions filled with existing [*vorhanden*] things given to begin with. This dimensionality of space is still cloaked in the spatiality of the at-hand. . . . All "wheres" are disclosed and exhibited round about us through the comings and

goings of everyday life, not ascertained and specified by reflective spatial measurement.[68]

Such generous quotation from the work of another scholar was commonplace in Cassirer's work. But this note, and the ones that followed addressing Heidegger's philosophy, were of unusual length. Cassirer, it seems clear, at first saw this new thinker as meriting serious attention.

Cassirer even saw their positions as complementary: "What distinguishes our own undertaking from that of Heidegger," he explained, "is above all that it does not stop at this stage of the at-hand and its mode of spatiality, but, without challenging Heidegger's position, goes beyond it [*ohne sie irgend zu bestreiten, über sie hinausfragt*]." Leaving Heidegger's contributions undisturbed, Cassirer proposed to "*follow the road leading from spatiality as a factor in the at-hand to space as the form of existence* and furthermore to show *how this road leads right through* [*hindurchführt*] the domain of symbolic formation." Cassirer thus saw the "pragmatic" theory of space as a theory of *the merely subjective structure of experience*. Dasein's spatiality was a hermeneutic horizon, he implied, but it was one that symbolic thought could feasibly surpass. Pragmatic space was not constitutive of Being as such; it was a mere way-station on the road to greater conceptual abstraction. On Cassirer's view, then, Heidegger had presented a welcome description of subjective-spatial conditions. But this description was to be supplemented by a theory of scientific spatial concepts that seemed to allow for a passage that could "lead-right-through" those subjective conditions to the conceptually constituted realm of objectivity "beyond."[69]

Cassirer presented a similar but even more emphatic reading of Heidegger's analysis of time. Again, the remarks suggest that Cassirer considered himself in basic accord with Heidegger regarding the structure of everyday and subjective experience. But, once again, without challenging the existential claim, Cassirer also wanted to make it clear that he was committed to a theory of symbolic conceptual capacity that *transcended* the subjective sphere. "The basic problem of the *Philosophy of Symbolic Forms*," Cassirer explained, "lies precisely in that territory which Heidegger expressly and intentionally excluded from the first volume of his book." The two philosophies were not in conflict, because the *Philosophy of Symbolic Forms* "does not deal with that mode of temporality which Heidegger elaborates as the original *Seinssinn des Daseins.*" The theories were therefore complementary, not opposed. In a few short lines, Cassirer summarized what he took to be his own rather modest and unexceptional modification to Heidegger's analysis:

> The Philosophy of Symbolic Forms *does not question* this temporality which Heidegger discloses as the ultimate foundation of existentiality and attempts to explain in its diverse factors. But our inquiry begins *beyond* this sphere, at precisely the point where a transition is effected from this existential temporality to the *form* of time. It aspires to show the conditions under which this form is possible, the conditions for the postulation of a "being" which *goes beyond the existentiality of "being-there."*[70]

Cassirer cast his own philosophy of form as *complementing* Heidegger's analysis. Hidden in this characterization, however, was a dramatic and potentially fatal verdict on the possibility for any further agreement between the two philosophers. As in his commentary on existential space, Cassirer read Heidegger's theory of existential temporality in a subjectivist fashion: existential temporality is applicable *only* to Dasein. But because the analysis addressed only Dasein and its attendant "sense" of Being, Cassirer felt free to describe it merely as a "stage" and to then supplement the analysis with his own theory of form: "In regard to time as to space," Cassirer wrote, the philosophy of symbolic forms sets forth a theory of the "*metabasis* from the meaning of existence to the objective meaning of the 'logos.'"[71] But this meant that existential temporality was little more than a *subjective* condition. It was merely a local and pragmatic "sphere," the antechamber to an objective "beyond" that was itself accessible only through conceptual forms.[72]

Cassirer seemed only dimly aware that this reading of Heidegger's analytic implied a deflationary account of so-called existential conditions: it meant that such conditions were limited merely to a subjective standpoint and that their "reduction" through purely functional concepts might still permit a mode of thinking correlated with objectivity. As noted above, Heidegger himself had helped to lend this interpretation of his work greater plausibility, thanks to his tentative references to a realm of time-free objects as disclosed by science. But as explained above, the meaning of such comments remained very much uncertain. They implied a commitment to metaphysical realism that was hardly consonant with Heidegger's greater effort to undo objectivist metaphysics and place the entire discipline of ontology on temporal-hermeneutic foundations.

Cassirer seemed to appreciate this larger project, and he acknowledged as much in a passing reference to Saint Augustine's theory of time as an "extension" of the mind: "Augustine's dictum still seems to retain its full force; time, which to the immediate consciousness is the most certain and most familiar of facts, shrouds itself in darkness the moment we seek to pass beyond this immediate givenness and draw into the sphere of reflective inquiry."[73] A proper interpretation of temporality, on Cassirer's view, thus required a theory of objectivity no longer conceivable in reference to metaphysical realism: "We find the Ariadne's thread that can lead us out of the labyrinth of time only when we express the problem in a fundamentally different form—only when we remove it from the realm of realistic-dogmatic ontology and place it within the framework of a pure analysis of the phenomena of consciousness."[74] But this, Cassirer observed, was precisely the Augustinian view later developed by Heidegger:

> In the structure of St. Augustine's thinking the time motif reveals its power in the very fact that it leads to a fundamental reorientation, a transformation of the question of being itself. Here it fulfills the same essential function as later in the development of modern "ontology," which also sees its task above all as the disclosure and authentic apprehension of time as the "horizon for all understanding and interpretation of being," and finds "the central problem of all ontology rooted" in the right view and explanation of the phenomenon of time (cf. Heidegger, "Sein und Zeit," esp. sec. 5).[75]

On Cassirer's view, Heidegger could rightly stand among the partisans of modern ontology, because he sustained a nonsubstantialistic and universal theory of temporal understanding: he performed a break with the "realistic dogmatic ontology" of Descartes and Newton, returning instead to the more fruitful Augustinian view of time as mental extension.

It is a remarkable testament to Cassirer as an early reader of Heidegger's philosophy that he was capable of perceiving both its potential merits and its potential moments of failure. It should be obvious, however, that Cassirer already found himself in a quandary: his own interpretation implied that Heidegger's existential analysis remained trapped in a kind of hermeneutic subjectivism that conceded to science a grasp of the objective world. As noted above, it was Heidegger himself who encouraged this interpretation, which found support in his highly ambiguous discussion concerning the status of scientific explanation. But Cassirer seemed to recognize that his own subjectivistic reading did not speak to Heidegger's greater ambition as an ontologist. After all, as Cassirer doubtless realized, Heidegger was not expounding a theory that concerned the merely human *perspective*. Rather, in the above passage from *Being and Time* that Cassirer cited with evident approval, Heidegger saw existential temporality as "the horizon for all understanding and interpretation of Being."

Cassirer could not resolve this difficulty. Nor did he seem especially concerned to lay the blame for its irresolution at Heidegger's feet. But a careful reader of Cassirer's work could not fail but note how his praise for Heidegger's analysis of existential space and time was conjoined throughout with a delicate insistence that those existential structures for which Heidegger claimed universal ontological application were in fact *merely pragmatic and subjective* and must therefore yield before the higher claims of conceptual space and time within the objective field of scientific explanation. This qualification would not have been possible had Heidegger himself not introduced the idea that scientific disclosure is a moment of epistemic "reduction"; but Cassirer saw reduction as an achievement, while Heidegger saw it as a loss of the existential world.

As noted above, Cassirer followed Hegel's lead in presenting the final volume of *The Philosophy of Symbolic Forms* as a "phenomenology" of human formative capacities: the path from myth to science was therefore dialectical and marked by crisis. It was an inevitable and seemingly irreversible process of mind. To Heidegger, however, this process was hardly inevitable. It was instead something rather more like a *lapse,* an uncommon breakdown in the otherwise constitutive structures of human significance.[76] The contrast was striking: what, for Cassirer, belonged to only the temporary patterns of myth was, for Heidegger, the constitutive pattern of human understanding as such. From Cassirer's point of view, this seemed to imply that Heidegger deemed the escape from myth a *historical impossibility.* One may therefore

appreciate the true significance of Cassirer's deflationary reading of Heidegger's work: by supplementing Heidegger's philosophy with a theory of
scientific concepts as correlated with metaphysical objectivity, Cassirer implied that those mythic structures were impermanent, and he thereby made
room within and beyond Heidegger's thinking for the possibility of modernity itself.

Existentialism and Aphasia

Of course, this was only Cassirer's first and most tentative assessment of
Heidegger's philosophy. Much later—after the Davos debates, after Heidegger's public declaration of support for National Socialism, and after
Cassirer himself had passed many years in exile—his assessment of Heidegger would emerge utterly transformed. This later and more aggressive
phase is the topic of Chapter 6, but we should note that certain themes of
Cassirer's earlier criticism would remain unchanged, notably, the claim that
the existential analytic captured an important but nonetheless *primitive* and
temporary stratum of human cognitive development. This claim already
bore within it a potentially violent criticism of Heidegger's entire philosophy, as the following example illustrates.

In the spring of 1931, at the annual meeting of the German Society for
Psychology in Hamburg, Cassirer presented a paper on "Language and the
Construction of the Object-World," which discussed at length John Hugh-
lings Jackson's neuroscientific contribution to the medical understanding
of brain damage, particularly aphasia. Jackson had claimed that to assess
the real extent of aphasic damage, it was not sufficient simply to note a
patient's loss of individual words. Aphasia was best measured by observing
a patient's difficulty in building full predicative sentences because, as
Cassirer explained, "The predicative-propositional 'sentence' ['*Satz*'] is the
vehicle for any manner and mode of objectivistic *placement* [*Setzung*], from
which there first emerges the actual objective world-picture [*Weltbild*].
Where language fails, however, so too our objective intuition sinks back, as
it were, to a lower level." This so-called lower-level understanding allowed for
little more than the "immediate *use* of the objects," and this capacity could be
retained almost entirely "even while there is no longer any success in apprehending the objects in their pure 'Being' ["*Sein*"] and determining their

'manner of Being' ["*So-sein*"]." The aphasic might be able to handle objects, but beyond and above this, he could not succeed in the more complex process of drawing simultaneously away from the object and facing them "objectively" ["*gegenüber*"] so as to relate to them as "represented" ["*vorstellig*"].[77]

Cassirer's interest was chiefly aroused at the philosophical lessons that might be drawn from the study of aphasia. He noted that the aphasic's representational incapacity was especially evident in spatial experience, which remained "a space of mere action and comportment [*ein bloßer Aktions- und Verhaltensraum*]" and could not rise to "a space of image or representation." The aphasic retained the ability of manipulation "within" space. So, for example, the aphasic could manipulate objects of "daily use" by placing them in their correct locations and intuitively grasping the coordination between them (as in, say, the pragmatic understanding of coordination among table, chair, and bed in a familiar room). Yet the aphasic had apparently lost the ability to make space *itself* present for apprehension as a totality or in its individual parts. Only this could explain why the aphasic might fail to identify individual things by name, while he retained the practical ability to use those things in the proper fashion. From this, Cassirer arrived at the philosophical lesson that an insult to one's linguistic capacity was also a blow against the very objectivity of the object-world. Experience surrendered its objectivity: "It draws back—to describe it, for brevity's sake, in Heidegger's terminology—from the sphere of 'Vorhandenheit' into the sphere of mere 'Zuhandenheit.'"[78]

For those who grasped even the most basic premises of Heidegger's existential analysis, this casual reference to the basic shift in ontological understanding—from presence-at-hand to readiness-to-hand—must have seemed counterintuitive at best. For as discussed above, Heidegger saw pragmatic spatial awareness as an essential component of Dasein's being-in-the-world. Indeed, he assigned it a primordial role in human ontological understanding overall. It followed, in the famous analysis of a breakdown in everyday comportment (as illustrated with the example of the hammer), that the shift from pragmatic spatial awareness to purely objectivized space brought a certain impoverishment in Dasein's understanding of the world as such. What was therefore so striking about Cassirer's appeal to existential terminology was that it introduced a silent *reversal* in Heidegger's assessment of the relation between pragmatic and theoretical understanding.

Whereas Heidegger described the shift to theory as a partial loss, Cassirer saw it as a cognitive achievement. More striking still, Cassirer's characterization of aphasia as a *withdrawal* from theoretical cognition *into* merely pragmatic understanding carried the bizarre implication: absent the capacity for higher objectification, what Heidegger characterized as the *primordial* experience of being-in-the-world actually resembled how the world might have appeared to someone who had suffered acute brain damage.

It would be naïve to think Cassirer did not recognize this reversal and all it implied. The earlier footnotes to *The Phenomenology of Knowledge* already betrayed his latent suspicion that Heidegger's analysis of human existence was fatally incomplete if it did not cede a higher and more privileged place to objective cognition. This was essentially the same complaint Cassirer had raised against Heidegger's reading of myth, and it reiterated the worry Cassirer had expressed at Davos, when he asked if Heidegger was actually willing to surrender objectivity. But the example of aphasia suggests a sharpening in Cassirer's judgment and a deepening awareness that the divide between them was perhaps insuperable. In the years leading up to their encounter at Davos, it may have been feasible to suppress this awareness. In the years that followed, it would prove altogether impossible.

6

After Davos:
Enlightenment, Politics, Religion

A hit, a very palpable hit.

—*Hamlet*, Act 5, Scene 2

Introduction

Shortly after his return from Davos, Heidegger confided in a letter to Elisabeth Blochmann that "my hope for the new powers of the youngest has grown more secure." But he also confessed that he feared that "the whole thing would turn into a sensation, given the strong tendency these days to interest oneself most of all in the person." He also felt irritation at Cassirer, who had been "exceptionally well-mannered and almost too obliging. I thus encountered too little opposition, which inhibited me from giving the problems the necessary sharpness of formulation." The fact of Cassirer's seemingly characterological resistance to public confrontation was further aggravated by the format of the event. "The questions were fundamentally too difficult by far for a public exposition," Heidegger explained, "Form and direction throughout the conversation could work merely by example."[1]

It is difficult to know how to judge such remarks. Can a philosopher be too polite? Was Cassirer actually "too obliging"? Or was Heidegger's complaint yet another sign of his widely noted irascible persona? Several eyewitnesses recall his behavior toward Cassirer as abrupt if not actually rude, though Heidegger himself certainly believed he had done nothing wrong. In fact, he would soon develop a theory to support his view that, in matters of philosophical discussion, vigorous and even aggressive debate was a prerequisite for genuine understanding.

In Chapter 5 we saw how the 1929 encounter at Davos was merely the culmination of a discussion between Cassirer and Heidegger that stretched back to the early 1920s. Specifically, it was argued that, despite their apparent consensus on the need for an analysis of the transcendental conditions for culture, they already diverged sharply in their respective judgments concerning the status of theoretical-scientific knowledge. Their disagreement was especially acute regarding the status of space and time as transcendental conditions for experience: Heidegger set forth an analysis of *existential space-time* as the ground for all further understanding, including scientific understanding. Cassirer, meanwhile, though he granted Heidegger's existentials a partial legitimacy as local and subjective conditions for everyday experience, nonetheless insisted that scientific knowledge achieved a *breakthrough* from existential to purely functional and objective space-time. Alongside this disagreement concerning the status of scientific concepts was a correlative dispute over the relation between myth and the modern world: Heidegger saw in mythic understanding one possible clue for the existential structure shared across all forms of human experience, whereas Cassirer posited a sharp break between mythic understanding and the self-consciousness that belonged (exclusively, in his view) to philosophical and scientific modernity. This chapter now moves forward in time to explore how, following their encounter at Davos, the conflict between Cassirer and Heidegger became increasingly ramified in its meaning and ultimately assumed a political significance that seemed to prohibit further dialogue. As we shall see, this conclusion was not foreordained. Had the Nazis not come to power, our memory of the Heidegger-Cassirer debate would appear very different indeed.

A Theory of Confrontation

In the months that immediately followed his return from Davos, Heidegger worked at an astonishing pace to complete the written text of his provocative reading of Kant, which he finished in a few brisk weeks over the summer and published later that same year as *Kant and the Problem of Metaphysics.* He had now reached a new level of prestige, and he inaugurated his professorship at Freiburg with the public lecture, "What Is Metaphysics?" delivered before the assembled philosophy faculty on July 24, 1929. The following summer, he offered a seminar, "On the Essence of Human Freedom: An Introduction to Philosophy," which consisted of a reexamination of the question of Being in ancient Greek thought, along with a protracted discussion of the problem of freedom as articulated by Kant. The seminar is of special interest here because it afforded Heidegger the opportunity to deepen his claims concerning the specifically metaphysical problem of freedom in Kant's practical philosophy, a question he had more or less neglected in his Davos lectures and in the Kant-book. As discussed above, freedom served as the key illustration for Cassirer's claim that Heidegger's Kant-interpretation failed to acknowledge the moment of metaphysical breakthrough—from finitude to infinity—that was a defining characteristic of Kant's philosophy overall. In the 1930 seminar, Heidegger now attempted to fill in this apparent lacuna with a careful consideration of human freedom as a genuinely metaphysical problem that could be properly understood only if it was set within the bounds of human finitude.

The seminar opened with an explicit promise to address freedom as the defining characteristic of the human being as a creature whose existence is "tiny, fragile, powerless, and transitory," as contrasted with both the "immeasurable duration of cosmic processes" and the "fates and fortunes" of world history. But Heidegger immediately warned his auditors that definitions of human freedom that remained fixed on questions of metaphysical contrast would only afford insight into negative rather than positive freedom: "For a long time," Heidegger explained, "the greatness of finitude has been downgraded through a false and deceptive infinity, such that we are no longer able to reconcile finitude and greatness. Man is not the image of a god conceived in the sense of the absolutely bourgeois, but this latter god is the ungenuine creation of man."[2] For Heidegger, philosophy would only begin to grasp the meaning of human freedom if it abandoned the premise that freedom resembles a causality—a law-giving unto oneself—a premise that conformed to the conventional picture of the human being as an entity confronting a metaphysically separate world of entities conceived as "objective." But any such confrontation was only possible given the prior *manifestness* of those entities, where this manifestation presupposed an original *comportment of human understanding in relation to what there is.* What Heidegger called the "letting-be-encountered" of entities thus presupposed a kind of freedom that was prior to and deeper than the Kantian conception of freedom as self-legislation. The genuine freedom of the human being was nothing less than "the condition of the possibility of the manifestness of the being of beings."[3]

This argument offered a subtle rejoinder to Cassirer's interpretation of Kantian freedom as providing access to an objectivity secured by the concepts of pure practical reason: objectivity was merely a derivative mode of making manifest the entities of Dasein's world, and as such it presupposed freedom as Dasein's basic mode of existence. Cassirer, of course, would have immediately countered this argument with the objection that it simply wasn't faithful to Kant's claims. But from Heidegger's perspective, textual fidelity was an ancillary concern and sometimes inhibited a properly philosophical grasp of what was truly at stake. To drive home this point, Heidegger warned his readers to resist the idol of historical accuracy and to embrace instead the possibility that genuine interpretation might demand "controversy," or *Auseinandersetzung*:

> As long as we hang on mere words, taking the Kantian philosophy, likewise every other great and genuine philosophy, as an interesting historical standpoint, as long as we do not resolutely enter into the occurrence of philosophy by means of a philosophical controversy, everything remains closed to us. . . . If true controversy takes place, however, it becomes irrelevant whether the categorical imperative is formulated by Kant or someone else.[4]

One could almost read this passage as Heidegger's attempt to justify his disagreement with Cassirer: "To be sure," Heidegger observed, "controversy does not mean what the common understanding assumes, i.e., criticizing and contradicting. Instead, it is a bringing back of the other, and thereby also of oneself, to what is primary and originary, to that which, as the essential, is itself the common, and thus not needful of any subsequent alliance."[5]

If this was indeed a reference to Cassirer, there was little need to mention him by name. He could appear as a nameless but necessary *other* of the philosophical controversy, the interlocutor who would be brought to something deeper and more "essential" than mere alliance. But the partners locked in such an *Auseinandersetzung* would have to agree that their common ground was the "originary" occurrence of philosophy as such and not the historical text that served as the pretext to their debate. The brute facts of the historical text were mere happenstance and could be sacrificed if they did not provide access to what was essential. *"Philosophical controversy,"* Heidegger concluded, *"is interpretation as destruction."*[6]

Academic Rivalry and Personal Prejudice

Not long after their encounter at Davos, academic conditions for Cassirer and Heidegger grew far more complex. On July 6, 1929, Cassirer was appointed as rector at the University of Hamburg for the length of the academic year, a position from which he would step down in the autumn of 1930. Even in his formal address of termination on November 10, he showed that Heidegger was still on his mind: In a lighthearted aside Cassirer compared the situation of the contemporary university to Heidegger's idea of "care" *(Sorge).*[7]

That very same year Heidegger also achieved a new prominence when he received an official offer from the state minister of science, art, and education, Adolf Grimme, informing him of the invitation to assume the Ernst Troeltsch Chair in Philosophy at the University of Berlin. Heidegger of course recognized the significance of this honor, but in a letter dated May 10, 1930, Heidegger informed Grimme that he would decline.[8] He had already made this decision with his wife Elfride, even before he travelled to Berlin to learn details.[9] As he explained to Elisabeth Blochmann, the Berlin offer came with financial terms that the Baden ministry could not match. But Heidegger had resolved to follow what he called "my inner voice," which counseled him to cherish inner peace over external rewards (though Baden did secure him two semesters of additional leave).[10] For Heidegger the offer was an indication of changing times. "My appointment," he wrote Elfride, "coincides with the rise of the young generation of Brüning, Treviranus and even Grimme too—in its general spiritual direction." Jaspers, too, was heartened by the signs of Berlin's philosophical awakening. "J[aspers] says he would definitely go, but fully respects my innermost decision." While he found colleagues there who appealed to him, his ultimate decision was reinforced by his distaste for Berlin life: "The sheer groundlessness [*Bodenlosigkeit*] of the place is dreadful," he wrote, "and yet it is *still* no genuine abyss for philosophy after all. Berlin must be *conquered from the outside*."[11]

The deliberations leading to the Berlin offer were supposed to be confidential. But during his Berlin visit Heidegger received a phone call from Kurt Riezler, who, after consulting with Windelband, had learned of a remarkable fact, which he now related to Heidegger: at first, the Berlin faculty had wished to nominate Ernst Cassirer. The nomination, moreover, had been *unico loco*. But as Heidegger later explained to Jaspers, Cassirer's nomination was immediately quashed by Nicolai Hartmann, who then nominated Heidegger instead, although Hartman expressed certain "reservations about youth etc." Heidegger then related to Jaspers, in strictest confidence, several of the further details he had learned about the Berlin deliberations: "After it was over with the appointment offer, several members of the faculty, among them [the classicist Werner] Jaeger, discovered that they actually would have wanted me—except the bigwigs [*die Bonzen*]. It is not for the first time that I doubt whether such cowards are the right people to help a new humanism get to its feet."[12]

The fact that *both* Heidegger *and* Cassirer were the final candidates for one of the most prestigious philosophy chairs in Germany should not surprise us, given their tremendous stature in the profession. In fact, this was not the only time that Heidegger and Cassirer were under consideration for the same position. Two years before, Cassirer had been the only serious contender when Husserl had vacated his Freiburg chair. There had also been substantive discussion among Jaspers and his colleagues at Heidelberg that Cassirer and Heidegger would be the two most likely candidates under consideration to succeed Heinrich Rickert upon his retirement. This means that Cassirer and Heidegger had competed for the same academic position *on at least three occasions.*

It may say something important about their relative standing in the philosophical community around 1930 that Cassirer was the preferred choice over Heidegger, and that Heidegger was nominated only once Cassirer's nomination was quashed. It is a commonplace of postwar philosophical memory that Heidegger emerged as the clear victor from his meeting with Cassirer at Davos. But the history of the Berlin chair suggests that this verdict fails to capture the true nuances of the situation. If we can trust the details of Grimme's account as reported by Heidegger, it was only the "bigwigs" (presumably the older and better-placed members of the faculty) who had preferred Cassirer. Heidegger further confided to his wife that he had

heard that older members of the faculty, including the neo-Kantian Windelband, were going to do their best to make certain the offer would collapse.
According to Grimme, the majority had apparently believed all along that
Heidegger was the better choice. Still, his knowledge of such details seem to
have left Heidegger feeling remarkably bitter. Summarizing the entire ordeal,
he wrote to Jaspers, "Thus they wanted to add to the four mediocrities and
inferiors a fifth who was harmless. It has now become downright fatal to be
expressly nominated by a Berlin faculty."[13]

Although Heidegger never seriously considered accepting the Berlin offer, it is nonetheless difficult to imagine he would have felt pleased to learn
after the fact that Cassirer had been the first and preferred nominee. But
Cassirer's nomination, Heidegger believed, was merely "convenient" and
"superfluous" since he suspected the Berlin faculty had calculated already
that Cassirer's appointment would ultimately be quashed.[14] More perplexing is Heidegger's further expression of doubt as to whether "such cowards"
(presumably, the Berlin faculty who wanted Heidegger but conceded to Cassirer's nomination) could help to inaugurate "a new humanism." Apparently, this was meant as a sarcastic comment on the personal character of
scholars who were ready to award institutional legitimacy to Cassirer's philosophical humanism *but only because they lacked the courage to oppose it.*

In all of this intrigue Heidegger believed he could detect troubling signs
that Germany's philosophical future remained uncertain. The offer, after all,
might have gone to Cassirer. For Heidegger this meant that philosophy *itself*
was in jeopardy, for Cassirer represented a strain of thinking that was
"harmless," that avoided the bracing questions of existence. But there were
other, less palatable reasons for Heidegger's resentment. In his struggle for
institutional advantage, he was prone to cynicism and his letters reveal a
somewhat calculating temperament. To be sure, debates over employment
rarely show professors in the most flattering light. But we cannot avoid the
unpleasant possibility that his understanding of this struggle may have been
tainted with anti-Jewish prejudice. Some months after his meeting with
Cassirer at Davos, in an October 1929 letter to Victor Schwoerer (then the
deputy president for the Society for the Support of German Science), Heidegger urged the Society to consider the grant candidatate Eduard Baumgarten, whose application was especially important because "we are faced with
a choice, either to provide our *German* intellectual life once more with real

talents and educators rooted in our own soil [*bodenständige*], or to hand over that intellectual life once and for all to the growing *Verjudung* [literally, Jewification] in the broad and narrow sense."[15] Very little in his personal or academic records lends credence to the charge that Heidegger was an anti-Semite in the *racial* sense. It would be hard to deny, however, that he subscribed to the fantastical belief that Jews posed an imminent threat to authentic German culture. In 1933, when he was rector at Freiburg, Heidegger would observe in an official letter that neo-Kantianism was a "leveling" philosophy "tailor made for liberalism," which could only be combated through an influx of what he called "native-born" teachers.[16] There may be no direct evidence that Heidegger's negative assessment of neo-Kantianism as a philosophical movement was intermingled with anti-Semitism.[17] But the call for "native-born" instructors *as against* neo-Kantians is suggestive, at the very least.

Nor were Heidegger's personal feelings toward Cassirer above suspicion. In her 1948 memoirs, Toni Cassirer described her and Ernst's shared apprehension in the days preceding the Davos conference: "We knew of Heidegger's remarkable appearance, and also his hostility toward the neo-Kantians, especially toward Cohen." Almost as an afterthought, she then wrote: "and his tendency toward anti-Semitism was not unknown to us."[18] Given what is now on record concerning Heidegger and his public-political behavior during the rectorship, this rather casual reference to his personal prejudices should not appear at all surprising. We should acknowledge that Toni Cassirer wrote her memoirs *after* Heidegger's official engagement with National Socialism and they are therefore burdened with all complications of historical hindsight. But we know from Heidegger's own letters that even in 1929 he was not free of anti-Semitism. This, at least, was the impression of Mrs. Cassirer, who also informs us that at Davos, Heidegger meant "to drag Cohen's work into the dust and, if possible, to destroy Ernst."[19] Her choice of terms—*vernichten* for "destroy"—is striking.

More ambiguous, but nonetheless suggestive, is Cassirer's public objection at Davos that "Neo-Kantianism is the scapegoat of the newer philosophy." (The term for "scapegoat," *Sündenbock,* has similar associations in German as in English.) Did Cassirer mean to suggest that Heidegger's own hostility toward neo-Kantianism was a mask for bigotry? The issue remains obscure. Cassirer's sensitivities at Davos about possible slights against neo-

Kantianism were no doubt heightened by a scandal that had transpired only a month before (on February 23, 1929) at the University of Munich, where the philosopher Othmar Spann had delivered a lecture at the behest of the *Kampfbund für deutsche Kultur* and an assortment of local Nazi-party acolytes. Newspapers later reported that Spann had begun by fulminating about the "crisis of culture" and had specifically attacked neo-Kantianism, a movement which in his words was led by the "foreigners" Cohen and Cassirer.[20]

The Rousseau Lecture at Freiburg

While the facts and inferences discussed above may appear quite damning, it is important to note that there is apparently no *direct* evidence that Heidegger's own anti-Semitism ever contaminated his dealings, personal or professional, with Cassirer. In fact, much that we know about Heidegger's behavior toward his colleague would suggest that the two remained on cordial terms.[21] About Heidegger, Toni Cassirer would later observe that

> his attitude toward Ernst after the Davos encounter became unclear. Somehow Ernst's personality had left an impression on him. In any event he never issued a rejoinder to Ernst's writing against him [a reference to Cassirer's 1931 review of *Kant and the Problem of Metaphysics*], nor did he ever write a critique of the third volume of the *Symbolic Forms,* which appeared in 1929.[22]

It would not have been at all surprising had Heidegger taken offense at Cassirer's review (which, after all, was quite negative, as will be discussed below). Nor could Heidegger be blamed had he disliked the third volume of *The Philosophy of Symbolic Forms,* given that it announced the necessity of surpassing Heidegger's analytic of existential space-time. Although Heidegger could have felt cause for retaliation, it would appear he never did so. Instead, in April 1932, he helped to secure an invitation for Cassirer to lecture in Freiburg before the Academic-Literary Society on "The Problem of Jean-Jacques Rousseau."[23]

Cassirer had spent much of 1931 in Paris, researching and writing his study on the philosophy of the Enlightenment; he and Toni would leave

Germany together in early 1933. The Rousseau lecture was to be Cassirer's last personal encounter with Heidegger and, in fact, one of Cassirer's last presentations before an assembly of German academics. In his immense corpus of published work, this lecture might seem negligible, were it not for the fact that it afforded him a final chance to restate his fundamental philosophical convictions directly in Heidegger's presence.

The opportunity was not to be squandered. Speaking through Rousseau, Cassirer delivered the rueful verdict that "philosophy had long since forgotten how to speak its native language." Philosophy, which should have been "the teaching of wisdom," now spoke, instead, "the language of the time, fitting itself into the thought and interests of the era." Rousseau, Cassirer continued, had complained long ago of humanity's penchant for conformity. The average human being was habituated to "constantly living outside himself." Uncertain of his own agency and opinion, the human being lived "only in the opinion of others" and could "gather awareness of his own existence solely through this derived and indirect method." Although Rousseau "shied away from the turmoil of the market place and the noise of battle," he remained, nonetheless, a fierce critic of his times. His essential demand—a demand that only Kant, of all his eighteenth-century contemporaries, fully understood—was "that men, instead of losing themselves in idle laments over the miseries of existence, should *understand their destiny and master it themselves.*"[24] From this requirement there flowed Rousseau's distinctive affirmation of a purely anthropocentric metaphysics:

> *Man cannot be relieved of the task of ordering his world; and in shaping and guiding it, he neither can nor ought to rely on help from above, on supernatural assistance.* The task has been put to *him*—he must solve it with his own, purely human means. But precisely as he penetrates into the character of the problem before him, he acquires the certainty that his self is not confined to the limits of the world of sense. From immanence and from ethical autonomy, *man now pushes forward into the core of "intelligible" being.*[25]

This was nothing less than a restatement of Cassirer's own philosophical precepts, as well as a reprisal of the debate over German philosophy's eighteenth-century inheritance that had served as the pretext for the encounter at Davos. Once again it was Kant who served as the philosophical authority behind the dispute: for of all Rousseau's contemporaries, it was Kant alone, Cassirer claimed, who had understood the Genevan completely and who had recognized the commitment to "ethical necessity" that unified all of his work.[26] Cassirer even permitted himself a subtle complaint against unnamed philosophers who would rather dwell on the "miseries of existence" than assume the burdens of worldmaking and the ethical imperatives that lay beyond all sensual bounds in a purely intelligible sphere. If this was an allusion to Heidegger, it was hardly a complaint about him alone. By this point, Cassirer had already developed a conscious and many-layered critique of the various currents of modern philosophy in which he discerned an incipient irrationalism and a fatalistic attraction to history or other reified categories resistant to practical reason. Cassirer's earlier attacks on the twin exponents of *Lebensphilosophie,* Scheler and Klages, had moved him to similarly bold pronouncements regarding the paramount significance of freedom in philosophy. Yet, much of the language would seem to suggest that, even where Heidegger was not the exclusive target, he was never far from Cassirer's thoughts.

If Heidegger recognized Cassirer's lecture as an implicit challenge, he betrayed no sign of having taken offense. In fact, the two philosophers got on quite well, as Cassirer related in a letter to Toni: "In Freiburg for my lecture the largest lecture hall in the University was packed full, and nearly the whole philosophy faculty appeared; afterwards I was at Gerhard Ritter's together with Fränkel, Schadewaldt, Heidegger, and others. The next morning I visited Heidegger and found him very open and straightforwardly friendly." Cassirer then added a perplexing remark: "Of the wild rumors spinning around him, in any event, I could ascertain nothing. He confessed to me that for a long time he had floundered over a review of my third volume, but for the time being still didn't know how he should grapple with the thing."[27]

Clearly, around 1932, there were traces of divided sentiment on both sides. It is evident that by this point, Cassirer disagreed sharply with Heidegger's philosophical claims and was even beset with suspicions that Heidegger as a man was perhaps not to be trusted. About the "wild rumors" he had heard, we can only guess at their likely meaning. Nor was Cassirer the only one who felt concerned. During the winter semester of

1932–1933, Heidegger wrote an angry and defensive letter to Hannah Arendt, in which he countered her query about rumors of his anti-Semitism by listing the great number of Jewish students he had advised and noting, too, his "personal relationships with Jews (Husserl, Misch, Cassirer, and others)."[28] Later in 1933 Heidegger would speak less ambiguously of a "dangerous international alliance of Jews," in a private conversation with Karl Jaspers (whose wife was Jewish). That he spoke in this fashion even when there was clearly no public advantage may suffice to prove that the rumors of his anti-Semitism were true after all.[29] Cassirer clearly had good reason to be suspicious. But we might also wonder at Heidegger's professed difficulties in writing a review of the third volume to Cassirer's *Philosophy of Symbolic Forms*. Was it only out of professional deference to Cassirer that Heidegger refrained from completing what would no doubt have been a negative review? It seems quite possible that Heidegger saw Cassirer through the distorted lens of his own prejudices. But it seems no less evident that Heidegger also esteemed Cassirer for his professional accomplishments and perhaps even felt something like personal admiration for his colleague—notwithstanding all that divided them.

Cassirer's Kant-Book Review

We must now turn back to the philosophical controversy itself. Throughout this chapter I have stressed repeatedly that in the years immediately following the Davos encounter Heidegger and Cassirer seem to have remained on more or less cordial terms, even if they felt increasingly apprehensive about their cultural (and, perhaps, political) differences. However, an important turning point came with the publication of Heidegger's book, *Kant and the Problem of Metaphysics*, in the late summer of 1929. As I noted in Chapter 5, the Kant-book provided a reprisal and elaboration of the arguments Heidegger had just presented in his public conversation with Cassirer only months before. So it is hardly surprising that Cassirer himself would have published one of the book's earliest reviews. Cassirer's long and highly critical assessment appeared in the early spring of 1931 as the lead essay in *Kantstudien*. Its publication exposed for the first time a deep and perhaps insuperable fault line between the two philosophers. Never before had Cassirer expressed his philosophical disagreement with Heidegger in such a sustained fashion, and never before had Cassirer implied that this philosophical disagreement was also the sign of a more ramified cultural-historical divide.

But even here we should not exaggerate its consequences. Despite its stringent tone, the review did very little to damage Heidegger's reputation. On the contrary, it would be more accurate to say that it marked Heidegger's arrival at a new plateau of academic legitimacy. In twenty-six densely set pages, it offered an assessment of the philosopher's work that was more extensive and engaged than anything that had yet been written concerning Heidegger's impact in either Germany or abroad.[30] Not even in the earlier published reviews of *Being and Time* had Heidegger seen his ideas subjected to such careful scrutiny. Nor should we forget that Heidegger had assumed his professorial position at Freiburg little more than two years before Cassirer's review. Heidegger was admittedly no longer a novice, but the Kant-book was only the second of his major works to be published. A prominent review of this sort in a leading journal brought unprecedented attention. Overall, Heidegger had good reason to take Cassirer's review to heart—and good reason to be dismayed by what he read.

Cassirer commenced his review by recalling a 1772 letter Kant sent to his colleague, the Berlin physician Marcus Herz, whom Kant had once praised (alongside Salomon Maimon) as among the few readers to have grasped the deeper principles of transcendental idealism. Kant had announced to Herz that he at last held in his hands "the key to the entire secret of the heretofore still-hidden metaphysics." The crucial element of this metaphysics was the problem of the "transcendental object," which promised to reorient all of metaphysics away from its traditional concerns with objects and toward the basic structure of thought itself. Cassirer observed that even in Kant's time, this new transcendental orientation met with considerable resistance, especially from members of the older generation who saw in Kant's solution nothing less than a wholesale "destruction" (*Zerstörung*) of metaphysics. Mendelssohn expressed a widespread sentiment of the age when he called Kant the "all-destroyer" (*Alleszermalmer*). Since Kant's time, the debate had not subsided: Did the transcendental turn promise a revivified and altogether novel approach to metaphysics? Or, instead, did it spell the death of metaphysics as such? "In the answer to this question," Cassirer observed, "*intellectuals and epochs are divided.*"[31]

From the very beginning, Cassirer wanted his readers to understand that his criticism of Heidegger was philosophical but also historical. Their disagreement itself rehearsed a division of intellectual orientations and "epochs" stretching all the way back to late eighteenth-century Germany. It could hardly have been accidental that Cassirer opened his review by recalling for his readers a moment in the history of German Enlightenment sociability when Germans and Jews were coming to recognize their political aspirations in common, and when Kant himself had looked to Marcus Herz, a German-Jewish physician, as his most intimate philosophical companion—it was perhaps a message that Cassirer understood how the world had changed. Yet the key to their disagreement was and would remain the question concerning the nature of philosophical inquiry itself: Cassirer believed that the original dispute over Kant's attitude toward metaphysics held a paradigmatic import insofar as it had remained the standard for all of modern philosophy since Kant's day. In Cassirer's estimation, the Kantian-Copernican revision of metaphysics into epistemology was now a settled matter, the philosophical consensus having emerged already with the neo-Kantians' anti-metaphysical teachings in the late nineteenth century. As Cassirer explained, most current scholars were in accord—if not on the substance of Kant's doctrine, then at least on its formal-logical and methodological character. Notwithstanding its diversity, the neo-Kantian school in particular agreed at least on this one point, that Kant's system was a *theory of knowledge* (*Erkenntnistheorie*), a theory that started with the facts of science and asked after their possibility. It was this epistemological orientation that marked the essentially "scientific" character of Kant's own efforts, and it was this scientific ideal that remained the desideratum for all philosophical inquiry within neo-Kantian circles well into the twentieth century. To illustrate this point, Cassirer recalled the philosopher Alois Riehl, whose 1883 inaugural address at Freiburg, "On Scientific and Non-Scientific Philosophy," introduced a sharp distinction between the properly critical questions of scientific or "rigorous" philosophy and those questions pertinent to individual life or subjective experience that he categorized as matters of worldview or *Weltanschauung*.[32] Riehl had taken care to note that while questions of worldview had their own legitimacy within the subjective sphere, they were forever banned from the circle of genuine philosophy.

Before considering the substance of Cassirer's review, we should pause to consider this opening provocation: we can already see how it ratified a set of uncompromising distinctions—dogmatic metaphysics *versus* modern epistemology, *Weltanschauung versus* scientific philosophy—by which Cassirer would judge and ultimately condemn Heidegger's work. At issue was not only a local issue of Kant-interpretation. This was only one specific dispute within what Cassirer described as the "opposition between Heidegger's interpretation of the central task of metaphysics and the mode of thought and philosophical sensibility of positivistic-inclined and oriented 'Criticism.'" But if the stakes of the opposition were truly this broad, then the explicit reference to Riehl in particular must have seemed especially provocative. For it could hardly have escaped the reader's notice that almost forty years after Riehl's *Antrittsrede* at Freiburg, Heidegger himself had assumed a permanent post on the same philosophical faculty. Implicit in Cassirer's remark was therefore the suggestion that Heidegger's Kant-book signaled a kind of regression, both institutional *and* methodological, to the "non-scientific" philosophy of mere worldview his Freiburg predecessors had labored to overcome.

Returning to his initial complaint at Davos, Cassirer again remarked on the vigor of Heidegger's antipathy toward Riehl and the entire neo-Kantian school: "Nothing is fought against so passionately and forcefully by Heidegger as this mode of thought—the assumption that for Kant the *essential* goal was to ground metaphysics in the 'theory of knowledge.'" On this point, Heidegger's purpose was unmistakable: the neo-Kantian epistemological orientation was to be, in Heidegger's own words, "'finally destroyed.'"[33] That Cassirer opened his review by quoting this bold statement from Heidegger's book was hardly incidental, for the rivalry of schools was to serve as a marker for a larger distinction—between "scientific" and "non-scientific" philosophy. And it thereby anticipated the final verdict of Cassirer's review, that the contrast between Heidegger and his neo-Kantian predecessors was part of a much larger, historico-cultural divide between a theologically inflected metaphysics and a modernist philosophy grounded in the sciences and the Enlightenment.

With these distinctions in place, Cassirer could now proceed to give a careful exposition and demolition of Heidegger's book. His ultimate verdict was clear: *Kant and the Problem of Metaphysics* offered a dramatic reprisal of the metaphysical reading the neo-Kantians had suppressed. Heidegger assumed that the first *Critique* should not be seen along neo-Kantian lines as an epistemological inquiry into the logical preconditions for the natural sciences but should be understood instead as a metaphysical inquiry into the human-ontological preconditions for raising the question of Being (i.e., for general ontology). The task was to investigate *human being* as the necessary foundation for understanding Being as such. It was this preparatory task—a "groundlaying for metaphysics"—that Heidegger termed "fundamental ontology." In Heidegger's view, this meant that any question concerning the knowledge of the world must begin with an analysis regarding the status of the kind of being that is capable of raising such a question. Thus: "All questions into Being overall must first proceed with the question into human being." Heidegger's conclusion was that metaphysical knowledge as such comes back to the earlier question concerning the being of human existence: the metaphysics of Dasein.[34]

From Cassirer's perspective, this initial turn—from epistemology to metaphysics—was already thick with controversy. Indeed, although he attempted to sustain a tone of scholarly neutrality, Cassirer could not refrain from voicing a certain skepticism concerning Heidegger's point of departure:

> It would be idle and pointless to quarrel with Heidegger on this first and original premise of his problem or to want to rectify him as to the choice of this starting point. If any sort of philosophical "confrontation" ["*Auseinandersetzung*"] is going to be in any sense *fruitful,* the critic must accordingly decide to stand upon the ground Heidegger has selected. Whether he can remain thereon is a question that can only be decided through the exposition itself—but he must take to that ground if criticism is not to degenerate into a mere polemic and an incessant talking-past-one-another [*Auseinandervorbeireden*].[35]

In these elaborate displays of philosophical fair-mindedness, the attentive reader could already detect a tone of strained equanimity. Cassirer took care to note that he was undisturbed at Heidegger's failure to grasp "the historical service of neo-Kantianism and especially the foundational interpretations offered by Hermann Cohen in his Kant-books." The misunderstanding was in any event natural because Heidegger wished to "unlearn"— Heidegger's own term—the basic epistemological premises of Marburg neo-Kantianism. More importantly, Cassirer wrote, although he dissented from Heidegger's metaphysical revision, it was nonetheless important when judging the book to obey Kant's own maxim that no philosophical position be held with "dogmatic certainty" lest in place of critical discussion philosophers indulge in a mere "playing-against-each-other" of rival "standpoints." But even this statement of seeming charity carried a critical thrust: in his readiness to renounce any combat of "standpoints," Cassirer issued a rejoinder (which, given his powerful control of allusion, we may assume was intended) to Heidegger's closing remark at Davos that "the differentiation of standpoints is at the root of philosophical endeavor." To invoke Kant as a guide for a nondogmatic method of philosophical interpretation was therefore to imply that Heidegger's own method of interpretation was un-Kantian, and, indeed, dogmatic.

To expose this element of dogmatism in Heidegger's reading, it was crucial to see how it emerged out of a creative misunderstanding of fundamental concepts in Kantian doctrine. The key to Heidegger's interpretation, Cassirer observed, was its attempt to characterize the first *Critique* as a disquisition on the finitude of human understanding. This interpretation had apparently solid textual foundations: Kant himself had distinguished between the divine intellect (*intuitus originarius*), which enjoys an unconditioned spontaneity and relates immediately to the being of objects in the very act of thought, and the human intellect, which is fundamentally receptive in virtue of its dependence on what is given through intuition. On Heidegger's view this insight into the essential dependency of the human mind remained in place throughout the first *Critique*. But, as Cassirer noted, this view was highly controversial in light of Kant's discovery that the mind makes its own "spontaneous" contribution to human knowledge in the form of the pure concepts of the understanding. Indeed, Kant himself had wished to safeguard this spontaneity by distinguishing between three faculties of mind: understanding, reason, and sensibility. Thus even while Kant granted that sensibility was a faculty dependent upon what is given, Kant could sustain this dependency *together with* his theory of rational spontaneity. But, on Heidegger's reading, the apparent spontaneity of the understanding was an illusion, for Kant himself ultimately reaffirmed the finitude of human knowledge insofar as he traced the three faculties to a single source in the transcendental imagination. And through an ingenious reading of the first *Critique*'s "schematism," Heidegger then claimed that at the root of this "mysterious" doctrine, there lay a hidden recognition that temporality itself served as the existential condition for imagination, and therefore for "meta-physics." Kant's most celebrated theory of mental spontaneity was therefore grounded in a deeper portrait of human temporality and finitude: "All thought as such," wrote Cassirer, "all, even the 'purely logical' use of the understanding already carries the stamp of finitude;—indeed, that is its genuine seal." It followed that human consciousness in all its efforts would never achieve the quasi-divine freedom of pure and unconditioned sponta-neity. This was the fundamental lesson of Heidegger's Kant-book, that "the chain of finitude is not to be broken."[36]

In Chapter 4, we saw that a major theme in the quarrel between Hei-degger and Cassirer concerned the essential finitude of human reason and the question as to whether, notwithstanding this limitation, our reason has the capacity to "break through" its finitude in either theoretical knowledge or ethics. In his review Cassirer once again emphasized that Heidegger re-mained committed to the doctrine of an *unbroken* finitude. Cassirer none-theless took care to acknowledge his agreement with Heidegger concerning the centrality of the transcendental imagination in Kant's theoretical phi-losophy. While other scholars had neglected the theme of imagination entirely, or had claimed it was nothing but a mere remnant of Kant's predi-lection for architectonic symmetry, Heidegger at least recognized that the doctrine of transcendental imagination and the concomitant theory of the "schematism" lay at the very core of Kantian doctrine. From Cassirer's point of view, this emphasis on the schematism was clearly among the greatest merits of Heidegger's book: its interpretation of the schematism exhibited an "extraordinary power," and the entire exposition displayed the "utmost sharpness and clarity."[37] Moreover, this was an emphasis Cassirer himself shared (as demonstrated by the careful discussion of transcendental imagi-nation in the third volume of his *Philosophy of Symbolic Forms*).[38] Yet, not-withstanding their agreement as to the importance of the transcendental imagination, the two philosophers would ultimately disagree as to what this importance entailed: Heidegger found in the doctrine of the sche-matism a further validation for his claim that human understanding is irretrievably finite. It was here, on Cassirer's view, that Heidegger's overall interpretation of Kantian doctrine began to run into serious and ultimately fatal difficulties.

As Cassirer explained, the suggestion that Kant's philosophy was anchored in a theory of human finitude could be justified *only* if one construed the notion of finitude according to the signature distinctions of transcendental philosophy, between the sensible and intelligible world, experience and idea, phenomena and noumena. Heidegger was certainly correct to observe that human knowledge exhibits a certain finitude in relation to the objects of knowledge insofar as the human mind does not *create* its objects but instead must *receive* them. But in attempting to make this a linchpin of Kantian doctrine, Heidegger missed the fact that transcendental philosophy, in Cassirer's words, "has nothing to do with the absolute existence of objects and the absolute ground of their Being." Kant's inquiry was *not* fixed directly on the objects and their origins but *only* on the modes by which those objects were understood. Once acknowledged, however, this transcendental distinction vitiated the force of Heidegger's repeated appeals to human finitude, which owed their apparent plausibility to an older, metaphysical rather than epistemological notion of objecthood. Heidegger attempted to justify the claim about human finitude with allusions to Kant's own contrast between human or *receptive* understanding and a "divine" or "*creative* understanding." But he failed to acknowledge that, according to Kant himself, the notion of a creative intellect was a mere "limit-concept," the possibility of which we could make "not even the slightest representation."[39] The notion of a divinely creative understanding, on Cassirer's interpretation, served an exclusively "negative" function in the first *Critique*. This meant that Heidegger had burdened Kantian epistemology with an illicitly metaphysical and dogmatic meaning that Kant himself would have denied.

More importantly, Cassirer claimed that by importing the premodern or theological distinction between divine and human intuition back into Kant's epistemological system, Heidegger was not only misreading the basic doctrine of the transcendental analytic, he was also giving the notion of human finitude an absolutist meaning that ultimately disabled Kant's own theory concerning reason's progressive acquisition of knowledge. Kant's distinctive view (as presented in the transcendental dialectic) was that although the "idea of the unconditioned" found no immediate use within the bounds of intuition, it was nonetheless a necessary principle of orientation by which reason conceived of an "absolute totality of the synthesis of conditions." Reason necessarily imposed this idea on itself as a presupposition of all empirical inquiry, although the idea as such corresponded to no possible sensible object and remained (in Cassirer's words) "purely *symbolic*." It was in this sense that human reason broke through its dependency on intuition and achieved a grasp of the infinite or the unconditioned. The view expounded by Kant's anti-critical contemporaries, such as F. H. Jacobi, that human reason remained forever trapped in a merely "receptive" function betrayed not only a basic misunderstanding of Kantian doctrine, it also illustrated the "typical opposition" between critical idealism and the "philosophy of faith" (*Glaubensphilosophie*).[40] Heidegger's own mischaracterization implicitly aligned him with the latter school and thereby obstructed any recognition for Kant's more "Platonist" confidence in the pure ideas of reason. For it was in the doctrine of the ideas, Cassirer explained, that "Kant burst free from the circle ... of merely-temporal existence [*bloß-zeitlichen Daseins*]."[41]

On Cassirer's view, Heidegger's basic misunderstanding of Kantian principles became even more evident when one considered the place of ethics in the Kantian system. Although theoretical reason from the Kantian perspective remained operative only within the bounds of empirical experience, this was decidedly not the case for practical reason: the unconditioned idea of freedom, as Cassirer explained, represented Kant's "ultimate step" beyond the limits of empirical experience and into the realm of the "purely-intelligible" and "supratemporal." As free agents, we give to ourselves laws, and in so doing (as Kant wrote in the first *Critique*), "disclose a spontaneity" linking us to an intelligible and no longer merely sensual world.[42] In Cassirer's words: "It is thus the unconditionality of the moral law which ultimately lifts us out from the circle of merely-phenomenal existence [*bloß-phänomenalen Daseins*]." Heidegger's attempt to read Kant's philosophy without reference to the unconditional character of its ethical concepts therefore expunged what Kant himself had called a "wonder in the phenomenal world," that is, the spontaneity of the will. For in Kant's ethics, wrote Cassirer, one's being is no longer conditioned ultimately by one's sensual being. Rather, "the 'I' is at bottom only what it makes of itself."[43]

Heidegger contrived to minimize and ultimately cancel out this radical spontaneity, but he could do so only by placing what Cassirer deemed an unwarranted stress on Kant's notion that the practical self relates to the moral law through a "feeling of respect," as if this somehow ratified Heidegger's own thematics of care-laden finitude. This reading was illegitimate, Cassirer argued, because it conflated ethical and psychological categories. One's empirical feeling of respect for the moral law did not first *constitute* or *ground* the moral law; it served merely as the *means* by which the moral law was *represented* within empirical-finite consciousness. To read Kant's ethical theory as applicable only to human beings and to read it as anchored in peculiarly human affective dispositions was to reduce it to a mere anthropology, thereby missing one of Kant's most crucial insights, that the moral law was indeed categorical insofar as it retained its validity "for all possible rational beings." Here, Cassirer made an oblique reference to Heidegger's remarks at Davos on the place of angels in Kant's system, noting that, by "rational beings," Kant had *not* meant to invoke "the loving angels" as Schopenhauer had implied. Kant meant only to underscore the universal-rational applicability of the moral law, the validity of which was unconstrained by any empirical and anthropological fact. Cassirer's conclusion was that throughout the Kant-book Heidegger tried illicitly to collapse the essential dualism in Kantian doctrine concerning reason's twofold application to the intelligible (noumenal) and the sensible (phenomenal) worlds. Heidegger's evident purpose in collapsing this dualism, Cassirer surmised, was to demonstrate an allegedly dramatic if rarely acknowledged truth, that Kant's critical philosophy brought reason back from its illusory transcendence and restored it to the "plane of temporal Dasein." But Heidegger's attempt to unify these two distinctive domains of reason (by grounding them both fully and decisively in the transcendental imagination) found no real warrant in Kant's text. In place of Kant's characteristic dualism, Heidegger had simply substituted what Cassirer termed a "monism of the imagination."[44]

The theme of unqualified finitude was therefore a reflection of Heidegger's own interests and had little to do with Kant's philosophy. "For [Kant's] problem," Cassirer concluded, "is not the problem of 'Being' and 'Time,' but rather the problem of 'Being' and 'Ought,' of 'Experience' and 'Idea.'" Although Cassirer agreed with Heidegger that the transcendental imagination served as a cornerstone to Kant's theoretical philosophy, any attempt to address the so-called metaphysics of Kant's philosophical system would need to move beyond the confines of the theoretical work to explain Kant's broader theory of ideas. The ultimate goal of the Kantian system, Cassirer declared, was not human Dasein in its incorrigible finitude and temporal isolation, but instead the "intelligible substrate of humanity."[45] The ultimate problem with Heidegger's reading was that it claimed to discover an ontology or a metaphysical account of human being where Kant meant only to lay down a "theory of experience" (an allusion to Cohen's *Kant's Theory of Experience*), which is to say, a theory that concerned the conditions for the objectivity of possible knowledge. Heidegger was especially mistaken to read Kant's theory of transcendental imagination as a metaphysical lesson about *human* existence, because that theory was meant to describe only a phenomenology of the *object* and not the subject: "The entire problematic concerning the temporality of the subject, the interpretation of human existence on the basis of temporality, of 'being toward death,' as Heidegger has laid out in *Being and Time*—: all this remains to Kant not merely factually but fundamentally alien."[46]

Cassirer was well aware of Heidegger's explanation as to why his reading appeared so exotic: Heidegger wished to bring to light *not* what Kant actually said but what remained *unsaid* as the hidden and metaphysical doctrine that had been suppressed by Kant and his neo-Kantian followers. And this meant resisting the apparent meaning of Kant's texts even to the point of contradicting its manifest content. In Heidegger's own words (as quoted by Cassirer), "any such interpretation must necessarily use *violence*."[47] From Cassirer's perspective, however, this apologia for violence simply opened the door to willful distortion. To claim with Heidegger that the first *Critique* contained a theory of "purely receptive spontaneity" was to import into Kant's lexicon a wholly foreign terminology that would have seemed, from Kant's own perspective, no less paradoxical than the concept of wooden iron. "Here," Cassirer wrote, "Heidegger speaks no longer as a commentator but as a usurper, who intrudes as it were on the Kantian system with force of arms to subject it and make it serve his [own] problematic."[48]

More troubling still was Heidegger's inference that Kant had "drawn back" from the radical and even "unsettling" consequences of the theory of human temporality as contained within the first (A) edition of the schematism-chapter and had therefore "suppressed" that theory in the second (B) revised edition so as to bolster the seeming sovereignty of human reason. From Cassirer's perspective, any such inference was strictly forbidden: citing Kant's own remarks on the use of "hypotheses" in transcendental philosophy, Cassirer noted that inferences of this variety were tools of mere polemic and "weapons of war."[49] Schopenhauer, Cassirer explained, had anticipated Heidegger in claiming that the second edition obscured Kant's true intentions—a revision motivated by Kant's "fear of humanity." While Heidegger's reading shared nothing in common with Schopenhauer's "foolish and coarse-grained" psychologism, it nonetheless introduced a "subjective and psychological" inference in place of objective explanation. Perhaps the most surprising thing about Heidegger's psychological argument was that Kant had rarely displayed any reluctance to forsake the consolation of metaphysical absolutes. Even in the pre-critical *Dreams of a Spiritseer,* Kant had declared himself an eager disciple of Socrates: "How many are the things of which I have no need!" He boldly disowned the "butterfly-wings of metaphysics" and embraced in his own fashion the "finitude" of this-worldly empirical experience. Kant's theory concerning an intelligible order of pure ideas did not stand in contradiction to this empiricism because it was not a theory of intelligible *substance* (and, moreover, because they cannot be schematized in a priori spatiotemporal intuition, such ideas were not actually "metaphysical" in the dogmatic sense). Kant neither imagined nor had any reason to fear anything like the "abyss" Heidegger discerned in his philosophy. Cassirer could therefore see little warrant for Heidegger's image of an "anxious Kant."[50]

From Cassirer's perspective, the ultimate difficulty in Heidegger's interpretation was that it ascribed to Kant a "fundamental mood" (*Grundstimmung*) that had little to do with the Königsberg philosopher's true "intellectual atmosphere" or historical-cultural sensibility. Kant, observed Cassirer, "strives after light and clarity even where he contemplates the deepest and most hidden 'grounds' of Being." To read a page of Kant was thus to feel (as Goethe remarked) as if one had entered a brightly lit room. During his remonstrations at Davos, Cassirer had quoted just one passage from the poem by Friedrich Schiller, "Das Ideal und das Leben," so as to illustrate the intellectual worldview expressed in Kant's philosophy. He now reproduced a full stanza:

Only the body owns those powers
That bind our dark fate,
But free from all time's force, . . .
The divine amongst divinities, is form.
If you would soar upon your wings,
Cast off from yourself the fear of earthly things.
Flee from the narrow, dull life,
Into the Ideal's Kingdom.[51]

This poem offered what Cassirer believed to be a perfect illustration of the broader historical-cultural values expressed in Kant's philosophy, its union of empiricism and idealism, and its undiminished fidelity to the pure ideas through which humanity might secure its own share of the infinite. With these values, Cassirer concluded, "Kant is and remains—in the most sublime and beautiful sense of this word—a thinker of the Enlightenment."[52] The *Stilprinzip,* or "principle of style," that Cassirer discerned in Heidegger's work stood in vivid contrast to the classical idealism that permeated Kant's philosophy. For the trademark themes of Heidegger's ontology—angst, fate, finitude, and so forth (many of which were on display in Heidegger's recent lecture "What Is Metaphysics?" from which Cassirer quoted liberally)—seemed expressive of the very darkness and limitation Schiller had urged us to transcend. Such themes served as standard currency only within "the world of Kierkegaard." In Kant's conceptual universe, however, they had no legitimacy whatsoever.

Cassirer's assessment of the Kant-book was remarkable not only for its content but also its tone. In this rare instance, Cassirer had gone vigorously on the offensive. His well-known equanimity was strained to such a degree that it seemed necessary to conclude by emphasizing once again that "in these reflections nothing lay further [from my intentions] than any kind of personal polemic."[53] He hastened to add that the Kant-book, "like all Heidegger's works," bore the stamp of a "genuinely philosophical sensibility" and was animated by a "true inner passion for its task." Its value overall "should not in any way be minimized or denied." But such reassurances only betrayed the strength of Cassirer's disapproval. His rejection of Heidegger's interpretation now appeared far more comprehensive and wide-reaching in its consequences than auditors at Davos would have suspected two years before. Most striking of all was Cassirer's new readiness to lend his philosophical disagreement a broader and more ramified cultural-historical meaning. Heidegger's philosophy was governed by a "stylistic principle" essentially at odds with Kant and the overall "spiritual atmosphere" of the Enlightenment. Cassirer left unstated a further but obvious inference: that Cassirer himself (and *not* Heidegger) was the more faithful interpreter of Kant's philosophy and more loyal to its actual "style." The explanatory value in this aesthetic-historical language was still far from clear, especially because both philosophers had agreed in principle that a philosophical difference should never be construed as a personalized and theatricalized conflict between one *Weltanschauung* and another. Cassirer thus ended the review by recalling, "I have already stressed in my conversations with Heidegger at Davos that I harbor neither the wish nor the hope of converting him to my 'standpoint.'" The true purpose of philosophical debate was, after all, the clarification of the concepts alone: "In all philosophical confrontation [*Auseinandersetzung*]," Cassirer advised, "what should be striven for is that one learn to *see* the contrasts correctly and that one should *understand* oneself precisely in these contrasts."[54]

Heidegger's Response

Not surprisingly, Heidegger took strong exception to Cassirer's review and also to the much shorter review by the neo-Kantian-trained philosopher Rudolf Odebrecht, which appeared in the *Blätter für deutsche Philosophie* later that same year.[55] In a handwritten paper covered with fragmentary notes, Heidegger sketched out a private rejoinder to both critics, devoting particular attention to Cassirer.[56] Although he only published his retort much later, the notes are especially instructive in that they offer a vigorous rejoinder to Cassirer's implication that the Kant-book was somehow an exercise in crypto-theology. Odebrecht, meanwhile, had gone so far as to suggest that Heidegger had "deduced" finite knowing from absolute or divine intuition. In his notes, Heidegger insisted that "absolute knowing is merely a constructed idea . . . that is, it comes from our knowing, in which the specifically finite has been separated and its essence has been freed." Nothing in his argument, however, *presupposed* the existence of God: "The actual knowledge of the actual Being-at-hand of absolute knowledge—which is to say *the Being of God himself*—is not needed here." The purpose of his appeals to the notion of a creative or infinite knowledge was merely to underscore the finitude of *human* understanding: "What are we to find, or do we want to find, from the comparison of our knowing with the absolute?" Heidegger queried. "Simply to explain what is meant by the finitude of *our* knowing."[57]

Most revealing of all, however, was Heidegger's emphatic defense of the idea of *thrownness*, which he clearly believed both critics had misunderstood. In the notes, Heidegger referred back to his own effort in the Kant-book to thematize thrownness as "the ground for the finitude of knowing," a phenomenon first manifest within human experience as "dependency upon beings other than ourselves." Cassirer and Odebrecht, however, had mistaken it for an epistemological problem: "Finitude is primarily not that of knowing," Heidegger objected, "rather, that is only *an essential consequence of thrownness [nur eine Wesesfolge der Geworfenheit].*"[58]

Thrownness, in other words, had been reduced from a metaphysical insight into a primarily epistemological problem. The bitter lesson of this misunderstanding was that, despite Heidegger's great efforts in attempting to restore Kant's transcendental philosophy to its properly metaphysical foundations, the predominant interpretation of the first *Critique* as a theory of knowledge still held sway. On this point, Heidegger expostulated, Cassirer's assessment of his book betrayed a thoroughgoing failure of comprehension: "What is supposed [to come of] the theorizing about the spontaneity of the understanding [*Spontaneität des Verstandes*]," Heidegger asked, "precisely where I have placed the power of imagination in the center?" By laying undue emphasis on spontaneity alone, Cassirer merely replicated and amplified the various commonplace prejudices of the Marburg School: "Only understanding and only logic," Heidegger exclaimed, "and intuition merely a fatal remnant that should disappear into an infinite process! Space and time as concepts of the understanding!"

Nor could the debate be resolved simply by appealing to the original text: "A *Kant in himself*," wrote Heidegger, "is a fundamental misunderstanding." Ultimately, what Cassirer failed to admit was that thrownness and finitude remained constitutive *problems* for the human being, and metaphysical problems could not be made to disappear simply by singing hymns to the creative powers of human reason. It was obvious that Cassirer had misunderstood Heidegger's most fundamental aims: "To philosophize in this way about finitude only because it turns up for one person or another, maybe in a moment of hangover [*Katzenjammer*], this is indeed no *philosophical* motivation," Heidegger complained. "It appears as if Cassirer has indeed *completely* missed the central theme!"[59]

But it was Heidegger himself who ultimately changed his mind. In subsequent editions of the Kant-book, he included prefatory notes that marked his own growing dissatisfaction with the book's original claims. In the second edition in 1950, he acknowledged, perhaps in oblique reference to Cassirer, that "readers have taken constant offence at the violence of my interpretation." Such allegations of violence are "supported" because there are laws for "thoughtful dialogue" that are too easily "damaged." In any such dialogue, "the possibility of going astray is more threatening, the shortcomings more frequent." Heidegger now admitted the "shortcomings of the present endeavor," but he added that "thinkers learn from their shortcomings to be more persevering." In the fourth edition's new preface in 1973, he seemed to echo Cassirer's early criticism, admitting that "I sought in Kant an advocate for the question of Being which I posed," though in truth "Kant's question is foreign [*fremde*] to it." Heidegger even granted that the book was in fact an "over-interpretation" (*Überdeutung*).[60] Cassirer had said precisely this more than forty years before. It was an ironic end to this brief chapter of the story. Heidegger had frequently insisted that genuine interpretation required controversy, but on this point, at least, he finally conceded that Cassirer had been right all along.

Cassirer's Unpublished Critique

Even before Cassirer had completed the third volume of his *Philosophy of Symbolic Forms,* he had already commenced laboring on a projected fourth volume, which he titled *The Metaphysics of Symbolic Forms.* A fragment of the fourth volume was initially meant to serve as the conclusion to volume 3, but it grew so massive, swelling to nearly 300 pages, that in 1929 Cassirer resolved to publish the third volume without the fragment. Over the coming years the drafts and sections intended for volume 4 continued to proliferate, but they remained unpublished in Cassirer's lifetime. For a deeper assessment of Cassirer's growing critique of Heidegger, however, these fragments are of enormous significance. In some of them, Heidegger appears by name; in others he remains a specter, though his presence is no less obvious.

In the first chapter of *The Metaphysics of Symbolic Forms,* Cassirer was already working out some of the critical reflections on *Lebensphilosophie* that he would present in his lectures at Davos. The chapter, titled simply "'Spirit' and 'Life'" ("'Geist' und 'Leben'"), purports to be an assessment of the most prominent early twentieth-century representatives of the philosophy of life, Georg Simmel and Ludwig Klages. But as would befit the conclusion to his three-volume philosophical system, it is evident that Cassirer had in mind a far broader target. He took aim not only at the life-philosophers but more generally at the many-headed hydra of philosophical irrationalism represented by Friedrich Nietzsche, Henri Bergson, and Wilhelm Dilthey, whose popularity in the 1920s he refused to dismiss as mere fashion (as was the verdict of Heinrich Rickert in his 1920 study, *The Philosophy of Life*).[61] From Cassirer's perspective life-philosophy was a capacious philosophical movement of far-reaching consequence; indeed, it was arguably the single most influential intellectual trend of the 1920s. Its message, moreover, stood in direct contradiction to the philosophical principles and ideals Cassirer himself wished to promote.

The life-philosophers, claimed Cassirer, were inclined to lament the unfortunate divide between "life" and "spirit," or intellectual cognition, even as they transformed this dualism into the founding dogma of a new and proudly irrational metaphysics. For Simmel the dualism was indeed a tragedy: the human being abandons the sphere of life and effects a "turn to the idea," reinforcing the notion that the intellect lies in a sphere transcendent and even adversarial to life.[62] Klages went even further with the quasi-Nietzschean declaration that all intellectual activity expresses the human drive to dominate life, an impulse that if left unchecked must eventually destroy the soul. Against the metaphysical extremism of all such views, Cassirer insisted that the life-philosophers' notion of a fatal antagonism between life and spirit was profoundly mistaken. Even their effort to comprehend and defend life against the dominance of the mind bore witness to the mind's capacity for comprehension. The so-called turn to the idea, Cassirer explained, "cannot be described as life bidding itself farewell into order to go forth into something foreign and distant from itself." From Cassirer's own philosophical perspective, the supposed dualism between intellection and life experience was merely an illusion. Even the experience of historical passivity—as typified, for example, by the life philosophers' quasi-mythical category of fate—was first intelligible only through human conceptual effort, and thus bore witness to human freedom. Life, wrote Cassirer, "must be seen as returned to itself, it 'comes to itself' in the medium of the symbolic forms. It possesses and grasps itself in the imprint of form as the infinite possibility of formation, as the will to form and the power to form. Even life's limitation becomes its own act; what is from outside seems to be its fate, its necessity, [but] proves to be a witness to its freedom and self-formation."[63]

Cassirer clearly meant to defend not only his own philosophy but all contemporary philosophies allied under the simple banner of "idealism." From this line of analysis, life-philosophy was only the most recent manifestation of an ancient tendency to denigrate the powers of human cognition in favor of some deeper and more irrational source of value. Against the rising tide of anti-intellectualism, he extolled an idealistic principle traceable to Nicholas of Cusa, who had theorized that, while God is the power that "gives Being," the human mind itself is the power that "lends and justifies values." For Cassirer this meant that *any* attempt to disown the mind and to celebrate Being as a deeper and more original authority must inevitably founder on a self-contradiction:

> The principle of the devaluation of the mind, no matter from what standpoint or authority this is attempted or carried out, has from the outset a definite limit to it. Every purely negative evaluation of the mind also affirms it in one of its highest, truly positive achievements. Even if the entire sphere of the intellect were conceived as something negative, even if all its activities were denied and rejected, the mere assigning of this negative meaning is itself a new act that holds us firmly in the sphere of *Geist* we had hoped to flee.[64]

Cassirer concluded that it was in vain that humanity attempted to disown its freedom for the false comfort of an unreflective and romanticized passivity. The supposed priority of Being or fate could be demonstrated only through an act of reflection that itself bore witness to spontaneity: "To pronounce something blissful or to demand it is only possible for something that is capable of negating itself, for this act of self-negation always also represents an act of self-assertion."[65] The very denial of freedom presupposed its reality.

This broad condemnation of life-philosophy and the intellectual trend in contemporary philosophy toward fatalism would reappear, with Heidegger now as the explicit target, in Cassirer's final work, *The Myth of the State*. Meanwhile, Cassirer continued, intermittently from 1928 and throughout the 1930s, to develop his criticism of Heidegger's philosophy well beyond what the brief encounter at Davos had allowed. At the time he published his critical review of *Kant and the Problem of Metaphysics*, Cassirer was also making sketches for a more elaborate and direct assessment of Heidegger's entire philosophy, which he hoped to include in the planned-for fourth volume to *The Philosophy of Symbolic Forms*, titled *The Metaphysics of Symbolic Forms*. The sketches, apparently composed around 1931, were subdivided into three sections, "3: Spirit and Life: Heidegger," "4: Heidegger and the Problem of Death," and "5: Time according to Bergson and Heidegger."

What emerges in these notes, perhaps more clearly than in any of the published criticism, is Cassirer's basic conviction that Heidegger's philosophy remained fatally disabled by premises it had carried over from theology. "For Heidegger, who comes . . . from the philosophy of religion," Cassirer observed, the controlling categories of his philosophy were not naturalistic like Bergson's but theological. This is true for whatever terms played roles comparable to *life* and *spirit*. For Heidegger "all temporality has its roots in the '*Augenblick*' [moment; literally, blink-of-an-eye] seen in a religious sense—for it is constituted through '*Sorge*' [care] and through the basic religious phenomenon of death—and '*Angst*' (cf. Kierkegaard)."[66] In Cassirer's judgment, the difficulty was that Heidegger's careful and even admirable attention to the innermost sphere of personal existence could not permit a passage beyond the individual into the realm of intersubjective and transpersonal truth. Heidegger drew the "power and depth" of his "religious purposes" from the "individualistic tendency" as thematized in both Luther and Kierkegaard, but without paying notice to the Christian promise of transcendence: "Heidegger moves through the sphere of life to that of personal existence, which he utilizes unremittingly for a religious purpose, but on the other hand he is also confined by this sphere."[67] Given his theological-individualistic beginnings, Heidegger remained deeply averse to the prospect of objectivity or intersubjectively ratified knowledge:

> The thought of "eternal truths" seems therefore to Heidegger almost as a kind of hubris, a reaching beyond human life, ignoring the primary phenomena of death. His whole analytic of existence has no other goal than to reverse this process—again to remove death from its "concealment" [*Verdeckung*] to make it truly visible again. . . . Here—we do not deny—a genuine religious tone becomes audible, as with Kierkegaard. As with Kierkegaard the concept of anxiety steps into the middle of this phenomenology—anxiety is essentially anxiety about finitude, about transitoriness, about annihilation.[68]

In these notes, Cassirer's overall verdict concerning Heidegger's philosophy turned on the argument that Heidegger had never truly abandoned the premises he inherited from theology. As confirmation, Cassirer cited a remark by Heidegger's neo-Kantian teacher Heinrich Rickert, apparently from a 1931 essay, who had complained about Heidegger's philosophy that he could not determine "what has an objective basis and what is a personal creed, and such confusions, under every circumstance, mean trouble."[69] But Cassirer hastened to qualify this verdict: although Heidegger's analytic of finite *Dasein* appleaed to religion for its image of the human being, it abstained resolutely from any theistic metaphysics. The promise of redemption as afforded by conventional religion therefore remained beyond its comprehension. The consequence was a schizophrenic philosophy, which accepted theism's description of the human predicament only to reject the expected theistic resolution. As Cassirer observed:

> With Heidegger, the problem seems to cut more deeply, insofar as his posing of the question was wholly determined by theological considerations, but the theological solution to the problem is rejected. He does not allow anxiety, as mankind's basic state of mind, to be pacified through either theological metaphysics or a religious Gospel of salvation.[70]

For Cassirer, in other words, the deeper flaw in Heidegger's philosophy lay *not* in its general recourse to religion but rather in its specific reliance on a quasi-Kierkegaardian interpretation of religious experience as irremediably subjectivistic. Such an interpretation, on Cassirer's view, wholly ignored the universalist dimension of Western monotheism, which promised a transformative salvation *from* the finitude of the mortal self:

> In opposition to [Heidegger's philosophy], we uphold, despite everything, the broader, more universal, *idealistic* meaning of religion and the idealistic meaning of history. In *it* we behold liberation and deliverance from the "anxiety" which is the signature, the basic "state-of-mind" of finite Dasein. But this anxiety signifies only the beginning, not the final, inevitable constraint on our finite *Dasein*.[71]

Not surprisingly, such remarks recall various claims Cassirer had already directed against Heidegger during their public meeting at Davos. But these remarks are not only more elaborate; they are far more disapproving. This was no doubt partly due to the fact that these were notes intended only for private consultation. Or, perhaps it is because, since the public exchange at Davos a few years earlier, sufficient time had passed for Cassirer to ruminate to a fuller degree upon what he believed were the true ramifications of Heidegger's work. He now exhibited greater comfort (which is not to say agreement) with Heidegger's unusual terminology. And his verdict was accordingly more decisive: the essential flaw in Heidegger's philosophy was that it remained trapped in radical subjectivism and understood the very Being of the world as dependent upon the finite self. For Cassirer this made Heidegger's philosophy a species of "Idealism" (a term he took care to place in quotation marks so as to distinguish it from both transcendental idealism and Hegelian or absolute idealism). Heidegger's quasi-idealism was individualistic in that it saw true selfhood as disclosed in anxiety and care for one's ownmost being-in-the-world. This individualism, moreover, not only failed to acknowledge any transpersonal reality; it actively *resisted* the public or social as a realm of leveling inauthenticity. As Cassirer wrote:

> Here, basically, is where we depart from him, because for us objective spirit is not exhausted by nor does it degenerate into the structure of everydayness. The "impersonal" does not consist merely in the pale, diluted social form of the average, the everydayness of the "one" [*das*

"Man" with Cassirer's quotation marks], but in the form of transpersonal meaning. For this transpersonal, Heidegger's philosophy has no access.[72]

By denying the possibility for a genuine yet shared social consciousness, Heidegger's philosophy could only interpret history as a field of meanings available *to and for* the individual. "To be sure," Cassirer granted, Heidegger's philosophy

> has a sense for historical life, but it takes all historical understanding as but mere repetition, the repetition-uplifting [*Wieder-Herauf-Holung*] of personal *Dasein,* personal destinies, personal fates. This feature of history [is] very deeply and very clearly seen. . . . But it is always a religious-individualistic comprehension of history that confronts us here. History as "history of culture" the "history of meaning" and "the life of the objective spirit" is not disclosed.[73]

The true subject of history in Heidegger's thought remained always and only the finite individual, for whom there remained but two options: either to assume with knowing resolve the opportunities given to him through historical inheritance, or to submit passively to the historical condition of being-thrown (*Geworfensein*).

It was here that Cassirer first introduced his critique of thrownness, a critique that would reappear more than a decade later in *The Myth of the State* as a key to his political judgment on the cultural consequences of Heidegger's doctrines in Germany. Here, Cassirer did little more than mention it in the rushed disorder of private note taking. He went on to express regret that, although Heidegger undeniably possessed an acute sensitivity to questions of historical existence, his broader philosophical acumen was disabled by a metaphysical and epistemological subjectivism that denied altogether the objective or transhistorical character of knowledge: "We understand the general not as the mere 'one' [*als blosses "Man"*]," Cassirer wrote, "but as 'objective spirit and objective culture.'" For Heidegger, "spirit has no access to such objectivity—even Logos, language, becomes to him a *merely* social phenomenon."[74] From Cassirer's perspective the banal and unobjectionable fact that human beings live *within* historical time provided no warrant for

dismissing the possibility that our claims might enjoy a *trans*historical validity. Heidegger had turned his back on objectivity and retreated into the
religiously derived cul-de-sac of radical subjectivism: "Being thrown [*Das
Geworfensein*], . . . Here we find the essential statement: for an entity that is
in time and which passes away in time, there can be no eternal truths."[75]

This critical focus on Heideggerian *Geworfenheit* would continue to
evolve well into the 1930s. In fact, in the years following the Nazi seizure of
power, Cassirer's preoccupation with themes of fate and historical destiny
seems to have only intensified, perhaps because the experience of forced
dislocation gave thrownness a vividly personal meaning. From his new
home in exile at the University of Göteborg in Uppsala, Sweden, Cassirer
began to make notes for a new kind of philosophical inquiry into so-called
basis phenomena, and in connection with this effort, he sketched rudiments
for a theory concerning the character of history and historical knowledge:
history, he now wrote, was composed of two phenomena, personal action
and fate (*Schicksal*). The contrast between these two poles remained ineradi-
cable, and it was crucial that philosophy acknowledge them both:

> A "fate," a Something, that "happens" to us, an accident, a foreign
> power, to which we are delivered in some fashion (Heidegger's *Gewor-
> fenheit*), and a Willing, which does not just cast itself [*unterwirft*] be-
> neath fate, the happenstance, the accident—but rather throws itself
> *against* it [*entgegen wirft*], which encounters the merely passive "*Gewor-
> fenheit*" with an independent and free "project" ["*Entwurf*"]—which
> takes it upon itself to steer the course of fate toward an determined *goal*
> it has willed.[76]

A notable irony of these reflections is that they exhibit a penchant for etymological variation one might more typically associate with Heidegger
rather than Cassirer. But in Cassirer's hands the wordplay remained relatively straightforward and served to reinforce a more or less obvious contrast between two images of human being: *thrownness* (*Geworfenheit*) implied that the self would "cast itself" (*sich unterwift*) beneath the wheels of
fate, whereas the individual endowed with agency could "throw itself
against" (*entgegen wirft*) fate and devote itself to a freely selected "project"
(*Entwurf*). The contrast—agency versus fatality—amounted to little more

than a repetition of themes central to the ongoing debate between the two philosophers. Cassirer still cleaved to Schiller's exhortation that we should "throw off" the anxiety that pervades our being-in-the-world, whereas Heidegger, from Cassirer's perspective, endorsed a species of fatalism steeped in mythic fear. Heidegger had surrendered the human being entirely to its historical thrownness, while making no acknowledgement of the human capacity for creating our own future in accordance with self-determined plans. For the time being the political implications of this charge remained merely implicit. In the coming years Cassirer would bring them boldly to the fore.

Retrieving the Enlightenment

In the early 1930s both Heidegger and Cassirer remained more or less consumed with work. Between 1931 and 1933 Heidegger made the initial steps of what would come to be known as the "Kehre," his methodological and thematic turning from the technical problems of modern philosophy and toward richer lines of reflection: problems of art and technology, the poetry of Hölderlin, the multi-year lectures on Nietzsche. But for the immediate two years his seminars focused almost exclusively on the Greeks: Aristotle's metaphysics (summer 1931), Plato's *Theateatus* and the theory of truth (winter 1931), and the so-called beginning of Western philosophy with Anaximander and Parmenides (summer 1932). These were some of the first courses in which Heidegger began to develop a deeper account of what had gone wrong even at the very inception of philosophical modernity, an epoch that now stretched back at least as far as Plato. By the time he composed his perhaps most enigmatic work, *Contributions to Philosophy* (written 1936–1938), Heidegger had begun to make reference to "the other beginning," a different path for philosophical reflection free of the metaphysical subjectivism he now saw as a fatal dispensation of nearly all of modern philosophy and culture.

Cassirer, meanwhile, showed no sign of slackening the pace of his own scholarly production. Over the next two years he would devote the greater share of his energy to exploring specific themes in the history of modern philosophy. For much of the summer semester of 1931, he lived in Paris to pursue research at the Bibliothèque Nationale for his new philosophical-historical study of the pan-European Enlightenment. A year later, he published not just one, but two distinctive historical works, *The Platonic Renaissance in England* and the much larger and more comprehensive *The Philosophy of the Enlightenment*. As even this brief summary suggests, the division of interests between Heidegger and Cassirer was growing wider: Heidegger would eventually conclude that the entire tradition of philosophical modernity was essentially corrupt and that the remedy lay in modes of poetic disclosure and in the "other beginning" of pre-Socratic thought. Cassirer meanwhile had written a synthetic tribute to the Enlightenment as a living resource for the modern world.

The Philosophy of the Enlightenment displayed Cassirer's consummate skill at intellectual-historical synthesis, in that it demanded both interpretative ability and an astonishing breadth of empirical knowledge regarding the details of modern intellectual history. But it also carried a specific contemporary resonance: Following shortly upon his composition of the review of Heidegger's Kant-book, his comprehensive effort to reconstruct the philosophy of the Enlightenment in general gave Cassirer the opportunity to amplify his earlier suggestion that Kant's philosophy, in particular, stood at the summit of modern philosophy. And, more specifically, it afforded Cassirer the opportunity to make a vigorous case for the relevance of the Enlightenment to the problems that now beset the twentieth century.

One might therefore characterize Cassirer's book as not only a reconstruction but a *retrieval* of Enlightenment philosophy. And on this very issue, the contrast between Cassirer and Heidegger could not have been more profound: While Heidegger was turning away from philosophical modernity as an era condemned to ontological oblivion, Cassirer now leapt forward to defend its honor and its continued importance as a philosophical resource for the modern world. In the preface to *The Philosophy of the Enlightenment,* Cassirer took special note of the "multitude of prejudices" concerning the apparent shortcomings of eighteenth-century thought, which "to this day are an obstacle to an impartial study and appraisal of Enlightenment philosophy." He disclaimed any overtly "polemical intentions" and sought to reassure readers that he was not aiming for the Enlightenment's "rescue." But it was obvious he hoped his book would dispel at least some of the misperceptions about the Enlightenment that had first arisen during the age of Romanticism and that had survived well into the twentieth century.

Cassirer mentioned one of these prejudices in particular: that the Enlightenment failed to understand historicity and historical difference (a criticism made famous in 1936 by the eminent historian Friedrich Meinecke).[77] Even if there was some validity to this specific charge (and Cassirer abstained from offering an opinion), it was nonetheless unfair to use this single flaw to condemn the entire epoch. "The slogan of the 'shallow Enlightenment' is still in vogue," Cassirer complained. "A major objective of this study would be achieved if it succeeded in silencing that slogan."[78]

The Philosophy of the Enlightenment is an immense and occasionally forbidding synthesis, far more than a mere catalogue or survey of various thinkers and ideas. As Cassirer himself noted, "the real philosophy of the Enlightenment is not simply the sum total of what its leading thinkers ... thought and taught." A book with philosophical objectives could not confine itself to mere summary and it would have to do more than "just string its various intellectual formations along the thread of time and to study them chronologically." Cassirer thought what was truly of philosophical significance in the Enlightenment was to be found in what he called "the form and manner [*Form und Art*] of intellectual activity itself." For among the many themes in Enlightenment philosophy that he saw as meriting defense, one alone served as the Enlightenment's unifying and transcendental principle:

> This philosophy believes ... in *an original spontaneity of thought;* it attributes to thought not merely an imitative function but the power of and the task of shaping life itself. Thought consists not only in analyzing and dissecting, but in actually bringing about that order of things which it conceives as necessary, so that by this act of fulfillment it may demonstrate its own reality and truth.[79]

This principle of mental spontaneity furnished the book's narrative cohesion and also the argumentative solution for each chapter's stated theme.

Perhaps most noteworthy in *The Philosophy of the Enlightenment* overall was the author's emphatic message that such spontaneity must be acknowledged as a specifically modern and historical achievement. Here the contrast between Cassirer and Heidegger came into sharpest relief: whereas for Heidegger, the defining flaw of philosophical modernity was its unwarranted confidence in the human subject as the creative force behind all things, for Cassirer it was just this confidence that most distinguished the Enlightenment and merited its ongoing defense. It was the Enlightenment itself that had "discovered and passionately defended the autonomy of reason" and that "firmly established this concept in all fields of knowledge." Cassirer concluded his prefatory remarks by invoking Kant's Enlightenment motto, "*Sapere Aude*" ("Dare to know") as an encouragement for his contemporaries to embrace historical knowledge. Just as there could be no reconstruction of history of philosophy without the guidance of present philosophical concepts, so, too, any such reconstruction of the past was bound to prompt contemporary comparisons and self-criticism. "More than ever before," Cassirer wrote, "the time is ripe for applying such self-criticism to the present-age, for holding up to it that bright clear mirror which was fashioned by the age of Enlightenment." Although he remained characteristically silent concerning the contemporary political challenges then facing Germany (or Europe in general), the urgency of his words was evident: "The age which venerated reason and science as man's highest faculty cannot and must not be lost even to us."[80]

On Cassirer's view the Enlightenment in general was animated by a basic commitment to self-determination and progressive development. It was united in its conviction that reason can "determine for itself the direction of its journey," but that reason's essence therefore cannot be known wholly a priori as an essence or substance but can be recognized only through its self-realization, its activity and "function." Reason is therefore "a concept of "agency" (*Tun*) and "becoming" and not "Being" (*Sein*).[81] In this sense Enlightenment natural science built upon the foundations of the Renaissance and its new conception of the relation between mind and world (first articulated by Giordano Bruno), according to which "the power of reason is our only access to the infinite," as it is by virtue of reason alone that humanity reaches out into the "great spectacle of the world."[82] With this new confidence in human reason as an active rather than merely receptive faculty, the Enlightenment effected a final break from the medieval conception of science, which had contented itself with merely "tracing the architectonics of Being." According to the older scholasticism, "all thinking knew itself to be sheltered by [an] inviolable order" within the "three great coordinates of Being" (God, soul, and world), which "it [was] not the task of thought to create but only to accept."[83] By contrast, the Enlightenment, and Newtonian theory in particular, validated the new notion that, while nature would furnish evidence, the mind alone would provide the theoretical principles. Hence, "in one and the same intellectual process of emancipation" the Enlightenment attempted to show "the self-sufficiency of both nature and intellect" as correlated directly and without the mediation of a transcendent power.[84] Yet, for Cassirer, it was Leibniz above all who furnished the Enlightenment with its most important model of reason, because with the monadology there emerged the new theory of rational development or "entelechy," which would eventually leave its mark on all fields of inquiry, from epistemology to politics and from religion to the philosophies of nature and history.[85]

Leibniz's views on epistemology and metaphysics remained of central importance for the entire span of Enlightenment philosophy. In the Leibnizian concept of the monad, the earlier static and merely receptive notion of substance as theorized by seventeenth-century psychologists such as John Locke, gave way to a dynamic notion of mental spontaneity. A psychology of impressions, wrote Cassirer, "misses the fundamental phenomenon of the mind, whose nature consists in activity not in mere passivity." The Leibnizian ego is not passive but enjoys a power to act and therefore a capacity for self-perfection. All being consists in "force" and the greater the intensity of this force, the more one discovers both "multiplicity from unity" and "unity from multiplicity." On Cassirer's view, these Leibnizian insights furnish the solid foundations for the German Enlightenment, in general, and remain of cardinal importance for Kant's philosophy, in particular, insofar as it too remained faithful to the key (originally Leibnizian) principle concerning the "spontaneity of the ego" (*Spontaneität des Ich*).[86]

Liebniz also inspired the theories of religion that developed during the Enlightenment. Gothold Ephraim Lessing's ideas concerning the "education of the human race," for example, would not have been possible without the ideas of perfection born from Leibnizian theodicy and the evolutionist metaphysics first articulated in the monadology.[87] The Enlightenment theory of history is likewise patterned after Leibnizian principles: just as the monad only achieves its identity insofar as it perfects its own inner nature through temporal development, so too every epoch and nation (according to both Lessing and Johann Gottfried von Herder) must realize through history its own individual character and spontaneous energy.[88] Perhaps only in the chapter on political thought did Cassirer momentarily stray from the general

thesis concerning the centrality of Leibnizian philosophy. Rather, the basic
principles animating the Enlightenment theories of law and contract were
found to derive from Grotius's insight that "the intellect can and should begin with fundamental norms, which it creates from within itself [*ursprünglichen Normen, die er aus sich selbst schöpft*]."[89] Even in Rousseau's political
philosophy, the Enlightenment's fundamental commitment to the "aprior-
ity of law" remains in place insofar as the state of nature serves as a perhaps
counterfactual "standard and norm" by which to judge "what is morally
obligatory" and what is "mere convention." Cassirer could accordingly declare that among Rousseau's many followers, Kant alone emerged as a revolutionary force whose philosophy both "overshadows the Enlightenment
even while it represents its final glorification."[90]

In the final chapter, Cassirer turned to a discussion as to how the Enlightenment effected a higher reconciliation between philosophy and aesthetics.
These distinct and seemingly opposed fields of knowledge were not immediately coordinated, and they first had to go through a "series of preliminary
stages" before their ultimate synthesis was to achieve their definitive shape
in the work of Kant.[91] This synthesis was realized not only in philosophy but
in poetry as well: the entirety of the Enlightenment eventually produced
both a new "logical method" (Kant) and a "new form of artistic creation"
(Goethe's poetry). The synthesis between them marked the close and the
climax of eighteenth-century culture.[92]

The book concluded with an extended discussion of Alexander Baumgarten's philosophy, which laid the foundations for both a new aesthetics and
for what Cassirer called a new "philosophical anthropology." Here, not surprisingly, there reemerged a central theme of Cassirer's ongoing dispute with
Heidegger; for the key element in Baumgarten's inheritance from Leibniz
was the latter's distinction between human and divine understanding, between the finite mind that remains dependent on sensory experience (*intellectus ectypus*) and the infinite mind that enjoys the special capacity for
"adequate ideas" that fully embrace the constitutive elements of every complex whole (*intellectus archetypus*). With this contrast, it became evident
that because the divine does not remain bound to sensory or aesthetic phenomena, any experience of beauty belongs exclusively to the human or finite
understanding. Baumgarten's conclusion, Cassirer averred, was that, although the human being remains necessarily enclosed within certain limits,

such a limitation nonetheless permits humanity to realize our higher aims: "Man should not transcend the finite, but explore it in all directions [*nicht über die Endlichkeit hinausschreiten, sondern er soll im Endlichen nach allen Seiten gehen*]."[93] Thus in Baumgarten's aesthetics (and in Lessing's after him), Cassirer discovered a "purely human ideal," according to which the Enlightenment "gradually learned to do without the 'absolute' in the strictly metaphysical sense," that is, "without the ideal of 'God-like knowledge.'"[94]

Cassirer's account of Baumgarten holds a special relevance here, insofar as it bears directly on the aftermath of the Davos encounter. As we saw earlier, at one point in Cassirer's and Heidegger's public exchange concerning the significance of human finitude, Cassirer had replied to Heidegger that for human beings, the true relation between finitude and infinity is not one of metaphysical opposition. For in human experience (Cassirer argued), "infinity" must be understood as the "totality" or the "fulfillment of finitude itself." To illustrate this idea, Cassirer had quoted Goethe's maxim, "If you want to step into infinity, just go in all directions into the finite." On Cassirer's view, it was inappropriate to regard human finitude as a *privative* condition (i.e., as lacking a divine attribute), because this was to judge human capacities by an improper and metaphysical standard. Although Kant himself had invoked this very same Leibnizian distinction between *intellectus ectypus* and *intellectual archetypus,* the notion of a divine intellect served in his own philosophy as no more than a "limit concept." But this meant that the distinction between finitude and infinity should be understood from within the bounds of human experience alone. And when judged in accordance with purely human standards, the notion of infinity was found to possess its own legitimate meaning, because it served as the regulative idea of "totality" or the thoroughgoing determination of all components of experience.[95]

The Philosophy of the Enlightenment reaches its denouement by returning once again to the theme of spontaneity as the governing paradigm for Enlightenment thought. In accordance with Cassirer's own philosophical conviction that the capacity for symbolic expression governs the entire spectrum of human activity—from science to art—the book closed with remarks concerning the larger importance of Baumgarten's aesthetics: Baumgarten, wrote Cassirer, understood that in beauty we come to realize the moment of "pure spontaneity" that dwells even in the senses. In this sense Baumgarten's aesthetics helped to lay the foundations for a new and truly secular *theory of the human being* as endowed with its own creative-artistic powers. Aesthetic creativity, therefore, is only one element within the broader theory of "creative activity" or human self-expression that brings to fruition a genuine reconciliation between mind and world, and thereby represents the ultimate fulfillment of the Enlightenment.[96]

As noted earlier, it is important to realize that Cassirer's study of the Enlightenment was not only a historical reconstruction but was also a philosophical retrieval of the Enlightenment and its basic principles. The normative image of humanity that had once animated the Enlightenment was, on Cassirer's view, of enduring and urgent relevance to the present historical moment. Only this can explain why Cassirer believed the Enlightenment could furnish the contemporary world with a "bright clear mirror" such that the comparison with the past could provide both a critique of present liabilities and also a reflection of present strengths. Indeed, the ultimate premise of Cassirer's book was that the Enlightenment remained not merely one but in fact *the* paradigm for modernity. Such an assumption was unlikely to arouse great disagreement among Cassirer's neo-Kantian contemporaries. In an essay from 1931, Kurt Sternberg had declared that the Enlightenment was not restricted in its meaning to the eighteenth century but in fact signified "the entirety of modern culture." At its summit stood Kant's philosophy itself, the "classical" meaning of which far outstripped the one-sided "logical-methodological" reading of its neo-Kantian epigones and embraced both Enlightenment *and* Romanticism. On Sternberg's view, it was this classicism that most promised to resolve the present intellectual crisis.[97]

The Philosophy of the Enlightenment was first published in Germany in the autumn of 1932. By this time, of course, the division between Cassirer and Heidegger had become more widely acknowledged, and it would not have seemed at all unnatural for critics to summon the comparison between the two philosophers as a means of dramatizing larger intellectual and cultural controversies of the day. In an early 1933 review, Ludwig Feuchtwanger (editor for the *Bayerischen Israelitischen Gemeindezeitung* and brother to better-known German-Jewish writer Lion Feuchtwanger) hailed Cassirer's book as a defense of the age of reason, "which today is treated so dismissively and with abuse." Its defense had a "double significance" insofar as the

Enlightenment alone illumined the path for the human sciences beyond "the false lights of *Seins- und Lebensphilosophie,* whether derived from Klages or Heidegger."[98]

Such politicizing interpretations of the ongoing quarrel between Cassirer and Heidegger should not obscure our appreciation for the internal and philosophical significance of their discussion. At the time, however, such interpretations with all of their *sotto voce* or explicitly political implications were in any case increasingly common. For by 1933 the divide between Cassirer and Heidegger was no longer confined to philosophy: Politics intruded, and with it, all the nuance and philosophical richness of their previous discussion at Davos was swept aside. On January 30, Hitler was named chancellor of Germany and the Nazis began their swift consolidation of power over the state bureaucracy, including the universities. On April 7, the Nazis passed the so-called Law for the Restoration of the Professional Civil Service, excluding from public office "non-Aryans," Social-Democrats, and other enemies of the new regime. In the universities, the law immediately decommissioned more than a thousand professors, including a great many philosophers of German-Jewish descent, many of whom were affiliated with the neo-Kantian movement. On April 22, 1933, Heidegger assumed his new post as rector at Freiburg University, and on May 3 he officially joined the National Socialist Party. On May 2, Ernst and Toni Cassirer left Hamburg for the last time to seek a new life abroad (first in Vienna, then Oxford, Sweden, and finally the United States). By July 28 Cassirer was officially relieved of his post according to the terms of the April 7 legislation, although he had quietly resigned a few days before. Neo-Kantianism had indeed become the scapegoat, not merely of the newer philosophers, but of the regime some of them—too many of them—endorsed.

A final example will show how dramatically the philosophical atmosphere had changed. In 1936 the nationalistic assault on Cassirer's interpretation of the Enlightenment reached its nadir with an essay by Max Wundt, "German Philosophy in the Age of Enlightenment," published in the newly founded *Zeitschrift für deutsche Kulturphilosophie.* (The journal was in fact the old journal *Logos,* but its new title telegraphed its nationalist credentials, and the editorial board was now purged of founding members such as Edmund Husserl.) Wundt began his essay with a polemic against an unnamed "newer presentation of the philosophy of the Enlightenment," according to which the "German Enlightenment" was "only a dependent and not altogether valuable supplement to the brilliant developments of the English and the French." Against this interpretation he promised to do justice to the German Enlightenment in its "own essence" and to explain how it "unfolded on German soil [*auf deutschem Boden*]."[99] Needless to say, the greatest central European historian of the Enlightenment was no longer permitted to live on German soil. Cassirer would compose his final work—an attack on political mythology—from the safety of exile in the United States.

The Myth of the State

In 1944 Cassirer had just reached his seventieth year. Having taught for several terms in New Haven at Yale, that July he would settle amid the swelling crowd of émigré intellectuals and refugees in New York City, where he would take up a final post in the philosophy department at Columbia. Accompanied by his wife Toni, he had spent the previous decade in transit—from Hamburg to Vienna, from Vienna to Oxford, and from Oxford to Sweden—and he had been in the United States as a professor at Yale only since his transatlantic passage by steamship in the autumn of 1941. This was to be his final period of production. For his American readers he had just completed *An Essay on Man: An Introduction to the Philosophy of Human Culture,* a shorter and more accessible summation of his formidable tripartite work, *The Philosophy of Symbolic Forms.* He had also nearly finished the manuscript of what would prove to be his final book, *The Myth of the State,* a massive indictment of ideologies of mythic fatalism, from ancient Greece to the Third Reich.

Cassirer completed the manuscript for *The Myth of the State* just a few days before his death in April 1945. The task of editing the manuscript for publication fell to his Yale colleague, the American-born philosopher Charles W. Hendel (1890–1982). Princeton educated, Hendel had also studied briefly at Marburg University before World War I, and he was therefore intimately familiar with the neo-Kantian movement in general and with Cassirer's specific contributions to the philosophy of science and culture. Hendel and his North American colleagues were frustrated that Cassirer had not authored any sustained work addressed to current politics. Though admired for his temperate judgment, the aging émigré philosopher seems to have impressed his new peers as the quintessence of central European erudition—an unpolitical *Ordinarius* with a perspective on contemporary events that was distant and even Olympian. Hendel recalled that occasionally friends would urge Cassirer, "Won't you tell the meaning of what is happening *today*, instead of writing about past history, science, and culture?"[100]

Certainly, in those years many other German-speaking émigrés were directing their attention to the political crisis. In the early 1940s, the exiled social theorists from Frankfurt, Max Horkheimer and Theodor Adorno, commenced work on their "philosophical fragments" a breathtaking transhistorical genealogy that portrayed fascism as the culmination of instrumental reason, which was first published as *Dialectic of Enlightenment* in 1947. Their associate, Franz Neumann, a fellow émigré also affiliated with the Institute for Social Research at Columbia University, published a more narrowly Marxist analysis, *Behemoth: The Structure and Practice of National Socialism,* in 1942. Meanwhile, Hannah Arendt had arrived in New York in 1941, and, after writing for several years for the German-language Jewish press, she commenced research on her own inquiry on *The Origins of Totalitarianism,* which would be published in 1951. It was therefore not surprising that friends and colleagues would expect from Cassirer some contribution to the growing literature by émigré intellectuals on the political catastrophe. Two years after his arrival in the United States, in the winter of 1943–1944, Cassirer set to work on the book that became known as *The Myth of the State.* A short selection first appeared in *Fortune* magazine in July 1944, and the finished manuscript was edited by Hendel and published by Yale in 1946, when its author was no longer alive.

The consuming task of the book is to comprehend how and why it proved possible for mythical thought, typically regarded as primitive, to reassert itself with such vigor at the very climax of European modernity. This question was especially perplexing for Cassirer because in 1925 he had devoted the second volume of his *Philosophy of Symbolic Forms* to the comparative study of mythical thought. We should recall that Cassirer's earlier work on myth had taken a generous view of its role as a spontaneous form of human understanding. It furnished anthropological evidence from ancient religions and native peoples for what seemed to be a universal capacity of human symbolization. Seen in this light, myth was a transcendental framework for human experience and no more dispensable than language itself. But as explained earlier, this inquiry into human symbolic capacities was premised on an evolutionary model: it assumed the dialectical advance of human expression through time from myth to modern science. Cassirer himself had argued in his third volume to *The Philosophy of Symbolic Forms* that modern and scientific cognition effected nothing less than a "crisis," a thoroughgoing rupture with earlier and primitive modes of human symbolization. The reemergence of myth in modern European politics was therefore not merely perplexing but seemed to signal a regression in human civilization. What Cassirer considered the most alarming feature of the modern crisis was that after "a short and violent struggle," mythical thought seemed to have won a "clear and definitive victory" over rational thought: "How," he asked, "was this victory possible?"[101]

To answer this question demanded a preliminary excursus on the place of myth in primitive society, a question already theorized by diverse anthropologists from Frazer and Spencer to Lévy-Bruhl, Boas, and Malinowski. Rejecting any facile disdain for myth as mere falsehood or primordial "idiocy" (*Urdummheit*), Cassirer was equally hostile to Freud's remarks in *Totem and Taboo* equating the psychic life of savages with modern neurosis. Such a dismissive view turned a universal human capacity into a psychopathology. On the contrary, Cassirer saw myth as a phenomenon akin to poetry and art, a foundational framework for meaning or a "symbolic form." Its substance or representational contents were therefore of less importance than its function in human social life, and it was therefore mistaken to regard myth as mere fantasy or emotion, for what was most significant in myth was that it served as an *expression* of emotion: "The expression of emotion is not the feeling itself," Cassirer explained, "it is emotion turned into an image."[102]

For Cassirer this difference was decisive. To grasp the true function of myth in primitive society, it was necessary to understand myth as a spontaneous and creative *formation* of experience by which "what was a passive state becomes an active process."[103] Moreover, myth was not a wholly private and could not be ascribed to individual fears or anxieties; it was shared across all human beings living within the same culture. Myth was therefore nothing less than *the objectification of man's social experience.* Citing Malinowski, Cassirer further claimed that myth served its greatest role in

organizing and rendering intelligible the otherwise overwhelming experience of mortality. By this transformation, "death ceases being a hard un-
bearable physical fact; it becomes understandable and supportable." In
mythical thought, Cassirer concluded, "the mystery of death is 'turned into
an image.'"[104]

Following this preliminary excursus, in the second and largest portion of
his book, Cassirer turned his attention toward the "struggle against myth" in
political philosophy from ancient Greece to nineteenth-century Europe. He
aimed chiefly to show how philosophers had attempted to developed rational
conceptions of human political agency that could supplant the older social-
organizational role of myth. It was with the Greeks that "logos" first appeared as a new cultural-political force that promised to vanquish "mythos"
and to displace mythological understanding with a rationally conceived
model of the state. In direct opposition to the mythic gods whose powers
surpass human control, Plato introduced the Idea of the Good as a higher
measure by which human beings could actively order their lives: "Of all
things in the world myth is the most unbridled and immoderate. It exceeds
and defies all limits; it is extravagant and exorbitant in its very nature and
essence. To banish this dissolute power from the human and political world
was one of the principle aims of the *Republic*."[105] In an apparent irony the
Republic reached its denouement with a new myth charting the soul's cycli-
cal return to the world. But Cassirer hastened to explain that in the original
myth, the human being was understood to be possessed *by* a good or evil
demon, whereas in Plato's revision the human being actively *chose* his demon.
This essentially Socratic ideal of self-direction was then transferred by Plato
to the *polis,* which was endowed with the same capacity for self-direction.
Rather than submitting passively to its fate as if before an unknown god, the
Greeks extolled our spontaneous capacity to *choose* our fate and thereby
remain authors of our political future.

In medieval political thought Cassirer discerned an almost insurmount-
able conflict between reason and faith. It was Augustine, in his treatise *De
magistro,* who expressed the turn away from the spontaneous intellectualism of ancient Greece with the objection that all knowledge is dependent on
divine illumination, and worldly knowledge itself is inconsequential if it
does not lead in the end to knowledge of God. The Mosaic idea of politics
presupposes a *lawgiver,* and without the revealed law, no human reason on

its own can reach eternal truth: "Here God is not, as in Greek thought, described as the summit of the intellectual world, as the highest object of knowledge, the knowledge of the Good. It is from God himself, from the revelation of his will, not from dialectic, that man has to learn good and evil."[106] Because in Hebrew and Christian monotheism God is the lawgiver and his essence is not an objectivity but a *will,* the polity as imagined by medieval theologians remains incorrigibly bound to a revelation from beyond human reason. Divine voluntarism stands opposed to Greek intellectualism: "The conflict between these two tendencies," wrote Cassirer, "pervades the whole scholastic philosophy and determines its course throughout the centuries from St. Augustine to Thomas Aquinas."[107] Notwithstanding the apparent stalemate, however, Cassirer also acknowledged the emergence of a different tendency in Aquinas that signaled a greater role for human autonomy. In the *Summa Theologica,* Aquinas claimed that the human being does not submit passively in the face of divine judgment. Although grace is a free gift from God, humanity nonetheless retains the power to at least prepare the way for its own salvation. For Cassirer, these concessions granted "new dignity" to man's own powers of political organization and pointed the way beyond the mythico-religious passivity that remained otherwise characteristic of medieval political thought.[108]

If Cassirer seemed unimpressed with the medieval attempt to navigate between politics and religion, the tone of his analysis changed markedly once he arrived at his study of the Renaissance. In Machiavelli's work in particular, Cassirer discerned the birth of a truly *secular* theory of politics. To be sure, Machiavelli's reflections on statecraft did not allow for a theory of thoroughgoing autonomy: it reserved government solely for the prince and not the people. But it was nonetheless an important step toward a *nonmythic understanding of agency.* At first glance, Machiavelli's notion of the goddess *Fortuna* seemed a concession to a mythic force beyond human knowledge or appeal. But the innovation in Machiavelli's theory was to claim that the skillful prince is not altogether helpless before Fortune but can in fact wrest some measure of rational mastery from the flux of events: "Man is not subdued to Fortune; he is not at the mercy of winds and waves. He must choose his course and steer his course. If he fails to perform this duty Fortune scorns and deserts him." For Cassirer this doctrine qualified as the "*secularization* of the symbol of Fortune."[109] Although Machiavelli himself was "the first philosophical advocate of a resolute militarism," his works were, in Cassirer's view, the fruits of "a clear, cool, and logical mind," and his theory of statecraft thus anticipated later, more rationalized ideals of political organization.

But it was in the rationalist political thought of the sixteenth and seventeenth centuries most of all that Cassirer located the true watershed for the emergence of a modern politics without myth. For the first time a rational understanding of the physical world came to serve as a model for political theory as well: the method of *mathesis universalis,* with its assumption that the natural order of all things can be measured and known through human reason, was applied not only to the physical environment but also to human nature. Spinoza's ethics presuppose the validity of a geometric method, and Christian Wolff, a discipline of Leibniz, composed a textbook on natural law that followed "a strict mathematical method." In these cases of political rationalism, Cassirer detected an early modern revival of Stoicism and its ideal of rational "autarky," according to which reason was "autonomous and self-dependent." It was "not in need of any external help; it could not even accept this help if it were offered." This neo-Stoic principle pervaded the theories of the sixteenth and seventeenth centuries, from Grotius to Bodin, and it culminated in the contractualist theory of Hobbes. In *De Corpore* Hobbes drafted an overall theory of knowledge that presupposed the human mind's capacity to know the first causes of all worldly things. For Cassirer this meant not an empirical study of generation but a purely mental process of construction, an *"origin in reason, not in time."*[110] When Hobbes applied this same method in *De Cive* and *Leviathan* to political phenomena, he meant to assess *not* the historical transition from the state of nature to society but its *validity.* And this meant that the very mechanism of the social compact was wholly susceptible to human understanding. Cassirer granted that for Hobbes himself the social compact, once realized, was irrevocable and the sovereign's power absolute. But this was, on Cassirer's view, a "gratuitous assumption" that stood in logical contradiction to the Stoic doctrine of natural rights:

> The contract of rulership which is the legal basis of all civil power has . . . its inherent limits. There is no *pactum subjectionis,* no act of submission by which man can give up the state of a free agent and

enslave himself. For by such an act of renunciation he would give up that very character which constitutes his nature and essence. He would lose his humanity.[111]

Here Cassirer's liberal commitments were transparent and so, too, was his strong antipathy toward any mythic foundations for politics. A theory of social contract supplanted the notion of submission to mythic forces with the doctrine of rational control. For once the political order was seen to be reducible to the action of free individuals and their voluntary submission to the polity, it followed that "all mystery is gone." But this implied that the mythical experience of dispossession could be fully dissolved into the experience of self-reflective reason. Contractualism thus signaled the endpoint of demythologization: a contract in principle was only valid if the signatory fully comprehended its meaning and consequences, and it therefore presupposed the fullest rational transparency and agency. As Cassirer observed, "There is nothing less mysterious than a contract."[112]

Heidegger and the Return of Myth

In the third and final part of his book, titled "The Myth of the Twentieth Century," Cassirer traced the nineteenth-century breakdown of the self-authorization ideal and the modernist reprisal of political myth. Of the diverse theories responsible for this process of political *re*mythologization, Cassirer singled out only two: Carlyle's theory of hero worship and Gobineau's theory concerning the inequality of races. Both in distinctive ways helped to restore to politics an attitude of blind submission—in Carlyle, a submission to the heroic leader, and in Gobineau, a submission to the fatalism of racial history—which would ultimately coalesce in the ideology of National Socialism. Gobineau's theories of racial superiority culminated in what Cassirer saw as a form of political religion, or "race worship."[113] But Gobineau's unrelieved hostility toward all forms of extant nationalism led to a fatalistic conviction that all races were destined to pass away. The modern myth of the state would therefore not have been possible were it not for one final and noxious modification: according to Hegel's philosophy of history, the state itself appeared as the worldly incarnation of the divine Idea. Although Cassirer knew very well that Hegel himself saw history as a rational process, he explained that the Hegelian conception of cosmic rationality permitted individual states to make their contribution to the unfolding historical truth through negativity and war. Hegel, wrote Cassirer, "did not attempt to do away with the evils, the miseries, and the crimes of the historical world. All this is taken for granted. Nevertheless he undertakes to justify this hard and cruel reality."[114] The truth of any given state was, in Hegel's notorious phrase, "not a moral one" but rather "the truth which lies in power."[115] About this doctrine Cassirer could barely restrain his venom: "These words written in 1801, about 150 years ago, contain the clearest and most ruthless program of fascism that has even been propounded by any political or philosophical writer."[116]

There is much ground for disagreement about Cassirer's various judgments on the pre-history of Nazi ideology.[117] But whatever our disagreements today with Cassirer's construction of the intellectual canon, there remains "The Technique of the Modern Political Myths," the stunning conclusion to his book. Cassirer addressed the central paradox of modern political myth—that it appeared as *both* a regression to primitive belief *and* a cynical instrument of mass propaganda. It was at once premodern *and* modern, both *mythos* and *techné.* On the one hand, mythic politics seemed a perfect illustration of Malinowski's anthropological insights into the importance of ritual magic in moments of mortal threat. As Cassirer observed, these insights applied "equally well to highly advanced stages of man's political life. In desperate situations man will always have recourse to desperate means—and our present-day political myths have been such desperate means. If reason has failed us, there remains always the *ultima ratio,* the power of the miraculous and mysterious."[118] Cassirer granted it would be naïve to think that mythical forms of social organization had been entirely displaced by principles of rational self-governance. Perhaps this was so in "quiet and peaceful times" and in "periods of relative stability," but in the modern world the experience of mortal danger was now a constant. In contemporary politics, Cassirer observed, "we are always living on volcanic soil."

> In all critical moments of man's social life, the rational forces that resist the rise of the old mythical conceptions are no longer sure of themselves. In these moments the time for myth has come again. For myth

has not been really vanquished and subjugated. It is always there, lurking in the dark and waiting for its opportunity. This hour comes as soon as the other binding forces of man's social life, for one reason or another, lose their strength and are no longer able to combat the demonic mythical powers.[119]

If this observation appeared to suggest that modern political myths were mere atavisms—a resurgence of the primitive—Cassirer was quick to note that no actual return was possible. For the peculiar predicament of modern man was that, even when seized by the most violent passions, he could not wholly deny the claims of rationality: "In order to believe he must find some 'reasons' for his belief; he must form a 'theory' to justify his creeds. And this theory, at least, is not primitive, it is, on the contrary, highly sophisticated."[120]

But this was only half of the story. Equally important for Cassirer's analysis was the further insight that modern political myths *were no longer the spontaneous expression of the collective as they had been for primitive society.* The difference was due to a historical transformation in human capacities for instrumentalist control: "Man began as *homo magus*," Cassirer explained, "but from the age of magic, he passed to the age of technics." It followed that the modern political leader could simultaneously embody *two distinctive activities and two epochs of civilization:* On the one hand, the mythic leader served as "the priest of a new, entirely irrational and mysterious religion." On the other hand, "when he has to defend and propagate this religion he proceeds very methodically." The new political myths, Cassirer concluded, "do not grow up freely; they are not wild fruits of an exuberant imagination. They are artificial things fabricated by very skilful and cunning artisans. It has been reserved for the twentieth century, our own great technical age, to develop a new technique of myth." The apparent paradox of the modern political myths—that they were both atavism *and* modern artifice—was thereby resolved: "Henceforth myths can be manufactured in the same sense and according to the same methods as any other modern weapon—as machine guns or airplanes."[121] We might note in passing that this argument bore some resemblance to the claims laid down by Adorno and Horkheimer, who concurred with Cassirer that myth was both a spontaneous expression *and* the final stage of instrumental reason: "Myth is already enlightenment," they claimed, "but Enlightenment reverts to myth."[122] The resemblance, however, was only superficial. The Frankfurt theorists condemned modern reason *itself* for its lapse into fatalistic repetition. Cassirer continued to distinguish between fascism as a modern manipulation of myths and reason's true promise to dispel them.

But who, in Cassirer's eyes, were the most recent prophets whose scientific and philosophical ideas had given the political myths their modern prestige? In the book's concluding pages Cassirer revisited this question a final time to explain how even the most sophisticated and technical modes of explanation could play a role in the resurgence of mythic thought. Of the many modern philosophers in Germany who might have been mentioned, Cassirer named only two: The first was Oswald Spengler, whose grand statements about the West's decline served to reinforce a mythic sense of fatalism and ratified the Nazis' wholesale revolution against liberal modernity. The second and final philosopher Cassirer named was Martin Heidegger.

For readers who had followed Cassirer's long career, this final attempt in his last book to revisit the philosophical contributions of his German colleague could hardly have come as a surprise. With characteristic generosity, Cassirer began by acknowledging the power of Heidegger's philosophical work. But he also noted that Heidegger had abandoned the logical rigor of Husserlian phenomenology: The ideal of philosophy as a "strict science" was cast aside in favor of a nonlogical strain of *Existenzphilosophie* that denied the possibility of universally valid truths and embraced only the truths of finite existence. The crucial lesson of Heidegger's philosophy, Cassirer explained, was that "existence has a historical character" and "is bound up with the special conditions under which the individual lives."

> In order to express his thought Heidegger had to coin a new term. He spoke of the *Geworfenheit* of man (the being-thrown). To be thrown into the stream of time is a fundamental and inalterable feature of our human situation. We cannot emerge from this stream and we cannot change its course. We have to accept the historical conditions of our existence. We can try to understand and interpret them; but we cannot change them.[123]

Whether this account of Heideggerian "thrownness" was philosophically precise seemed unimportant because Cassirer did not wish to indict Heidegger's philosophy itself. Rather, he was concerned solely with its cultural consequences: "I do not mean to say that these philosophical doctrines had a direct bearing on the development of political ideas in Germany. Most of these ideas arose from quite different sources." At issue in other words was not whether Heidegger was philosophically correct, but whether his ideas had *contributed to the new mood of political fatalism.* On this point Cassirer's lesson was clear: The "new philosophy" had helped to "enfeeble and slowly undermine the forces that could have resisted the modern political myths." Spengler and Heidegger were both culpable, *not* as philosophers but as mythologists of submission:

> A philosophy of history that consists in somber predictions of the decline and inevitable destruction of our civilization and a theory that sees in the *Geworfenheit* of man one of his principal characteristics has given up all hopes of an active share in the construction and reconstruction of man's cultural life. Such a philosophy renounces its own fundamental theoretical and ethical ideals, it can be used, then, as a pliable instrument in the hands of the political leaders.[124]

This was to be Cassirer's final verdict on Heidegger. In the early 1920s it was already apparent that Cassirer and Heidegger were divided by a key difference of philosophical premises. Cassirer endorsed a Kantian model of mental spontaneity where Heidegger insisted on the temporal throwness of human existence. In the end, Cassirer no longer articulated his claims against Heidegger in philosophical terms: existentialism itself now seemed to Cassirer a mere symptom for the mythic-political resurgence he summarized as "the return of fatalism in our modern world."[125]

What is perhaps most striking about this conclusion is the implication that philosophies mattered at least as much for their ideological effects as for their truth claims. This argumentative shift—from conceptual truth to pragmatic efficacy—becomes rather more evident in a 1944 lecture Cassirer delivered at Connecticut College, which follows closely the arguments of *The Myth of the State.* The lecture repeats almost verbatim the book's attempt to indict Heideggerian "thrownness" along with Oswald Spengler's theories of cultural decline as signals of Germany's atavistic return to the "general mythical concept . . . of fate." Cassirer now clarified that philosophy must fulfill "its most important educational task," which is to "teach man how to develop his active faculties in order to form his individual and social life." But the Heideggerian doctrine of submission to historical Being could not fulfill this mission. "As soon as philosophy no longer trusts its own power," Cassirer claimed,

> as soon as it gives way to a merely passive attitude, . . . *it cannot teach man how to develop his active faculties in order to form his individual and social life.* A philosophy that indulges in somber predications about the decline and inevitable destruction of human culture, a philosophy whose whole attention is focused on the *Geworfenheit,* the Being-thrown of man, can no longer do its duty.[126]

Years before Cassirer had condemned Heidegger's 1929 work, *Kant and the Problem of Metaphysics,* for overthrowing Kant's Enlightenment in favor of darkly religious motifs distilled from Kierkegaard. But Cassirer now recast the philosophical complaint against theological fatalism as an indictment of the *uses* to which Heidegger's political-mythological ideas could be put. Strictly speaking, however, this was not a philosophical objection. After years of mounting disagreement, the philosophical quarrel had finally transformed into a public dispute over the status of philosophy as ideology.

In a brief postscript, Cassirer warned that modernity's greatest achievements—in the sciences, poetry, and art—were only the "upper layer" for a "much older stratum that reaches down to a great depth." This was especially true of the conflict between spontaneity and fatalism, because the principle of political self-authorization through reason was a fragile ideal that could barely withstand the dark forces of myth: "We must always be prepared," Cassirer warned, "for violent concussions that may shake our cultural world and our social order to its very foundations." As illustration, Cassirer chose (not without irony) to end his book by resorting to a Babylonian myth: Marduk, the highest god, wished to create the world, but to do so, he had to first vanquish the serpent Tiamat and other dragons of darkness. From the limbs of the serpent, Marduk could then fashion the cosmos and humanity: "He formed the world and gave to it its shape and its order."

Here, Cassirer observed, was a myth that portrayed the struggle against myth: "The world of human culture" could not arise until the agencies of myth were subdued. But the subterranean powers still persist. Humanity holds in its possession "superior forces" that keep the mythic powers at bay: "As long as these forces, intellectual, ethical, and artistic, are in full strength, myth is tamed and subdued. But once they begin to lose their strength chaos is come again. Mythical thought then starts to rise anew and to pervade the whole of man's cultural and social life."[127]

It was a stunning conclusion. A book whose consuming task was to indict the noxious entwinement of modern politics and myth came to a close by affirming its own mythology, as if Marduk were liberalism's god. Heidegger himself was no longer an individual philosopher but a mere servant among the dark fellowship of Tiamat. It was a paradoxical way for Cassirer to end his book, as it appealed to the key instruments of mythological understanding that liberal rationalists were supposed to disown. Readers were left with a lingering doubt: had Tiamat won after all?

Cassirer, Heidegger, and Political Theology

By the time Cassirer published *The Myth of the State,* the debates in Germany over political theology were already well advanced, and to appreciate the ultimate lessons of his book in relation to Heidegger's philosophy it may prove helpful to look briefly at this wider context. It is of course well known that theoretical interest in the relation between religion and politics is due most of all to Carl Schmitt's 1922 *Politische Theologie,* in which he claimed that "all significant concepts of the modern theory of the state are secularized theological concepts."[128] Crucial to Schmitt's authoritarian critique of liberalism was the inference that just as God's sovereignty is recognizable by his capacity to intervene with miracles in the order of nature, so too, the sovereign within any political order is he who has the power to intervene at decisive moments of extralegal exception. Because no legal system or parliamentary structure can evade the need for such decision, all political legitimacy must ultimately appeal to a sovereign event of irrational discontinuity. Schmitt's more notorious theories would come later when his sympathies for decisionism and the emergency provisions of Weimar's notorious Article

48 eventually brought him into official alignment with the Third Reich. Although he was excommunicated from the Church, Schmitt continued to believe in the importance of religion. A key theme in his work was that all political orders rest upon irrational foundations and exhibit a logic that cannot be understood without reference to their political-theological foundations. In his 1938 study, *Der Leviathan in der Staatslehre des Thomas Hobbes: Sinn und Fehlschlag eines politischen Symbols,* Schmitt observed that without some visible "substance," the state cannot stand, and such a substance was supposed to be found in some kind of "myth." Although the book is stained with anti-Semitism, its core argument bears notice: Schmitt's criticism of Hobbes was that the Leviathan itself was the wrong myth because it reinforced a purely mechanistic understanding of both the state and the human being.[129]

Schmitt was not alone in his insistence on the need for mythic foundations in any political regime. In 1938 the political theorist Erich Voegelin published *The Political Religions,* his boldest attack on the ideology of National Socialism. The first edition in Vienna was immediately confiscated by the Nazis but reappeared a year later in Stockholm. Voegelin disagreed with Schmitt on many points (it should be remembered, for instance, that Voegelin was a student of Hans Kelsen, the neo-Kantian author of the so-called pure theory of law, whose work Schmitt subjected to unrelenting criticism). But Voegelin nonetheless agreed with Schmitt on the theological foundations of modern political regimes. In *The Political Religions,* Voegelin observed:

> the life of men in a political community cannot be defined as a profane sphere, in which we only have to deal with questions of organizations, of law, and of power. The community is also a realm of religious order, and the recognition of a political situation is incomplete in one decisive point if it does not also embrace the religious forces of the community and the symbols in which they find expression; or indeed, if it embraces them but does not recognize them as such, but rather translates them into areligious categories. Man lives in the political community with all aspects of his being from the corporal to the spiritual and religious.[130]

Voegelin agreed with Schmitt that modern politics must always rest upon mythic foundations. The pathology of National Socialism was thus due *not to its political theological character as such* but rather to the fact that it tried to break free of the *original* foundation of Western politics in Christianity and strove instead to create new and ostensibly *areligious* foundations. The consequence of such an innovation was to introduce what Voegelin called a purely "temporal religiosity," that is, the worship of things fabricated by the human being alone. But any such worship presupposed that man without God could be an independent source of good, a naïve belief in human autonomy born, or so Voegelin claimed, from the Enlightenment. Despite Voegelin's antipathies toward Nazism, he therefore endorsed the deeper premises of political theology. His own etiology of Nazi ideology ruled out Cassirer's ideal of autonomy as merely a liberal myth.

Voegelin made this point clear when he reviewed *The Myth of the State* in 1947.[131] Commenting on the "melancholy task" of assessing the late thinker's final work, Voegelin wrote that, "It is a cause for reflection that the generation which carried an important phase in modern philosophy, that is the neo-Kantian movement, is passing away." What Voegelin seemed to find most touching yet also naïve in Cassirer's analysis was its incorrigibly rationalist conviction that "the human mind evolves historically from an earlier mythical phase towards an increasingly rational penetration of the world; the idols of myth give way to reason and science." Yet for Cassirer the entire history of humanity seemed to display an eternal conflict between reason and myth, a drama which resembled "an Eastern struggle between the forces of Light and Darkness." Here Voegelin detected a paradox Cassirer had ostensibly missed: to portray Enlightenment modernity as locked in *mythic* struggle against unreason implicated Cassirer's own argumentation in the mythological landscape he was trying to escape. Cassirer's own appeal to myth seemed to dismantle reason's triumph, a paradox which, at the very least, cast "a curious ambivalence on [Cassirer's] concrete analysis." But Voegelin's final claim struck at the very heart of Cassirer's political testament, in which Voegelin could find "no awareness that the myth is an indispensable forming element of social order." Voegelin concluded darkly that

the overcoming of the "darkness of myth" by reason is in itself a problematical victory because the new myth which inevitably will take the place of the old one may be highly unpleasant. *The Myth of the State* is written as if it had never occurred to the author that tampering with a myth, unless one has a better one to put in its place, is a dangerous pastime.[132]

To this criticism Cassirer could only have responded that Voegelin's political-theological premise was incorrect: Myth was not indispensable but only the *first* and *provisional* foundation of political life. With humankind's emergence from what Kant had called its "self-incurred immaturity" (*selbst-verschuldete Unmündigkeit*), it was indeed not only possible, but a matter of political urgency for human beings at last to forego any appeal to unknown forces and to conduct their affairs on their own. On this point Cassirer sounded a theme that his fellow émigré Karl Löwith (now at the Hartford Theological Seminary) would repeat in his book *Meaning in History* just a few years later. As Löwith explained, the political evils of the modern world (including the evil he discerned in his teacher Heidegger's crypto-religious fatalism) were due precisely to the calamitous union between the mythico-religious temporality and secular history, between *Heilsgeschichte* and *Weltgeschichte*.[133]

More devastating, however, was the brief 1947 review of Cassirer's book by political philosopher Leo Strauss. It is common knowledge that Strauss, who had studied with both Cassirer and Heidegger back in the 1920s, retained a keen interest in his teachers and was unusually attentive to the significance of their quarrel. Under Cassirer's supervision, he had received his doctorate from the University of Hamburg in 1921 with a thesis on the counter-Enlightenment philosophy of F. H. Jacobi. But the very next year Strauss made the not only geographical, but also philosophical, move to Freiburg, where he was drawn into the circle of Husserl's disciples and first encountered the young Heidegger, whose philosophical rigor and charismatic manner impressed him deeply. In 1925, when Heidegger moved to Marburg, Strauss's close friend Jacob Klein attended Heidegger's seminars on a regular basis. Concerning their shared experience, Strauss would later observe that "nothing affected us as profoundly in the years in which our minds took their lasting direction as the thought of Heidegger," whose "speculative intelligence," he added, "surpasses . . . all his contemporaries."[134] Strauss owed a heavy but unpaid debt to Cassirer, but by the time Strauss

read *The Myth of the State,* its author was deceased, and in his review Strauss
made it clear that he meant not to praise his teacher but only to bury him.
Cassirer, Strauss wrote, had understood himself as a frank an uncritical
partisan of the Enlightenment, and he had embraced without reserve the
Enlightenment's self-image as an intellectual struggle against myth. Here
already, Strauss detected a fatal error in Cassirer's work: *The Philosophy of
Symbolic Forms* was evidently designed as a modernist *extension* of the
Enlightenment's unfinished labor, but notwithstanding its pretensions, it
remained little more than an exercise in innocent aestheticism, because it
ignored the deeper normative purposes of philosophy. Were Cassirer to adequately confront the modern political myths as developed by Heidegger et al.,
Strauss argued, this confrontation would have required a genuinely moral
response rather than a merely epistemological analysis. Such a response
would have required a "radical transformation" of the philosophy of symbolic forms into "a teaching whose center is moral philosophy." Ultimately it
would have had to entail "something like a return to Cassirer's teacher Hermann Cohen, if not to Kant himself."[135]

Strauss, of course, did not believe this transformation was at all likely. A
philosophical project such as Cassirer's revealed what Strauss considered
Weimar liberalism's abject failure to provide a muscular defense of liberal
norms against its various enemies, among whom Strauss counted Heidegger.
But this failure had its roots in what Strauss by the later 1940s had come to
regard as liberalism's deepest and most insoluble predicament, a faith in
reason whose own rationalist skepticism robbed it of the principles by
which to explain why that faith alone survived reason's corrosive scrutiny.
Strauss hinted at the possibility that Cassirer might have redressed this
failure in his philosophy by restoring its neglected premise—the primacy
of practical reason—a premise that both Kant and neo-Kantians such as
Hermann Cohen had acknowledged. Just why this would have solved the
aporias of Cassirer's Weimar liberalism remains unclear. If Strauss believed
that liberal nihilism was the culmination of the Enlightenment's single-
minded affirmation of instrumental reason (as he implied in the indictment of Weberian rationalism in *Natural Right and History*), then presumably, liberal nihilism was an unavoidable consequence, absent some appeal
to a nonrational principle transcending the sphere of disenchanted modernity. What Strauss did not mention (though he implied it through his char-

acteristic device of indirection) was that any such "return" to Cohen would therefore have entailed a return to the *religious principles* that served as the groundwork to Cohen's normative defense of modernity. But for Strauss the broader lesson was clear: Cassirer exemplified the anemic liberal rationalism of the Weimar era that had cast aside the one needful resource of ethical-religious foundationalism that might have served as its defense against nihilism. Cassirer had retreated into epistemology, and Heidegger had won.

The Ethico-Political Status of Monotheism

Strauss's verdict on Cassirer's philosophy was, of course, excessive. It is critical to note, *pace* Strauss, that Cassirer did in fact recognize the crucial place of religion within his own philosophy, a fact apparent to even the most casual reader of *The Philosophy of Symbolic Forms,* where monotheism was portrayed as turning dialectically against its mythological origins.[136] That Strauss neglected this crucial moment in Cassirer's historical-philosophical narrative was perhaps unsurprising: the fable of Davos—of Cassirer's toothless rationalism suffering a decisive defeat by Heidegger's irrationalism—was a treasured conceit in Strauss's postwar critique of liberal modernity. In this fable there was little room for appreciating Cassirer's own contributions to the philosophy of religion.

But there was other evidence as well. Cassirer was a private man and typically reticent about his felt attachments to religion. So it was perhaps from some sense of fortified solidarity with the émigré community that in 1944 he agreed to publish an essay for the *Contemporary Jewish Record* under the title "Judaism and the Modern Political Myths." Although the essay is a mere eleven pages, it speaks volumes, not only about Cassirer's own views on contemporary politics, but also about the broader tradition of German-Jewish culture that was just then reaching a violent end: "In our life, in the life of a modern Jew," he wrote, "there is no room left for any sort of joy or complacency, let alone exultation or triumph":

> All this has gone forever. No Jew whatsoever can and will ever overcome the terrible ordeal of these last years. The victims of this ordeal cannot be forgotten; the wounds inflicted upon us are incurable. Yet

amidst all these horrors and miseries there is, at least, one relief. We may be firmly convinced that all these sacrifices have not been made in vain. What the modern Jew had to defend in this combat was not only his physical existence or the preservation of the Jewish race. . . . We had to represent all those ethical ideals that had been brought into being by Judaism and found their way into general human culture, into the life of all civilized nations. . . . These ideals are not destroyed and cannot be destroyed. They have stood their ground in these critical days. If Judaism has contributed to break the power of the modern political myths, it has done its duty, having once more fulfilled its historical and religious mission.[137]

This religious testament had several noteworthy features. The first and most obvious was its belated paean to Judaism as a religion of ethical idealism. A modern variant of mission-theory according to which the Israelites serve as a "light-unto-the-nations," the notion that Judaism bore a distinctively ethical and universalistic gift for humanity came into special prominence among the great German-Jewish historians of the nineteenth century, such as Heinrich Graetz, and reached its philosophical apogee with Hermann Cohen's tribute to Judaism as the wellspring to the prophetic doctrine of universalist ethics he called "religion of reason." One might call this conception belated because it may seem surprising that Cassirer could still have cleaved to it with such evident passion at the midpoint of the twentieth century. Its apologetic universalism, though well suited to the age of emancipation, had yielded by Cassirer's time to new strains of existentialist and nationalist assertion. Most of all, Cassirer's image of Judaism harkened back to the late religious philosophy of his teacher, Hermann Cohen (notwithstanding the fact that in his own philosophy of culture Cassirer had advanced well beyond the neo-Kantian doctrines of the nineteenth century). Second and less obvious, perhaps, was Cassirer's claim that Judaism helped to "break the power" of modern political myth. This was an unusual statement in that it assigned the Jewish religion a special place in what might be called a *narrative of political demythologization*. The implication was not only that Judaism bore an ethical universalist content, but also that this content worked as a *solvent* against the illicit efforts by modern political regimes to reintroduce mythological elements into politics.

The intellectual context for these claims is complex and bears closer examination. Like many émigrés, Cassirer was understandably perplexed at the ferocity of Nazi anti-Semitism, and he grasped eagerly at various theories. He granted a partial validity to the theory of "scapegoating," the primitive ritual for the expulsion of evil analyzed by late nineteenth-century Scottish anthropologist James Frazer in his comparative study of world religion, *The Golden Bough,* which Cassirer cited at length.[138] But Cassirer felt the need for greater precision: although Frazer catalogued diverse and ingeniously brutal cases of scapegoating from ancient Abdera to modern Peru, the existence of the generic phenomenon left unexplained why any one victim or group was selected on a given occasion over another. A theory of socially regulative scapegoating therefore failed to address the historically specific riddle as to why the Jews in particular served as the preferred objects of Nazi persecution. For Cassirer the answer was clear: it was Judaism that had first effected "the decisive step that led from a *mythical* to an *ethical* religion." Insofar as Nazism was itself a political *myth,* it was therefore inevitable that those who bore witness to Judaism's ethico-religious message would come to be seen as Nazism's mortal enemy. The Jews were therefore not arbitrarily chosen as victims but were in fact a peculiar threat to Nazism as a political mythology: "In the history of mankind," Cassirer explained, the Jews "had been the first to deny and to challenge those very conceptions on which the new state was built." However perverse their reasoning, the Nazis were therefore in a sense correct to discern in the Jewish religion a specific threat to the Third Reich's mythological foundations.[139]

This argument was a direct homage to Hermann Cohen. And it should move us to qualify Strauss's rather brittle contrast between Cohen's theological ethico-political fortitude and Cassirer's ostensibly superficial retreat into aestheticism. In June 1935, only two years into his period of exile from Germany, Cassirer delivered a lecture in English before the Oxford Jewish Society on the topic of "Cohen's Philosophy of Religion," in which he outlined some of the key principles of his late teacher's writings on Judaism. As Cassirer explained, Cohen readily acknowledged the foundational significance of myth in human experience and social order: "In all positive, in all concrete religion there is contained a mythical element. In a certain sense we may even say, that the mythical thought is not only the beginning and origin of religion, but the origin of all civilization." As

Cohen himself observed, "All civilization . . . , in all its different fundamental directions has unfolded from mythical elements."[140] Thus far it appeared that Cassirer consented to Voegelin's suggestion that myth served as the requisite foundation for politics. But Cassirer hastened to cancel this impression. Notwithstanding its initial importance, myth furnished only the most primitive elements for human experience and these were destined to be overcome into a "purer form of religious thought," which expressed a "new relation to the ethical ideal of humanity."[141] Here, the difference between myth and the Jewish religion stood for a difference between two distinctive conceptions of social cohesion:

> Myth—says Cohen—has nothing in common with this ideal. Myth is interested in clan, in tribe, in nation, but no heathen myth ever directed its view upon humanity. . . . The idea of humanity is the fruit and issue of the unity of God. The prophets by defying the mythical relation between God and men could by this implant the correlation between man and man into the original soil of prophetic religion. It was only by the idea of the unity of God that they were able to discover the unity of mankind—that highest thought of morality.[142]

Whereas myth remained bound within limited concepts of the sacred and therefore contented itself with notions of redemption through national belonging or race, monotheism, for the very first time in the history of human consciousness, broke free of mythical particularism, and through its universal concept of God, was able to conceive a truly universal humanity.[143] For Cohen, Judaism had thereby achieved (in Cassirer's paraphrase) "the decisive and the most difficult step in the development of religious thought . . . *the transition from the mere mythical concept of the Deity to its moral concept.*"[144]

This conception of Judaism perhaps is of special interest here insofar as it casts Cassirer's debate with Heidegger in a new and unfamiliar light. A recurrent theme in their debate was that Cassirer argued for the possibility of a *breakthrough* from the finitude of Heideggerian or existential space-time to the unbounded sphere of scientific or theoretical space-time. And, as we have seen, Cassirer seemed to affirm the discoveries of Heidegger's existential analytic only to then insist that these discoveries were applicable *solely within the primitive stratum of mythic consciousness,* a stage in historical development that humanity had eventually surpassed as it began to grasp its surroundings through functional symbolization rather than substantial and sensualistic images. The striking consequence of this criticism was that, from Cassirer's perspective, Heidegger's philosophy itself seemed to offer an accurate portrait of the world *but only as it was experienced within the bounds of myth.* In his final book, Cassirer had also condemned Heidegger for helping to fortify the legitimacy of Nazism as a modern political myth. Against this diagnosis of myth as both an existential framework and a political experience, Cassirer now conceived Judaism as the vehicle of an intellectual revolution: The Jewish religion, he argued, was first and foremost the agent for history's triumphant breakthrough from mythic tribalism to a universal concept of humanity

Cassirer had traveled a long way from the Marburg neo-Kantian philosophy of his earliest years. But at the end of his life, he made what we might call a *spiritual return* to Marburg by endorsing, if not its philosophy, then at least its idea of the Jewish religion. It is worth noting that in at least one important essay Cohen went so far as to assert an "inner affinity" (*innere Beziehung*) between Judaism and Kantianism.[145] Cassirer was of course hardly alone among the refugee Jewish intellectuals from central Europe who extolled Judaism for its revolutionary break from the world of pagan myth. In 1939, Sigmund Freud himself, also a refugee in England, turned Moses into an Egyptian but in the very same breath praised the Second Commandment as "a triumph of intellectuality over the senses."[146] This was yet another variation on the common theme, that Judaism is a religion of pure intellect whose revolutionary and universalist message effects a total rupture from the mythological world of sensual imagination. Cassirer merely recapitulated this line of analogies and ranked Heidegger among the forces of atavistic paganism. Unnoticed in this argument, however, was a strange logic that not only condemned Heidegger's philosophy but also implied that the Jewish religion retained the special and transhistorical power to break Heidegger's mythic spell: if Heidegger belonged to the legions of Tiamat, Judaism was Marduk's enlightened heir.

One could well ask, of course, whether Heidegger's philosophy had ever played so powerful a role in German interwar culture as Cassirer supposed.

And we may wonder too whether his spiritualized understanding of Judaism was wholly accurate. But we may forgive Cassirer if he looked for solace in an idealized image of the Jewish religion at a historical moment of unrelenting violence. And we might also record a last, bitter detail: In September 1942, Martha Cohen, Hermann Cohen's widow, was murdered in Theresienstadt—one individual among the millions who died as victims of the modern political myths.

7

Philosophy and Memory

The play's the thing . . .

—*Hamlet*, Act. 2, Scene 2

A Visit to Todtnauberg

In the autumn of 1945, two envoys of reemergent French intellectual life, Maurice de Gandillac and Alfred de Towarnicki, made their way eastward from Paris to Freiburg to visit Martin Heidegger, who was now living with his wife Elfride under the more or less casual watch of the French occupation. His future career was uncertain, and his past would soon become the object of official scrutiny: It was well known that Heidegger had served as rector at Freiburg during the first year of National Socialist rule. But while he would attempt to mitigate his guilt with a report to the de-Nazification committee in December 1945, rumors were beginning to swell concerning the true meaning and extent of his collaboration.[1] For the time being, he was forbidden from teaching and travel, and he was grateful for the coffee and other assorted gifts sent his way by post from old friends and students who were now living abroad. The two young men thus arrived at Heidegger's home as unofficial agents of judgment, and possibly of reconciliation, between German and French culture, and, more specifically, as ambassadors *sans papier* from Jean-Paul Sartre, who seemed in those years the very embodiment of the French intellectual resistance, and in whose fledgling journal, *Les Temps Modernes*, they would publish the record of their visit some months later, in January 1946.[2]

In the published text of their visit, de Gandillac relates that he and his companion were shown into Heidegger's study, where the conversation began in a subdued mood. Heidegger had once been seen as perhaps the greatest philosopher of his generation, but he now endured something like house arrest, and what students attending his seminars and lectures had once discerned in the German thinker as a near-magical charisma seemed now to have vanished entirely. To ease their conversation, de Gandillac reminded the philosopher that they had met on at least one previous occasion: It was around Easter 1929, when de Gandillac, then a student, had made a pilgrimage along with many of his cohort to Davos to witness in person an intellectual clash of the titans—the meeting between the two great philosophers of the age, Heidegger and Cassirer. "This memory," de Gandillac wrote, "restored him somewhat to his good humor." He then related Heidegger's memory of the event: "At that time then," de Gandillac recounted Heidegger saying, "he had not hesitated, after long discussions concerning Kant, 'to shake publicly the hand of the Jew Cassirer.' Compromising expressions, but which today have become, as it were, certificates of an upstanding life and morality." De Gandillac continued: "At this precise moment, Heidegger opens a drawer and takes from it, without having to search, a paled photograph that recalls those innocent times." De Gandillac could not resist a wry remark: "I doubt that, at that still-so-recent epoch, when everywhere there reigned a fear of the Gestapo, he could have found this small token of faith quite so easily."[3]

Even by the end of World War II, the Davos disputation between Cassirer and Heidegger had already begun to assume in philosophical memory a near-allegorical significance for the history of European ideas. In previous chapters, we have seen how contemporary witnesses to the dispute ascribed it a pivotal importance in the transformation of interwar philosophy. Even today, the Davos encounter remains a touchstone for intellectual-historical narratives of the twentieth century. Scholars from a variety of disciplines and ideological camps frequently regard it as a final moment of rupture—between humanism and anti-humanism, enlightenment and counter-enlightenment, or rationalism and irrationalism—as if the defining struggles of twentieth century thought were crystallized in this single event. What are we to make of such judgments? What can it mean when a philosophical dispute becomes so richly embroidered with historical meaning? How can we recover its actual significance when the intervening years have brought a subtle transformation of philosophical and political perspective? Here I have tried to sustain the distinction between philosophy and history. Indeed, one might say it is a desideratum for philosophy that its arguments should be resolved by philosophical means only and without reference to the nonphilosophical world. On this view, philosophy would seem to demand a kind of *askesis*, the principled attempt to hold thought apart from all that is mundane. In deference to this principle (which, admittedly, is stated here in the boldest and least qualified fashion), I have tried in the foregoing chapters to move carefully and with deliberation through the complex history of the Cassirer-Heidegger debate so as to appreciate just what was at stake in philosophical terms.

But, as we have seen, philosophical meaning cannot be easily disentangled from cultural and political memory. Philosophy partakes of common memory the moment it begins to ramify into the broader narrative of human affairs. This mutual entanglement between philosophy and memory may seem both obvious and benign, and typically it *is* benign. But a difficulty may arise when the memory of historical injustice remains so vivid that it presses on one's conscience and refuses to be silenced. When this happens, the habitual posture of philosophical *askesis* may seem indefensible and even inhuman. It is at this point that memory may begin to reshape our understanding of the philosophical past. Can this transformation be reversed? Can the allegories be undone? Can we restore to philosophy its innocence in the face of historical disruption? While I appreciate the longing, the *necessity,* even, for such restoration of original meaning, its prospects seem to me dubious at best: Our interpretation of past philosophical debate is marked, inevitably, by what has transpired between past and present. What I have here called *ramification* is not something we can evade, and it would indeed be foolish to believe in a pristine moment of philosophical meaning. But we can nevertheless try to understand how memory has done its work.

A Little Spectacle

The challenge of understanding the confrontation between Heidegger and Cassirer in strictly philosophical terms is made all the more difficult once we recall that its symbolic ramifications were evident from the very beginning. Eyewitness commentators on the dispute remarked on its drama and its intriguing study in contrasts. As we saw in Chapter 2, reporters likened the debate to the conversation between Settembrini and Naphta (partisans

of the Enlightenment and romantic revolution, respectively) in Thomas
Mann's Davos-situated novel of ideas, *The Magic Mountain*. For the assembled students the theatricality of the occasion was especially pronounced,
and a number of them revived an old custom of restaging the dispute as
light entertainment before an assembled crowd. For this *petit spectacle* the
role of Cassirer was played by none other than the young philosophy student
Lévinas, while Bollnow played the role of Heidegger. Several newspaper reports made reference to this little event and none of them implied there was
anything unusual to the occurrence, though today such play-acting would
strike us as highly inappropriate. In a 1987 interview, Lévinas recalled that
he had at that time an abundance of black hair, which he dipped in white
powder so as to better resemble "the noble gray coiffure of the master [Cas-
sirer]." Lévinas also wrote the dialogue for their exchanges. To Bollnow, he
gave lines "that seemed to me to caricature Heidegger's etymological inven-
tions [for example]: 'for interpretation [*interpretari*] is to place something
on its head.'"[4] Later, in a 1992 interview, Lévinas added the detail that Heidegger was "constantly attacking" Cassirer's statements. To capture Cassirer's "non-combative and somewhat desolate attitude," Lévinas made his
Cassirer-persona repeat several times, "I am a pacifist." Lévinas adds a further, rather surprising fact: both Cassirer and Heidegger were present in the
audience and looked on as their students reduced their philosophical dialogue to low comedy.[5]

We do not know how the two philosophers felt about this bathetic reenactment. It has been said that Cassirer suffered greater ridicule and perhaps
even took personal umbrage at Lévinas's caricature. There is no record of
Heidegger's response. We do know, however, that Lévinas came to regret his
early admiration for Heidegger, and he especially regretted making Cassirer
the object of abuse: Lévinas taught as a visiting professor at Johns Hopkins
University in the fall of 1973 under the auspices of the French department.
Richard Sugarman, professor of philosophy at the University of Vermont,
travelled in the company of two colleagues to Baltimore, where they all met
with the French philosopher and his wife and passed the afternoon in conversation. According to Sugarman, Lévinas himself raised the topic of the
Davos disputation: "You know the debates they have in the academy, where
you ridicule the opponent?" (Sugerman and his colleagues said no.) "Well,"
continued Lévinas, "Heidegger invited me to go to Davos. I did such a great

job, Cassirer was too easy to mimic, in fact; he had hair like an ice-cream cone. I'm afraid I did much better than I would have liked to." He then added: "I always said that if I came to the United States I would ask pardon of Mme. Cassirer. I had no idea, we could not have known, what would take place in 1933. This was the author of *Being and Time* . . . you cannot bypass Heidegger as a thinker." Sugarman remembers quite clearly that Lévinas then added (in reference to Heidegger): "No friend of ours." Summarizing the conversation, Sugarman observed that, "It was evident to me that Lévinas was conflicted, even mortified."[6] Others have written that Lévinas had been planning to speak at Yale during his U.S. visit and hoped to find Toni Cassirer so that he might apologize to her in person. It is not known if Lévinas persisted in his search, but his efforts would have been in vain: she had died in 1961.

Why was Lévinas so consumed with remorse? It is hard to imagine that the play alone was the thing, and it is also worth noting that he was by no means the only member of the audience to poke fun at the philosophers. The logical positivist Rudolf Carnap was arguably even more insulting, and his criticism was of greater significance philosophically. Having sat through all three of Heidegger's Kant-lectures at Davos, Carnap seems to have been more impressed by the philosopher's odd terminology than by the substance of the interpretation: a twenty-two-year old student named Ernst Benz (who would later become a distinguished theologian) recalled many years afterward that, in the afternoon following one of Heidegger's lectures, a handful of the guests decided to take in the local scenery by riding the cable car that ascended from the valley of Davosplatz to the high, snow-covered peak of the Jakobshorn. Pressed together in the cabin and swaying slightly as it rose were a number of professors and students, including both Cassirer and Carnap. Cassirer turned to his neighbor: "Herr Kollege," he asked, "How would you express the content of today's lecture by Herr Heidegger in the language of mathematical logic?" And Carnap responded: "Quite simple: Bi-ba-bum!"[7]

The joke requires little explanation as its aim was simply to demonstrate that Heidegger's philosophy could be reduced to nonsense. Carnap's dismissive "gloss" resembles both the clang of church bells and, perhaps, the crazed counter-semantics of Dada poets such as Hugo Ball.[8] More likely, Carnap was referring to the turn-of-the-century German poet Christian Morgenstern's

quasi-metaphysical verse, which drank from the same well as the British
nonsense poets Lewis Carroll and Edward Lear. (Morgenstern had in fact
authored a strange little poem, "Bim, Bam, Bum," which was published in
the 1905 collection, *Gallows Songs*.) While jokes often condense a manifold
of unmentionable meanings and serve as vehicles for hidden aggression,
Carnap's withering report on the philosophical content of Heidegger's lectures served as more than mere ridicule: it anticipated the critique of Heidegger's "metaphysical pseudo-sentences" that Carnap would include in his
famous essay, "The Overcoming of Metaphysics through the Logical Analysis of Language," the first draft of which he completed by November 1930.
We know from Michael Friedman that Carnap's attitude toward Heidegger
was anything but dismissive: Friedman quotes a diary entry written at
Davos and dated March 18, 1929, in which Carnap observed that "Cassirer
speaks well, but somewhat pastorally . . . Heidegger, serious and objective,
as a person very attractive." The following year (by which time he had read
Being and Time), Carnap participated in a discussion group and colleagues
were "astonished that I was capable of interpreting Heidegger." But notwithstanding the serious efforts he made to comprehend Heidegger's philosophy,
Carnap would ultimately conclude that it was shot through with unverifi-
able sentences, such as "The Nothing itself nothings," which were therefore,
from his "scientific" perspective, without meaning.[9]

Carnap's verdict was unusually severe and not everyone was inclined
to be so dismissive. But even the most casual recollections of the Davos encounter have something to tell us about the mutual entwinement of philosophy and memory and about the way historical and political evaluations of
intellectual debates are first granted an independent life. What Lévinas
called the *petit spectacle* deserves notice, not because it is a piece of intellectual gossip, but because it affords us a small if imperfect glimpse into the
processes by which individual as well as collective memories help to shape
our larger and more canonical judgments concerning the philosophical
past. The young Heidegger was already lionized for his creative readings of
the philosophical tradition, but even his most admiring students seemed
quick to tease him for a style of interpretation that turned a text violently on
its head even to the point of apparent "nonsense." Cassirer by contrast was
seen by nearly all who met him as a distinguished if somewhat distant figure, a philosophical and political moderate who was reluctant to engage in

any sort of polemic. Symbolically he was a "pacifist." What merits consideration is that this sort of contrast could so easily be turned to the purposes of historical and political allegory. Not all philosophical debates lend themselves to caricature and political symbolism of this kind. But if it has proven difficult to appreciate the Davos encounter purely on philosophical terms, this is partly because it was already susceptible to political dramatization from the very beginning.

Earliest Memories, 1929–1934

There is yet another fact about the earliest reports that deserves mention: *They make no mention whatsoever of political conflict.* Lévinas only later came to regret having preferred Heidegger to Cassirer, and he admitted that he "could not have known . . . what would take place in 1933."[10] Indeed, no eyewitness reports written in the immediate aftermath of the disputation make even the slightest suggestion that the two men were in fact divided by politics. Many reports interpret the dispute as a contrast between two eras in philosophical history. A writer for the *Frankfurter Zeitung* noted that it was "not merely an academic quarrel between professors" but actually "a confrontation between representative envoys of two epochs."[11] One could not fail to admire the "imposing" Cassirer with his "white crown of hair" and his "masterful, completely clear lecture," but most auditors felt more closely aligned with Heidegger, whose philosophizing implied that *"tua res agitur"* (this is of personal concern). Cassirer's lectures on philosophical anthropology left the impression that his work had no bearing on a "specifically modern problematic," while Heidegger's whole manner of questioning, despite its opacity, struck the audience as devoted to philosophical concerns of "present-day humanity." The difference was indeed dramatic and "far more fundamental than their statements let be known." Both practiced philosophy, but they practiced it "with entirely different premises and goals" because their respective philosophies developed from a "wholly distinctive portrait of the human being" *(ein verschiedenes Bild des Menschen)*:

> Behind Cassirer's philosophy stands an image of man who breaks through the constraints of his finitude and climbs upward into the world of free spirit. Heidegger says by contrast that the essence of philosophy lies not

in what it says but rather what it does not say, in what occurs. One could say that Cassirer's philosophy is a philosophy of the answer, Heidegger's a philosophy of the question. Its aim is not a cultural philosophy, which is only presentation, but rather he sees it as the task of philosophy, "to forge readiness for the leap of man into existence." Its fundamental problem is that of the finitude and bondage of humanity.[12]

This is admittedly impressionistic, but it is hardly an inaccurate assessment of the exchange. It is worth noting that its author, Hermann Herrigel, also styled himself as a philosopher and had published several enthusiastic if superficial tracts excoriating the older generation of neo-Kantians (especially Natorp), while heaping praise on the Weimar philosophical trend known as "the new thinking."[13] What is most noteworthy in his report is that although it provides a fair sketch of the philosophical contrast between the two participants, it makes no allusion whatsoever to conflicts of either a personal or political nature. The dispute, on his view, concerned a "fundamental contrast" not in politics but in philosophical models of what it is to be human. Nor were there any signs of personal discomfort. Echoing Heidegger's complaint to Blochmann (mentioned earlier), Herrigel actually mentions with regret that the usual codes of academic etiquette were too pronounced: "Unfortunately, one must say that a somewhat too far-reaching generosity of both opponents ultimately did not allow the opposition between them to be seen in its full sharpness."[14]

Others saw things differently. A reporter for the *Neue Zürcher Zeitung* observed that "instead of seeing two worlds clash against one another . . . one enjoyed at most a theatrical performance, two spoken monologues, between a very nice man and a very violent man, who, however, made a terrible effort himself to be nice."[15] Impressions of personal conflict only magnified the widespread sense that the two men embodied "two philosophical generations."[16] Given the small age gap between them, it is surprising that Cassirer and Heidegger were taken as emblems for two successive but radically opposed epochs in German thought. But for several critics, the difference of historical and philosophical perspective was so immense that it prohibited genuine dialogue. Franz Josef Brecht (Heidegger's student from Freiburg) observed that "for most of the participants in this year's Davos

Hochschulkurse," Heidegger and Cassirer stood as "the greatest representatives of the two, last, fundamental positions in philosophy, for whom mutual discussion was logically no longer possible." Indeed, their debate symbolized "the situation of contemporary philosophy" overall: Heidegger represented "a new daring and questioning," a new "metaphysical courage and existential seriousness," which introduced a "new philosophical disposition of *man,*" as against the disposition of "science with its orderly rules."[17] The entire Kantian legacy had reached its end: the idealizing tendency of Kant's philosophy had "robbed the world of its substantiality and had transformed it into a function of knowing consciousness." But now "the category of substance in reference to the object-world asserts its deep rights against the functionalist theory of knowledge." Against the philosophical idealism that had predominated throughout the previous decades, a new "realist tendency" was now apparent in both Heideggerian and Schelerian phenomenology. The transformation was not due merely to a shift in philosophical fashion or *Weltanschauung* but was instead born from the inner problematic of philosophy itself and the new emergence of a "metaphysics" that burst the bounds of subject-centered idealism. Whereas "in Marburg neo-Kantianism the logical subject had the character of a world-producing, object-determinative activity, now Being itself with its specific power presses itself upon consciousness and thus its generative dynamism is essentially reduced." After Davos, it was clear that "the primacy of the subject has been shaken."[18]

Some critics recognized that the debate between Heidegger and Cassirer was perhaps not nearly so unprecedented as it seemed. For Erich Przywara, the Jesuit philosopher who had participated in the 1929 Davos *Hochschulkurse,* the disputation was merely the latest manifestation of a problematic stretching back as far as the pre-Socratics and reappearing throughout the history of philosophy, in Thomas Aquinas and again in Kant, whose doctrine represented an uneasy union between an empiricist's one-sided theory of receptivity and a rationalist's exaggerated confidence in spontaneity. Contemporary criticism of Kant's philosophy was now divided between those who emphasized receptivity and therefore appealed to Kant's theory of human finitude and those who instead emphasized Kant's theory of spontaneity and made it the cornerstone for modernist doctrines of humanistic creativity.[19] Cassirer was therefore attacked as both too modern and not modern enough. While scholars like Przywara were quick to disparage Cassirer for an excessive confidence in the natural sciences and a seemingly dogmatic rationalism, others condemned him as out of step with the intellectual fashion they celebrated as a "resurrection of metaphysics." Such opinions were confirmed by the Italian philosopher Armando Carlini (a participant at Davos), who also saw Kant as the most decisive figure in modern European thought but saw in Heidegger "a decisive overcoming" *(un decisivo superamento)* of all preceding schools.[20]

But critics with greater sympathy for Cassirer were quick to observe that his philosophy of symbolic forms had little to do with the one-sided scientism of his Marburg neo-Kantian teachers and in fact had opened up a viable path for future philosophy. Joachim Ritter (who had studied with Heidegger but received his 1925 doctorate with Cassirer) was especially eager to note that Cassirer's most recent turn to culture represented a decisive break from the constraints of Marburg "scientism" while it also resisted the superficial fashions of Scheler's philosophical anthropology. Cassirer's position was nonetheless firmly based upon an idealistic confidence in the "primacy of reflection," as the author of *The Philosophy of Symbolic Forms* himself affirmed in his methodological introduction: "all contents of culture . . . have as their premise *an original act of mind* [*eine ursprüngliche Tat des Geistes*]." For Ritter this idealistic confidence in the creative capacities of human consciousness marked the decisive difference between Cassirer's philosophy of culture and the rival trends in ontological and metaphysical inquiry that Ritter most associated with Scheler and Heidegger.[21]

It bears repeating that nowhere in the contemporary reports before 1933 was there any intimation that the actual philosophical discussion between Heidegger and Cassirer bore an overtly political meaning. Joachim Ritter himself returned to the Davos *Hochschulkurse* in the early spring of 1931 and remarked on the constant discussion of a *Bildungskrise* (crisis in education) as a phenomenon afflicting all of European thought. Numerous scholars described this crisis as an "alienation between thought and life," and they pronounced their diagnoses in the jargon of existentialism and philosophical anthropology.[22] If there was a political valence to such reports, Ritter and his peers failed to take notice.

But the Nazi seizure of power in 1933 brought a dramatic change in philosophical perspective. Heidegger assumed his post as rector at Freiburg and officially declared his allegiance to the Third Reich, while Cassirer was dismissed from his Hamburg professorship. Accompanied by his wife, he fled Hamburg, and the prestigious chair in philosophy that he had held for many years was converted by the Nazis into a regular *(Ordinarus)* position for racial science *(Rassenkunde)*.[23] Meanwhile, in that same year, Joachim Ritter assumed de facto the responsibilities for instruction in history of philosophy that his teacher Cassirer had left behind.

It is in this suddenly altered political context that in February 1933 Ritter gave his inaugural address at Hamburg, "The Meaning and Limits of the Theory of the Human Being," in which he attacked both Scheler and Heidegger for having introduced irrationalist and metaphysical themes into contemporary philosophy in general and philosophical anthropology in particular. Reviving claims Cassirer had directed against his interlocutor at Davos just a few years before, Ritter excoriated Heidegger's "metaphysical anthropology," warning it would lead Continental philosophy into a cul-de-sac of "scepticism, subjectivism, and mysticism," where it would lose its bond with science and culminate in "the absolutization of one's own ego." Heidegger's metaphysical investigations into the ontological status of the human being, Ritter warned, would bring a baleful turn from science to mere *Weltanschauung*. Whereas philosophy since the ancients had fought against metaphysics and had aligned itself with science, the new metaphysical anthropology threatened an end to "rational clarity" and the abandonment of philosophy as a "critical" discipline.[24]

It would of course be misleading to interpret Ritter's inaugural address as a simple reprisal of Cassirer's critique of Heidegger at Davos and in the 1931 *Kantstudien* review. But the striking coincidence of themes suggests that Ritter retained a sense of philosophical alliance with his teacher, whose professorship at Hamburg would soon be dissolved on April 7, 1933, by Nazi decree. The moral complexities of Ritter's own career are too elaborate for discussion here.[25] As early as November 1933, Ritter would join ranks with approximately one thousand professors and *Dozenten* to sign the "Loyalty Oath of Professors in the German Universities and Institutes of Higher Learning to Adolf Hitler and the Nationalsocialist State" (among whose signatories were twenty-two philosophers, including Arnold Gehlen and Hans-Georg Gadamer).[26] In October 1934 the dean of the philosophical faculty at Hamburg would grant Ritter a prestigious lectureship in "the history of

late-antique and medieval philosophy."[27] But while Ritter advanced with
relative ease, his political relations with the Nazi regime remained strained
due to his open avowal of Marxism in the 1920s and his first marriage to a
woman of Jewish descent. As late as 1939, an official memo warned that
Ritter was less than trustworthy because he had once received instruction
from "a Jewish teacher."[28] Whether Ritter remained genuinely faithful to his
teacher's ideal of philosophy as a "critical" and "scientific" discipline is a
question best left to moralists and not historians. But it seems clear that
when speaking in 1933, he saw in Heidegger's philosophy a certain betrayal
of the ideals Cassirer wished to promote.

This was a rare and still-early sign of a coming transformation in memory. By late autumn of 1934, the scandal of Heidegger's Nazism was widely
known. Retroactively, it introduced a new strain of political judgment into
the memory of the Davos encounter. In an essay for French readers, Maurice
de Gandillac described his experiences in postwar Germany, when a mood
of catastrophe had seized the population "like an epidemic" and spawned a
vogue for philosophical pessimists who "instead insisted most of all on the
paradox of life and excluded from true existence the traditional order of
everyday life and social restraint." He then recalled a memory from Davos:

> Even for superficial readers, there was an accent there, a resonance that
> corresponded better with their neurosis than the cheerful and liberal
> neo-Kantianism of old-fashioned professors. Well before Hitlerism,
> in 1929, at the *Semaines Universitaires de Davos,* in listening to the dis-
> courses over long hours by Ernst Cassirer, an historian so admirably
> intelligent, so balanced, so discreet, and on the other side, the "wood-
> cutter" Heidegger, paradoxical, lyrical, passionately one-sided, we were
> struck to see how the scales tipped from the very beginning, and the
> mass of German students fell prey to the charms of the vehement phi-
> losopher a bit in the same manner that those beyond the Rhine listen-
> ing today fall prey to the magnetism of the Führer.[29]

Here was an early and powerful specimen of the allegory of European philosophy that would emerge with greater strength only after the war: in
de Gandillac's portrait what functioned as memory was now interlaced
with political judgment—Cassirer fell into dignified obsolescence, while

Heidegger prefigured Hitler—although what passed for mere recollection in this scenario referred to events that at the time of the dispute were as yet unknown. It is important to note that de Gandillac had not committed a serious violation of historical narrative. He no doubt understood that by commingling two moments in time, he indulged little more than a rhetorical analogy. But the comparison seemed hardly to require justification: Heidegger's politics, after all, had not emerged ex nihilo. The dramatic confrontation at Davos therefore seemed an appropriate scenario for tracing the origins of a political narrative the consequences of which still lay in the future.

Postwar Memory, 1945–1956

In the years following Ernst Cassirer's death in April 1945, recollections of the Davos disputation began to solidify into a political allegory. The impression that Heidegger had defeated his opponent (though clearly an exaggeration) came to serve as a condensed and highly affecting personal history that symbolized political events of the years to come. An especially rich and poignant illustration can be found in Toni Cassirer's 1948 memoir, *My Life with Ernst Cassirer,* which documents the enduring bond between the philosopher and the wife who was his intellectual equal and companion. Describing Ernst's preparations for the debate, she wrote,

> before our trip to Davos Ernst occupied himself with the details of Heidegger's writings, to which until that point he had not actually dedicated his attentions. Heidegger's abstruse language, which he used so as to extract the "needful" element from the centuries-old customary philosophical terminology, repelled Ernst; but after a little time he had learned what he called this new language, and he treasured Heidegger's works even while in principle he repudiated them.[30]

Toni Cassirer's account of the Cassirers' relations with Heidegger tells us little about the philosophical exchange itself, but it reveals a great deal about the personal unease that would mark their encounter. "We had been expressly prepared for Heidegger's remarkable appearance," she wrote, "his repudiation of every social convention was known to us, as well as his enmity [*Feindschaft*] toward the neo-Kantians, especially against Cohen."

And she adds, almost as if it were an afterthought: "Nor was his tendency toward anti-Semitism unknown to us [*Auch seine Neigung zum Antisemitismus war uns nicht fremd*]."[31]

Toni Cassirer seems to have possessed an uncommon confidence. Born in 1883 into an Austrian-Jewish family in Vienna, she described her father as a well-to-do bourgeois who placed "full trust in assimilation," and she noted that, of five children, she was the only one who regarded this trust with skepticism. Her memoir begins with the revealing comment that her sole political memory from childhood was the Dreyfus Affair. This sensitivity to the challenges facing European Jewry seems to have given her a strong drive to confront cases of apparent anti-Semitism even in polite company. Concerning Heidegger at Davos, she had strong recollections that deserve to be quoted at length:

> His animosity and combativeness were plain to see. The problem, as I understood it, was how I could pass the next fourteen days as the neighbor to this remarkable nemesis when I recognized him as such. But I hoped for Ernst's aid, since he was to be sitting at my right and, I assumed, would lead the table conversation. But things turned out differently. The next morning, following his first lecture, Ernst contracted a powerful flu with a high fever and had to stay in bed for many days. So I now sat together twice daily with this peculiar fellow, who had resolved to drag Cohen's achievements in the dust and, if possible, to vanquish Ernst.[32]

What is remarkable in the passages above is the direct acknowledgment (typically unmentioned in other contemporary memoirs) that Heidegger's anti-Semitism was common knowledge. Even more striking, however, is Toni Cassirer's determination to embarrass the philosopher until she could awaken his hidden sympathy:

> Then the thought occurred to me that I might outwit this sly fox—for so he was reputed to be. I began a naïve conversation with him, as if I knew not the slightest thing about either his philosophical or his personal antipathies. I asked him about all manner of common acquaintances, most of all about his familiarity with Cohen as a person, and in my manner of posing the questions I already took for granted his ready

acknowledgement. Unprompted, I described for him Ernst's relation with Cohen; I spoke of the scandalous treatment which this preeminent scholar had experienced as a Jew; I told him how not a single member of the Berlin faculty had accompanied his burial casket. I divulged to him, his agreement naturally assured, all sorts of particulars about Ernst's life, and I had the pleasure of watching this hard biscuit dissolve as if dipped in warm milk. When Ernst rose from his sickbed Heidegger found himself in a difficult situation for carrying through with his planned hostilities, since he knew personally so much about him. Of course Ernst too, with his goodwill and the respect he granted him, made a frontal assault no easy matter. The battle dissipated into respectable relations, which must have caused wonder amongst the mob of Heidegger elites who followed him.[33]

Did Toni Cassirer actually believe that her conversation with Heidegger had broken through the hard shell of his prejudice? This seems unlikely. She was evidently a woman of formidable intelligence and it is clear that she found him a thoroughly disagreeable person: among the many attributes that repulsed her, she made special mention of Heidegger's "deadly seriousness" and his "complete lack of humor." (Ernst's humor, by contrast, comes through strongly in her memoir, a fact one would hardly suspect given the unrelieved sobriety of his own philosophical writings.) We are permitted to ask, however, whether her postwar recollections of Heidegger benefit from hindsight. She concluded her description by noting that,

on the whole, to the students Heidegger emerged as the victor, because he approached the events of the day quite differently than Ernst. I could sense quite well, what the opposition to the Marburg school and also to Ernst consisted in. *And it was not hard to recognize which direction this man pointed.* When two years later he became the first National-Socialist rector, it did not surprise me so much as it frightened me. For Heidegger's great gift was undeniable, and he was more dangerous than any of the other supporters.[34]

Much of what Toni Cassirer wrote about Heidegger is corroborated elsewhere in memoirs and contemporary reports. In *The Myth of the State* Ernst Cassirer, too, claimed that Heidegger was more dangerous than his colleagues because his philosophical gifts were more powerful; his ideas of fatalism and thrownness helped to weaken the self-confidence of philosophy as a critical and emancipatory instrument. We might also grant that Heidegger "pointed" toward Germany's political descent. More worrisome, however, is the implication that Heidegger "won" and Cassirer "lost" *because of the political differences between them.* This sort of retroactive judgment permits us to dissolve the philosophical disagreement into a political conflict, even if, paradoxically, this is just the self-abandonment of philosophy to political power that Cassirer himself most feared.

A Disputed Detail

After twenty years, the memory of the Davos disputation was now richly laden with historical symbolism and it was now commonplace to describe the debate as an allegory for political events that in 1929 still lay in Germany's future. A notable example can be found in the postwar essay, "Recollections of Ernst Cassirer," written by the Dutch linguist Hendrik J. Pos for publication in the 1949 critical anthology on Cassirer's thought, edited by Paul Arthur Schilpp. As a witness and participant at the Davos *Hochschulkurse,* Pos was well placed to paint an evocative portrait of the two philosophers. He described Cassirer as "the representative of the best in the universalistic traditions of German culture, a man for whom Idealism was the victorious power which is called to mold and spiritualize human life." He was "the heir of Kant" and he

> stood there tall, powerful, and serene. His effect on his audience lay in his mastery of exposition, in the Apollonian element. From the beginning he had within him the liberal culture of Central Europe, the product of a long tradition. In both spiritual lineaments and external appearance, this man belonged to the epoch of Kant, of Goethe, and of Kleist, to each of whom he had dedicated some of his literary efforts.

This is an ennobling portrait. Now here is Pos's memory of Heidegger:

> And over against him stood an altogether different type of man, who struggled with Cassirer over the deepest intentions of Kant's writings.

This man too had a gigantic intellect. As a man, however, he was completely different. Of *petit bourgeois* descent from southeast Germany, he had never lost his accent. In him this was readily forgiven, being taken as a mark of firm-rootedness and peasant genuineness. . . . In his youth he was destined for the priesthood. . . . He ran away, however, and became a renegade. At home as almost no one else in Aristotle and the scholastics, in Kant and Hegel, he constructed for himself a philosophy which, on the side of method, came close to the phenomenology of his teacher, Husserl. In point of content, however, this philosophy was of course entirely his own: There lay feelings at the base of it where were concealed by the gigantic intellectual superstructure. But when one listened to his lectures, listened to this gloomy, somewhat whining and apprehensive tone of voice, then there flowed forth the feelings which this man harbored or at least which he knew how to awaken. These were feelings of loneliness, of oppression, and of frustration, such as one has in anxious dreams.[35]

We must remember that the Dutch linguist greatly admired Cassirer so we should not find the above contrast so surprising. It is nonetheless remarkable that when he recalls the closing moment of the *Arbeitsgemeinschaft,* Pos introduces a startling new detail: "The magnanimous man offered his hand to his opponent: but it was not accepted."[36]

This would have been a strong insult and a striking confirmation of other stories concerning Heidegger's incivility. Pos further noted that this conclusion was "not without human symbolism." It is, of course, not *completely* implausible that things happened this way. From many reports we know that Heidegger did not observe the usual academic proprieties. That he lectured at least once in his ski suit sufficed to make him a scandalous presence. But to fail to grasp his interlocutor's hand at the end of the debate when it was extended to him would have been not only a grotesque violation of convention but also a truly personal affront.

The problem is that there would appear to be no confirmation from any of the other sources that this actually happened. No one else among the many eyewitnesses records this detail. Toni Cassirer did not mention it, though given her meticulous eye for everything that passed between Heidegger and her husband, the omission would be baffling. It is, of course, possible that

Pos was the only one to see it happen. Maybe, for example, it took place some time after the audience had dispersed, or maybe the play of gestures was overly subtle and lost on the other guests. Another possibility would be that Pos was describing only a *symbolic* insult, that Cassirer made *intellectual* gestures of reconciliation that Heidegger refused. (But this would be redundant, for why would Pos note that the insult was "not without human symbolism"?) A further possibility is that Pos was mistaken or had misremembered the event. On balance, the latter seems most probable. Given all that Pos knew about Heidegger's disagreeable personality, and given all that had happened over the intervening two decades, his inclusion of this one detail might be forgiven as a small embellishment of memory. Even more perplexing is the fact, already noted above, that when Heidegger met with de Gandillac and de Towarnicki in the fall of 1945, he actually told them that "he had not hesitated, after long discussions concerning Kant, 'to shake publicly the hand of the Jew Cassirer.'"

It is worth noting that these are words de Gandillac assigns to Heidegger, though de Gandillac places them in quotation marks. It is indeed odd that Heidegger mentioned this detail about Davos to his French guests: Why would he have thought this was an important bit of information when it would have been conventional behavior at an academic conference in 1929 between two esteemed European philosophers? Perhaps, as de Gandillac implies, Heidegger meant to ward off postwar accusations of anti-Semitism. But if so this seems an unimpressive piece of evidence and the infelicitous phrase, "the Jew Cassirer" does little to inspire our confidence that Heidegger was wholly without prejudice. Or, perhaps, Heidegger *himself may have been aware of another story* according to which he had *not* shaken Cassirer's hand. De Gandillac, in his 1998 memoir, also mentions this conflict of memories, about which he says that "if there were a refusal of the extended hand, no trace of it has been left to us, as proven by the enthusiastic lines by Cavaillès that summarize an 'ardent' exchange that for us seemed never to have trespassed the habitual limits of academic courtesy."[37]

Whatever our suspicions about this mystery, we are confronted with contradictory evidence and no sure means of resolving the contradiction. Both narrators are unreliable: Heidegger, because he would soon be asked to defend himself before authorities who could decide whether his right to teach might be reinstated, and Pos, because he felt strongly partial to Cassirer.

Heidegger's grounds for insisting on the truth of his own memory obviously carried greater consequences for his personal career. But that does not mean he was actually telling the truth, nor does it suggest he was lying. Pos, by contrast, had little to gain from falsifying such a detail, except that it served as a fitting conclusion for his story. He was indeed inclined toward symbolism: he ended his recollection with the observation that "The Davos conversations were symbolical of the tragic decline toward which Germany philosophy was hastening."[38]

Tillich and Strauss

Two final accounts from the immediate postwar decade, by Paul Tillich and Leo Strauss, help us to understand a bit more about the place of the Davos debate in European philosophical memory. Tillich, born in 1886, was a Lutheran minister and philosopher with strong sympathies for socialism. He taught theology at the University of Frankfurt from 1929 until 1933, when the Nazis came to power and he was forced to flee to the United States, where he joined the faculty at the Union Theological Seminary in New York City, after which he moved to Harvard Divinity School (1955–1962) and then to the University of Chicago, where he remained on the faculty from 1962 until his death. Tillich knew Cassirer quite well from the early 1920s, when they had both been affiliates in Hamburg at the Warburg Library.[39] History brought them together once again as exiles in New York City, where Tillich helped to convene deliberations for Germany's postwar intellectual reconstruction. Cassirer himself declined to participate in these meetings, partly because he believed the Germans would have to undertake democratic reform on their own, but also because, in Toni Cassirer's words, Ernst "could not share Tillich's optimism" concerning Germany's postwar prospects.[40]

Tillich was also well acquainted with Heidegger from a short period from 1924 to 1925, when they had both taught at the University of Marburg. Although Tillich could boast of a rich understanding of both philosophers and their achievements, he was not himself present at the Davos encounter. However, in late March of 1954 at the Cooper Union Forum in New York, Tillich delivered a public address in which he offered a handful of reflections on Heidegger, his performance at Davos, and his broader role in the history of philosophy. After a brief excursus on general themes of Heidegger's philosophy, Tillich moved on to explain what to him seemed its key—the concept of resoluteness, or *Entschlossenheit*—and then attempted to relate this concept to Heidegger's embrace of the Third Reich. Tillich hastened to note that "one should not judge the worth of a philosopher only in terms of the personal shortcomings of one's life." The example of Plato, who was "foolish enough to become an advisor to the Hitler of his time, the Tyrant of Syracuse," was sufficient to show that great philosophers could make great political errors.[41]

Yet Tillich himself could not resist drawing a connection between Heidegger's political decision in early 1933 and his philosophy, specifically, the idea of resoluteness: With the Nazi seizure of power, Tillich declared, "Heidegger found a lot of resolve, more than he had ever found before." The problem was that Heidegger's resolve was cast adrift without normative orientation: his "resoluteness was, as *we* would say, demonic: that is, it was destructive, antiessential, and without moral justification. And it was this way precisely because Heidegger had no criterion by which to measure his resolve." Tillich then drew a surprising connection:

> Two years [*sic*] prior to Hitler's coming to power there was a very interesting discussion in Switzerland between Cassirer and Heidegger. This discussion probably reveals as much about the situation as can be shown, namely, the conflict between one who, like Cassirer, came from Kantian moral philosophy with rational criteria for thinking and acting, and one who, like Heidegger, defended himself on the notion that there are no such criteria. A year later Cassirer was in exile and Heidegger was the rector of Freiburg.[42]

For Tillich, then, the contrast between Heidegger and Cassirer was not merely of biographical interest, it also held a philosophical significance because it was vivid proof that "pure existentialism cannot provide any answers in the area of moral philosophy and ethics."[43] For Tillich, the Davos debate has primarily an ethico-poliitical rather than an anthropological-metaphysical meaning: ignoring the fourth and foundational question from Kant's *Logic* ("What is Man?"), Tillich claimed that the debate turned chiefly on Kant's normative question, "What should I do?" To this question Cassirer could provide a ready answer in the form of a universally valid ethical law, whereas Heidegger, because his thinking extolled finitude in place of universality, there could be no answer besides a normatively vaccuous re-solve. Needless to say, Tillich's indictment of Heideggerian existentialism, already articulated in roughly the same fashion by Heidegger's student Karl Löwith in an essay for *Les Temps Modernes* in 1946, missed a crucial feature of Heidegger's philosophy: that one's resolution occurs only *in the midst of thrownness*. It also took for granted the principle that it is a necessary task for philosophy to furnish human beings with ethical instruction.[44] Given this premise, Tillich could describe the 1929 encounter as a kind of proving ground for the ethical challenges to come, when Heidegger's philosophy would be "exposed" as a species of political nihilism, while Cassirer's phi-losophy, though politically vanquished, would stand revealed as the last best hope for universalism in the wake of the European catastrophe. That such an interpretation transformed philosophy into a quasi-mythic struggle be-tween darkness and light did little to inhibit its appeal.

The political philosopher Leo Strauss gave these themes an even more radical interpretation in 1956 in a memorial lecture for Kurt Riezler, which he first delivered before the graduate faculty of the New School for Social Research in New York.[45] As already noted in Chapter 2, Riezler was a close friend of Strauss's and had given a paper at the 1929 Davos *Hochschulkurse*. Strauss himself was not actually present at Davos (though several historians have incorrectly placed him there). In the early 1920s both Riezler and Strauss, like so many students of philosophy at that time, felt drawn to Hei-degger's radical manner of thought, and it seems fair to say that one cannot comprehend the theories of political right that later made Strauss the titular head of a prominent (though admittedly controversial) school without under-standing *both* his attraction to Heidegger's philosophy *and* his ultimate dis-illusionment when Heidegger's philosophy culminated in a political deci-sion favoring the Third Reich. In his 1956 address Strauss acknowledged Heidegger's charismatic effect on his friend: "It would be an understate-ment," observed Strauss, "to say that Heidegger was the greatest contempo-rary power which Riezler ever encountered." Following a pattern already well established among Heidegger's students, Strauss praised his teacher's originality but lamented the paralysis of critical thinking he induced in so many followers:

> Heidegger surpasses all his contemporaries by far. This could be seen long before he became known to the general public. As soon as he

appeared on the scene, he stood in its center and he began to dominate it. His domination grew almost continuously in extent and in intensity. He gave adequate expression to the prevailing unrest and dissatisfaction because he had clarity and certainty, if not about the whole way, at least about the first and decisive steps. The fermentation or the tempest gradually ceased. Eventually a state has been reached which the outsider is inclined to describe as paralysis of the critical faculties; philosophizing seems to have been transformed into listening with reverence to the incipient *mythoi* of Heidegger.[46]

This was a familiar indictment: It closely resembled Cassirer's claim a decade earlier in *The Myth of the State* that Heidegger had solidified the hold of political myth over modern German consciousness. But Strauss strayed from the usual indictments of Heidegger's philosophy when he explained that the deeper fault for the decay of philosophy in the modern world lay not with Heidegger's existentialism but with the liberal rationalism that should have blocked its ascent.[47] To drive this claim home, Strauss quoted a passage from Virgil's *Aeneid,* extolling a "grave and pious man" who is capable of silencing the bloodthirsty mob.

Strauss's implication was clear: the tragedy of philosophy in Germany was that no one among Heidegger's opponents could speak with equal moral authority. In an earlier period, students had looked to Hermann Cohen as their paradigm of philosophical charisma and ethical instruction. But in the 1920s only Heidegger conveyed the same passion for genuine philosophy, though Heidegger was bent on destroying the foundations on which Cohen and his rationalist protégés had built their vaunted ideals. And Cassirer in particular was no match for Heidegger. For Strauss's friend, the outcome at Davos seemed almost foreordained: "Riezler took the side of Heidegger without any hesitation. There was no alternative. Mere sensitivity to greatness would have dictated Riezler's choice." Heidegger was for Strauss a *great* philosopher; Cassirer was not: "Cassirer represented the established academic position. He was a distinguished professor of philosophy but he was no philosopher. He was erudite but he had no passion. He was a clear writer but his clarity and placidity were not equaled by his sensitivity to the problems." In the symbolic confrontation at Davos, it was Cassirer who most deserved reproof, because he typified what Strauss saw as the retreat of modern liberalism into political quietism and its abandonment of philosophy's highest ethical mission:

> Having been a disciple of Hermann Cohen he had transformed Cohen's philosophic system, the very center of which was ethics, into a philosophy of symbolic forms in which ethics had silently disappeared. Heidegger on the other hand explicitly denies the possibility of ethics because he feels that there is a revolting disproportion between the idea of ethics and those phenomena which ethics pretended to articulate.[48]

Strauss evidently felt little but disdain for Cassirer's work, given what he saw as its insufficient devotion to the *political* questions that for him were the highest and perhaps the *only* serious questions of philosophy. Because Cassirer had ceded this terrain to his opponent without a struggle, Heidegger was free to declare in vain all further attempts to provide a transcendental grounding for political norms. It remained uncertain whether Strauss himself *accepted* this nihilistic verdict as applying to *all* political norms, or whether instead (as seems more likely), Strauss simply believed that Cassirer's apparent defeat signaled the need to provide modern politics with new and decisively *non-liberal* foundations. In any event, what Strauss called intellectual "probity" and political prudence required that his deeper intentions would remain in principle difficult to fathom. But his apparent hostility toward historicist anti-foundationalism and his manifest attempt to revive a premodern tradition of natural right suggest that, for Strauss, the Davos debate served as perverse evidence that Straussian doctrine was correct.

In Living Memory

More recently, the memory of the Davos disputation has come to symbolize a division in Continental thought that is political *and* philosophical at once. For Otto Friedrich Bollnow, who drafted the transcript of the *Arbeitsgemeinschaft* along with Ritter, memories of the dispute remained still vivid even a half century later: Heidegger had invited Bollnow, along with Eugen Fink, to attend the conference, and Bollnow would later recall the feeling of tense anticipation as the audience waited for the discussion to begin. The

conversation between the two philosophers seemed to embody "the philosophical situation of the time." It was a meeting between two distinctive
eras in philosophical history: "a tradition that had arrived at a rich flourish-
ing was once again embodied in Cassirer's imposing figure," while in Heidegger, Bollnow saw "a new time breaking through with the consciousness
of a radical new beginning."[49] The conversation did not flow smoothly: "So
far as I can trust my memory," Bollnow writes, "Cassirer began every time
in a quite congenial fashion by insisting that they were ultimately of one
opinion, and Heidegger answered him, with a sharpness bordering on im-
polite, that one must first of all clearly recognize the differences between
them." Most noteworthy is Bollnow's assertion that the debate ended "without consequence [*ohne Ergebnis*]," a claim that contrasts with the majority's
view that Heidegger emerged as the clear victor. Bollnow also notes—and he
is the only one to mention this—that it was proposed to continue the conversation the following day but Heidegger did not wish to do so.[50]

The case of Emmanuel Lévinas is more complex. In a handful of inter-
views published toward the end of his life, he shared his rich memories of
the debate and the two philosophers whose conversation had impressed the
young student as "the creation and the end of the world."[51] For Lévinas, perhaps more than any other eyewitness, the disputation was to represent a
true milestone in his career, and his complicated assessment of its significance reveals a great deal about both his own divided consciousness as a
philosopher and the greater division of European history he had witnessed
firsthand. Lévinas shared the widespread impression that Cassirer symbolized "an order that was going to be defeated."[52] In an interview with François Poirié, Lévinas recalled Cassirer as

> a refined humanist of patrician bearing, neo-Kantian, great disciple of
> Hermann Cohen, modern interpreter of Kant starting out from the
> intelligibility of the sciences, very close to our own Léon Brunschvicg;
> and, like him, in line with the tradition of rationalism, aesthetics, and
> political ideas deriving from the nineteenth century. Very far, of course,
> from the positivism and quite banal scientism, but who was persuaded
> nonetheless like our teacher Léon Brunschvicg that invention in math-
> ematics had been inner life itself, and that meditating upon the inevita-
> bility of death is not the first thought of a philosopher.

It is clear that Lévinas admired Cassirer, whose philosophy, for Lévinas, stood for the most cherished values of modern European philosophy and whose diminished stature after Davos signalled "the end of a certain humanism."[53] As Lévinas explained, "it was following this historic confrontation that the thoughts inspired by Kant and the heritage of the Enlightenment as represented principally by Cassirer vanished from Germany."[54] But it is apparent from his words that Lévinas could only recall Cassirer with a certain distanced admiration. Not so his memory of Heidegger:

> Then standing on the other side there was Heidegger, the philosopher who did not depart from exact science, of physico-mathematical science taken as the source of intelligibility and for the direction of thinking. But the Heidegger at Davos brings me round to Heidegger at Freiburg, for whom Being was understood from its verbal form as an event of Being that is at issue for the human being. A necessary sense for the understanding of every being. For Heidegger, science is of course one of the modes of intelligibility—but it is already a derivative modality. He searched for the origin in the human being, whose being consists precisely in its understanding of Being, and from that point at which the Being of beings takes its sense. There was a new path, a radicalization of philosophical questioning, a priority over and against mathematical-physical scientific reflection. A thinking whose repercussions one certainly must not fail to acknowledge for all of the philosophy of our century. A new culmination for Greek thinking, which appeared not only as the twilight of modern science but as the awakening of the question of Being and perhaps also as the site of its initial perplexities. But today also perplexities indicating lines that are in their own way necessary and dramatic, never simple errors or deviations. A new pathos of thought.[55]

Lévinas's memory of the encounter remained troubled. In his major works of the postwar era, Lévinas would develop a sophisticated critique of Heidegger's philosophical legacy, and each step only magnified the distance he had traveled, both philosophically and politically, from his earliest years of apprenticeship in Freiburg, when he had still counted as an admiring member of the phenomenological circle. Already by the time he composed

Existence and Existents (in captivity between 1940 and 1945), he announced a need to "leave the climate of that philosophy," while insisting that "we cannot leave it for a philosophy that would be pre-Heideggerian."[56] And even in his last years he could never accept the view that Heidegger's philosophy might be simply dismissed. Many years later, when speaking with Richard Sugarman, he declared that "you cannot bypass Heidegger as a thinker."[57] His own debts aligned him with the teacher who had explored "a different direction than the . . . Kantian" and "problems more important and more fundamental than those of the grounding of the sciences."[58]

But Lévinas also confessed that in 1929 he had felt something like a "shudder" *(frémissement)*. Despite his philosophical alignment with Heidegger, he later claimed to have known *at the time* that Cassirer represented "an order that was going to be defeated." Yet he acknowledged that retroactive judgment came with a certain risk:

> Nowadays one has a certain shift in perspective that perhaps falsifies one's memories; I think that Heidegger announced a world that was going to be overturned. You know who he was going to join three years later: one would nonetheless have needed to have the gift of prophecy in order to foresee this already at Davos. I felt for a long while—during the terrible years—that I had sensed it then, despite my enthusiasms. The judgments of value attached to both the one and the other have certainly needed to change with the times. And I had greatly reproached myself during the Hitlerian years for having preferred Heidegger at Davos.[59]

Given all we have learned about Heidegger's complicity with Nazism, it is hardly surprising that Lévinas's memory of the dispute reveals a troubled and deeply divided conscience. But it would be wrong to simplify our political understanding of the past through a facile realignment of the two sides, by insisting, for example, that Lévinas and Cassirer were *both* simply exponents of "humanism" confronting Heidegger's "anti-humanism."[60] Terms of such magnitude are an easy temptation but they lead us to falsify both memory and philosophy. What made the memory so difficult for Lévinas was the *impossibility* of resolving the dispute to his own satisfaction. And the truth is that he was riven in two, between his admiration for Cassirer as an exponent of ethical universalism, and his unshakable conviction that the future for European philosophy lay with Heidegger, even though the fulfillment of Heidegger's legacy also required its overcoming. Perhaps for this reason Lévinas confessed skepticism that the problems of the Davos disputation would ever be resolved. To him it signified an "impassable antinomy," a division that was "of a profound antiquity" and that concerned not only a specific moment in modern European history but actually the whole of what he called "our civilization."[61] Lévinas could hardly look upon this division in Continental philosophy from a safe distance, for the truth is that Lévinas himself was divided in two.

A similarly complex and historically expansive view was given by Hans Blumenberg (1920–1996), the great German historian of philosophy who drew inspiration from Cassirer's philosophy and was perhaps best known for his contributions to the study of myth and his theoretical debate with Karl Löwith concerning the processes of secularization and the "legitimacy of the modern age." In a brief essay (published posthumously), Blumenberg offered the intriguing if highly speculative suggestion that the Davos disputation might be seen as reprising the theological controversy that took place in Marburg 400 years earlier between Martin Luther and Ulrich Zwingli over the character of Christ's presence in the Eucharist: "Being *or* sense, substance *or* function, reality *or* meaning." For Blumenberg, the concepts at issue between Heidegger and Cassirer appeared to be a more-than-coincidental "reproduction" of the Protestant controversy concerning "realism" and "docetism," between the orthodox view that the body of Christ is really present in the host, and the contrarian view (commonly regarded as heretical) that Christ's embodiment is merely an illusion and that the bread and wine can only be said to signify his body and blood though they are not literally so. For Cassirer, too, the problem of substance had been displaced by the problem of function: modern science had arrived at a point where it dealt with only a symbolic order without reference to a metaphysical substrate of independent reality. Cassirer was also to this extent, in Blumenberg's eyes, a distant cousin to Husserl, whose investigations were confined to intentional phenomena as acts of *meaning.* Heidegger, by contrast, understood phenomenology not as the study of mental acts of meaning but as a contemplative study of that which "shows itself," thereby signaling a shift of the subject's position from agency to receptivity and a shift in the "dignity

of the questioner's position." Husserl's own struggle against all varieties of
worldly reductionism, such as historicism, psychologism, and anthropolo-
gism, could analogously be understood as recapitulating the ancient Gnos-
tic's hostility toward all doctrines of secularization that spoke of divine
incarnation in an impure world. It remained for Heidegger to restore the
impurity of worldly existence, bringing phenomenology into direct conflict
with Cassirer. As Blumenberg explained:

> Against the disjunction between the concepts of "substance" and
> "function" which had already been introduced by Cassirer in 1910,
> Heidegger decided with Luther, in favor of substance as the first and
> the *unique* category, against the functional propagation of categories
> into "symbolic forms"—and thus in favor of . . . the conventions of the
> "realists." But at issue now was Being itself—and who wouldn't want to
> be in its vicinity?[62]

We can admire Blumenberg for his acuity of insight into broad lineages of
intellectual history, even if we remain skeptical as to his attempt at comparing the Heidegger-Cassirer debate to hoary quarrels over the body of Christ.
But we should also welcome his interpretation insofar as it ventures beyond
the customary reading of the Davos dispute as a political allegory. He struck
with greater precision with his suggestion that Cassirer's preference for the
symbolic presupposed the primacy of human agency, whereas Heidegger's
modification of phenomenology into a study of what "shows itself" cast the
human being into a largely receptive position.

Unfortunately, Blumenberg did not further develop this interpretation
but only obscured its importance by returning to politics as the ultimate
meaning of the debate. The historical outcome of the Davos encounter, he
claimed, could not be dismissed as merely "a fact of contingent rhetorical
capacities or the mentality of the time or bids for dominance between
schools." Blumenberg actually saw its political consequences as so self-
evident that he brought his essay to an abrupt conclusion with a verdict favoring politics over philosophy: "Whoever listens with forewarning at the
rectoral address of 1933 will be able at least to agree, however reluctantly—
that it was about politics and not about philosophy, or about the one as a
mere instrument [*Organon*] of the other." Even for those who insisted as

a matter of philosophical principle on their "blindness for 'meaning'" could hardly fail to admit that Davos was itself just like Being: it "shows itself."[63] The danger in such interpretations is they exhibit a peculiar readiness to evacuate philosophical meaning in favor of political consequences, relying on the sort of metaphysical assumption Blumenberg made explicit, that political events are *real* while philosophical arguments are merely *meaningful*. Whether Blumenberg actually meant this as a serious argument remains uncertain. But it seems most probable he wished only to drive home his political verdict by means of parody, making history into a theater for the transsubstantiation of political realities across time.

Bourdieu and Habermas

The last two decades have seen a resurgence of interest in the Davos *Auseinandersetzung*. No doubt this is due in part to renewed debate over the nature and extent of Heidegger's support for Nazism, and in part to the revival of enthusiasm for Cassirer's philosophical legacy, which for many years fell into eclipse but now seems to be enjoying a true renaissance of scholarly attention, especially in Germany. The literature addressing their encounter is now extensive. While a comprehensive analysis of all recent contributions to the discussion concerning the significance of the Heidegger-Cassirer debate would no doubt prove valuable, it would also require superhuman patience, for both the author and the reader as well. Here it must suffice to take a closer look at only two very different cases, both of which may prove instructive for understanding just what the Davos encounter has signified—and continues to signify—for both memory and history of recent Continental ideas.

In 1988, the French sociologist Pierre Bourdieu intervened in the then-raging controversy in French philosophical circles over Heidegger's Nazism with an extended essay, *The Political Ontology of Martin Heidegger*.[64] A sophisticated theorist of culture and social power whose so-called reflexive sociology combined insights from phenomenology and structuralist Marxism and anthropology, Bourdieu, by socioeconomic origin an outsider, was especially attentive to the way that education and cultural sophistication functioned as modes of "symbolic capital," and he used his considerable skills as a polemicist to puncture the inflated pretensions of the

French intellectual elite. His aggressive yet slender book offered a brisk re-tort to the diverse group of French Heideggerians whom he suspected of minimizing the extent of the German philosopher's complicity with the Third Reich so as to safeguard their own intellectual inheritance.

Bourdieu's sociological insight into the Davos disputation is quite reveal-ing. To understand his intervention in greater detail, it may be helpful to re-call the peculiar role Heidegger played in French intellectual life throughout the later twentieth century. While the French philosophical establishment has always been riven with intense disagreement concerning its various schools and traditions, it is nonetheless fair to say (as shown in the philo-sophical and historical studies by Tom Rockmore and Ethan Kleinberg) that beginning in the 1930s, Heidegger stood as a preeminent model or *maître-penseur* for many French thinkers of various political persuasions.[65] While the scandal of Heidegger's collaboration with the Nazis was a matter of in-tense discussion, even in the immediate postwar period (when the fascist as-sociations of German existential phenomenology proved especially worri-some for Jean-Paul Sartre and the existentialist writers surrounding *Les Temps Modernes*), the controversy reignited with even greater passion in 1987 with the French publication of a book by the Chilean historian Victor Farias bear-ing the title *Heidegger et le nazisme.*[66] Farias's study provoked much outrage, and legitimately so, because it seemed to develop a wholesale indictment of Heidegger's philosophical legacy by an associative logic, exposing, for exam-ple, the young Heidegger's interest in the Catholic theologian Abraham a Santa Clara and then demonstrating that the latter was a notorious anti-Semite. Following the publication of Farias's book, the controversy in France exploded, eventually spreading to Germany as well as the English-speaking world.[67] For some time it appeared as if French intellectuals' discussion of Heidegger's politics would never cease.

What therefore made Bourdieu's intervention in this debate so unusual is that, unlike most of the commentaries, it was written from a *sociological* perspective: Heidegger's work was to be understood not as body of argu-mentative claims but rather as a repertoire of strategic possibilities, the purpose of which was to secure advantage within the finite system of sym-bolic power that Bourdieu termed the "philosophical field." The governing premise of this sociological perspective was that the philosophical field is an arena of symbolic struggle that serves to express sociopolitical commitments. But because the philosophical discipline understands itself as obeying a set of system-immanent rules, sociopolitical commitments cannot be expressed directly but must pass instead through a matrix of disciplinary "censorship." For Bourdieu it followed that even the more subtle points of philosophical argumentation could be understood as *encrypted* forms of symbolic power. Concerning Heidegger's philosophy in particular, Bourdieu set out to prove that it served as the coded and strategic expression of Heidegger's own historically conditioned position as an exponent of "conservative revolution." And because Bourdieu believed that the philosophical field necessarily permits only a finite set of strategic options, Heidegger's debate with Cassirer served as an empirical illustration for how this symbolic game of domination was actually played out against one strategically significant opponent. Heidegger's philosophical assault on Cassirer's neo-Kantianism, claimed Bourdieu, was revealed as a strategic gesture within the larger context of the conservative-revolutionary assault on Weimar-era liberalism. Thus, for example, Heidegger's technical remarks in *Being and Time* laying down a preference for genuine "care" *(Sorge)* as against a degraded "solicitude" *(Fürsorge)* could be understood as a philosophically encrypted statement of radical-conservative protest against the Weimar Republic's social-welfare legislation.

Bourdieu was justly celebrated both for the originality of his theoretical and empirical sociology and for his bracing manner of composition, which often seemed to hover strangely between densely reasoned scholasticism and political polemic. Yet even champions of Bourdieu's method will likely agree that *The Political Ontology of Martin Heidegger* is not one of his most successful efforts. The difficulty may have something to do with the reflexive discomfort of a book that itself owes a methodological debt to phenomenology—Bourdieu's early work reveals the serious influence of both Husserl and Merleau-Ponty—even while it purports to explain not just phenomenology but *all* of philosophy with the instruments of sociological disenchantment. Bourdieu was keenly aware that his own intellectual formation and sociological theory could not claim immunity from the corrosive analysis of "symbolic capital" he had pioneered.[68] But there is a difference between a reflexive analysis that sees one's own theory as a strategy among others and the reflexive dissonance that occurs when one's own theory claims to possess a certain political status—in Bourdieu's case, his

theory asserted a proud alliance with the post-Marxian political Left—
while the reflexive operation of those methods revealed their quite different
political origins. How, in other words, could Bourdieu attack phenomenology for its specifically reactionary political markings when his own theory
demonstrated it could be put to different political ends? The implicit answer, forced on Bourdieu by his own sociological achievement, was that the
temporary alliance he discerned between Heidegger's philosophy and the
Weimar-era ideology of conservative revolution was little more than a *contingent* realization of possibilities that were themselves constantly changing and becoming available for creative reappropriation. This meant that
Bourdieu's sociological findings had little relevance to current debates over
the political legitimacy of Heidegger's philosophy in contemporary France.
Bourdieu's own success at integrating phenomenology into his left-oriented
sociological method therefore revealed the deflationary lesson, that any
claim by sociology to reduce the meaning of a philosophy to a single,
political-historical matrix was bound to fail.

The unfortunate lapse into performative self-contradiction that marked
Bourdieu's sociological interpretation of the Davos encounter may serve as a
useful illustration for the more general aporias that may arise when philosophy comes into contact with political memory.[69] The attempt to bypass
philosophical meaning *entirely,* by decrypting its claims into historically
conditioned gestures of power, runs a serious risk insofar as it cannot explain how any meaning, including its own, will survive the analysis. This
aporia shows itself in various forms depending on one's discipline: where
the sociologist may appeal to a deeper "knowledge" unavailable to the participants, regarding the social power underlying their argumentation, the
historian may be tempted to claim possession of a different species of privileged insight in the form of the future, about which the participants could
have little knowledge. Blumenberg revealed the true limitations of this
quasi-historical method when he claimed that the political outcome of the
Davos disputation already showed itself in 1929 (although this claim was
only possible given premonitory knowledge).

A salutary alternative to the above methods was offered by Jürgen Habermas in a speech on "The Liberating Power of Symbols," delivered at the
University of Hamburg in 1995 at the convergence of two ceremonial events,
both honoring Jewish intellectuals who had fled Germany a half century

before: the dedication of the newly restored Warburg Library for Cultural Studies and a commemoration for Ernst Cassirer on the fiftieth anniversary of his death. With an unparalleled sensitivity for the philosophical as well as the political significance of what he called Cassirer's "humanistic legacy," Habermas made use of this occasion to exceed the customary rituals of public memory by reintroducing some of the key themes and principles from *The Philosophy of Symbolic Forms,* which he summarized as a "semiotic transformation of Kantian transcendental philosophy."[70] Evident throughout this theory, Habermas explained, was a model of the mind as a "world-projective spontaneity," which creates for itself a plurality of symbolic domains. Although Cassirer had derived this understanding of the mind as a creative faculty chiefly from Kant, Habermas also took care to note the influence of Wilhelm von Humboldt's linguistic theories (implicitly acknowledging his own debts to Cassirer's philosophy of language). But notwithstanding this relatively sympathetic overview, Habermas did not refrain from criticizing what he considered a central weakness in Cassirer's thought—that while it struggled to overcome the Kantian dualism between subject and object, it nonetheless retained "an epistemological standpoint" in the sense that it interpreted "linguistic world-disclosure on the model of the transcendental constitution of objects of possible experience."[71] For Habermas, this meant that Cassirer never managed to surmount the Kantian-transcendental presupposition that spontaneity, which itself constitutes reality, lies beyond its sphere of expression as an unconditioned and "extramundane mind."[72] This proved ultimately fatal for Cassier, because he could not theorize his own discursive position.

To Habermas, this apparent vulnerability in Cassirer's philosophy was revealed at Davos: Heidegger himself had already touched upon the crucial weakness in Cassirer's transcendental presuppositions when he observed that for Cassirer "the terminus a quo is utterly problematical." Cassirer, in other words, could offer no theoretically convincing account of the character of the human subject from which the creative action of symbolization first emerged. Had Cassirer tried to explain the character of this human being without lapsing into metaphysical dogma, Habermas reasoned, Cassirer "would have had to give language and the lifeworld a central position in the construction of symbolic forms." However, because he failed to take this step into the social- and life-philosophical constitution of the human subject,

Cassirer could never overcome his "epistemologically constricted vision." Nor could he develop a satisfactory theory concerning the normative premises and implications of the philosophy of symbolic forms:

> This may be the systematic reason why the controversy in Davos did not touch on the real crux of the dispute. The conflict between Cassirer and Heidegger, which extended into the political domain, was not played out. The opposition between the decent, cultured spirit of a cosmopolitan humanism, and that fatal rhetoric set on throwing man back into the "hardness of his fate," was reflected only in a contrast of gestures and mentalities.[73]

In the Davos disputation Habermas saw lessons of potential relevance to both philosophy and politics. But insofar as neither participant seemed willing to develop his philosophical doctrine into an explicit theory of social existence, the political lessons were accessible only via the philosophical debate. Any possible social-theoretical consequences of the dispute passed without recognition within a nonpolitical contest between anthropological types, fatalism *versus* spontaneity. And because both Heidegger and Cassirer had failed to make these consequences explicit, the political significance of their confrontation remained obscure, revealing itself only in a dumb show of conflicting "gestures and mentalities," precisely the sorts of signs and rudimentary metaphors of politics and persona that first tempted their own contemporaries in the 1930s to transform the debate into a cultural-political allegory.

With this conclusion, Habermas tried to acknowledge the latent political ramifications of the Davos debate without sacrificing its manifest philosophical content. This was a subtle interpretation indeed. But it is crucial to note its deeper irony, that it already presupposed that the disengaged standpoint of Cassirer's epistemology was more or less mistaken: In his political sympathies, of course, Habermas would continue to see himself as Cassirer's ally, insofar as he shared the earlier philosopher's passion for a modernist and emancipatory politics grounded in critical reason. In his philosophical sympathies, however, Habermas appears here in a rather different light: for while he retains a fidelity to reason that Heidegger would have strenuously resisted, Habermas seems to have taken on board

Heidegger's view that neo-Kantianism suffers from a decontextualized and implicitly metaphysical model of the human being. Though Habermas seems unwilling to say so directly, his interpretation of Cassirer's philosophical difficulties thus presupposes that Heidegger was on this crucial point correct. Indeed, it may be that we have yet to appreciate the depth of Heidegger's enduring influence on Habermas, who, preceding the scandals born from the postwar publication of *An Introduction to Metaphysics*, could still praise Heidegger as "my most influential teacher." Habermas responded to these early scandals in an essay, "Thinking with Heidegger against Heidegger," a title which, as he later acknowledged, still revealed the younger author as a "devoted Heidegger disciple."[74] The Habermasian critique of Cassirer's conception of transcendental consciousness thus emerges from a critique of metaphysics that retains a subterranean debt to Heidegger that Habermas himself seems unwilling to disavow. Even Habermas, it seems, could not wholly succeed in closing the gap between philosophy and politics.[75]

This is yet another irony in the ongoing *Auseinandersetzung* with the memory of the Davos encounter. The notion that we might ever close that gap without destroying the very substance of intellectual life remains, I believe, dubious at best. Even today, readings of the Davos debate as discerning as Habermas's remain exceptional. More typical are those that commit what I have called an allegorical strategy of interpretation, whereby a disagreement concerning a philosophical problem is treated as if it were nothing but an outward manifestation of political struggle. The true danger in allegory, however, is that by dissolving the philosophical into the political, it threatens to divest us of any remaining criteria by which to decide intellectual debate other than the anti-intellectual contingencies of sheer power. For the ultimate tragedy of the Davos encounter is not that it ended in victory for politics of the wrong kind. The deeper tragedy is that it ended in politics at all.

Conclusion

What a piece of work is a man, how noble in reason, how infinite in faculties, in form and moving how express and admirable, in action how like an angel, in apprehension how like a god! the beauty of the world, the paragon of animals—and yet, to me, what is this quintessence of dust?

—*Hamlet,* Act. 2, Scene 2

In the *Jäsche Logic* Kant is recorded as saying that the three great questions of critical philosophy—"What can I know?" "What should I do?" and "What may I hope?"—find supplementation and grounding in a fourth question, "*Was ist der Mensch?*" or "What is the human being?"[1] In the more than two centuries that now separate us from Kant's pathbreaking contributions to modern philosophy, the urgency of this question has grown only more pronounced, even while it seems we have barely progressed toward a consensus as to its possible resolution. If anything, our grasp of its significance and its status had only grown more obscure. Is it even a proper question for philosophy? If so, then in what form would its answer appear? If it is empirical, which sorts of evidence does it require? If it is transcendental, what is to prevent an aporia among the various factions who claim already to possess a priori knowledge of its solution?

For Continental philosophy in the postwar era, this anthropological question retains a special poignancy. Insofar as Continental philosophy today can still claim to be a coherent intellectual tradition, its identity is bound to history and is therefore burdened by the memory of events, the unresolved meaning of which constitutes something like a permanent crisis in human self-understanding. Philosophy and memory remain in this sense intertwined. As I have tried to suggest in the preceding pages, the memory of the Heidegger-Cassirer dispute continues to play an important role in this anthropological and philosophical crisis. The dispute itself, of course, did not end in a decisive manner with the victory of one philosopher over the other. But it may be precisely *because* their conversation remains undecided that it seems still to offer an instructive allegory for a series of philosophical questions that themselves remain unanswered and, perhaps, unanswerable.

The *Letter on "Humanism"* and the *Essay on Man*

In 1944, from the safety of his newfound home in the United States, Cassirer completed his penultimate work and his last summation of his symbolic-forms philosophy, *An Essay on Man: An Introduction to the Philosophy of Human Culture,* the very title of which expressed his hopes of addressing a new audience in the Anglophone world. In its pages he observed that modern philosophy now found itself in a "strange situation," that even as the empirical human sciences made steady progress each within their own domains, all hope seemed to have been lost of appealing to an established authority who might coordinate their efforts so as to reach some consensus on the essential nature of humanity. "Our technical instruments for observation and experimentation have been immensely improved," Cassirer wrote, "and our analyses have become sharper and more penetrating. We appear, nevertheless, not to have found a method for the mastery and organization of this material." Cassirer granted that this crisis in anthropological understanding not wholly new: in the late 1920s Max Scheler had observed that humankind confronted itself as an enigma. But Cassirer understood that in the intervening years the crisis had grown far more acute and had assumed truly civilizational proportions: the anarchy in rival conceptions of the human being was not merely a "theoretical problem," Cassirer warned, it represented "an imminent threat to the whole extent of our ethical and cultural life."[2]

   In 1946 Heidegger issued his own contribution to this revived debate over philosophical anthropology in the so-called *Letter on "Humanism,"* a densely written address to a postwar European readership that, much like Cassirer's own *Essay on Man,* served as both a summation and a subtle modification of philosophical claims its author had first introduced twenty years before. Heidegger, too, professed to recognize the urgency of the new era. To the query from his French colleague Jean Beaufret, *"Comment redonner un sens au mot 'Humanisme'?"* ("How can one restore sense to the

word 'humanism'?"), Heidegger responded that perhaps it was time to move
beyond terms freighted with such an obviously metaphysical meaning. For
the philosophical and cultural stance to which some wished to assign the
vaunted name "humanism" was actually a mask for metaphysical subjectivism according to which the human being reigned supreme as the principle
and ground for all reality. Such a subjectivism, Heidegger warned, could
proffer no solution to the modern crisis. Heidegger hastened to explain that
his dissent did not signal a political rejection of an essentially humane world:
"Because we are speaking against 'humanism,'" he wrote, "people fear a defense of the inhuman and a glorification of barbaric brutality." Nor did he
mean to endorse what some might fear was a species of "irrationalism." He
acknowledged the concern that his own emphasis on ontology could appear
to displace logic, but this was because logic as conventionally understood
remained trapped in representational thinking. He also acknowledged the
worry that *Being and Time* might seem to have neglected ethics, but this was
because he wished to cast light on a mode of thinking that preceded the
distinction between practical and theoretical philosophy. "It is time to break
the habit of overestimating philosophy and of thereby asking too much of
it," Heidegger concluded. "What is needed in the present world crisis is less
philosophy, but more attentiveness in thinking."[3]

We may regard both of these statements—the *Letter on "Humanism"* and
the *Essay on Man*—as early interventions in the multivalent controversy
over humanism that would preoccupy Continental philosophers in the
immediate postwar era.[4] That Heidegger played a major role in this controversy is of course well known insofar as his statement was meant as a corrective to Sartre's effort to define existentialism as a humanism. That Cassirer,
too, played a role in this controversy is rarely acknowledged, an omission
due in part to the fact that, following his exile in 1933 and his death in 1945,
his very name suffered a fractional eclipse and, for at least a generation, was
rarely heard in European philosophical conversation. But in revisiting these
two texts, one discerns almost immediately how they remain locked in
controversy.

Cassirer sought to justify his discussion of the "anthropological question"
with the observation that its status was not only theoretical but in fact practical and actually of urgent ethical relevance for the contemporary world. Heidegger insisted on the contrary that the emphasis on practical significance

was misplaced. He objected *even to the distinction* between theoretical and practical reflection and called instead for a mode of philosophy whose very action would be simply the recollection of Being: thinking, he declared, "acts insofar as it thinks." Yet this difference should not obscure the fact that both Cassirer and Heidegger wrote in full awareness that contemporary philosophy was in a state of crisis, and both believed that a true resolution to this crisis would require a deepened understanding of what it is to be human. Their essential disagreement was as follows. For Cassirer, the human being is essentially a being endowed with a distinctive capacity for spontaneous creation. This creative capacity is

> man's highest power and it designates at the same time the natural boundary of our human being. In language, in religion, in art, in science, man can do no more than to build up his own universe—a symbolic universe that enables him to understand and interpret, to articulate and organize, to synthesize and universalize his human experience.

Human culture as a whole could therefore be described as "the process of man's progressive self-liberation." And the evidence of our capacity for symbolization would reveal itself wherever humanity turned its gaze: "This *spontaneity* and *productivity*," Cassirer averred, "*is the very center of all human activities.*"[5] For Heidegger, however, the essence of the human being was to be found not in a capacity for production but rather in a special kind of receptivity by virtue of which the human being stood within what he called "the openness of Being." The emphasis on spontaneity was therefore misplaced, insofar as the essence of human existence was something more "enigmatic." As Heidegger explained, "But here the enigmatic shows itself: the human being is in thrownness [*der Mensch ist in der Geworfenheit*]. This means that the human being, as the ek-sisting counterthrow [*Gegenwurf*] of being, is more than *animal rationale* precisely to the extent that he is less bound up with the human being conceived from subjectivity. The human being is not the lord of beings. The human being is the shepherd of Being."[6] Heidegger objected to the image of spontaneity because it seemed to install the human being as the unconditioned "lord of beings," that is, as the metaphysical ground and point of origin for all reality. While he granted that "Being is cleared for the human being in ecstatic projection

[*Entwurf*]," he hastened to add that "this projection *does not create being*."
Heidegger concluded that the human being "stands out" into the "clearing
of Being" and does so only and precisely "out of its thrown essence [*aus sei-
nem geworfenen Wesen*]."[7]

Thrownness or Spontaneity?

As Cassirer and Heidegger understood, both conceptions of the human
being have deep and ancient roots in the philosophical tradition. But we
should not find it surprising that it was Kant's philosophy most of all that
furnished ample resources for their debate. For one could argue that Kant
himself combined in his philosophy precisely these two countervailing
models of humanity under the terms *spontaneity* and *receptivity*. Already in
the Third Antinomy Kant recognized a fundamental division between two
rival conceptions of the world, one that allowed for the possibility of human
freedom and another that dictated that, according to the rules of human
understanding, we may rightly conceive only the unbroken causality of nature. Kant therefore characterized human freedom as "an absolute causal
spontaneity beginning from itself," but between this absolute spontaneity
on the one hand and thoroughgoing naturalistic determinism on the other,
his system left almost no room for compromise.[8] In his theory of the faculties, however, Kant brought these two concepts into a more harmonious relation, the spontaneous faculty of understanding, or *Verstand*, working in
cooperation with the receptive faculty of sensibility, or *Sinnlichkeit*, so as to
furnish the foundations for all possible experience.

One might surmise that the quarrel between Cassirer and Heidegger
arose in part because in their own philosophical doctrines they lay more
pronounced stress on only one of the two opposed sides of Kant's divide:
Cassirer carried over from Cohen's logic a wholly productive conception of
the mind. He gathered space and time into the spontaneous understanding
alone and thereby dispensed with the seemingly metaphysical commitment
implied by the notion of a faculty receptive to the merely given. Heidegger,
by contrast, tried to reverse the exorbitant intellectualism of the Marburg
School with the radical suggestion that Kant's epistemology was in fact
grounded primarily in receptivity, though he transfigured this receptivity
beyond all recognition and, via the phenomenological theory of intuition,

disavowed any ties to empiricism. More striking still, he suggested that Kant's philosophy (specifically, its theory of imagination as found in the schematism) rested upon a deeper and barely acknowledged theory of human finitude according to which the human being was thrown incorrigibly into time. Today Heidegger's Kant-interpretation may strike most readers as implausible. But we should at least acknowledge that it was born as a corrective to a perceived asymmetry in neo-Kantian doctrine.

Yet the debate's true origins are both much older and more enduring than any technical matters of philosophical interpretation. As we have seen, Cassirer and Heidegger ultimately came to see their disagreement as part of a far broader conversation about what it is to be a human being. For Cassirer it is to be an *animal symbolicum,* an animal distinguished by the spontaneous capacity for symbolic expression. This capacity, moreover, has developed *historically:* As the human being passes from the mythic to the modern-scientific understanding of the cosmos, it undergoes a process of enlightenment, an emancipatory awakening to its role as creator of its own symbolic reality. It is therefore a process of disenchantment and a retrieval of powers, theoretical and moral, once assigned to divine beings, and it thus requires a casting aside of whatever obstacles may prevent humanity from recognizing itself as the author of its own historical condition. For Heidegger, the human being that appears under the name of *Dasein* is not so much a *capacity* as a *clearing* or an opening upon the world. The theoretical and functionalist conception of reality that Cassirer sees as a cognitive achievement is, from Heidegger's point of view, a historical impoverishment in human understanding. Our *Seinsvergessenheit* or "oblivion of Being" has only abetted the human drive for mastery, and it has conspired to obstruct our recognition of ourselves as thrown into an existence where historical mastery is an impossibility. Where Cassirer sees an increase in our capacity for self-legislation, Heidegger sees only a forgetting of the "nullity" that lies deeper than any apparent freedom. What Cassirer calls spontaneity is for Heidegger merely a metaphysical conception of the human being that underwrites the drive to technological domination. What Heidegger calls thrownness is for Cassirer merely a primitive and mythic conception of humanity destined to be surpassed.

The contrast between these two rival conceptions of humanity is indeed profound, and in this book I have not proposed any definitive claims on behalf of one or the other. My goal has been more modest: to explore some of the terms of their conflict and to show how, in one particular instance, considerations of their respective merits became intertwined with larger conflicts of political history. I have also suggested that the politicization of this debate was a *tragedy,* not a grandly Shakespearean tragedy, to be sure, though a tragedy all the same, because it conspired to obscure our appreciation for the substantive questions at issue. It is one of the lessons of this book that the mutual entwinement of philosophy and politics was itself contingent, as all history is contingent, and it therefore cannot be used as a moralist's solution to what was at core a disagreement between two normative images of humanity.

To be sure, both conceptions of the human being explored here still have their philosophical advocates, and hope for an eventual reconciliation between them remains a prominent theme in philosophical discussion. But one is tempted to ask whether a true resolution of this conflict is at all likely or even possible. For in fact these two philosophical principles, thrownness and spontaneity, mark the opposing facets of a conceptual divide, the very persistence of which might be understood as the historical predicament of philosophy itself. We must of course remember that *neither* Cassirer *nor* Heidegger can be rightly understood as an unremitting advocate for only one of these two principles, even if, as we have seen, their conversation at Davos and its ensuing transformation into a political allegory surely enhanced the appearance of an unbridgeable division. The debate between Cassirer and Heidegger may remain a permanent fixture in the memory of Continental philosophy, perhaps because it embodies a controversy we cannot hope to resolve to our complete satisfaction. Borrowing a term from Kant, we might describe it as an *antinomy* in our concepts of humanity. But an antinomy is not a conflict to be resolved in favor of one contestant only. Even Prince Hamlet, poised in indecision, could not find a means of settling the quarrel between "nobility" and "dust." To force its resolution, or to foreclose prematurely upon its continued debate, would be to deny what may very well be an essential tension of the human condition.

Abbreviations for Frequently Cited Texts

Works by Cassirer

EC: Rev. of KPM   "Kant und das Problem der Metaphysik: Bemerkungen zu Martin Heideggers Kantinerpretation." KS 36 (1931): 1–26.

EM   *An Essay on Man.* New Haven: Yale University Press, 1944.

ECW 17   *Gesammelte Werke: Hamburger Ausgabe,* Bd. 17: *Aufsätze und Kleine Schriften, 1927–1931.* Ed. Birgit Recki. Hamburg: Felix Meiner, 2004.

ECW 18   *Gesammelte Werke: Hamburger Ausgabe,* Bd. 18: *Aufsätze und Kleine Schriften, 1932–1935.* Ed. Birgit Recki. Hamburg: Felix Meiner, 2004.

FuF   *Freiheit und Form: Studien zur deutschen Geistesgeschichte.* 2nd ed. Berlin: Bruno Cassirer, 1922.

GL   "'Geist' und 'Leben' in der Philosophie der Gegenwart." *Die Neue Rundschau* 41 (1930): 244–264.

GL, English   "'Spirit' and 'Life' in Contemporary Philosophy." Trans. R. W. Bretall and P. A. Schilpp. In Schilpp, 855–880.

HCE   "Hermann Cohen und die Erneuerung der Kantischen Philosophie." KS 17 (1912): 252–273.

ICRP   *The Individual and the Cosmos in Renaissance Philosophy.* Trans. Mario Domandi. New York: Dover, 2000.

MS   *The Myth of the State.* New York: Doubleday & Co., 1955.

PE   *The Philosophy of the Enlightenment.* Trans. Fritz
        Koellen and James Pettegrove. Boston: Beacon
        Press, 1955. In German as *Die Philosophie der
        Aufklärung.* Tübingen: Mohr, 1932. (G,—) for
        German references.

PK   *The Problem of Knowledge: Philosophy, Science and
        History since Hegel.* Trans. William H. Woglom
        and Charles W. Hendel. New Haven: Yale Univer-
        sity Press, 1950.

PSF, I   *The Philosophy of Symbolic Forms.* Vol. 1: *Language.*
        Trans. Ralph Manheim. New Haven: Yale Univer-
        sity Press, 1955. In German as *Die Philosophie der
        Symbolischen Formen.* Vol. 1: *Die Sprache.* Berlin:
        Bruno Cassirer, 1923. (G,—) used for German
        references.

PSF, II *The Philosophy of Symbolic Forms.* Vol. 2: *Mythical
        Thought.* Trans. Ralph Manheim. New Haven: Yale
        University Press, 1955. In German as *Die Philoso-
        phie der Symbolischen Formen.* Vol. 2: *Das
        Mythische Denken.* Berlin: Bruno Cassirer, 1925.
        (G,—) for German references.

PSF, III *The Philosophy of Symbolic Forms.* Vol. 3: *The
        Phenomenology of Knowledge.* Trans. Ralph
        Manheim. New Haven: Yale University Press,
        1957.

PSF, IV *The Philosophy of Symbolic Forms.* Vol. 4: *The
        Metaphysics of Symbolic Forms.* Ed. John Michael
        Krois and Donald Phillip Verene. Trans. John
        Michael Krois. New Haven: Yale University Press,
        1996.

QJJR   *The Question of Jean-Jacques Rousseau.* 2nd ed. Ed.
        and trans. Peter Gay. New Haven: Yale University
        Press, 1989.

SF, Swabey/ETR, Swabey *Substance and Function and Einstein's Theory of
        Relativity.* Trans. William Curtis Swabey and
        Marie Collins Swabey. Chicago: Open Court, 1973.

Works by Heidegger

BP   *Basic Problems of Phenomenology.* Trans. Albert
       Hofstadter. Bloomington: Indiana University
       Press, 1982.

BT   *Being and Time.* Trans. John Macquarrie and
       Edward Robinson. New York: Harper and Row,
       1962.

EHF   *The Essence of Human Freedom: An Introduction to
       Philosophy.* Trans. T. Sadler. New York: Contin-
       uum, 2002.

FCM   *The Fundamental Concepts of Metaphysics: World,
       Finitude, Solitude.* Trans. W. McNeill and N.
       Walker. Bloomington: Indiana University Press,
       1995.

GA   *Gesamtausgabe.* Frankfurt am Main: Vittorio
       Klostermann, 1975–.

HCT   *History of the Concept of Time.* Trans. Theodore
       Kisiel. Bloomington: Indiana University Press,
       1985.

KPM   *Kant und das Problem der Metaphysik.* 4th ed.
       Frankfurt am Main: V. Klostermann, 1973.

KPM, English   *Kant and the Problem of Metaphysics.* 4th ed. Trans.
       Richard Taft. Bloomington: Indiana University
       Press, 1990.

LH   "Letter on 'Humanism.'" In *Pathmarks.* Ed. William
       McNeill. Cambridge: Cambridge University Press,
       1998, 239–276.

MH: Rev. of PSF, II   "Review of Mythic Thought." In *The Piety of Think-
       ing: Essays by Martin Heidegger.* Trans. James
       Hart and John Maraldo. Bloomington: Indiana
       University Press, 1976, 32–45.

MFL   *The Metaphysical Foundations of Logic.* Trans.
       Michael Heim. Bloomington: Indiana University
       Press, 1984.

SZ   *Sein und Zeit.* 11th ed. Tübingen: Niemeyer, 1967.

WM   *Was ist Metaphysik?* 14th German ed. Frankfurt am
       Main: V. Klostermann, 1992.

WM, English   "What Is Metaphysics?" In *Pathmarks.* Ed. William
       McNeill. Cambridge: Cambridge University Press,
       1998, 82–96.

Other Works

Schilpp   *The Philosophy of Ernst Cassirer.* The Library of
           Living Philosophers, 6. Ed. Paul Arthur Schilpp.
           La Salle, IL: Open Court, 1949.

DR   "Bericht über die II. Davoser Hochschulkurse 17.
      März–6. April." Special issue of *Davoser Revue.* IV.
      Jahrgang. Nr. 7 (April 15, 1919).

DH   *Die II. Davoser Hoschschulkurse 17 März bis 6. April.
      Les II'mes cours universitaires de Davos, du 17 Mars
      au 6 Avril.* Davos: Kommissionsverlag, Heintz,
      Neu & Zahn, 1929.

FZ   Frankfurter Zeitung

KdrV   Immanuel Kant, *Kritik der reinen Vernunft: Zehnte
        Auflage.* Leipzig: Felix Meiner, 1913. English
        quotations from Critique of Pure Reason. Ed. Paul
        Guyer and Allen Wood. Cambridge: Cambridge
        University Press, 1998.

KS   *Kantstudien*

NZZ   *Neue Zürcher Zeitung*

Notes

Preface

1. Peter E. Gordon, *Rosenzweig and Heidegger: Between Judaism and German Philosophy* (Berkeley: University of California Press, 2003).

2. Dominic Kaegi and Enno Rudolph, eds., *Cassirer—Heidegger. 70 Jahre Davoser Disputation,* Cassirer-Forschungen 9 (Hamburg: Felix Meiner, 2002); Michael Friedman, *A Parting of the Ways: Carnap, Cassirer, and Heidegger* (Chicago: Open Court, 2000).

3. Nelson Goodman, *Ways of Worldmaking* (Indianapolis: Hackett, 1978), 1.

Introduction

1. Hermann Herrigel, "Denken dieser Zeit: Fakultäten und Nationen treffen sich in Davos," FZ, April 22, 1929, Abendblatt: Hochschulblatt, 4; O. F. Bollnow, "Gespräche in Davos," in *Erinnerung an Martin Heidegger,* ed. Günther Neske (Pfullingen: Neske, 1977), 25–29; François Poirié, *Emmanuel Lévinas: Qui êtes-vous?* (Lyon: La Manufacture, 1987), 78.

2. To be sure, the distinction between these two styles of philosophic inquiry should not be overdrawn: some of the most creative and insightful work happens at their intersection. But that is another story. For Michael Friedman, the Davos debate brought into relief a "parting of the ways" between analytic philosophy (as symbolized by Carnap) and Continental philosophy (as represented by Heidegger), with Cassirer offering the promise of philosophical mediation between the two traditions. See Friedman, *A Parting of the Ways: Carnap, Cassirer, and Heidegger* (Chicago: Open Court, 2000).

3. The great historian of philosophy Hans Blumenberg wrote in a similar fashion about root paradigms that govern human thought. The term *image* as I use it here carries over some, though by no means all, of the insights from his work. One of his insights was that such paradigms manifest themselves through irreducibly poetic symbols or forms, such as the symbol of a ship or shipwreck, which

was the subject of his very last book. See Blumenberg, *Shipwreck with Spectator: Paradigm of a Metaphor for Existence,* trans. Steven Rendall (Cambridge, MA: MIT Press, 1997).

4. Taylor Carman develops a similar view of the Cassirer-Heidegger disagreement as involving a basic contrast between thrownness and spontaneity. See Carman, "Heidegger's Anti-Neo-Kantianism," in *The Philosophical Forum.* Vol. 41, Number 1 (Spring, 2010),131-142. Other crucial works of philosophical commentary include Frank Schalow, "Thinking at Cross Purposes with Kant: Reason, Finitude, and Truth in the Cassirer–Heidegger Debate," KS, 87 (1996), 198–217; Calvin O. Schrag, "Heidegger and Cassirer on Kant," KS 58 (1967), 87–100; Dennis A. Lynch, "Ernst Cassirer and Martin Heidegger: The Davos Debate," KS 81 (1990), 360–70; Wayne Cristaudo, "Heidegger and Cassirer: Being, Knowing and Politics," KS 82 (1991), 469–83; John Michael Krois, "Aufklärung und Metaphysik: Zur Philosophie Cassirers und der Davoser Debatte mit Heidegger," *Internationale Zeitschrift für Philosophie* (Stuttgart: J. B. Metzler), Heft 2 (1992), 273–89. Pierre Aubenque, "Le Débat de 1929 entre Cassirer et Heidegger," in *Ernst Cassirer: De Marbourg 'a New York, L'itinéraire philosophique,* ed. Jean Seidengart (Paris: Les 'Editions du Cerf, 1990), 81–96; and Karlfried Gründer, "Cassirer und Heidegger in Davos, 1929," in *Über Ernst Cassirers Philosophie der symbolischen Formen,* ed. Hans-Jürg Braun, Helmut Holzhey and Ernst Wolfgang Orth (Frankfurt am Main: Suhrkamp Verlag, 1988), 290–302.

5. Heidegger, FCM, 184; in German see GA, Band 29/30, 272.

6. My thanks especially to John Michael Krois for his numerous papers drawing attention to this phase in Cassirer's work.

7. For an extension of this historicized theory of a priori principles, see Michael Friedman, *Dynamics of Reason* (Stanford, CA: CSLI Publications, 2001).

8. Ernst Cassirer, "Der Begriff der Symbolischen Form im Aufbau der Geisteswissenschaften," in *Vorträge der Bibliothek Warburg,* 1921/1922 (Leipzig: B. G. Teubner, 1923), 11–39, quotation at 15; emphasis added.

9. Recall that the third volume of Cassirer's *The Philosophy of Symbolic Forms* was first published in 1929 as *The Phenomenology of Knowledge.* On Cassirer's largely Hegelian understanding of "phenomenology," see Friedman, *A Parting of the Ways,* esp. 135 n. 184.

10. PSF, III, 16; emphasis added.

11. See Felix Kaufmann, "Cassirer's Theory of Scientific Knowledge," in Schilpp, 183–213, esp. 203.

12. PSF, III, 20–21. For a largely negative assessment of Cassirer's "anti-realism" as tending toward "relativism" and "nihilism" [*sic*], see William Curtis Swabey, "Cassirer and Metaphysics," in Schilpp, 121–148.

13. Ernst Cassirer, "Mythic, Aesthetic, and Theoretical Space," trans. Donald Phillip Verene and Lerke Holzwarth Foster, *Man and World* 2.1 (1969): 3–17, quotation at 5; trans. of "Mythischer, äesthetischer, und theoretischer Raum," in

Vierter Kongress für Äesthetik und allgemeine Kunstwissenschaft, ed. Hermann Noack (Stuttgart: Ferdinand Enke, 1931).

14. For a characterization of Cassirer's general theory of science as a process of abstraction, see, for example, Felix Kaufmann, "Cassirer's Theory of Scientific Knowledge," in Schilpp, 183–213, esp. 198.

15. PE, 15.

16. SF, Swabey, 167.

17. SF, Swabey, 71.

18. PSF, III, chap. 5, "Symbolic Pregnance," 191–204, esp. 202.

19. SF, Swabey, 317.

20. ETR, Swabey, 379.

21. FuF, xv.

22. FuF, 167.

23. FuF, 167.

24. FuF, 283; Cassirer is citing Schiller's letter to Körner, February 18, 1793; emphasis added.

25. FuF, 286; Cassirer is again citing phrases from Schiller's letter to Körner, February 18, 1793.

26. For a recent study of Cassirer's relations with Warburg and Panofsky, see Emily Jane Levine, "Culture, Commerce, and the City: Aby Warburg, Ernst Cassirer, and Erwin Panofsky in Hamburg, 1919–1933," doctoral dissertation submitted to the Department of History, Stanford University, 2008.

27. Fritz Saxl, "Ernst Cassirer," in Schilpp, 47–51, quotation at 47–48.

28. Erwin Panofsky, *Perspective as Symbolic Form,* trans. Christopher S. Wood (New York: Zone Books, 1991), trans. of "Die Perspektive als 'Symbolische Form,'" in *Vörtrage der Bibliothek Warburg* 4, 1924/5 (Leipzig: Teubner, 1927), 258–330.

29. Panofsky, *Perspective as Symbolic Form,* quotations at 3 and 66, respectively.

30. Panofsky, *Perspective as Symbolic Form,* 72.

31. The comparison between Carnap and Cassirer is a prominent theme in Friedman, *A Parting of the Ways;* on Carnap's conception of the relation between cultural modernism, socialism, and logical positivism, see Peter Galison, "Aufbau/Bauhaus: Logical Positivism and Architectural Modernism," *Critical Inquiry* 16.4 (1990): 709–752.

32. On Cassirer's relationship with the Warburg Institute, see most especially Silvia Ferretti, *Cassirer, Panofsky, and Warburg: Symbol, Art and History,* trans. Richard Pierce (New Haven: Yale University Press, 1989); E. H. Gombrich, *Aby Warburg: An Intellectual Biography* (London: The Warburg Institute, 1970); Eveline Pinto, "Cassirer et Warburg: De l'histoire de l'art à la philosophie de la culture," in *Ernst Cassirer: De Marbourg à New York,* ed. Jean Seidengart (Paris: Éditions du Cerf, 1990), 261–275.

33. On Heidegger's reading of Albert Schweitzer's humanistic reading of Christianity, see Theodore Kisiel, *The Genesis of Heidegger's* Being and Time

(Berkeley: University of California Press, 1995), 522 n. 22. Also see Theodore Kisiel and Thomas Sheehan, eds., *Becoming Heidegger: On the Trail of His Early Occasional Writings, 1910–1927* (Evanston, IL: Northwestern University Press, 2007), 475 n. 8.

34. Ernst Cassirer, *Die Idee der Republikanischen Verfassung: Rede zur Verfassungsfeier am 11 August 1928* (Hamburg: Friederichsen, de Gruyter and Co., 1929), 31.

35. For Heidegger's discussion of the relationship between his own understanding of ontology and the ontological premises of his phenomenological teachers, including Husserl, see, for example, MFL, 150.

36. BT, 23; SZ, 4.

37. BT, 221; SZ, 177.

38. For Heidegger's remarks on Augustine, Luther, and Kierkegaard on anxiety and fear, see especially BT, 292 n. iv; SZ, 190.

39. For Heidegger on Kierkegaard and authenticity, see Hubert L. Dreyfus, *Being-in-the-World: A Commentary on Heidegger's* Being and Time, Division I (Cambridge, MA: MIT Press, 1991). Also see Allan Janik, "Haecker, Kierkegaard, and the Early Brenner: A Contribution to the History of the Reception of *Two Ages* to the German-Speaking World," in *Søren Kierkegaard: Critical Assessments of Leading Philosophers,* vol. 4: *Social and Political Philosophy: Kierkegaard and the "Present Age,"* ed. Daniel W. Conway with K. W. Gover (London: Routledge, 2002), 123–147, esp. 142.

40. Martin Heidegger, "Augustine and Neo-Platonism," in *The Phenomenology of Religious Life,* trans. M. Fritsch and J. Anna Gosetti-Ferencei (Bloomington: Indiana University Press, 2004), 113–184, quotation at 151–153.

41. WM, 38; WM, English, 93.

42. WM, 38; WM, English, 93.

43. WM, 93; WM, English, 93.

44. BT, 330; SZ, 284–285.

45. Charles Bambach, *Heidegger, Dilthey, and the Crisis of Historicism* (Ithaca, NY: Cornell University Press, 1995), esp. chap. 5.

46. BT, 417; SZ, 366.

47. BT, 333; SZ, 287.

48. BT, 435; SZ, 384.

49. BT, 435; SZ, 384.

50. Karl Löwith, "My Last Meeting with Heidegger, Rome 1936," in *Mein Leben in Deutschland vor und nach 1933,* trans. Richard Wolin (Stuttgart: Metzler Verlag, 1986), 56–58.

51. For a discussion of the methodological problems concerning formalism and the difference between "negative" versus "positive" implication in relating Heidegger's philosophy to National Socialism, see Julian Young, *Heidegger, Philosophy, Nazism* (Cambridge: Cambridge University Press, 1998).

52. BT, 435; SZ, 384.

53. On "community," "people" *(Volk),* and "generation," see BT, 436; SZ, 385.

54. On this theme see Gregory Fried, *Heidegger's Polemos: From Being to Politics* (New Haven: Yale University Press, 2000).

55. Emmanuel Lévinas, as recollected by Richard Sugarman, phone interview with the author, July 23, 2008.

56. For the details of this initial meeting, see Thomas Meyer, *Ernst Cassirer* (Hamburg: Ellert & Richter, 2006), 154.

57. Martin Heidegger, *Introduction to Phenomenological Research,* trans. Daniel O. Dahlstrom (Bloomington: Indiana University Press, 2005), 208–209.

58. BT, Div. I, chap. 1, n. xi, 490; SZ, Div. I, chap. 1, n. xi; emphasis added.

59. BT, 490 n. xi; SZ, 51.

60. Martin Heidegger, "Ernst Cassirer, *Philosophie der symbolischen Formen.* 2. Teil: *Das mythische Denken.* Berlin, 1925" (Review), originally published in *Deutsche Literaturzeitung* 5.21 (1928): 1000–1012; reprinted as appendix II in *Kant und der Problem der Metaphysik,* 5th exp. ed. (Frankfurt am Main: V. Klostermann, 1991), 255–270; reprinted in English as "Review of Mythic Thought," in *The Piety of Thinking: Essays by Martin Heidegger,* trans. James Hart and John Maraldo (Bloomington: Indiana University Press, 1976), 32–45.

61. BT, 206; SZ, 163.

1. Philosophy in Crisis

1. Paul Valéry, "La Crise de l'esprit," originally published in two parts as "The Spiritual Crisis," and "The Intellectual Crisis," in *The Athenaeum,* April 11, 1919, and May 2, 1919, and in French in *Variété,* August 1, 1919; reprinted in Valéry, *The Outlook for Intelligence,* trans. Denise Foliot and Jackson Mathews (New York: Harper and Row, 1962), 23–36.

2. Georg Simmel, "Die Krisis der Kultur," FZ, February 13, 1916, Drittes Morgenblatt, 1–2.

3. Rosa Luxemburg, *Die Krise der Sozialdemokratie* (Berlin: A. Hoffmann, 1919); Eugen Varga, *Die Krise der kapitalistischen Weltwirtschaft* (Hamburg: Kommunistischen Internationale, 1921).

4. Richard Nicolaus Coudenhove-Kalergi, *Krise der Weltanschauung* (Vienna: Pan-Europa, 1923); Alfred Weber, *Die Krise des modernen Staatsgedankens in Europa* (Stuttgart: Deutsche Verlags-Anstalt, 1925).

5. Hans Tietze, *Lebendige Kunst-Wissenschaft: Zur Krise der Kunst und der Kunstgeschichte* (Vienna: Krystall, 1925); Hermann Platz, *Das Religiöse in der Krise der Zeit* (Waldshut: Benziger & Co., 1928); Karl Bühler, *Die Krise der Psychologie,* 2nd ed. (Jena: G. Fischer, 1929).

6. Louis Reynaud, *La crise de notre littérature: Des romantiques à Proust, Gide et Valéry* (Paris: Hachette, 1929).

7. Rudolf Pannwitz, *Die Krisis der europäischen Kultur* (Nuremberg: H. Carl, 1917).

8. For an important summary of "crisis-consciousness," see Charles Bambach, *Heidegger, Dilthey, and the Crisis of Historicism* (Ithaca, NY: Cornell University Press, 1995), and Andras Gedo, *Crisis Consciousness in Contemporary Philosophy,* trans. Salomea Genin (Minneapolis: Marxist Educational Press, 1982). Also see Reinhart Koselleck, *Critique and Crisis: Enlightenment and the Pathogenesis of Modern Society* (Cambridge, MA: MIT Press, 1998), and Koselleck, "Some Questions Regarding the Conceptual History of 'Crisis,'" in *The Practice of Conceptual History,* trans. Todd Samuel Presner (Stanford, CA: Stanford University Press, 2002), 236–247.

9. Ernst Troeltsch, "Die Krisis des Historismus," *Die Neue Rundschau* 33 (1922): 572–590; also see Troeltsch, *Der Historismus und seine Probleme* (Tübingen: Mohr, 1922), and Karl Heussi, *Die Krisis des Historismus* (Tübingen: Mohr, 1932).

10. For a summary see Dirk Kaesler, *Max Weber: Eine Einführung in Leben, Werk, und Wirkung* (Frankfurt am Main: Campus Verlag, 2003), 236; and see the discussion in Peter Novick, *That Noble Dream: The "Objectivity Question" and the American Historical Profession* (Cambridge: Cambridge University Press, 1988), 157.

11. Karl Barth, *Epistles to the Romans,* trans. Edwyn C. Hoskyns (London: Oxford University Press, 1933). Despite Barth's frequent recourse to the language of "crisis," especially in the *Epistle to the Romans* (1919), it has been argued that "'crisis' is used by Barth to describe a theological subject-matter, and not a cultural state of affairs." Bruce L. McCormack, *Karl Barth's Critically Realistic Dialectical Theology: Its Genesis and Development, 1909–1936* (Oxford: Oxford University Press, 1995), 212 n. 11. Nor was the crisis of historicism confined only to Christianity. Modern Jewish thinkers such as Franz Rosenzweig and Emmanuel Lévinas were affected as well. On this, see Samuel Moyn, *Origins of the Other: Emmanuel Levinas between Revelation and Ethics* (Ithaca, NY: Cornell University Press, 2005), and David Myers, *Resisting History: Historicism and Its Discontents in German-Jewish Thought* (Princeton, NJ: Princeton University Press, 2003).

12. Hermann Weyl, "On the New Foundational Crisis of Mathematics," in *From Brouwer to Hilbert: The Debate on the Foundational Metaphysics in the 1920s,* ed. Paolo Mancosu (New York: Oxford University Press, 1998), 86–118, reprint and trans. of "Über der neue Grundlagenkrise der Mathematik," *Mathematische Zeitschrift* 10 (1921): 37–79. For an overview of the foundations crisis in mathematics in relation to political events, see Sanford L. Segal, *Mathematicians under the Nazis* (Princeton, NJ: Princeton University Press, 2003), esp. chap. 2.

13. Albert Lewkowitz, "Die Krisis der modernen Erkenntnistheorie," *Archiv für systematischen Philosophie* 21.2 (1915): 186–196.

14. For an overview of the debates over German Idealism, neo-Hegelianism, and neo-Kantianism in the Weimar era, see Peter E. Gordon, *Rosenzweig and*

Heidegger: Between Judaism and German Philosophy (Berkeley: University of California Press, 2003), esp. 1–118.

15. Karl Joël, *Die philosophische Krisis der Gegenwart,* Rektoratsrede (Leipzig: Felix Meiner, 1914); Arthur Liebert, *Die geistige Krisis der Gegenwart* (Berlin: Pan-verlag R. Heise, 1923).

16. BT, 29; SZ, 9.

17. EM, 228, quotation at 21–22.

18. The philosopher Arthur Liebert, a neo-Kantian and a former editor of *Kantstudien,* was only one of many German-Jewish scholars who found themselves stateless after the Nazi seizure of power. Exiled to Belgrade, he published *Die Krise des Idealismus* (Zürich: Rascher, 1936).

19. Edmund Husserl, "Philosophy and the Crisis of European Humanity," originally presented to the Vienna Cultural Society, May 7 and 10, 1935, followed six months later by the similarly named lecture in Prague, later expanded into Husserl's last, posthumously published work: Edmund Husserl, *The Crisis of the European Sciences: An Introduction to Phenomenological Philosophy,* trans. David Carr (Evanston, IL: Northwestern University Press, 1970), 299.

20. Fritz Jellinek, *Die Krise des Bürgers* (Zürich: Europa, 1935).

21. Alfred Rosenberg, *Krisis und Neubau Europas* (Berlin: Junker und Dünnhaupt, 1934).

22. Hans Sluga, *Heidegger's Crisis: Philosophy and Politics in Nazi Germany* (Cambridge, MA: Harvard University Press, 1993).

23. For an insightful assessment of Heidegger's political vision for university reform, see Iain D. Thomson, *Heidegger on Ontotheology: Technology and the Politics of Education* (Cambridge: Cambridge University Press, 2005). For a general overview, see Claudia Koonz, *The Nazi Conscience* (Cambridge, MA: Belknap Press of Harvard University Press, 2003), chap. 3, "Allies in the Academy."

24. Joachim Ritter, "Bildungskrise in Davos: Bemerkungen zu den IV. Davoser Hochschulkursen vom 22. März bis 11 April, 1931," *Neue Jahrbücher für Wissenschaft und Jugendbildung* 7.7 (1931): 661–665.

25. Fritz Heinemann, *Neue Wege der Philosophie: Geist, Leben, Existenz* (Leipzig: Quelle und Meyer, 1929), x.

26. The most successful historical narrative to deploy this theme in a psychoanalytic mode is Peter Gay, *Weimar Culture: The Outsider as Insider* (New York: Harper and Row, 1968); also crucial are Robert Wohl, *The Generation of 1914* (Cambridge, MA: Harvard University Press, 1979), and Detlev Peukert, *The Weimar Republic: The Crisis of Classical Modernity,* trans. Richard Deveson (New York: Hill and Wang, 1989).

27. Karl Mannheim, "The Problem of Generations" (1927), in *From Karl Mannheim,* 2nd exp. ed., ed. Kurt Wolff (New Brunswick, NJ: Transaction Publishers, 1993), 351–395, quotation at 380.

28. Wilhelm Dilthey, "Über das Studium der Geschichte der Wissenschaft vom Menschen, der Gesellschaft und dem Staat" (1875), in *Gesammelte Schriften,* vol. 5: *Die geistige Welt: Einleitung in die Philosophie des Lebens,* 2nd ed. (Stuttgart: Teubner, 1957), 31–73, quotation at 36–37.

29. BT, 41; SZ, 20.

30. BT, 436; SZ, 384–385.

31. Mannheim, "Problem of Generations," 381.

32. Wilhelm Pinder, *Das Problem der Generation in der Kunstgeschichte Europas* (Berlin: Frankfurter Verlags-Anstalt, 1926).

33. E. Günther Gründel, *Die Sendung der jungen Generation: Versuch einer umfassenden revolutionären Sinndeutung der Krise* (Munich: Beck, 1932).

34. Husserl, *Crisis of the European Sciences,* 6.

35. Summaries of these talks may be found in DH, esp. Ludwig Englert, "Als Student bei den zweiten Davoser Hochschulkursen," 5–64, and DR, 181–205.

36. Hermann Herrigel, "Denken dieser Zeit: Fakultäten und Nationen treffen sich in Davos," FZ, April 22, 1929, Abendblatt: Hochschuleblatt, "Für Hochschule und Jugend," 4.

37. Franz Josef Brecht, "Die Situation der gegenwärtigen Philosophie," *Neue Jahrbücher für Wissenschaft und Jugendbildung* 6.1 (1930): 42–58, quotation at 42.

38. Ernst Howald, "Betrachtungen zu den Davoser Hochschulkursen," NZZ, April 10, 1929, Morgenausgabe, 1.

39. The original manifesto was by Otto Liebmann, *Kant und die Epigonen: Eine kritsche Abhandlung* (Stuttgart: C. Schober, 1865). For a sociological and historical overview of the entire movement, see Klaus Christian Köhnke, *The Rise of Neo-Kantianism: German Academic Philosophy between Idealism and Positivism,* trans. R. J. Hollingdale (Cambridge: Cambridge University Press, 1991). Still valuable is Thomas Willey, *Back to Kant: The Revival of Kantianism in German Social and Historical Thought, 1860–1914* (Detroit: Wayne State University Press, 1978). On the politics of the Marburg School, see Timothy Keck, "Kant and Socialism: The Marburg School in Wilhelminian Germany (PhD diss., University of Wisconsin at Madison, 1975).

40. Hermann Cohen, *Logik der reinen Erkenntnis* (Berlin: Bruno Cassirer, 1902); Cohen, *Ethik des reinen Willens* (Berlin: Bruno Cassirer, 1904); Cohen, *Aesthetik des reinen Gefühls* (Berlin: Bruno Cassirer, 1912).

41. For a discussion of the philosophical debates concerning Cohen's *Religion of Reason,* see Gordon, *Rosenzweig and Heidegger,* chap. 1; and see Hermann Cohen, *Religion der Vernunft aus den Quellen des Judentums* (Darmstadt: Joseph Melzer, 1966).

42. HCE, 255.

43. HCE, 257–261.

44. HCE, 264.

45. HCE, 272–273.

46. Hans-Georg Gadamer, *Philosophical Apprenticeships,* trans. Robert R. Sullivan (Cambridge, MA: MIT Press, 1985), 7.

47. Martin Heidegger, "Zur Geschichte des philosophischen Lehrstuhles seit 1866," in *Die Philipps-Universität zu Marburg, 1527–1927* (Marburg: N. G. Elwert'sche Verlagsbuchhandlung [G. Braun], 1927), 681–687; republished as appendix VI in KPM, 304–311.

48. Fritz-Joachim von Rintelen, "Kant-Studien und Kant-Gesellschaft," KS 52 (1960–1961): 258–270; von Rintelen is quoting A. Gardeil here. Also see Gerhard Funke, "Kantstudien, 1896–1996," KS 87, Heft 4 (1996): 385–389; and Christopher Adair-Toteff, "Vaihinger's Kant-Studien," KS 87, Heft 4 (1996): 390–395.

49. Thomas Meyer, *Ernst Cassirer* (Hamburg: Ellert & Richter, 2006), 179.

50. For a complete summary of the Bauch affair, see Ulrich Sieg, "Deutsche Kulturgeschichte und Jüdischer Geist: Ernst Cassirer's Auseinandersetzung mit der Völkischer Philosophie Bruno Bauchs. Ein Unbekanntes Manuskript," followed by the unpublished essay by Cassirer, "Zum Begriff der Nation: Eine Erwiderung auf den Aufsatz von Bruno Bauch," *Bulletin des Leo Baecks Instituts* 88 (1991): 59–71, 73–91.

51. Meyer, *Ernst Cassirer,* 78.

52. Peter Wust, *Auferstehung der Metaphysik* (Leipzig: Felix Meiner, 1920); Heinrich Kerler, *Die auferstandene Metaphysik: eine Abrechnung,* 2nd ed. (Ulm: Verlag Heinrich Kerler, 1921).

53. Gadamer, *Philosophical Apprenticeships,* 48.

54. For a summary, see Lanier Anderson, "The Debate over the *Geisteswissenschaften* in German Philosophy," in *The Cambridge History of Philosophy 1870–1945,* ed. Thomas Baldwin (Cambridge: Cambridge University Press, 2003), 221–234; for details concerning Rickert and Windelband's methodology, see Bambach, *Heideger, Dilthey, and the Crisis of Historicism.*

55. Alois Riehl, "Über wissenschaftliche und nichtwissenschaftliche Philosophie, Eine akademische Antrittsrede (Freiburg 1883)," in *Philosophische Studien aus vier Jahrzehnten* (Leipzig: Quelle & Meyer, 1925), 227–253.

56. Richard Kroner, *Kant's Weltanschauung,* trans. John E. Smith (Chicago: University of Chicago Press, 1956).

57. Kroner, *Kant's Weltanschauung,* 4.

58. Kroner, *Kant's Weltanschauung,* 56–57. The reference is to Kant, *Religion within the Limits of Reason Alone,* trans. T. M. Greene and H. H. Hudson (Chicago: Open Court, 1934), 58, in which Kant quotes Albrecht von Haller's poem, "Über den Ursprung des Übels" (1734): "Denn Gott liebt keinen Zwang, die Welt mit ihren Mängeln / Ist besser als ein Riche von Willen-losen Engeln" ("For God loves not compulsion; the world with all its faults / Is better than a realm of will-less angels"). For an explanation of Kant's purposes, see Kant, *Lectures on Philosophical Theology.* trans. Allen W. Wood and Gertrude M. Clark (Ithaca, NY: Cornell University Press, 1978). See esp. Wood's comments at 116 n. 5.

59. Heinrich Rickert, *The Limits of Concept Formation in Natural Science,* trans. Guy Oakes (London: Cambridge University Press, 1986).

60. On Dilthey's philosophy of historical understanding, see Bambach, *Heidegger, Dilthey, and the Crisis of Historicism,* and Rudolf A. Makkreel, *Dilthey: Philosopher of the Human Studies* (Princeton, NJ: Princeton University Press, 1992).

61. BP, 169.

62. On Heidegger and the Southwestern neo-Kantians' theory of history, see the excellent elucidations in Bambach, *Heidegger, Dilthey, and the Crisis of Historicism.*

63. BT, 31; SZ, 11. For a negative appraisal of Heidegger's attitude toward regional ontology, see Herman Philipse, *Heidegger and the Question of Being: A Critical Interpretation* (Princeton, NJ: Princeton University Press, 1998), esp. 37–39.

64. BT, 31; SZ, 10–11.

65. BT, 31; SZ, 10.

66. BT, 329–330; SZ, 284–285.

67. Ernst Cassirer, ed., *Immanuel Kants Werke,* in Gemeinschaft mit Hermann Cohen, Artur Buchenau, Otto Buek, Albert Görland, Benzion Kellermann (Berlin: Bruno Cassirer, 1912–1922); Cassirer, *Kants Leben und Lehre* (Berlin: Bruno Cassirer, 1918).

68. Arthur Liebert, "Besprechung: Ernst Cassirer, *Kants Leben und Lehre,*" KS 25.2–3 (1920): 233–237.

69. Toni Cassirer, letter to Aby Warburg, April 28, 1924, Warburg Archive, London.

70. These facts taken from Edward L. Schaub, "The Kantfeier in Königsberg," *Philosophical Review* 33.5 (1924): 433–449.

71. Friedrich Myrho, "Zum Geleit," preface to *Kritizismus: Eine Sammlung von Beiträgen aus der Welt der Neu-Kantianismus,* ed. Friedrich Myrho (Berlin: Rolf Heise, 1926), iii–vi, quotation at iii. Note that the publication of this volume was delayed for two years after the Kant bicentennial.

72. Heinrich Rickert, *Kant als Philosoph der modernen Kultur* (Tübingen: J. C. B. Mohr [Paul Siebeck], 1924), 6. For his own critical assessment of life-philosophy, see Heinrich Rickert, *Die Philosophie des Lebens: Darstellung und Kritik der philosophischen Modeströmungen unserer Zeit,* 2nd ed. (Tübingen: Mohr-Siebeck, 1922).

73. Rickert, *Kant als Philosoph der modernen Kultur,* 153.

74. Søren Kierkegaard, *Gesammelte Werke,* 12 vols., ed. and trans. Hermann Gottsched and Christoph Schrempf (Jena: Eugen Diedrichs, 1909–1922).

75. Fritz Heinemann would later write that during the Davos *Hochschulkurse,* Heidegger personally rebuffed him for proposing the term *Existenzphilosophie.* See the preface in Heinemann, *Existenzphilosophie, lebendig oder tot?* 2nd ed. (Stuttgart: Kohlhammer, 1954).

76. Charles Guignon, "Introduction," in *The Cambridge Companion to Heidegger,* 2nd ed., ed. Charles Guignon (Cambridge: Cambridge University Press,

2006), 1–40, 40 n. 29. On Kierkegaard and Dostoyevsky as influences on Heidegger, see Otto Pöggeler, *Martin Heidegger's Path of Thinking*, trans. D. Magurshak and S. Barber (Atlantic Highlands, NJ: Humanities Press, 1987), 265. Also see Leo Löwenthal, "The Reception of Dostoevski's Work in Germany, 1880–1920," in *The Arts in Society,* ed. Robert Neal Wilson (Engelwood Cliffs, NJ: Prentice-Hall, 1964), 122–147. On the Kierkegaard reception in Weimar Protestant theology, see Matthias Wilke, *Die Kierkegaard-Rezeption Emanuel Hirschs: Eine Studie über die Voraussetzungen der Kommunikation christlicher Wahrheit* (Tübingen: Mohr-Siebeck, 2005). Emmanuel Hirsch would eventually publish a series of "Kierkegaard studies" between 1930 and 1933; see Hirsch, *Kierkegaard-Studien* (Gütersloh: C. Bertelsmann, 1930–1933).

77. Erich Przywara, S.J., *Kant Heute: Eine Sichtung* (München: Oldenbourg, 1930), 28.

78. See Przywara, *Kant Heute,* 10, for his discussion of spontaneity and receptivity; for his summary of Heidegger, see 92–96.

79. Przywara, *Kant Heute,* 99.

80. Hans Vaihinger, "Kant—ein Metaphysiker?" in *Kritizismus, eine Sammlung von Beiträgen aus der Welt des Neu-Kantianismus,* ed. Friedrich Myrho (Berlin: Rolf Heise, 1926), 64–73.

81. For a historical summary and a thematic characterization of the entire tradition, see Joachim Fischer, *Philosophische Anthropologie: Eine Denkrichtung des 20. Jahrhunderts* (Freiburg: Karl Alber, 2008).

82. Helmut Plessner, *Die Aufgabe der philosophischen Anthropologie* (1931), in *Zwischen Philosophie und Gesellschaft* (Frankfurt: Suhrkamp, 1979), 141ff., quoted from Herbert Schnädelbach, *Philosophy in Germany, 1831–1933,* trans. Eric Matthews (Cambridge: Cambridge University Press, 1984), 223–224.

83. Quotation from Plessner in Schnädelbach, *Philosophy in Germany,* 223–224.

84. Fritz Heinemann, *Neue Wege der Philosophie: Geist, Leben, Existenz* (Leipzig: Quelle und Meyer, 1929), 363.

85. The second edition was printed in its integrity as Max Scheler, *Der Formalismus in der Ethik und die materiale Wertethik: Neuer Versuch der Grundlegung eines ethischen Personalismus,* 2nd ed. (Halle: Max Niemeyer, 1921), trans. Manfred S. Frings and Roger L. Funk as *Formalism in Ethics and Non-Formal Ethics of Values: A New Attempt toward the Foundation of an Ethical Personalism* (Evanston, IL: Northwestern University Press, 1973).

86. Heidegger, "In Memoriam Max Scheler," in MFL, 50–52.

87. For a comparative study of Scheler and Heidegger, see Manfred S. Frings, *Person und Dasein: Zur Frage der Ontologie des Wertseins* (The Hague: Martinus Nijhoff, 1969).

88. See Eugene Kelly, *Structure and Diversity: Studies in the Phenomenological Philosophy of Max Scheler* (Dordrecht: Kluwer, 1997), 177.

89. Heinemann, *Neue Wege,* 374.

90. Heidegger, "In Memoriam Max Scheler," 50–52.

91. Max Scheler, *Die Stellung des Menschen im Kosmos* (Darmstadt: Reichl, 1928), trans. Hans Meyerhoff as *Man's Place in Nature* (New York: Noonday, 1961).

92. It is worth noting that Scheler repeated almost verbatim Heidegger's call for a destructive interpretation of the philosophical tradition: "Ein gewisser 'Fortschritt' ist daher schon durch die Tradition möglich. Doch beruht alle echt menschliche Entwicklung wesentlich auf einem zunehmenden *Abbau* der Tradition." Scheler, *Die Stellung des Menschen,* 25.

93. See, for example, Jakob von Uexküll, *Umwelt und Innenwelt der Tiere,* 2nd ed. (Berlin: Julius Springer, 1921), and his *Theoretische Biologie* (Berlin: Paetel, 1920). For a judicious historical treatment, see Anne Harrington, *Reenchanted Science: Holism in German Culture from Wilhelm II to Hitler* (Princeton, NJ: Princeton University Press, 1996).

94. Scheler, *Die Stellung des Menschen,* 32–34.

95. Scheler, *Die Stellung des Menschen,* 55–56, 62.

96. Scheler, *Die Stellung des Menschen,* 65–67.

97. For Scheler's full discussion of Klages and the latter's opposition between spirit and life, see Scheler, *Die Stellung des Menschen,* 65–67; in English, 81 and 87.

98. Scheler, *Die Stellung des Menschen* 68; in English, 89–90.

99. Scheler, *Die Stellung des Menschen,* 68.

100. BT, 73; SZ, 47–48.

101. For Heidegger's credit to Scheler on this point, see the discussion in BT, 178; SZ, 139. Also see the homage to Scheler's personalism in BT, 492 n. vi; and SZ, 272. For Heidegger's more specific remarks on Scheler and sympathy, see BT, 491 n. i; SZ, 116 n. i.

102. See esp. Heidegger's remarks in §37, "The Problem of Philosophical Anthropology," in KPM, English, 142–145.

103. For a recent assessment, see John Michael Krois, "'A Passion Can only Be Overcome by a Stronger Passion': Philosophical Anthropology before and after Ernst Cassirer," *European Review* 13.4 (2005): 557–575; also see Gerald Hartung, *Philosophische Anthropologie* (Stuttgart: Reclam, 2008), and Gerald Hartung, "Anthropologische Grundlagen der Kulturphilosophie: Zur Entstehungsgeschichte von Ernst Cassirers Essay on Man," in *Kulturwissenschaftliche Studien* (Leipzig: Passage-Verlag, 2001), 2–18.

104. PSF, IV, 45.

105. Cassirer, "On the Metaphysics of Symbolic Forms," in PSF, IV, 3–114.

106. PSF, IV, 45.

107. PSF, IV, 43.

108. PSF, IV, 46.

109. Edmund Husserl, "Letter to Alexander Pfänder (January 6, 1931)," trans. Burt Hopkins, in *Becoming Heidegger: On the Trail of His Early Occasional Writings, 1910–1927,* ed. Theodore Kisiel and Thomas Sheehan (Evanston, IL: Northwestern University Press, 2007), 400–404.

110. Husserl, "Letter to Alexander Pfänder," 400–404.

111. Husserl, "Letter to Alexander Pfänder," 402.

112. Husserl, "Letter to Alexander Pfänder," 401–402.

113. Husserl, "Letter to Alexander Pfänder," 403; emphasis added.

114. Martin Heidegger, "For Edmund Husserl on His Seventieth Birthday (April 8, 1929)," trans. Thomas Sheehan, in *Edmund Husserl: Collected Works,* vol. 6: *Psychological and Transcendental Phenomenology and The Confrontation with Heidegger (1927–1931),* ed. and trans. Richard E. Palmer and Thomas Sheehan (Dordrecht: Kluwer, 1997), 475–477.

115. The WM lecture was not published until the following December. On Husserl's response, see Richard E. Palmer, "Husserl's Debate with Heidegger in the Margins of *Kant and the Problem of Metaphysics,*" *Man and World* 30 (1997): 5–33.

116. Husserl, "Letter to Alexander Pfänder," 403.

117. Husserl, "Letter to Alexander Pfänder," 403.

118. For a related argument, see Dan Zahavi, *Husserl's Phenomenology* (Stanford, CA: Stanford University Press, 2003), esp. 141.

119. Edmund Husserl, "Husserl's Marginal Remarks in Martin Heidegger, *Being and Time,*" trans. Thomas Sheehan, in *Edmund Husserl: Collected Works,* vol. 6: *Psychological and Transcendental Phenomenology,* 263–422, quotation at 296–297.

120. Palmer, "Husserl's Debate with Heidegger," 23.

121. Palmer, "Husserl's Debate with Heidegger," 14.

122. Edmund Husserl, "Phenomenology and Anthropology," trans. Thomas Sheehan and Richard Palmer, in *Edmund Husserl: Collected Works,* vol. 6: *Psychological and Transcendental Phenomenology,* 485–500.

123. Dorion Cairns, *Conversations with Husserl and Fink* (The Hague: Martinus Nijhoff, 1976), 9, as cited in *Edmund Husserl: Collected Works,* vol. 6: *Psychological and Transcendental Phenomenology,* 30.

124. Edmund Husserl to Roman Ingarden, *Briefwechsel* (April 19, 1931), 274, as cited in *Edmund Husserl: Collected Works,* vol. 6: *Psychological and Transcendental Phenomenology,* 30 n. 118.

125. For Cassirer's assessment of Natorp, see Ernst Cassirer, "Paul Natorp. 24. Januar 1854–17. August 1924," KS 30.3–4 (1925): 273–298.

126. For Natorp's summation of Cohen's legacy, see Paul Natorp, "Hermann Cohens philosophische Leistung unter dem Gesichtspunkte des Systems," in *Philosophische Vorträge veröffentlicht von der Kant-Gesellschaft* 21, ed. Arthur Liebert (Berlin: Reuther & Reichard, 1918); and Paul Natorp, "Hermann Cohen als Mensch, Lehrer und Forscher," *Marburger Akademische Reden* 39 (Marburg: Elwert, 1918).

127. Paul Natorp, "Kant und die Marburger Schule," KS 17.3 (1912): 193–221, quotation at 218–219.

128. Gadamer's commemorative address was later published as Hans-Georg Gadamer, "Die philosophische Bedeutung Paul Natorps," in *Philosophische Lehrjahre* (Frankfurt am Main: V. Klostermann, 1977), 60–68.

129. For an analysis of Natorp's late turn toward ontology and the comparison with Heidegger, see Christoph von Wohlzogen, "'Es gibt': Heidegger und Natorps 'Praktische Philosophie,'" in *Heidegger und praktische Philosophie*, ed. Annemarie Gethmann-Siefert and Otto Pöggeler (Frankfurt am Main: Suhrkamp, 1988), 313–337; and von Wohlzogen, *Die autonome Relation: Zum Problem der Beziehung im Spätwerk Paul Natorps. Ein Beitrag zur Geschichte der Theorien der Relation* (Würzburg: Königskausen & Neumann, 1984); also see Markus Brach, *Heidegger-Platon: Vom Neukantianismus zur existentiellen Interpretation des "Sophistes"* (Würzburg: Königshausen & Neumann, 1996).

130. Heinemann, *Neue Wege*, 93.

131. Kurt Sternberg, "Cassirer, Ernst. Prof. an der Universität Hamburg: *Die Begriffsform im mythischen Denken*," review, KS 30 (1925): 194–195, quotation at 194.

132. Joachim Ritter, "Ernst Cassirers Philosophie der symbolischen Formen," *Neue Jahrbücher für Wissenschaft und Jugendbildung* 6.7 (1930): 593–605, quotation at 593.

133. See, for example, the negative assessments of both Cassirer and Rickert in Gershom Scholem, *Walter Benjamin: The Story of a Friendship*, trans. Harry Zohn (New York: Schocken Books, 1981), 21.

134. Karl Jaspers to Martin Heidegger, Letter 24 (July 21, 1925), in *Briefwechsel, 1920–1963*, ed. Walter Biemel and Hans Saner (Frankfurt am Main: V. Klostermann, 1990), 51–52.

2. Setting the Stage

1. For a complete documentation of Davos as a *Kurort*, see Jules Ferdmann, *Die Anfänge des Kurortes Davos bis zur Mitte des XIX: Jahrhunderts* (Davos: Verlag der Davoser Revue, 1938).

2. Peter L. Berger, "The Cultural Dynamics of Globalization," in *Many Globalizations: Cultural Diversity in the Contemporary World*, ed. Peter L. Berger and Samuel P. Huntington (New York: Oxford University Press, 2002), 1–17.

3. Thomas Mann, *The Magic Mountain*, trans. H. T. Lowe-Porter (New York: Vintage Books, 1969), 586.

4. Volker Gürke, *Davos Entdecken: Wege zu einem ungewöhnlichen Ort* (Davos: Genossenschaft Davoser Revue, 1997), 72.

5. Ludwig Englert, "Als Student bei den zweiten Davoser Hochschulkursen," in DH, 36–37.

6. The reporter notes that temporality had become one of the most meaningful issues of the "philosophy of the age," as well as on the "magic mountain" (*Zauberberg*). Hans Barth, "Davoser Hochschulkurse 1929," NZZ, March 30, 1929, 1.

7. Karlfried Gründer, "Cassirer und Heidegger in Davos, 1929," in *Über Ernst Cassirers Philosophie der symbolischen Formen,* ed. Hans-Jürg Braun, Helmut Holzhey, and Ernst Wolfgang Orth (Frankfurt am Main: Suhrkamp, 1988), 290–302.

8. William Clark, *Academic Charisma and the Origins of the Research University* (Chicago: University of Chicago Press, 2006), chap. 3.

9. Grisebach professed a strong admiration for Heidegger's philosophy, especially its analysis of death. See Eberhard Grisebach, *Gegenwart: Eine kritische Ethik* (Halle-Saale: Max Niemeyer, 1928), esp. 556–557.

10. Albert Einstein, *Ideas and Opinions* (based on *Mein Weltbild,* ed. Carl Seelig), trans. Sonja Bargmann (New York: Crown Publishers, 1954).

11. The sketch is reproduced in Gürke, *Davos Entdecken,* 75.

12. Quoted from Ernst Howald, "Betrachtungen zu den Davoser Hochschulkursen," NZZ, April 10, 1929, Morgenausgabe, 1.

13. On the third conference, see the report by F. K., "Internationale Hochschulkurse in Davos," FZ, February 17 1930, 4.

14. Quoted from Professor G. Salomon, "Rückblick auf Davos, 1930," FZ, May 25, 1930, Zweites Morgenblatt, 6.

15. Hermann Herrigel, "Internationale Davoser Hochschulkurse: Bildung des praktischen Menschen," FZ, April 26, 1931, Zweites Morgenblatt, 8.

16. A roster of *Hochschulkurse* participants was published in the *Davoser Blätter* as a supplement to the complete schedule of lectures. See the *Davoser Blätter,* Jahrgang 58, Numbers 11–14 (March 15–April 19, 1929). This roster can be cross-checked against visitors' lists of new arrivals in the public hotels and sanatoria. These lists offer no guarantee that a visitor also attended the lectures, but they at least indicate an individual's presence in town during the *Hochschulkurse.* The visitors' list was published on a weekly basis as *Journal des Etrangers. Fremdenliste. Visitors List. New Arrivals. Neuangekommene. Nouvelles arrivées.* See esp. *Davoser Blätter,* Jahrgang 58, Numbers 11–15 (March 15–May 3).

17. Przywara's writings included *Gottgeheimnis der Welt: Drei Vorträge über die geistige Krisis der Gegenwart* (Munich: Theatiner, 1923); *Kant Heute: Eine Sichtung* (Munich: R. Oldenbourg, 1930); and *Christliche Existenz* (Leipzig: J. Hegner, 1934). Further biographical information can be found in Gustav Wilhelmy, ed., *Erich Przywara, 1889–1969: Eine Festgabe* (Düsseldorf: Patmos, 1969), 19–20.

18. Erich Przywara, "Vorwort zur ersten Auflage von *Analogia Entis,* I," in *Analogia Entis,* 2nd ed., *Schriften,* Bd. 3 (Einsiedeln: Johannes, 1962), 7–10.

19. For a summary of the conversation among Tillich, Grisebach, and Przywara, see Gerhard Kulhmann, "Allmächtigkeit oder Alleinwirksamkeit der Gnade: Ein theologisches Nachwort zu den Davoser internationaler Hochschulkursen," *Theologische Blätter,* N. 5, Jahrgang 7 (Mai 1928), 122–123.

20. DR, 199.

21. On Riezler's political career in the early years of the Weimar Republic, see Wayne C. Thompson, *In the Eye of the Storm: Kurt Riezler and the Crises of Modern Germany* (Iowa City: University of Iowa Press, 1980). Also see Fritz Stern, "Bethmann Hollweg and the War: The Limits of Responsibility," in *The Responsibility of Power*, ed. Leonard Krieger and Fritz Stern (New York: Doubleday, 1969), 271–307.

22. DR, 199–201.

23. Leo Strauss's essay, "Kurt Riezler," was an enlarged version of a memorial lecture delivered at the Graduate Faculty of the New School for Social Research in New York City. First published in *Social Research* 23.1 (1956): 3–32; republished as "Kurt Riezler (1882–1955)," in Leo Strauss, *What Is Political Philosophy? and Other Studies* (Glencoe, IL: The Free Press, 1959), 233–260, the version cited here.

24. Strauss, "Kurt Riezler," 245–246.

25. Strauss, "Kurt Riezler," 246.

26. Strauss, "Kurt Riezler," 245–246.

27. DR, 199–201. Also see the summary by Hans Barth, "Davoser Hochschulkurse, 1929," NZZ, March 27, 1929, Morgenausgabe, 1–2.

28. DR, 204.

29. For a complete list of all of the participants, see note 16 above.

30. Michael Friedman, *A Parting of the Ways: Carnap, Cassirer, and Heidegger* (Chicago: Open Court, 2000), 7.

31. Rudolf Carnap, "Overcoming Metaphysics" (1932), as quoted in Friedman, *A Parting of the Ways,* 12.

32. Jean Grondin, *Hans-Georg Gadamer: A Biography,* trans. Joel Weinsheimer, (New Haven: Yale University Press, 2003), 146.

33. Eugen Fink, "The Phenomenological Philosophy of Edmund Husserl and Contemporary Criticism," in *The Phenomenology of Husserl: Selected Critical Readings,* ed. R. O. Elveton (Chicago: Quadrangle Books, 1970), 73–147, quotation at 145; trans. of "Die phänomenologische Philosophie Edmund Husserls in der gegenwärtigen Kritik," *Kantstudien* 38 (1933): 319–383; quotations from Elveton.

34. Edmund Husserl, Preface to Eugen Fink, "The Phenomenological Philosophy of Edmund Husserl and Contemporary Criticism," in Elveton 73–75, quotation at 73.

35. Ronald Bruzina, *Edmund Husserl and Eugen Fink: Beginnings and Ends in Phenomenology, 1928–1938* (New Haven: Yale University Press, 2004).

36. François Poirié, *Emmanuel Lévinas, Qui êtes-vous?* (Lyons: La Manufacture, 1987), 74.

37. Emmanuel Lévinas, "Introduction," in *The Theory of Intuition in Husserl's Phenomenology,* trans. André Orianne (Evanston, IL: Northwestern University Press, 1973), esp. xxxiv.

38. The 1949 French anthology of Lévinas's early essays was published as *En découvrant l'Existence avec Husserl et Heidegger* (Paris: Vrin, 1949).

39. Emmanuel Lévinas, "Martin Heidegger et l'ontologie," originally published in *La Revue philosophique de la France et de l'étranger* 57 (1932): 395–431; reprinted, without this introductory passage, in *En découvrant l'Existence,* 53–76. The original essay from *La Revue philosophique* has been helpfully translated by the Committee of Public Safety as "Emmanuel Lévinas: Martin Heidegger and Ontology," in *Diacritics* 26.1 (1996): 11–32.

40. Emmanuel Lévinas, "Entretien avec Roger-Pol Droit," in *Les imprévus de l'histoire,* ed. Pierre Hayat (Montpellier: Fata Morgana, 1994), 203–210; originally published in *Le Monde* 2 (June 1992): 2.

41. On Lévinas as Heidegger's student, see Peter E. Gordon, "Fidelity as Heresy: Levinas, Heidegger, and the Crisis of the Transcendental Ego," in Samuel Fleischacker, ed., *Heidegger's Jewish Followers: Essays on Hannah Arendt, Leo Strauss, Hans Jonas, and Emmanuel Levinas* (Pittsburgh: Duquesne University Press, 2008), 187–203.

42. The photo can be found in Poirié, *Emmanuel Lévinas,* 56. Other photographs of participants at the Davos *Hochschulkurse* may be found in *Davos: Die Sonnenstadt im Hochgebirge,* Emil Schaeffer, hrsg. Schaubücher, Band 38 (Zürich: Orell Füssli Verlag, 1932).

43. Maurice de Gandillac, *Le Siècle traversé: Souvenirs de neuf décennies* (Paris: Albin Michel, 1998), 132–133.

44. Otto Friedrich Bollnow, "The Human Meaning of Crisis and Critique," in *Crisis and New Beginning: Contributions to a Pedagogical Anthropology,* trans. Donald Moss and Nancy Moss (Pittsburgh: Duquesne University Press, 1987), 1–27, quotation at 4–5; trans. of *Krise und neuer Anfang* (Heidelberg: Quelle und Meyer Verlag, 1966).

45. Otto Friedrich Bollnow, "Gespräche in Davos," in *Erinnerung an Martin Heidegger,* ed. Günther Neske (Pfullingen: Neske, 1977), 25–29.

46. Bollnow, "Gespräche in Davos," 25–29.

47. Bollnow, "Gespräche in Davos," 25–29.

48. Quoted from Otto Friedrich Bollnow, *Existenzphilosophie: Vierte Erweiterte Auflage* (Stuttgart: W. Kohlhammer, 1955), 131. First a student of physics and later philosophy, Bollnow contributed chiefly to hermeneutics, existentialism, and the philosophy of education. In the postwar era he taught at University of Tübingen. Representative publications include: *Dilthey* (1936); *Das Wesen der Stimmungen* (1941); *Existenzphilosophie* (1943); *Deutsche Existenzphilosophie* (1953); *Neue Geborgenheit* (1955); *Die Lebensphilosophie* (1958); *Existenzphilosophie und Pädagogik* (1959); *Mensch und Raum* (1963); *Sprache und Erziehung* (1966); *Philosophie der Erkenntnis* (vol. 1, 1970; vol. 2, 1975); and *Studies in Hermeneutics* (Freiburg and Munich, 1982, 1983).

49. Joachim Ritter, *Hegel und die französische Revolution* (Köln: Westdeutscher, 1957).

50. See, for example, Ritter's favorable review of Cassirer's *Philosophy of Symbolic Forms*: Joachim Ritter, "Ernst Cassirers Philosophie der symbolischen Formen," *Neue Jahrbücher für Wissenschaft und Jugendbildung* 6.7 (1930): 593–605.

51. Joachim Ritter, "Bildungskrise in Davos: Bemerkungen zu den IV. Davoser Hochschulkursen vom 22. März bis 11 April, 1931," *Neue Jahrbücher für Wissenschaft und Jugendbildung* 7.7 (1931): 661–665.

52. Toni Cassirer, *Mein Leben mit Ernst Cassirer* (Hildesheim: Gerstenberg, 1981), 205.

53. My thanks to John Michael Krois for the information on Ritter's relation to Cassirer. On Ritter's life and politics, see Hans Jörg Sandkühler, "'Eine lange Odyssee'—Joachim Ritter, Ernst Cassirer, und die Philosophie im 'Dritten Reich,'" *Dialektik* 1 (2006): 1–40. On Cassirer's *Lehrstuhl*, see Josef Meran, "Die Lehrer am Philosophischen Seminar der Hamburger Universität während der Zeit des Nationalsozialismus," in *Hochschulalltag im "Dritten Reich": Die Hamburger Universität 1933–1945,* ed. Eckart Krause, Ludwig Huber, and Holger Fischer (Berlin: Reimer, 1991), 459–482.

54. Ritter is quoted from Gunter Scholtz, "Joachim Ritter als Linkshegelianer," in *Joachim Ritter zum Gedenken,* ed. Ulrich Dierse (Stuttgart: Franz Steiner, 2004), 147–162, quotation at 158–159. Scholtz is cited in Sandkühler, "'Eine lange Odyssee,'" 21–22.

55. Joachim Ritter, *Über den Sinn und die Grenze der Lehre vom Menschen* (Potsdam: Alfred Protte, 1933). This is a largely unchanged reproduction of Ritter's *Antrittsrede* delivered in February 1933 at Hamburg University (hereafter *Antrittsrede*). Also see Sandkühler, "'Eine lange Odyssee,'" 33.

56. Ritter, *Antrittsrede,* 6.

57. Ritter, quoting from Max Scheler, "Mensch und Geschichte" (1929), in *Philosophische Weltanschauung* (Bonn: F. Cohen, 1929), 15–46, quotation from *Antrittsrede,* 15.

58. On this theme, also see Theodor Haering, "Die philosophische Bedeutung der Anthropologie," *Blätter für Deutsche Philosophie* 3.1 (1929): 1–32.

59. Ritter, *Antrittsrede,* 28.

60. Ritter, *Antrittsrede,* 30.

61. A complete biography can be found in *Gedenkschrift Joachim Ritter, zum Gedenkfeier zu Ehren des am 3. August 1974 verstorbenen em. Ordentlichen Professors der Philosophie Dr. phil. Joachim Ritter* (Münster: Aschendorff, 1978).

62. Heidegger, "Vorwort zur Vierten Auflage," in KPM, xiii–xv, xv. Although not included in the original Cohen Verlag edition, the transcript itself was later printed as Anhang IV: "Davoser Disputation zwischen Ernst Cassirer und Martin Heidegger," in KPM, 274–296.

63. Martin Heidegger, *Letters to His Wife, 1915–1970,* selected, edited, and annotated by Gertrud Heidegger, trans. R. D. V. Glasgow (Malden, MA: Polity Press, 2008); translated from *"Mein liebes Seelchen!" Briefe Mein Heideggers an seine Frau Elfride, 1915–1970,* Gertrud Heidegger, hrsg. (München: Deutsche Verlags-Anstalt, 2005), letter from Davos (March 21, 1929), 119.

64. From March 1 to April 1, 1929, Davos was also the location for a spring skiing expedition; see "Aus der Schweiz: Dies und das aus Davos," FZ, March 2, 1929, "Bäder Blatt," 10. The general contrast between skiers and students was especially striking; see Hermann Herrigel, "Internationale Davoser Hochschulkurse: Bildung des praktischen Menschen," FZ, April 26, 1931,

65. Heidegger, *Letters to His Wife,* 119.

66. See Henry Hoek, "Frühlings-Skifahrten," in DR, 207.

67. Martin Heidegger to Elisabeth Blochmann, in *Briefwechsel, 1918–1969,* ed. Joachim W. Storck (Marbach am Neckar: Deutsche Schillergesellschaft, 1989), 29.

68. Heidegger, *Letters to his Wife,* letter from Davos (March 21, 1929), 119.

69. "Bei den Studenten," in DR, 205–207.

70. Ernst Howald, "Betrachtungen zu den Davoser Hochschulkursen," NZZ, April 10, 1929, Morgenausgabe, 1.

71. Howald, "Betrachtungen zu den Davoser Hochschulkursen," 1.

72. Heidegger, *Letters to His Wife,* letter from Davos (March 23, 1929), 120; German from *"Mein liebes Seelchen!"* 161–162.

73. On Heidegger's persona, see the portrait by Pos described in "A Disputed Detail" in Chapter 7 of this volume.

74. Heidegger, *Letters to His Wife,* letter from Davos (March 26, 1929), 120–121.

75. The mood of the opening day is summarized in Howald, "Betrachtungen zu den Davoser Hochschulkursen," as well as DR, 191.

76. DR, 189.

77. DR, 181.

78. DR, 185.

79. DR, 186.

3. The Independent Lectures

1. Heidegger documents this in a letter to Elfride: "Cassirer is going to try to get up today, so the 'study group' won't take place until Monday or Tuesday." Heidegger, *Letters to His Wife*. letter from Davos (March 23, 1929), 120.

2. The contents of the three lectures (delivered on three consecutive Monday mornings, before Heidegger's afternoon lectures on Kant) closely track Cassirer's paper published the following year: "'Geist' und 'Leben' in der Philosophie der Gegenwart," *Die Neue Rundschau* 41.1 (1930): 244–264 (hereafter GL), translated

as " 'Spirit' and 'Life' in Contemporary Philosophy," trans. R. W. Bretall and P. A. Schilpp, in Schilpp, 855–880 (hereafter GL, English).

3. Hermann Herrigel, "Denken dieser Zeit, I," FZ, April 22, 1929.

4. See esp. BT, §10.

5. BT, 71–72; SZ, 45–46.

6. Jacob von Uexküll, *Umwelt und Innenwelt der Tiere* (1909; 2nd ed., Berlin: Julius Springer, 1921); for Heidegger's discussion of von Uexküll, see, for example, the 1929–1930 lecture course, in FCM, 261–264.

7. On Heidegger's gradual shift in terminology from "life" to "Dasein," see the excellent analysis in Theodor Kisiel, *The Genesis of Heidegger's* Being and Time (Berkeley: University of California Press, 1995), esp. 141–142.

8. BT, 178; SZ, 139.

9. DR, 196.

10. DR, 196.

11. DR, 197; my English summary is not verbatim but closely tracks the German report here.

12. DR, 197.

13. DR, 197.

14. DR, 198.

15. For full historical and editorial remarks on the projected "conclusion" to *The Philosophy of Symbolic Forms,* see John Michael Krois and Donal Phillip Verene, "Introduction," in PSF, IV, esp. xii–xiii. For my own analysis of this fourth volume, see chap. 6, "Cassirer's Unpublished Critique."

16. Max Scheler, *Die Stellung des Menschen im Kosmos* (Darmstadt: Reichl, 1928).

17. GL, 33.

18. Ludwig Klages, *Der Geist als Widersacher der Seele,* 5th ed. (Bonn: Bouvier, 1972); originally published in three volumes from 1929–1932; quotation from GL, 34.

19. GL, English, 860.

20. GL, 36; GL, English, 860–861.

21. Georg Simmel, "The Concept and Tragedy of Culture," in *Simmel on Culture: Selected Writings,* ed. David Frisby and Mike Featherstone (London: Sage Publications, 1997), 55–75; Georg Lukács, *Soul and Form,* trans. Anna Bostock (Cambridge, MA: MIT Press, 1974).

22. GL, English, 865.

23. GL, 49–50; GL, English, 872.

24. GL, 52; GL, English, 874–875.

25. GL, English, 869.

26. GL, English, 871.

27. The implied critique of Heidegger is recorded in the summary of Cassirer's lecture in DR, 196.

28. Ernst Cassirer, "Erkenntnistheorie nebst den Grenzfragen der Logik und Denkpsychologie," in *Erkenntnis, Begriff, Kultur,* ed. Rainer A. Bast (Hamburg: Felix Meiner, 1993), 77–154, originally published in *Jahrbücher der Philosophie* 3 (1927): 31–92. For further elucidation, see Gregory Moynahan, "Hermann Cohen's *Das Prinzip der Infinitesimalmethode,* Ernst Cassirer, and the Politics of Science in Wilhelmine Germany," *Perspectives on Science* 11.1 (2003): 35–75, esp. 68.

29. GL, 55; GL, English, 877.

30. BT, 32; SZ, 12.

31. The seminar material was later published in GA 25: *Phänomenologische Interpretation von Kants Kritik der reinen Vernunft* (Frankfurt am Main: V. Klostermann, 1977), trans. Parvis Emad and Kenneth Maly as *Phenomenological Interpretation of Kant's Critique of Pure Reason* (Bloomington: Indiana University Press, 1997). Heidegger's reference to the 1928 lecture in Riga can be found in his "Preface to the First Edition," KPM, xvi; KPM, English, xvii.

32. KPM, xiv; KPM, English, xvi.

33. See BT, esp. §6, "The Task of Destroying the History of Ontology," 41–44; SZ, 20–23.

34. This similarity supports Blattner's reading of Heidegger as an idealist about the entities disclosed via temporal understanding; see William D. Blattner, *Heidegger's Temporal Idealism* (Cambridge: Cambridge University Press, 1999).

35. BT, 251; SZ, 208; see Heidegger's larger discussion of idealism in BT, §43, "Dasein, Worldhood, and Reality."

36. Frank Schalow has observed that Heidegger later changed his mind about Kant (see, e.g., Heidegger's later work, *Die Frage nach dem Ding: Zu Kants Lehre von den transcendentalen Grundsätzen,* GA, Band 41, 1984); also see Schalow, "Thinking at Cross Purposes with Kant: Reason, Finitude, and Truth in the Cassirer-Heidegger Debate," KS 87 (1996): 198–217.

37. See Peter E. Gordon, "Science, Finitude, and Infinity: Neo-Kantianism and the Birth of Existentialism," *Jewish Social Studies* 6.1 (2000): 30–53; for further detail, see Peter E. Gordon, *Rosenzweig and Heidegger: Between Judaism and German Philosophy* (Berkeley: University of California Press, 2003), chap. 1, esp. 42–51; also see Amos Funkenstein, "The Persecution of Absolutes: On the Kantian and Neo-Kantian Theories of Science," in *The Kaleidoscope of Science: The Israel Colloquium for the History and Philosophy of Science,* vol. 1 (Dordrecht: Kluwer Academic Publishers, 1986), 329–348.

38. KPM, Anhang III: "Kants *Kritik der reinen Vernunft* und die Aufgabe einer Grundlegung der Metaphysik," 271–273; KPM, English, "Davos Lecture: Kant's *Critique of Pure Reason* and the Task of a Laying of the Ground for Metaphysics," 169–171. The outline was originally published in DR, 194–196.

39. KPM, 21; KPM, English, 15.

40. KPM, 48–49; KPM, English, 32, quoting Kant, KdrV, A34/B50.

41. KdrV, A141/B181; for insightful commentary, see Calvin O. Schrag, "Heidegger and Cassirer on Kant," KS 58 (1967): 87–100, quotation at 94.

42. KPM, 176; KPM, English, 120.

43. KPM, 169; KPM, English, 116.

44. KPM, 201; KPM, English, 137–138; emphasis added.

45. KPM, 273; KPM, English, 171. The opening phrase—"The point of departure in reason has thus been broken asunder. With that Kant himself, through his radicalism, was brought to the brink of a position from which he had to shrink back"—is repeated almost precisely in the published text of the Kant-book. See KPM, 168; KPM, English, 115.

46. KPM, 273; KPM, English, 171. For a helpful discussion of the quarrel over cultural philosophy, see John Michael Krois, "Why Did Cassirer and Heidegger Not Debate in Davos?" in *Symbolic Forms and Cultural Studies: Ernst Cassirer's Theory of Culture,* ed. Cyrus Hamlin and John Michael Krois (New Haven: Yale University Press, 2004), 244–262, esp. 251.

47. FCM, 75–76; emphasis added.

48. FCM, 75–76; emphasis added.

49. FCM, 77; emphasis added.

4. The Davos Encounter

1. Original Davos transcript by Otto Friedrich Bollnow and Joachim Ritter, "Davos Disputation zwischen Ernst Cassirer und Martin Heidegger," in KPM, 274–296. A complete English translation by Richard Taft can be found in the appendix, "Davos Disputation between Ernst Cassirer and Martin Heidegger," in KPM, English, 171–185. The text used here is based on the German transcript by Bollnow and Ritter. While I have consulted Taft's English version, I have most often retranslated from the German.

2. The passages quoted are from BT, 22; SZ, 3, and BT, 251; SZ, 207–208, respectively.

3. FCM, 184; in German, GA 29–30.

4. Martin Heidegger and Heinrich Rickert, *Briefe, 1912 bis 1933, und andere Dokumente,* ed. Alfred Denker (Frankfurt am Main: V. Klostermann, 2002), 60–63. The letter from Rickert is dated July 17, 1929; the response by Heidegger is dated July 25, 1929.

5. KdrV, A50/B75–A64/B88.

6. KdrV, A60/B85.

7. KdrV, A141/B181.

8. KPM, 168; KPM, English, 115–116.

9. KPM, 153; KPM, English, 105.

10. KPM, 187; KPM, English, 128.

11. KPM, Anhang III (Heidegger's Davos handout), 273; KPM, English, 171.

12. In Heidegger, see KPM, 105; in Cassirer, see, for example, PSF, III, 9, where Cassirer refers to "spontaneity," and 159, where Cassirer refers to a "spontaneity" of the imagination that demonstrates "a basic productive function of the spirit" that "can never be fully explained by merely reproductive processes."

13. PSF, III, 162–163.

14. KdrV, A137/B176–A147/B187.

15. KdrV, A141/B180–A142/B182.

16. Cassirer also developed this theme in the pivotal chapter on "Symbolic Pregnance" in PSF, III, 191–204.

17. PSF, III, 193–194.

18. Immanuel Kant, *Critique of Practical Reason*, in *Practical Philosophy*, trans. Mary J. Gregor (Cambridge: Cambridge University Press, 1996), 133–271, quotation at 193; emphasis added.

19. Kant, *Critique of Practical Reason*, 165; emphasis added.

20. Kant, *Critique of Practical Reason*, 262.

21. On breakthrough and objectivity, see Michael Friedman, "The Davos Disputation and Twentieth-Century Philosophy," in *Symbolic Forms and Cultural Studies: Ernst Cassirer's Theory of Culture*, ed. Cyrus Hamlin and John Michael Krois (New Haven: Yale University Press, 2004), 227–243, esp. 228.

22. Kant, *Critique of Practical Reason*, 196.

23. Kant, *Critique of Practical Reason*, 133–134.

24. KdrV, Preface, A, vii.

25. On this aspect of Kant's philosophy, see Michael Friedman, *Kant and the Exact Sciences* (Cambridge, MA: Harvard University Press, 1998).

26. Immanuel Kant, "Prolegomena to Any Future Metaphysics," trans. Gary Hatfield, in Kant, *Theoretical Philosophy after 1781,* rev. ed., ed. Henry Allison and Peter Heath et al. (Cambridge: Cambridge University Press, 2002), §§6–13.

27. Kant, "Prolegomena to Any Future Metaphysics," §13 n. 1.

28. The preface to PSF, III, is dated "End July, 1929," that is, just after the Davos disputation.

29. PSF, III, 149 n. 4 and 163 n. 2. For a fuller explanation of Cassirer's argument see the discussion in chapter 4 on "Myth, Crisis, Science,"

30. KdrV, A845/B873.

31. KdrV, A247/B303; emphasis added.

32. Kant, *Critique of Practical Reason*, 200.

33. Immanuel Kant, "Drittes Hauptstück: Von den Triebfedern der reinen praktischen Vernunft," in *Kritik der praktischen Vernunft, Philosophische Bibliothek* 38 (Hamburg: Felix Meiner, 1990), 140–142; Kant, *Critique of Practical Reason,* 204.

34. Kant, *Kritik der praktischen Vernunft,* §7, "Grundgesetz der reinen praktischen Vernunft," 57–58; Kant, *Critique of Practical Reason,* 165.

35. "Still less are we justified in laying down laws for such imaginary rational beings in the abstract. To talk of rational beings apart from man is as if we attempted to talk of heavy beings apart from bodies. *We cannot help suspecting that Kant here gave a thought to the dear little angels, or at any rate counted on their presence in the conviction of the reader*" (emphasis added). Arthur Schopenhauer, *On the Basis of Morality*, trans. E. F. J. Payne (Indianapolis: Hackett, 1998), 63–64.

36. Immanuel Kant, *Anthropology from a Pragmatic Point of View*, ed. and trans. Robert B. Louden (New York: Cambridge University Press, 2006), 71.

37. On Kant's *Religion* and the reference to Haller, see my foregoing remarks in Chapter 1 in "Southwestern and Marburg Neo-Kantianism."

38. Martin Heidegger, "What Are Poets For?" in *Poetry, Language, Thought*, trans. Albert Hofstadter (New York: Harper & Row, 1971), 134, originally published as *"Wozu Dichter?"* GA 5: *Holzwege*, ed. Friedrich-Wilhelm von Herrmann (Frankfurt: V. Klostermann, 1977), 312.

39. Heidegger to Löwith, in *Im Gespräch der Zeit*, vol. 2: *Zur philosophischen Aktualität Heideggers*, ed. Dietrich Papenfuss and Otto Pöppeler (Frankfurt: V. Klostermann, 1990), 27–32.

40. Martin Heidegger, "The Question Concerning Technology," in *The Question Concerning Technology and Other Essays*, trans. William Lovitt (New York: Harper Perennial, 1982), 35. The later writings are replete with references to both God and the gods, an indeterminacy that should warn off simpleminded characterizations of the later Heidegger as exclusively *either* a "pagan" *or* a "Christian" philosopher.

41. See, for example, Franz Rosenzweig's suggestion that Heidegger, an "Aristotelian scholastic," bore a secret philosophical debt to the later Hermann Cohen's philosophy of religion. The claim can be found in Rosenzweig's own commentary on the Davos debate, "Vertauschte Fronten," originally printed posthumously in the journal *Der Morgen* 6.6 (1930): 85–87; reprinted in Franz Rosenzweig, *Der Mensch und sein Werk: Gesammelte Schriften*, vol. 3, ed. Reinhold Mayer and Annemarie Mayer (Dordrecht: Martinus Nijhoff, 1984), 235–238.

42. KPM, 22–29; KPM, English, 16–20.

43. Kant, *Anthropology from a Pragmatic Point of View*, §28.

44. The Latin, *constitutivum* means a "constitutive feature," or necessary mark. See, for example, Immanuel Kant, *Notes and Fragments*, ed. Paul Guyer, trans. Paul Guyer, Curtis Bowman, and Frederick Rauscher (Cambridge: Cambridge University Press, 2005), 202–203, 234.

45. This point is repeated almost verbatim in KPM, 25–26; KPM, English, 17.

46. BT, 32; SZ, 12.

47. For a rich account of this theme, see Daniel O. Dahlstrom, *Heidegger's Concept of Truth* (Cambridge: Cambridge University Press, 2001).

48. BT, 256–273; SZ, §44, 213–230.

49. BT, 263; SZ, 221. For an explanation of the claim that Dasein "*is* its disclosedness," see Robert Brandom, "Heidegger's Categories in *Being and Time*," in *Heidegger: A Critical Reader,* ed. Hubert L. Dreyfus and Harrison Hall (Oxford: Blackwell, 1992), 45–64.

50. BT, 264; SZ, 222.

51. BT, 75; SZ, 50.

52. For dating the composition of "What Is Metaphysics?" see "Vorwort zur dritten Auflage, 1949," *Wegmarken* 123 (Preface to the Third Edition [1949] of "On the Essence of Ground"), in which Heidegger says these two lectures were written at the same time, in 1928. Both essays first came to public attention a year later: "What Is Metaphysics?" as a public lecture at Freiburg on July 24, 1929, subsequently published (Bonn: Friedrich Cohen, 1929), and "On the Essence of Ground" in the *Festschrift* presented to Edmund Husserl on his seventieth birthday, *Ergänzungsband zum Jahrbuch für Philosophie und phänomenologische Forschung* (Halle: Max Niemeyer, 1919), 71–110.

53. See, for example, BT, 26–27, and SZ, 7–8, regarding the claim that "we already live in an understanding of Being"; for further remarks also see §4, "The Ontical Priority of the Question of Being."

54. Karl Jaspers, *Psychologie der Weltanschauungen* (Berlin: Springer, 1919). On Heidegger's relation to Jaspers, see Alan M. Olson, ed., *Heidegger and Jaspers* (Philadelphia: Temple University Press, 1993).

55. See Martin Heidegger, "Critical Comments on Karl Jaspers' *Psychology of Worldviews*," in *Becoming Heidegger: On the Trail of His Early Occasional Writings, 1910–1927,* ed. Theodore J. Kisiel and Thomas Sheehan (Evanston, IL: Northwestern University Press, 2007), 110–149.

56. See Martin Heidegger, "Wilhelm Dilthey's Research and the Current Struggle for a Historical Worldview," in *Becoming Heidegger,* 238–274.

57. BP, §2, "The Concept of Philosophy, Philosophy and Worldview" (1927 lecture), 4–11, quotations at 9 and 10.

58. It is instructive to note that Heidegger genuinely believed in this principle even as applied to his own philosophical labor. See, for example, his famous remarks from the letter to Karl Löwith, August 19, 1921, that "I work in a concretely factical manner, from out of my 'I am'—from out of my spiritual, indeed factical heritage/milieu/life contexts, from out of that which thereby becomes accessible to me as the living experience in which I live." Quoted from Karl Löwith, *Martin Heidegger and European Nihilism,* ed. Richard Wolin, trans. Gary Steiner (New York: Columbia University Press, 1998), 236.

59. MFL, 17.

60. MFL, 18.

61. MFL, 18.

62. "Freundlos war der große Weltenmeister, / Fühlte Mangel—darum schuf er Geister, / Sel'ge Spiegel seiner Seligkeit!- / Fand das höchste Wesen schon kein

gleiches, / Aus dem Kelche des ganzen Seelenreiches / Schäumt ihm—die Unendlichkeit." Friedrich Schiller, "An die Freundschaft," in *Schiller's Sämmtliche Werke,* Bd. 8, ed. Robert Borberger (Berlin: Grote'sche Verlagsbuchhandlung, 1878), 21–22. Note that Cassirer says "strömt" and not "schäumt." A variant of this final stanza appears in Schiller's *Philosophische Briefe* (1786), in the section "God." The concluding two lines of the variant run as follows: "Aus dem Kelche des ganzen Wesenreiches schäumt ihm die Unendlichkeit." Hegel uses this phrase as the concluding lines to *The Phenomenology of Spirit.*

63. Johann Wolfgang von Goethe, *Sämtliche Werke: Briefe, Tagebücher und Gespräche,* ed. Dieter Borchmeyer et al., Frankfurter Ausgabe, ser. 1, vol. 2 (Frankfurt am Main: Deutscher Klassiker, 1985), 380.

64. ICRP, 189–191. The very same quotation from Goethe about exploring the finite in all directions also appears in the introduction to PSF, III, 41.

65. EM, 15.

66. BT, 435; SZ, 384.

67. Friedrich Schiller, *Werke,* vol. 3: *Gedichte, Erzählungen,* ed. Dieter Schmidt (Frankfurt am Main: Insel, 1966), 99–103.

68. Kuno Fischer, *Schiller-Schriften,* vols. 3–4: *Schiller als Philosoph: In zwei Büchern* (Heidelberg: Carl Winter, 1891); Friedrich Albert Lange, *Einleitung und Kommentar zu Schillers philosophischen Gedichten* (Leipzig: Velhagen und Klasing, 1919), xv; Karl Vorländer, "Schiller's Verhältnis zu Kant in seiner geschichtlichen Entwicklung," *Philosophischen Monatshefe* 30 (1894), reprinted in *Kant-Schiller-Goethe: Gesammelte Aufsätze,* 2nd ed. (Leipzig: Felix Meiner, 1923; orig. pub. 1906). Also see Peter E. Gordon, *Rosenzweig and Heidegger* (Berkeley: University of California Press, 2003), 143–147, and Frederick Beiser, *Schiller as Philosopher: A Re-Examination* (New York: Oxford University Press, 2005).

69. Heidegger writes that "Dasein is *authenticity itself* in the primordial individualization of the reticent resolutement which exacts anxiety of itself." For in Dasein's reticence, "it 'is' that thrown entity as which it can authentically *be.*" BT, 369; SZ, 323. Elsewhere Heidegger explains that Dasein's freedom occurs "always within the limitations of its thrownness." BT, 417; SZ, 366.

70. Hendrik J. Pos, "Recollections of Ernst Cassirer," in Schilpp, 63–72, quotations at 67.

71. PSF, III, 149.

72. KdrV, A805/B833.

73. Immanuel Kant, *Jäsche Logic,* trans. Robert S. Hartman and Wolfgang Schwarz (New York: Dover, 1974), 29. On Kant's anthropology, see Manfred Kuehn's introductory remarks in Kant, *Anthropology from a Pragmatic Point of View,* vii–xxix, esp. xi–xiii.

74. Traces of the debate with Cassirer survive in the book, where, for example, Heidegger writes that anthropology "determines in particular either the goal of philosophy or its point of departure or both at once. If the goal of philosophy lies

in the working-out of a world-view, then an anthropology will have to delimit the 'place of man in the cosmos'" (a reference to Max Scheler's *Die Stellung des Menschen im Kosmos*). See KPM, esp. §37: The Idea of a Philosophical Anthropology." Quotation from KPM, English, 144.

75. See, for example, BT, §9, "The Theme of an Analytic of Dasein," 42–47; and BT, §40, "The Basic State-of-Mind of Anxiety as a Distinctive Way in which Dasien Is Disclosed." For fleeing as "fleeing-toward-worldly-entities," see esp. BT, 233; SZ, 189.

76. PSF, I, 77–78 (G, 8–9).

77. EM, 143–144.

78. On the theme of the "ontico-ontological priority of Dasein" *(der ontisch-ontologischen Vorrang des Daseins),* see BT, 34; SZ, 14.

79. BT, 435; SZ, 384.

80. KdrV, A773/B801. Another reference to *ignava ratio* can be found at A689/B717.

81. FCM, 77.

82. See the similar remark in *Being and Time:* "Once one has grasped the finitude of one's existence, it snatches one back from the endless multiplicity of possibilities which offer themselves as closest to one—those of comfortableness, shirking, and taking things lightly—and brings Dasein into the simplicity of its *fate.*" BT, 435; SZ, 384.

83. Johann Gottlieb Fichte, "Foundations of the Entire Science of Knowledge," in *Science of Knowledge,* 2nd ed., ed. and trans. Peter Heath and John Lachs (Cambridge: Cambridge University Press, 1982), 16.

84. PSF, I, 285 (G, 252); emphasis added.

85. PSF, I, 88 (G, 21).

86. "All these symbols lay claim to objective value. . . . They themselves regard their symbols not only as objectively valid, but for the most part as the very core of the objective and 'real.'" "Not only science, but language, myth, art and religion as well, provide the building stones from which the world of 'reality' is constructed for us." PSF, I, 88, 91 (G, 21, 24).

87. See John Michael Krois, "Cassirer, Neo-Kantianism, and Metaphysics," *Revue de métaphysique et de morale* 4 (1992): 436–453.

88. See, for example, BT, 31; SZ, 11.

89. BT, 31; SZ, 11.

90. Hermann Herrigel, "Denken dieser Zeit: Fakultäten und Nationen treffen sich in Davos," FZ, April 22, 1929, Abendblatt, 4.

5. Before Davos

1. In the preface to PSF, III (written in Hamburg and dated July 1929), Cassirer wrote that "the manuscript of the volume was completed at the end of 1927

and that publication was delayed only because at that time I still planned to include the final, critical chapter. Consequently, I have been able to take into account only a few of the works published in the last two years." PSF, III, xvii.

2. In *An Essay on Man,* Cassirer affirmed that "space and Time are the framework in which all reality is concerned. We cannot conceive of any real thing except under the conditions of space and time." But "we must analyze the forms of human *culture* in order to discover the true character of space and time in our human world." For despite the unified human *capacity* on display in human culture, "there are fundamentally different *types* of spatial and temporal experience." EM, 42.

3. The phenomenological study of *Sinn* recalls Frege's classic distinction between sense and reference. For Frege's impact on Husserlian phenomenology, see Michael Dummett, *Origins of Analytic Philosophy* (Cambridge, MA: Harvard University Press, 1993). As Cristina Lafont observes, there is an important connection between Frege's theory and the tradition of linguistic hermeneutics that Charles Taylor has called the "H-H-H" tradition: see Taylor, "Theories of Meaning," in *Human Agency and Language: Philosophical Papers,* vol. 1 (Cambridge: Cambridge University Press, 1985), 248–292; and Lafont, *Heidegger, Language, and World-Disclosure,* trans. Graham Harman (Cambridge: Cambridge University Press, 2000).

4. For Husserl's defense of phenomenology as a merely descriptive science, see, for example, Husserl, *Ideas Pertaining to a Pure Phenomenology and to a Phenomenological Philosophy,* vol. 1: *General Introduction to Pure Phenomenology,* §75, "Phenomenology as Descriptive Theory of the Essence of Pure Experiences," 209–211. On differences between Husserl and Heidegger on bracketing, see Herbert Spiegelberg, *The Phenomenological Movement: A Historical Introduction* (The Hague: Nijhoff, 1960).

5. For an excursus on the problem of formal indication, see Daniel O. Dahlstrom, *Heidegger's Concept of Truth* (Cambridge: Cambridge University Press, 2001), esp. 245–252.

6. See BT, §14.

7. BT, 66; SZ, 66.

8. For an interpretation of "dealings," translated as "coping" and construed as the central category of analysis for the entirety Division One, see Hubert L. Dreyfus, *Being-in-the-World: A Commentary on Heidegger's* Being and Time, *Division I* (Cambridge, MA: MIT Press, 1991), esp. chap. 4.

9. BT, 97–98; SZ, 68–69.

10. I am indebted here to the analysis of space in Jeff Malpas, "Uncovering the Space of Disclosedness: Heidegger, Technology, and the Problem of Spatiality in *Being and Time,*" in *Heidegger, Authenticity, and Modernity: Essays in Honor of Hubert L. Dreyfus,* vol. 1, ed. Mark Wrathall and Jeff Malpas (Cambridge, MA:

MIT Press, 2000), 205–228, esp. 211. Also see Dreyfus, *Being-in-the-World*, 43, as cited in Malpas, "Uncovering the Space of Disclosedness," 209.

11. BT, 122; SZ, 88; emphasis added.

12. BT, 122; SZ, 88; emphasis added in the final sentence.

13. BT, 136; SZ, 103.

14. This term is translated by John Macquarrie and Edward Robinson as *de-severance*. For their justification of this neologism, see BT, 138–139.

15. BT, 140; SZ, 105.

16. BT, 142–143; SZ, 108.

17. BT, 147; SZ, 112–113.

18. BT, 147; SZ, 112; emphasis added in all places except "Unworlding," which is emphasized in the original.

19. Bernard Williams, *Descartes: The Project of Pure Enquiry* (Hassocks, England: Harvester Press, 1978).

20. Max Weber, "Science as a Vocation," in *From Max Weber: Essays in Sociology*, ed. and trans. H. H. Gerth and C. Wright Mills (New York: Oxford University Press, 1946), 129–156, quotation at 142.

21. Robert J. Dostal, "Time and Phenomenology in Husserl and Heidegger," in *The Cambridge Companion to Heidegger*, ed. Charles Guignon (Cambridge: Cambridge University Press, 1993), 141–169.

22. "The primordial unity of the structure of care lies in temporality." BT, 375; SZ, 327.

23. BT, 63; SZ, 39.

24. Saint Augustine, *Confessions*, trans. R. S. Pine-Coffin (London: Penguin Books, 1961), 274. Quotations from Kant in KdrV, "Transcendental Aesthetic, 'Von der Zeit,'" §§4–8, A31/B46.

25. Edmund Husserl, "Phenomenological Time and the Time-Consciousness," in *Ideas Pertaining to a Pure Phenomenology*, vol. 1, §81, 234–239, quotation at 235.

26. SZ, 437; my translation; emphasis added.

27. SZ, 437; my translation.

28. HCT, 320; emphasis added.

29. BP, 170. For this example I am grateful to Robert Dostal's paper, "Time and Phenomenology in Husserl and Heidegger," in *The Cambridge Companion to Heidegger*, ed. Charles Guignon (Cambridge: Cambridge University Press, 1993), 120–148.

30. There is much controversy surrounding the extent to which Heidegger was an anti-realist, that is, whether he believed that all, only some, or no entities are dependent for their essential characteristics on Dasein's mode of disclosure and, most especially, to what degree scientific, present-at-hand entities are so dependent. See William Blattner, "Is Heidegger a Kantian Idealist?" *Inquiry* 37 (1994):

185–201; Blattner, "Decontextualization, Standardization, and Deweyian Science," *Man and World* 28 (1995): 321–339; Blattner, *Heidegger's Temporal Idealism* (Cambridge: Cambridge University Press, 1999); and David R. Cerbone, "World, World-entry, and Realism in Early Heidegger," *Inquiry* 38 (1995): 401–421. For a summary of the controversy and the defense of Heidegger as a robust realist about natural-scientific entities, see Hubert L. Dreyfus, "How Heidegger Defends the Possibility of a Correspondence Theory of Truth with Respect to the Entities of Natural Science," in *The Practice Turn in Contemporary Theory,* ed. Theodore R. Schatzki, Karin Knorr Cetina, and Eike von Savigny (London: Routledge, 2001), 151–162.

31. For a fine reconstruction of this distinction, see Dahlstrom, *Heidegger's Concept of Truth.*

32. BT, 269; SZ, 226–227; emphasis added.

33. PSF, II, 91 (G, 117); emphasis added in English.

34. PSF, II, 95–97 (G, 122–124).

35. Cassirer continued: "Every mythically significant content, every circumstance of life that is raised out of the sphere of the indifferent and the commonplace, forms its own ring of existence, a walled-in zone separated from its surroundings by fixed limits, and only in this separation does it achieve an individual religious form." PSF, II, 103–104 (G, 131–132).

36. PSF, II, 89 (G, 113–114).

37. PSF, II, 105–106 (G, 133).

38. PSF, II, 105–106 (G, 133).

39. PSF, II, 110–111, (G, 141).

40. BT, 76–77; SZ, 51.

41. Bronoslaw Malinowski, *Myth in Primitive Psychology* (New York: W. W. Norton and Company, 1926), 108.

42. Malinowski, *Myth in Primitive Psychology,* 82.

43. BT, 76; SZ, 51.

44. Both Heidegger and Durkheim believed that the focus on "primitive" belief had a methodological advantage in that it disclosed the structure of human meaning in a "simpler" and more vivid fashion. Primitive religion, Durkheim argued, was "crude and rudimentary" and not yet "elaborated" to the point of obscuring its deeper structure. See Durkheim, *The Elementary Forms of Religious Life,* trans. Karen Fields (New York: The Free Press, 1995), 7.

45. BT, chap. 1, 490 n. xi; SZ, 51 n. 1.

46. BT, chap. 1, 490 n. xi; SZ, 51 n. 1.

47. See the perceptive comments by Jaspers in his letter to Heidegger, in *Briefwechsel, 1920–1963,* ed. Walter Biemel and Hans Saner (Frankfurt am Main: V. Klostermann, 1990), Letter 69 (July 8, 1928), 102.

48. MH: Rev. of PSF, II, 43.

49. MH: Rev. of PSF, II, 43.

50. MH: Rev. of PSF, II, 45; emphasis added.

51. MH: Rev. of PSF, II, 42

52. BT, 67; SZ, 42.

53. An excellent analysis of the dispute, specifically on the imagination, is Calvin O. Schrag, "Heidegger and Cassirer on Kant," *Kantstudien* 58 (1967): 87–100.

54. PSF, III, 16; emphasis added.

55. PSF, III, 27.

56. See esp. PSF, II, Part IV, "The Dialectic of the Mythical Consciousness," 235–261 (G, 287–320).

57. PSF, II, 239 (G, 294).

58. PSF, II, 252 (G, 309).

59. On the origins of Lévinas's Heidegger-criticism, see Samuel Moyn, "Judaism against Paganism: Emmanuel Lévinas' Response to Heidegger and Nazism in the 1930s," *History and Memory* 10.1 (1998): 25–58.

60. SF, Swabey, 91; emphasis added on the words *reduction* and *constructed by*.

61. PK, 27.

62. ETR, Swabey, 356.

63. ETR, Swabey, 439; emphasis added. As Felix Kaufmann noted, with this remark, Cassirer moves from naïve realism toward a kind of coherantism. See Felix Kaufmann, "Cassirer's Theory of Scientific Knowledge," in Schilpp, 183–213, esp. 192–193, 198, 206, and 211. For Einstein's own discussion of space and time and the distinction between "subjective" time and time as measured transpersonally in physics, see Albert Einstein, *Vier Vorlesungen über Relativitätstheorie: Gehalten im Mai 1921 an der Universität Princeton,* 2nd ed. (Braunschweig: Friedrich Vieweg und Sohn, 1922), esp. 1–2.

64. SF, Swabey, 104–105; emphasis added.

65. PSF, II, 85 (G, 109–110).

66. ETR, 379.

67. PK, 26–27.

68. PSF, III, 149 n. 4.

69. PSF, III, 149 n. 4.

70. The footnote begins with a subtle qualification: "The following chapter was written before the appearance of Heidegger's recent analysis of 'time' and 'temporality' ('Sein und Zeit,' *Jahrbuch für Philosophie und phänomenologische Forschung* 7 [1927]), which in many respects points to entirely new roads. Here I shall not attempt a detailed critical discussion of this analysis. Such a discussion will be possible and fruitful only when Heidegger's work is available as a whole." PSF, III, 163 n. 2. All emphases mine, except for Cassirer's on "beyond."

71. PSF, III, 163 n. 2.

72. This reading of Heidegger's work as a theory of merely "subjective" phenomenological horizons made sense, especially if one considered Heidegger's work as an interpretation within the Husserlian school. Hence, Cassirer's footnote: "On the difference between phenomenological time and objective 'cosmic' time, cf.

Edmund Husserl, *Ideen zu einer reineen Phänomenologie und phänomenologischen Philosophie* (Halle, 1928), secs. 81ff. I have unfortunately been unable to take into account the penetrating analysis of the temporal consciousness given by Martin Heidegger, 'Edmund Husserls Vorlesungen zur Phänomenologie des inneren Zeitbewusstseins,' *Jahrbuch für Philosophie und phänomenologische Forschung*, 9 (1928), 367–498, on the basis of Husserl's lectures." PSF, III, 173 n. 16.

73. PSF, III, 163.

74. PSF, III, 167.

75. PSF, III, 167 n. 8.

76. On Cassirer's general conflict with the modern phenomenological tradition, see Fritz Kaufmann, "Cassirer, Neo-Kantianism, and Phenomenology," in Schilpp, 799–854.

77. Ernst Cassirer, "Die Sprache und der Aufbau der Gegenstandswelt," in ECW 18, 111–122, quotation at 121; quotation marks around "gegenüber" and "vorstellig" in original.

78. Cassirer, ECW 18, 120–122.

6. After Davos

1. Martin Heidegger to Elisabeth Blochmann, in *Briefwechsel, 1918–1969*, ed. Joachim W. Storck (Marbach am Neckar: Deutsches Literaturarchiv, 1989), 29.

2. EHF, 94.

3. EHF, 205.

4. EHF, 198.

5. EHF, 198.

6. EHF, 198.

7. See the text of Cassirer's concluding rectoral speech in ECW 17, 375–384; the reference to Heidegger can be found at 380. My gratitude to Thomas Meyer for calling this reference to my attention.

8. Heidegger's letter to Adolf Grimme, dated May 10, 1930, explaining this refusal is published as "Entscheidung gegen Berlin," GA 16, 61–62.

9. Details of the Berlin trip can be found in Heidegger's letter to Elfride, from Berlin (April 6, 1930), in Martin Heidegger, *Letters to His Wife, 1915–1970*, selected, edited, and annotated by Gertrud Heidegger, trans. R. D. V. Glasgow (Malden, MA: Polity Press, 2008); translated from *"Mein liebes Seelchen!" Briefe Martin Heideggers an seine Frau Elfride, 1915–1970*, Gertrud Heidegger, hrsg. (München: Deutsche Verlags-Anstalt, 2005), 123.

10. Martin Heidegger to Elisabeth Blochmann, in *Briefwechsel, 1918–1969*, Letter 24 (May 10, 1930), 35–36.

11. Heidegger, *Letters to His Wife* (April 6, 1930), 123.

12. In a later letter to Jaspers (May 17), Heidegger wrote that he learned of these details from Grimme. This was quite possibly a misrepresentation meant to

protect Riezler from his role in revealing the details of the confidential deliberations. See Martin Heidegger/Karl Jaspers, in *Briefwechsel, 1920–1963,* ed. Walter Biemel and Hans Saner (Frankfurt am Main: V. Klostermann, 1990), 132–133.

13. Martin Heidegger to Karl Jaspers, in *Briefwechsel, 1918–1969,* Letter 102 (May 24, 1930), 134, and Letter 108 (July 25, 1931), 141–143.

14. Heidegger, *Letters to His Wife* (April 6, 1930), 123.

15. For a summary of this letter and its historical context, see Ulrich Sieg, "Die Verjudung des deutschen Geistes," *Die Zeit,* December 22, 1989, "Feuilleton," 52.

16. Martin Heidegger, "Hönigswald aus der Schule des Neukantianismus" (letter, from Freiburg, June 25, 1933), reprinted in GA 16, 132–133.

17. On Heidegger's personal attitude toward and treatment of Jewish students and peers, see Thomas Sheehan, "'Everyone Has to Tell the Truth': Heidegger and the Jews," *Continuum* 1.1 (1990): 30–44.

18. Toni Cassirer, *Mein Leben mit Ernst Cassirer* (Hildesheim: Gerstenberg, 1981), 182; originally appeared as *Aus Meinem Leben mit Ernst Cassirer,* privately issued in New York in 1950.

19. Toni Cassirer, *Mein Leben mit Ernst Cassirer,* 183.

20. For a summary of this incident see the balanced assessment by John Michael Krois, "Why Did Cassirer and Heidegger Not Debate in Davos?" in *Symbolic Forms and Cultural Studies: Ernst Cassirer's Theory of Culture,* ed. Cyrus Hamlin and John Michael Krois (New Haven: Yale University Press, 2004), 244–262, 247.

21. Thomas Meyer writes that Cassirer valued Heidegger "as an important thinker" and "accepted him as a person." See Thomas Meyer, *Ernst Cassirer* (Hamburg: Ellert & Richter, 2006), 174.

22. Toni Cassirer, *Mein Leben mit Ernst Cassirer,* 184.

23. Cassirer first delivered the lecture in French, as "L'Unité dans l'oevre de Jean-Jacques Rousseau," to the Société Française de Philosophie on February 27, 1932. The essay was first published in German later in 1932 as "Das Problem Jean Jacques Rousseau," *Archiv für Geschichte der Philosophie* (1932): in two installments, 177–213, and 479–513. An English translation appeared with an illuminating commentary by Peter Gay as *The Question of Jean-Jacques Rousseau,* 2nd ed., ed. Peter Gay (New Haven: Yale University Press, 1989) (hereafter QJJR).

24. QJJR, 46, 81; emphasis added.

25. QJJR, 115; emphases added.

26. QJJR, 58.

27. Toni Cassirer, *Mein Leben mit Ernst Cassirer,* 184.

28. Martin Heidegger and Hannah Arendt, *Letters, 1925–1975,* ed. Ursula Ludz, trans. Andrew Schields (Orlando: Harcourt, 2004), letter dated Winter 1932–1933, 52–53.

29. Thomas Sheehan, "Reading a Life: Heidegger and Hard Times," in *The Cambridge Companion to Heidegger,* ed. Charles Guignon (Cambridge: Cambridge

University Press, 2006), 70–96, quotation at 87; Sheehans is quoting from Karl Jaspers, *Philosophical Autobiography,* exp. ed. (Munich: Piper, 1977), 101.

30. One exception is the early and admiring essay by Emmanuel Lévinas, "Martin Heidegger et l'ontologie," in *En découvrant l'existence avec Husserl et Heidegger* (Paris: Vrin, 1949), 53–76; abridged version of original publication in *La Revue philosophique de la France et de l'étranger* 57 (1932): 395–431.

31. EC: Rev. of KPM, 2; emphasis added.

32. Alois Riehl, "Über wissenschaftliche und nichtwissenschaftliche Philosophie," in Riehl, *Philosophische Studien aus vier Jahzehnten* (Leipzig: Quelle und Meyer, 1925), 227–253.

33. EC: Rev. of KPM, 3; Cassirer is quoting from KPM, 221.

34. EC: Rev. of KPM, 3

35. EC: Rev. of KPM, 4.

36. EC: Rev. of KPM, 7.

37. EC: Rev. of KPM, 9

38. See PSF, III, esp. Part II.

39. EH: Rev. of KPM, 9; here Cassirer invokes the distinction introduced at KdrV, B72.

40. EC: Rev. of KPM, 12.

41. EC: Rev. of KPM, 13.

42. KdrV, B430; translation modified in accordance with Cassirer's German.

43. EC: Rev. of KPM, 14

44. EC: Rev. of KPM, 16.

45. EC: Rev. of KPM, 18.

46. EC: Rev. of KPM, 19.

47. EC: Rev. of KPM, 17, quoting from KPM, 192.

48. EC: Rev. of KPM, 17.

49. Cassirer cited in KdrV, B804.

50. EC: Rev. of KPM, 23.

51. "Nur der Körper eignet jenen Mächten, / Die das dunkle Schicksal flechten; / Aber frei von jeder Zeitgewalt, / Die Gespielin seliger Naturen, / Wandelt oben in des Lichtes Fluren / Göttlich unter Göttern die *Gestalt. /* Wollt Ihr hoch auf ihren Flügeln schweben / Werft die Angst des Irdischen von euch, / Fliehet aus dem engen dumpfen Leben / In des Ideales Reich!" Quoted from Friedrich Schiller, *Werke,* vol. 3: *Gedichte, Erzählungen* (Frankfurt am Main: Insel Verlag, 1966), 99–103.

52. EC: Rev. of KPM, 24.

53. EC: Rev. of KPM, 25.

54. EC: Rev. of KPM, 26.

55. Rudolf Odebrecht, "Martin Heidegger, *Kant und das Problem der Metaphysik,*" review, *Blätter für deutsche Philosophie* 5.1 (1931–1932): 132–135. Odebrecht's philosophy was deeply marked by his neo-Kantian training—like Cassirer,

Odebrecht had studied with Simmel in Berlin. He received his doctorate from Erlangen with a dissertation on Hermann Cohen's philosophy of mathematics. See Rudolf Odebrecht, *Hermann Cohens Philosophie der Mathematik,* diss., Friedrich-Alexander-Universität Erlangen-Nürnberg (Berlin: Universitäts-buchdr. von Gustav Schade [O. Francke], 1906). For biographical information, see Christian Tilitzki, *Die deutsche Universitätsphilosophie in der Weimere Republik und im Dritten Reich* (Berlin: Akademie, 2002), 337–338.

56. The notes remained unpublished until 1973, when they appeared in an appendix to the fourth German edition of *Kant and the Problem of Metaphysics.* See KPM, Anhang V, "Zu Odebrechts und Cassirers Kritik des Kantbuches," 297–303; also translated in the fifth English edition of KPM, 208–212.

57. KPM, Anhang V, 296–303, quotation at 296.

58. KPM, 298; emphasis added.

59. KPM, 300.

60. KPM, "Vorwort zur Zweiten Auflage" and "Vorwort zur Vierten Auflage," xiii–xviii. Heidegger uses the term *fremde* (foreign), the same word Cassirer used throughout his review to describe Heidegger's attempt to read ontology into Kant's theoretical philosophy.

61. Heinrich Rickert, *Die Philosophie des Lebens: Darstellung und Kritik der philosophischen Modeströmungen unserer Zeit* (Tübingen: Mohr, 1920).

62. Cassirer addresses his criticism here chiefly to Simmel's book, *Lebensanschauung: Vier metaphysische Kapitel* (Munich: Duncker und Humblot, 1918), esp. the chapter titled "Die Transcendenz des Lebens."

63. PSF, IV, 19.

64. PSF, IV, 32.

65. PSF, IV, 33.

66. PSF, IV, 200–201.

67. PSF, IV, 203.

68. PSF, IV, 206.

69. The editors of the English translation of PSF, IV, John Michael Krois and Donald Phillip Verene, have surmised that Cassirer was referring to Heinrich Rickert's essay, "Die Logik des Prädikats und das Problem der Ontologie," in *Sitzungsberichte der Heidelberger Akademie der Wissenschaften* (Heidelberg: Universitätsverlag C. Winter, 1930–1931), 1–236, quotation at 230. Krois has noted that this is only a surmise, hence the editorial statement that *in general* these manuscripts date from *circa* 1928. My thanks to John Michael Krois for clarifying this matter. Cassirer quotes Rickert at PSF, IV, 207.

70. PSF, IV, 206; emphasis added.

71. PSF, IV, 203–204.

72. PSF, IV, 202.

73. PSF, IV, 202–203.

74. PSF, IV, 202.

75. PSF, IV, 205–206.

76. Ernst Cassirer, *Nachgelassene Manuskripte und Texte,* Bd. 3: *Geschichte, Mythos,* ed. Klaus Christian Köhnke, John Michael Krois, and Oswald Schwemmer (Hamburg: Felix Meiner, 2002), 87.

77. Friedrich Meinecke, *Die Entstehung des Historismus* (Munich: R. Oldenbourg Verlag, 1936).

78. PE, xi.

79. PE, viii; emphasis added.

80. PE, xi (G, xiv); translation altered in accordance with German original.

81. PE, 14 (G, 16).

82. PE, 38.

83. PE, 39 (G, 51); translation modified.

84. PE, 45.

85. PE, 83–87.

86. PE, 125 (G, 166).

87. PE, 191–192.

88. PE, 228–233.

89. PE, 238.

90. PE, 274.

91. PE, 276.

92. Here Cassirer acknowledges a remark by Windelband that Kant's *Critique of Judgment* "constructs, as it were, *a priori* the concept of Goethe's poetry." PE, 278.

93. PE, 354 (G, 474).

94. PE, 353–354.

95. For more on the distinction between *intellectus archetypus* and *intellectus ectypus,* see the discussion on "the ideational content of the sign," in PSF, I, esp. 112–113.

96. PE, "pure spontaneity" from 356 (regarding Baumgarten); "creative activity" from 360, in the last sentence of the book (regarding Lessing).

97. Kurt Sternberg, "Aufklärung, Klassizismus und Romantik bei Kant," KS 36 (1931): 27–50.

98. Meyer, *Ernst Cassirer,* 179.

99. Max Wundt, "Die deutsche Philosophie im Zeitalter der Aufklärung," *Zeitschrift für deutsche Kulturphilosophie* 2 (1936): 225–250.

100. Charles Hendel, preface, in MS, v–xii, quotation at ix.

101. MS, 1.

102. MS, 52.

103. MS, 52.

104. MS, 60.

105. MS, 92.

106. MS, 99.

107. MS, 99.

108. MS, 143.

109. MS, 199.

110. MS, 218; emphasis added.

111. MS, 219.

112. MS, 216.

113. MS, 309.

114. MS, 323.

115. MS, 335.

116. MS, 315.

117. It is Cassirer's verdict on Hegel's statism that has fared worst of all. Indeed, the myth of Hegel as a "Prussian militarist" was already demolished in 1941 by Herbert Marcuse, *Reason and Revolution: Hegel and the Rise of Social Theory* (New York: Routledge, 1986).

118. MS, 350.

119. MS, 351–352.

120. MS, 353.

121. MS, 355.

122. Theodor W. Adorno and Max Horkheimer, *Dialectic of Enlightenment: Philosophical Fragments,* ed. G. S. Noerr, trans. E. Jephcott (Stanford, CA: Stanford University Press, 2002), xviii.

123. MS, 368–369.

124. MS, 369; emphasis added.

125. MS, 369.

126. "Philosophy and Politics," in Donald Philip Verene, ed., *Symbol, Myth and Culture: Essays and Lectures of Ernst Cassirer, 1935–1945* (New Haven: Yale University Press), 230; emphasis added.

127. MS, 375.

128. Carl Schmitt, *Political Theology: Four Chapters on the Concept of Sovereignty,* trans. George Schwab (Cambridge, MA: MIT Press, 1985), 36.

129. Carl Schmitt, *Der Leviathan in der Staatslehre des Thomas Hobbes: Sinn und Fehlschlag eines politischen Symbols* (Stuttgart: Klett-Cotta, 1995). On Schmitt's political theology, see Heinrich Meier, *Carl Schmitt and Leo Strauss: The Hidden Dialogue,* trans. J. Harvey Lomax (Chicago: University of Chicago Press, 1995), and Hent de Vries and Lawrence Sullivan, eds., *Political Theologies* (New York: Fordham University Press, 2006).

130. Erich Voegelin, *The Political Religions,* in *Modernity without Restraint: Collected Works of Erich Voegelin,* vol. 5. ed. Manfred Henningsen (Columbia: University of Missouri Press, 2000), 70.

131. Erich Voegelin, *"The Myth of the State,* by Ernst Cassirer," review, *The Review of Politics* 9.3 (1947): 445–447.

132. Voegelin, *"The Myth of the State,* by Ernst Cassirer," 447.

133. Karl Löwith, *Meaning in History* (Chicago: University of Chicago Press, 1949), 203 and 207.

134. Leo Strauss, "An Unspoken Prologue to a Public Lecture at St. John's," *Interpretation* 7 (1978): 2.

135. Leo Strauss, "Review of Ernst Cassirer, *The Myth of the State*," *Social Research* 14.1 (1947): 125–128.

136. PSF, II, esp. Part Four, "The Dialectic of Mythical Consciousness," 233–262.

137. Ernst Cassirer, "Judaism and the Modern Political Myths," *Contemporary Jewish Record* 7.2 (1944): 115–126; reprinted in Verene, *Symbol, Myth and Culture*, 233–241, quotation at 241.

138. Sir James Frazer, *The Golden Bough: A Study in Magic and Religion*, 2nd ed. (London: Macmillan, 1900), see esp. chap. 3.

139. Cassirer, "Judaism and the Modern Political Myths," 240.

140. Ernst Cassirer, "Cohen's Philosophy of Religion," *Internationale Zeitschrift für Philosophie* 1 (1996): 89–104; transcribed by Dominic Kaegi, who notes that the quotations are from Hermann Cohen, "Religion und Sittlichkeit: Eine Betrachtung zur Grundlegung der Religionsphilosophie (1907)," in *Jüdische Schriften*, Bd. 3: *Zur jüdischen Religionsphilosophie und ihrer Geschichte*, ed. Bruno Strauss (Berlin: Schwetschke, 1924) 98–168, quotation at 119.

141. In his last work, the *Religion of Reason*, Cohen had written that "Myth overall is the dawning phase of culture [*Der Mythos ist überall das Morgenrot der Kultur*]." Cohen claimed ethics emerged not from myth but only from the *Quellen des Judentums*. Hermann Cohen, *Religion der Vernunft aus den Quellen des Judentums* (Darmstadt: Joseph Melzer, 1966), 291.

142. Cassirer, "Cohen's Philosophy of Religion," 101–102. Quoted from Cohen, "Religion und Sittlichkeit," 139–141.

143. See, for example, Cohen, "Religion und Sittlichkeit," 165.

144. Cassirer, "Cohen's Philosophy of Religion," 101.

145. Hermann Cohen, "Innere Beziehungen der Kantischen Philosophie zum Judentum," in *Jüdische Schriften*, vol. 1: *Ethische und religiöse Grundfragen* (Berlin: Schwetschke, 1924), 284–305. For an insightful analysis, see Paul Franks, "Jewish Philosophy after Kant: The Legacy of Salomon Maimon," in *The Cambridge Companion to Modern Jewish Philosophy*, ed. Michael Morgan and Peter Gordon (New York: Cambridge University Press, 2007), 53–79.

146. Sigmund Freud, *Moses and Monotheism*, trans. Katherine Jones (New York: Vintage Books, 1967), 144, translation modified. For an analysis of this passage, see Richard Bernstein, *Freud and the Legacy of Moses* (New York: Cambridge University Press, 1998), 33.

7. Philosophy and Memory

1. Heidegger took special care to emphasize that he had rejected the official biological racism of the Nazi Party. See Martin Heidegger, "Schreiben Heideggers an den Vorsitzender des politischen Bereinigungsauschusses Prof v. Dietze (15 Dez. 1945)," GA 16, 414.

2. Maurice de Gandillac and Alfred de Towarnicki, "Deux Documents sur Heidegger," *Les Temps Modernes* 1.4 (1946): 713–724; de Gandillac, "Entretien avec Martin Heidegger," 713–716; de Towarnicki, "Visite à Martin Heidegger," 717–724.

3. De Gandillac, "Entretien avec Martin Heidegger," 714.

4. François Poirié, *Emmanuel Lévinas, Qui êtes-vous?* (Lyon: La Manufacture, 1987), 76.

5. Emmanuel Lévinas, "Entretien Avec Roger-Pol Droit," in *Les imprévus de l'histoire*, ed. Pierre Hayat (Montpellier: Fata Morgana, 1994), 203–210; originally published in *Le Monde* 2 (June 1992): 2.

6. Richard Sugarman, professor of philosophy, University of Vermont, notes from personal phone interview with the author on July 23, 2008.

7. Ernst Benz, *Urbild und Abbild: Der Mensch und die mythische Welt. Gesammelte Eranos-Beiträge* (Leiden: E. J. Brill, 1974), 515. My thanks to John Michael Krois for this reference.

8. The comparison to Dada verse is not mine; it can be found in Rüdiger Safranski, *Heidegger: Between Good and Evil*, trans. Ewald Osers (Cambridge, MA: Harvard University Press, 1999). Needless to say, the comparison is philosophically without much interest.

9. Michael Friedman, *A Parting of the Ways: Carnap, Cassirer, and Heidegger* (Chicago: Open Court, 2000), 7; see esp. chap. 2, "Overcoming Metaphysics: Carnap and Heidegger," 11–23.

10. Sugarman, interview with the author.

11. Hermann Herrigel, "Denken dieser Zeit: Fakultäten und Nationen treffen sich in Davos," FZ, April 22, 1929, Hochschulblatt, 4.

12. Herrigel, "Denken dieser Zeit," 4.

13. Hermann Herrigel, *Das neue Denken* (Berlin: Lambert Schneider, 1928).

14. Herrigel, "Denken dieser Zeit," 4.

15. Ernst Howald, "Betrachtungen zu den Davoser Hochschulkursen," NZZ, April 10, 1929, Morgenausgabe, 1.

16. Franz Josef Brecht, "Die Situation der gegenwärtigen Philosophie," *Neue Jahrbücher für Wissenschaft und Jugendbildung* 6.1 (1930): 42–58.

17. Brecht, "Die Situation der gegenwärtigen Philosophie," 42.

18. Brecht, "Die Situation der gegenwärtigen Philosophie," 51–52.

19. Erich Przywara, *Kant Heute: Eine Sichtung* (München: Verlag von R. Oldenbourg), 28.

20. Armando Carlini, *Orientamenti della filosofia contemporanea* (Rome: Critica Fascista, 1931), 88.

21. Joachim Ritter, "Ernst Cassirers Philosophie der symbolischen Formen," *Neue Jahrbücher für Wissenschaft und Jugendbildung* 6.7 (1930): 593–605, quotations at 595 and 605.

22. Joachim Ritter, "Bildungskrise in Davos: Bemerkungen zu den IV. Davoser Hochschulkursen vom 22. März bis 11. April, 1931," *Neue Jahrbücher für Wissenschaft und Jugendbilding* 7.7 (1931): 661–665.

23. On the history of Cassirer's chair and its fate during the Nazi-Zeit, see Josef Meran, "Die Lehrer am philosophischen Seminar der Hamburger Universität-während der Zeit des Nationalsozialismus," in *Hochschulalltag im "Dritten Reich": Die Hamburger Universität, 1933–1945*, ed. Eckart Krause, Ludwig Huber, and Holger Fischer (Berlin: Reimer, 1991), 459–482.

24. Joachim Ritter, *Über den Sinn und die Grenze der Lehre vom Menschen* (Potsdam: Alfred Protte, 1933), 29–30.

25. Hans Jörg Sandkühler, "'Eine lange Odyssee'—Joachim Ritter, Ernst Cassirer und die Philosophie im 'Dritten Reich,'" *Dialektik* 1 (2006): 1–30.

26. Sandkühler, "'Eine lange Odyssee,'" 16. On the "Bekenntnis" for the Third Reich signed by professors at both Hamburg and Marburg, also see Thomas Laugstien, *Philosophieverhältnisse im deutschen Faschismus* (Hamburg: Argument, 1990), 202.

27. Sandkühler, "'Eine lange Odyssee,'" 24.

28. Sandkühler, "'Eine lange Odyssee,'" 26.

29. Maurice de Gandillac, "Kierkegaard, le Pascal du Nord," *La Revue universelle* 59.15 (1934): 371–376, quotation at 371.

30. Toni Cassirer, *Mein Leben mit Ernst Cassirer* (Hildesheim: Gerstenberg, 1981), 181.

31. Toni Cassirer, *Mein Leben mit Ernst Cassirer*, 182.

32. Toni Cassirer, *Mein Leben mit Ernst Cassirer*, 182.

33. Toni Cassirer, *Mein Leben mit Ernst Cassirer*, 183.

34. Toni Cassirer, *Mein Leben mit Ernst Cassirer*, 182–183; emphasis added.

35. Hendrik J. Pos, "Recollections of Ernst Cassirer," in Schilpp, 61–72, 68.

36. Pos, "Recollections of Ernst Cassirer," 69.

37. Maurice de Gandillac, *Le Siècle traversé: Souvenirs de neuf décennies* (Paris: Albin Michel, 1998), 135.

38. Pos, "Recollections of Ernst Cassirer," 69.

39. Thomas Meyer, *Ernst Cassirer* (Hamburg: Ellert & Richter, 2006), 101–104.

40. Toni Cassirer, *Mein Leben mit Ernst Cassirer*, 323–325.

41. Paul Tillich, "Heidegger and Jaspers," in *Heidegger and Jaspers*, ed. Alan M. Olson (Philadelphia: Temple University Press, 1994) 16–28, quotation at 24. The talk was originally given at the Cooper Union Forum in New York, March 25, 1954.

42. Tillich, "Heidegger and Jaspers," 25.

43. Tillich, "Heidegger and Jaspers," 25.

44. Karl Löwith, "Les implications politiques de la philosophie de l'existence chez Heidegger," originally published in *Les Temps Modernes* 14 (1946), reprinted with some emendations in Löwith, *Sämtliche Schriften,* Band 8 (Stuttgart: Meltzer, 1984), 61–68.

45. Leo Strauss, "Kurt Riezler (1882–1955)," in *What Is Political Philosophy? and Other Studies* (Glencoe, IL: Free Press, 1959), 233–260. The written text is an enlarged version of a memorial lecture delivered at the Graduate Faculty of the New School for Social Research in New York City; it was originally published as "Kurt Riezler," *Social Research* 23.1 (1956): 3–34.

46. Strauss, "Kurt Riezler," 245.

47. The lines are from Virgil's *Aeneid,* lines 151–152: "tum, pietate gravem ac meritis si forte virum quem/conspexere, silent, arrectisque auribus adstant." Strauss does not provide this reference in the lecture or the published text.

48. Strauss, "Kurt Riezler," 246.

49. Otto Friedrich Bollnow, "Gespräche in Davos," in *Erinnerung an Martin Heidegger,* ed. Günther Neske (Pfullingen: Neske, 1977), 28.

50. Bollnow, "Gespräche in Davos," 28.

51. Poirié, *Emmanuel Lévinas,* 78.

52. Poirié, *Emmanuel Lévinas,* 78.

53. Poirié, *Emmanuel Lévinas,* 78.

54. Lévinas, "Entretien Avec Roger-Pol," 203–210.

55. Poirié, *Emmanuel Lévinas,* 78.

56. Lévinas, *Existence and Existents,* trans. Alphonso Lingus (Dordrecht: Kluwer, 1995), 19.

57. Sugarman, interview with the author.

58. Poirié, *Emmanuel Lévinas,* 78.

59. Poiré, *Emmanuel Lévinas,* 79.

60. Richard A. Cohen, "Humanism and Anti-humanism—Levinas, Cassirer, and Heidegger," in *Humanism of the Other* by Emmanuel Lévinas, trans. Nidra Poller (Chicago: University of Illinois Press, 2003), viii–xliv.

61. Poiré, *Emmanuel Lévinas,* 76ff.

62. Hans Blumenberg, "Affinitäten und Dominanzen," in *Ein mögliches Selbstverständnis: Aus dem Nachlaß* (Stuttgart: Philipp Reclam, 1996), 161–168.

63. Blumenberg, "Affinitäten und Dominanzen," 166.

64. Pierre Bourdieu, *L'Ontologie politique de Martin Heidegger* (Paris: Editions de Minuit, 1988).

65. Tom Rockmore, *Heidegger and French Philosophy: Humanism, Anti-Humanism, and Being* (New York: Routledge, 1995); Ethan Kleinberg, *Generation Existential: Heidegger's Philosophy in France, 1927–1961* (Ithaca, NY: Cornell University Press, 2005).

66. Victor Farias, *Heidegger and Nazism,* trans. Gabriel R. Ricci (Philadelphia: Temple University Press, 1989); originally published in French as *Heidegger et le nazisme,* trans. Myriam Benarroch and Jean Baptiste Grasset (Paris: Verdier, 1987).

67. Most relevant for the French debate of the later 1980s were Jean-François Lyotard, *Heidegger et "les juifs"* (Paris: Galilée, 1988); Philippe Lacoue-Labarthe, *La fiction du politique* (Paris: C. Bourgois, 1987), trans. as *Heidegger, Art, and Politics: The Fiction of the Political,* trans. Chris Turner (Cambridge, MA: Blackwell, 1990); Dominique Janicaud, *L'ombre de cette pensée* (Grenoble: Jérôme Millon, 1990); Jacques Derrida, *De l'esprit: Heidegger et la Question* (Paris: Flammarion, 1990).

68. For his reflexive understanding of his own intellectual work, see, most recently, Pierre Bourdieu, *Sketch for a Self-Analysis* (Chicago: University of Chicago Press, 2008).

69. On performative contradiction, see Martin Jay, "The Debate over the Performative Contradiction: Habermas versus the Poststructuralists," in *Force Fields: Between Intellectual History and Cultural Critique* (New York: Routledge, 1992), 25–37.

70. Jürgen Habermas, "The Liberating Power of Symbols: Ernst Cassirer's Humanistic Legacy and the Warburg Library," in *The Liberating Power of Symbols: Philosophyical Essays,* trans. Peter Dews (Cambridge, MA: MIT Press, 2001), 1–29.

71. Habermas, "The Liberating Power of Symbols," 15.

72. Habermas, "The Liberating Power of Symbols," 21.

73. Habermas, "The Liberating Power of Symbols," 23.

74. Habermas, "Public Space and Political Public Sphere—The Biographical Roots of Two Motifs in My Thought," in *Between Naturalism and Religion: Philosophical Essays,* trans. Ciaran Cronin (Malden, MA: Polity Press, 2008), 19–20.

75. On this theme see Cristina Lafont, "World-Disclosure and Critique: Did Habermas Succeed in Thinking with Heidegger and against Heidegger?" *Telos* 145 (2008): 161–176.

Conclusion

1. Immanuel Kant, *Jäsche Logic,* trans. Robert S. Hartman and Wolfgang Schwarz (New York: Dover, 1974), 29.

2. EM, 21–22.

3. LH, 276.

4. For the debate over humanism and anti-humanism, see Stefanos Geroulanos, *An Atheism That Is Not Humanist Emerges in French Thought, 1926–1954* (Stanford, CA: Stanford University Press, 2010).

5. EM, 220–221; emphasis added.

6. LH, 260; in *Wegmarken*, in GA, Band 9, 313–364, quotation at 342; English quotation slightly modified.

7. LH, 266; in *Wegmarken,* 350.

8. KdrV, A446/B474.

Acknowledgments

In writing this book I have incurred a great number of debts to both scholars and friends. For their generous comments and criticism on the manuscript, I am grateful most of all to Taylor Carman, Martin Jay, John Michael Krois, Thomas Meyer, Samuel Moyn, Thomas Sheehan, and Hans Sluga. My warm thanks as well to the following colleagues, whose ongoing conversation, criticism, and inspiration have enriched this book in ways too manifold to specify here: Terry Aladjem, David Armitage, Charles Bambach, Frederick Beiser, Warren Breckman, Andrew Chignell, Hubert Dreyfus, Michael Friedman, Peter Galison, Stefanos Geroulanos, Sean D. Kelly, Ethan Kleinberg, James Kloppenberg, Benjamin Lazier, Mark Lilla, Louis Menand, Gregory Moynahan, Hilary Putnam, Anson Rabinbach, Tommie Shelby, Eugene Sheppard, Alison Simmons, Jerrold Seigel, Judith Surkis, Iain Thomson, Dana R. Villa, and Mark Wrathall.

I would also like to thank the anonymous readers for the journal *Modern Intellectual History,* where I first published an essay on the Davos disputation ("Continental Divide: Heidegger and Cassirer at Davos, 1929—An Allegory of Intellectual History," *Modern Intellectual History* [Cambridge University Press] 1.2 [August 2004]: 1–30). I owe a special thanks to the editors there, especially Charles Izenberg, Charles Capper, and Anthony La Vopa. Thanks also to my coeditors at *New German Critique,* where I published a primitive variant of arguments contained in Chapter 6 ("Myth and Modernity: Cassirer's Critique of Heidegger," *New German Critique* no. 94 [Winter 2005]: 127–168). I must also thank the members and cosponsors of the New York Area Intellectual History Colloquium, where I first presented some of the further material in Chapter 5. Lastly, I would like to thank the participants in the Cornell conference on neo-Kantianism in September

2007, where I first presented my insights on Cassirer's interpretation of the Enlightenment, later published as "Neo-Kantianism and the Politics of Enlightenment," *Philosophical Forum* 39.2 (2008): 223–238. All previously published material is reprinted with permission.

The photograph of Heidegger and Cassirer used in this book is reproduced from the Privatarchiv Dr. Henning Ritter, courtesy of the Dokumentationsbibliothek Davos. My sincere thanks to Timothy Nelson at the Dokumentationsbibliothek Davos for verifying permissions.

Research for this book has taken me to libraries and archives both in Europe and North America, as follows: the Beinecke Rare Books Library, Yale University; the Bibliothéque Nationale de Paris; the Freie Universität, Berlin; the philosophy library, Humboldt Universität, Berlin; the fantastical boat-shaped Staatsbibliothek, Berlin; the Warburg Library, London; Green Library, Stanford University; Widener Library, Harvard University; and the Andover-Harvard Theological Library, Harvard University. For their help in locating the photograph of Cassirer and Heidegger reproduced in this book I am especially grateful to Eckart Marchand and Claudia Wedepohl at the Warburg Library, London. For material support I am grateful most of all to Harvard University, along with the Clarke Fund for faculty research, which afforded me two years of sabbatical leave. I am further grateful to Richard Sugarman for a personal phone interview regarding his meeting with Emmanuel Lévinas. For help at various phases of research, my thanks to Thomas Dolinger, and also Alexander Bevilacqua, André Lambelet, Vessela Hristova, and Rolf A. George. I owe a special debt to my research assistant Juliana Rhee for her scrupulous aid with references. At Harvard University Press I would like to express my deepest gratitude to Lindsay Waters and to Phoebe Kosman. And my thanks to John Donohue and Roberta Dempsey for their painstaking labor in editing the full manuscript. Finally, I extend warmest thanks to Noah Rosenblum, who produced the book's index with his characteristic intelligence and energy.

To my wife, Lucy, I would like to express my heartfelt gratitude, for her critical acumen in all matters philosophical and for her constant companionship throughout the trials of composition. For you I am truly blessed.

There are two last individuals to mention here; my mother, Elaine, and my father, Milton (ז״ל). Sadly, my father passed away as this book was still taking shape. All that can be said would not suffice. This book is dedicated to them.

Index